CONTEMPORARY AUDITING:
ISSUES AND CASES

SECOND EDITION

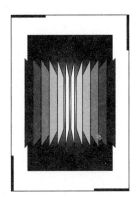

CONTEMPORARY AUDITING:
ISSUES AND CASES

Second Edition

Michael C. Knapp
University of Oklahoma

West Publishing Company
Minneapolis/St. Paul ■ New York ■ Los Angeles ■ San Francisco

Production, Prepress, Printing and Binding by West Publishing Company.

 TEXT IS PRINTED ON 10% POST CONSUMER RECYCLED PAPER    Printed with **Printwise** Environmentally Advanced Water Washable Ink

British Library Cataloguing-in-Publication Data. A catalogue record for this book is available from the British Library.

Copyeditor: Joan Torkildson
Composition: Carlisle Communications, Ltd.

COPYRIGHT © 1996 by WEST PUBLISHING COMPANY
610 Opperman Drive
P.O. Box 64526
St. Paul, MN 55164-0526

Library of Congress Cataloging-in-Publication Data
Knapp, Michael Chris, 1954–
    Contemporary auditing : issues and cases / Michael C. Knapp.—2nd ed.
        p.   cm.
    Includes bibliographical references and index.
    ISBN 0-314-06121-5 (soft : alk. paper)
    1. Corporations—United States—Auditing—Cases studies.
  2. Auditing—Corrupt practices—Case studies. 3. Auditors––Professional ethics—United States. 4. Auditing—Law and legislation—United States—Cases. I. Title.
HF5686.C7K62 1996
657'.95—dc20

DEDICATION

To Carol, Jessi, John, and Lindsay

ACCOUNTING TEXTBOOKS FROM WEST EDUCATIONAL PUBLISHING

Listed alphabetically by author

Jesse T. Barfield, Cecily A. Raiborn, and Michael R. Kinney: *Cost Accounting, Traditions and Innovations, 2E*

Leonard J. Brooks: *Professional Ethics in Accounting*

John G. Burch: *Cost and Management Accounting: A Modern Approach*

Janet Cassagio, Dolores Osborn & Beverly Terry: *College Accounting*

James Doak and Christine Kloezeman: *Computerized Accounting Principles*

James A. Hall: *Accounting Information Systems*

Bart P. Hartman, Robert M.J. Harper, Jr., James A Knoblett, and Philip M. Reckers: *Intermediate Accounting*

William H. Hoffman, Jr., William A. Raabe, James E. Smith and David M. Maloney: *West's Federal Taxation: Corporations, Partnerships, Estates and Trusts, 1996 Edition*

William H. Hoffman, Jr., James E. Smith, and Eugene Willis: *West's Federal Taxation: Individual Income Taxes, 1996 Edition*

Michael C. Knapp: *Contemporary Auditing: Issues and Cases, Second Edition*

Michael C. Knapp: *Financial Accounting: A Focus on Decision Making*

Larry F. Konrath: *Auditing Concepts and Applications: A Risk Analysis Approach, 3E*

Joseph G. Louderback, G. Thomas Friedlob, and Franklin J. Plewa: *Survey of Accounting*

Kevin Murphy with Rick L. Crosser and Mark Higgins: *Concepts in Federal Taxation, 2E*

William A. Raabe, Gerald E. Whittenburg, and John C. Bost: *West's Federal Tax Research, 3E*

Cecily A. Raiborn, Jesse T. Barfield, and Michael R. Kinney: *Managerial Accounting, 2E*

James E. Smith: *West's Internal Revenue Code of 1986 and Treasury Regulations: Annotated and Selected, 1996 Edition*

Gerald E. Whittenburg and Martha Altus-Buller: *Income Tax Fundamentals, 1996 Edition*

Eugene Willis, William H. Hoffman, Jr., David M. Maloney, and William A. Raabe: *West's Federal Taxation: Comprehensive Volume, 1996 Edition*

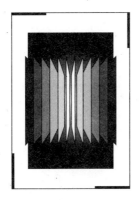

CONTENTS

SECTION ONE   COMPREHENSIVE CASES   1

Case 1.1   Mattel, Inc.   3

To sustain Mattel's impressive sales and earnings trends in the early 1970s, the company's top executives engaged in a massive scheme to distort the company's operating results.

Key Topics: Assessment of inherent risk, revenue recognition, the use of sales cutoff tests, effectiveness of the audit review process, auditing the reserve for inventory obsolescence, and auditor-client disagreements regarding year-end adjusting entries.

Case 1.2   ESM Government Securities, Inc.   15

The ESM scandal rocked the international financial markets and resulted in one state imposing the first "banking holiday" in the United States since the Depression.

Key Topics: Performance pressure exerted on auditors, the use of audit confirmation procedures, quality control in an auditing practice, and discovery of financial statement errors following the issuance of an audit report.

Case 1.3   United States Surgical Corporation   29

An SEC investigation disclosed that officials of this company went to great lengths to conceal pervasive irregularities in the company's accounting records from its independent auditors.

Key Topics: The use of analytical procedures, accounting for fixed assets and research and development expenses, implications of the imbalance of power in the auditor-client relationship, and evaluation of conflicting audit evidence.

Case 1.4   ZZZZ Best Company, Inc.   41

Barry Minkow, the "boy wonder" of Wall Street, created a $200 million company that existed only on paper.

Key Topics: Identification of key management assertions, limitations of audit evidence, importance of candid predecessor-successor auditor communications, client confidentiality, and client-imposed audit scope limitations.

Case 1.5   Lincoln Savings and Loan Association   55
Charles Keating's use of questionable accounting methods allowed him to manufacture huge paper profits for Lincoln.
Key Topics: Substance-over-form rule, detection of fraud, identification of key management assertions, collegial responsibilities of auditors, assessment of control risk, and auditor independence.

Case 1.6   Crazy Eddie Inc.   69
"Crazy Eddie" Antar oversaw a highly profitable chain of consumer electronics stores on the East Coast during the 1970s and 1980s. After massive fraud was discovered in the company's accounting records, Antar fled the country, leaving behind thousands of angry stockholders and creditors.
Key Topics: Auditing inventory, inventory control procedures, management integrity, the use of analytical procedures, and the hiring of former auditors by audit clients.

Case 1.7   Penn Square Bank   79
The collapse of Penn Square Bank in 1982 triggered a series of financial crises at some of the nation's largest financial institutions.
Key topics: Opinion shopping, client confidentiality, internal control reporting, and auditor independence.

Case 1.8   IFG Leasing   91
The spectacular growth of this company in the early 1980s was largely a result of unsound business decisions made by overly aggressive executives.
Key Topics: Auditing receivables and the allowance for uncollectible accounts, auditors' responsibility for "other financial information," factors influencing inherent risk, and audit evidence evaluation issues.

Case 1.9   The Fund of Funds, Ltd.   101
Bernie Cornfeld, John McCandish King, and Robert Vesco were among the parties associated with this once high-flying mutual fund.
Key Topics: Detection of fraud, client confidentiality, materiality of financial statement errors, and auditors' legal exposure under the Securities Exchange Act of 1934.

Case 1.10   Wedtech Corporation   115
The former auditors of this now infamous company were charged with numerous breaches of the accounting profession's ethical code.
Key Topics: Auditor independence issues, auditors' responsibilities related to illegal acts and accounting irregularities perpetrated by client, and the percentage-of-completion method of accounting for long-term construction projects.

SECTION 2 AUDITS OF HIGH-RISK ACCOUNTS AND INTERNAL CONTROL ISSUES   123

Case 2.1   Doughtie's Foods, Inc.   125
Inadequate inventory observation procedures prevented this company's auditors from discovering a materially overstated inventory balance.

Case 2.2   Flight Transportation Corporation   129
This company grossly overstated its revenues. Failure to investigate several major internal control weaknesses prevented the company's auditors from uncovering this fraud.

Case 2.3   The Trolley Dodgers   135
Control deficiencies in the Dodgers' payroll transaction cycle allowed an accounting manager to embezzle several hundred thousand dollars.

Case 2.4   J. B. Hanauer & Co.   137
This case focuses on the audit objectives related to the use of confirmation procedures and illustrates inappropriate methods of applying these procedures.

Case 2.5   Berkshire Hathaway, Inc.   143
The lack of a definitive accounting rule for recognizing profits on "proportionate redemptions" of stock led to a stormy confrontation between executives of Berkshire Hathaway and the company's independent auditors.

Case 2.6   Giant Stores Corporation   147
Numerous intentional understatements of this company's accounts payable and the failure of its auditors to discover these irregularities was the focus of an intensive SEC investigation.

Case 2.7   Howard Street Jewelers, Inc.   155
Given the susceptibility of cash to theft, companies typically establish rigorous internal controls for their cash processing functions. In this case, the high price of failing to implement such controls is documented.

Case 2.8   E. F. Hutton & Company, Inc.   159
This large brokerage firm's auditors were criticized by regulatory authorities and the financial press for failing to expose a massive and illegal cash management system.

Case 2.9   J. B. Lippincott Company   171
Inadequate confirmation procedures were largely responsible for the failure of this company's auditors to discover material overstatements in various receivables accounts.

Case 2.10   Porta-John Corporation   175

Porta-John's auditors "flip-flopped" on the important issue of when the company should recognize revenues received from its franchisees. The company's owner alleged that this indecision on the part of the auditors contributed to Porta-John's subsequent financial problems.

Case 2.11   Four Seasons Nursing Centers of America, Inc.   179

The misuse of the percentage-of-completion method of accounting for long-term construction contracts allowed Four Seasons to distort its operating results.

SECTION 3   ETHICAL RESPONSIBILITIES OF AUDITORS AND ACCOUNTANTS   185

Case 3.1   Cardillo Travel Systems, Inc.   187

A top executive of Cardillo pressured three accountants—the company's controller and two partners of public accounting firms—to misrepresent the nature of a large payment received by the company from United Airlines.

Case 3.2   Creve Couer Pizza, Inc.   193

Intrigue and espionage seem far removed from accounting ... but not in this case. The accountant for Creve Couer Pizza was actually a double agent. While providing various accounting services to his client, the accountant was also supplying incriminating evidence regarding the client to the IRS.

Case 3.3   The PTL Club   197

The officers of PTL convinced a partner of their independent audit firm to maintain a secret check register in his office to record illicit disbursements being made by the organization.

Case 3.4   Leigh Ann Walker, Staff Accountant   201

In this case, a staff accountant employed by a Big Six accounting firm was dismissed after serious questions arose regarding her integrity.

Case 3.5   Phillips Petroleum Company   205

Rather than compromise the confidentiality of his client's accounting records, the partner in charge of the annual Phillips audit was found in contempt of court and jailed.

Case 3.6   Laurel Valley Estates   209

A staff accountant wrongfully accused a client official of criminal conduct—an accusation that resulted in the official suing the staff accountant's employer.

Case 3.7   Whittaker Corporation   213

This company and its audit firm were reprimanded by the SEC for failing to disclose a set of circumstances that threatened the audit firm's independence.

Case 3.8   Suzette Washington, Accounting Major   217

Suzette Washington was a college senior majoring in accounting when she came face-to-face with an important ethical decision. Since accounting majors are entering a profession with a rigorous code of ethics, do they have a greater responsibility than other students to behave ethically?

SECTION 4   Professional Issues   219

Case 4.1   Hopkins v. Price Waterhouse   221

This case focuses on the unique problems faced by women pursuing a career in public accounting.

Case 4.2   When Auditors Become Lobbyists   231

Some of the largest public accounting firms have been charged with deferring to the economic interests of their clients when it comes to new accounting standards proposed by the FASB. This case examines this issue in the context of the recent FASB proposal regarding accounting for stock options.

Case 4.3   Tommy O'Connell, Audit Senior   241

A new audit senior is quickly exposed to the challenging responsibilities of his professional work role when he is assigned to supervise a difficult audit engagement. During the course of this engagement, the audit senior must deal with the possibility that a staff accountant is not completing his assigned audit procedures.

Case 4.4   Sarah Russell, Staff Accountant   245

Sexual harassment is a sensitive subject that many companies and professional firms have been forced to cope with in recent years. This case recounts the experiences of a staff accountant who was harassed by an audit partner.

Case 4.5   When Auditors Change Sides   249

The hiring of auditors by their clients is an important and controversial issue facing the public accounting profession. This case, which was originally a *New York Times* article, explores this issue.

Case 4.6   Bill DeBurger, In-Charge Accountant   253

"To sign off" or "not sign off" was the issue facing Bill DeBurger at the end of an audit of a client's most important account. An unpleasant confrontation with the audit engagement partner made Bill's decision even more difficult.

Case 4.7   First Blood Associates   257

In recent years, the accounting profession has been pressured to become more involved in the preparation of financial forecasts. This case illustrates the legal exposure that accounting firms assume when they accept such a responsibility.

SECTION 5   CLASSIC LITIGATION CASES   261

Case 5.1   Fred Stern & Company, Inc. (*Ultramares Corporation v. Touche et al.*)   263

This 1931 legal case established the Ultramares Doctrine, which six decades later still has an important influence on auditors' civil liabilities under the common law.

Case 5.2   BarChris Construction Corporation   271

Factors influencing materiality decisions, auditors' responsibilities when accounting standards do not provide definitive guidelines for certain client transactions, and the due diligence responsibilities of auditors under the Securities Act of 1933 are the key issues addressed by this case.

Case 5.3   1136 Tenants Corporation   281

The need for an explicit contractual agreement between a client and audit firm was made clear in this landmark case.

Case 5.4   Yale Express System, Inc.   285

In the course of a consulting engagement, the audit firm of Yale Express discovered that the company's prior year financial statements were materially in error, although an unqualified opinion had been issued on those statements.

Case 5.5   First Securities Company of Chicago (*Ernst & Ernst v. Hochfelder et al.*)   293

In reviewing this case, the Supreme Court defined the degree of auditor misconduct that must be present before a client can recover damages from an auditor in a lawsuit filed under the Securities Exchange Act of 1934.

Case 5.6   Equity Funding Corporation of America   301

The huge Equity Funding scandal demonstrated the critical need for auditors to maintain a high level of skepticism when planning and carrying out an audit.

Index   307

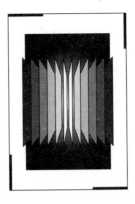

PREFACE

Pervasive changes are under way in accounting curricula across the nation. Criticism of the accounting profession by regulatory authorities, the financial press, and the general public has forced the profession to reassess its societal purpose and future direction. One result of this reassessment has been a call for exploring ways of improving accounting education. Critics suggest that accounting educators should employ a broader array of instructional resources, particularly resources that are experiential in nature and designed to stimulate active learning by students. A primary objective of the Accounting Education Change Commission is to encourage the development of those types of materials for use in accounting courses. This casebook provides instructors with a source of such materials that can be used in both undergraduate and graduate auditing courses.

This casebook stresses the "people" aspect of independent audits. So-called problem audits seldom result from the failure of audit technology. Instead, problem audits typically result from the presence of one, or both, of the following two conditions: (1) client personnel who intentionally subvert an audit and (2) auditors who fail to carry out the responsibilities assigned to them. The purpose of this text is not to criticize the individuals who have been involved in these audits, but rather to allow students to learn from these cases. Students who have been exposed to problem audits will be better equipped to recognize the red flags that often accompany these situations. Students also receive a dose of reality when they are exposed to the serious consequences that can result from audit failures for both auditors and other parties.

The cases in this text also acquaint students with the work environment of auditors. After studying these cases, students will better understand the subtle pressures and nuances that complicate the work roles of independent auditors. Client pressure—both explicit and implicit—peer pressure, and time budgets are among job-related variables that can frustrate auditors. These and related variables are interwoven in the cases in this text. Also depicted in these cases are the ambiguity and lack of structure with which auditors must cope each day. Missing documents, conflicting audit evidence, the dual obligation to the client and to financial statement users, and the lack of definitive professional standards for many situations are aspects of the audit environment that are integrated into these cases.

Several suggested changes recommended by adopters of the first edition have been incorporated in this second edition. For example, a number of the original cases, such as Lincoln Savings and Loan Association and Penn Square Bank, have been updated for new events and circumstances arising since the publication of the first edition. The most apparent change in this edition is the addition of thirteen new cases. Because several adopters indicated a particular desire for additional short cases, many of the new cases in this edition are fairly brief and can be adequately covered in class in no more than twenty to thirty minutes. Another change in this edition is a refocusing of the fourth section. This section is now entitled Professional Issues. Included in this section are several cases that concern developing or emerging issues facing auditing firms. Also included are cases that illustrate the nature of specific work roles assumed by auditors. These cases, such as Bill DeBurger, In-Charge Accountant, are designed to provide students with a better appreciation of the nature and responsibilities of the work roles many of them will be assuming in the next few years.

Among the other new cases incorporated in this second edition are Crazy Eddie, Inc., a comprehensive case, and J. B. Hanauer & Co., which demonstrates the use or misuse of confirmation procedures. New cases focusing on ethical issues include Phillips Petroleum Company and Creve Couer Pizza, Inc. The Phillips case describes a series of events resulting in an audit partner being jailed for refusing to breach the confidentiality of his client's accounting records. In contrast, a CPA in the Creve Couer case funneled incriminating evidence regarding a client to the IRS. Included in the Professional Issues section is a new case highlighting the controversy surrounding the FASB's recent exposure draft intended to change the method of accounting for certain stock options. The key issue addressed in this latter case is whether audit firms should lobby rule-making bodies on behalf of positions supported by their major clients.

This casebook can be used as a supplemental text for the undergraduate auditing course or as a primary text for a graduate-level seminar in auditing. Listed in the instructor's manual are additional readings that instructors can assign if the casebook is being used as a primary text for a graduate auditing course. A syllabus for such a course is included in the instructor's manual. This casebook can also be used in the capstone professional practice course that is incorporated in many five-year accounting programs.

The following are the five groups of cases included in this casebook, along with a brief overview of the cases in each group. In addition, the table of contents for the second edition of this casebook provides a short description of each case.

Comprehensive Cases

Most of these cases deal with high-profile problem audits including ESM Government Securities, ZZZZ Best Company, and Lincoln Savings and Loan Association. These cases address a wide range of auditing, accounting, and ethical issues.

Audits of High-Risk Accounts and Internal Control Issues

In contrast to the cases in the prior section, the cases in this group are more focused, generally addressing only one or two auditing issues or concepts. For example, the focus of the Doughtie's Foods case is inventory observation audit procedures, while Howard Street Jewelers addresses internal control issues related to the cash processing function of a small retail business.

Ethical Responsibilities of Auditors and Accountants

Integrating ethics into an auditing course requires much more than simply discussing the AICPA's Code of Professional Conduct. This section presents actual situations in which auditors and accountants have faced perplexing ethical dilemmas. Students who study these cases and consider the context in which ethical issues arise should be better prepared to deal with similar situations in their own professional careers. One of the new cases in this section, Suzette Washington, Accounting Major, concerns a college senior majoring in accounting who is faced with an ethical dilemma in her work role as an inventory clerk.

Professional Issues

Because of the dynamic nature of the public accounting profession, several important changes have recently occurred in the work environment of public accountants and the nature of the services they provide. The cases in this section address many of these changes. For example, the Hopkins v. Price Waterhouse case discusses the unique problems faced by women pursuing a career in public accounting. A few decades ago, this was not a widely discussed issue in the profession, since relatively few women at that time chose careers in public accounting. This section also includes several cases focusing specifically on the nature of the various professional work roles assumed by auditors and the key responsibilities related to these roles. For example, Tommy O'Connell, Audit Senior, provides students with important insights on the professional work role of audit seniors.

Classic Litigation Cases

Most auditing textbooks focus almost exclusively on the legal liability issues inherent in the classic auditing-related litigation cases that have arisen over the past several decades. In this text, the underlying auditing issues or controversies inherent in these cases, as well as the pertinent legal liability issues, are presented.

The Customized Casebook Option: *Westext*

To maximize the flexibility of using these cases, West Publishing Company is including *Contemporary Auditing: Issues and Cases* in its custom publishing program, *Westext*. This program makes it possible for adopters to select among the cases included here and create a customized casebook ideally suited to their needs. For more information on how to design your customized casebook, please contact your West sales representative.

I greatly appreciate the insight and suggestions provided by the following reviewers of the first and second editions of this casebook. First edition: Ed Blocher, University of North Carolina; Kurt Chaloupecky, Southwest Missouri State University; Ray Clay, University of North Texas; Mary Doucet, University of Georgia; Donald McConnell, University of Texas at Arlington; Heidi Meier,

Cleveland State University; Don Nichols, Texas Christian University; Rajendra Srivastava, University of Kansas; and Jim Yardley, Virginia Polytechnic University. Second edition: Barbara Apostolou, Louisiana State University; Jane Baird, Mankato State University; Ray Clay, University of North Texas; Ruth Engle, Lafayette College; Laurence Johnson, Colorado State University; and Marcia Niles, University of Idaho. This project also benefited greatly from the guidance and patience of Rick Leyh and Jessica Evans of West Educational Publishing, as well as the editorial assistance of my sister, Paula Conatser. Finally, I would like to acknowledge the contributions of my students, who have provided invaluable comments and suggestions on the content and use of these cases.

SECTION ONE
COMPREHENSIVE CASES

Case 1.1   Mattel, Inc.

Case 1.2   ESM Government Securities, Inc.

Case 1.3   United States Surgical Corporation

Case 1.4   ZZZZ Best Company, Inc.

Case 1.5   Lincoln Savings and Loan Association

Case 1.6   Crazy Eddie, Inc.

Case 1.7   Penn Square Bank

Case 1.8   IFG Leasing

Case 1.9   The Fund of Funds, Ltd.

Case 1.10 Wedtech Corporation

CASE 1.1
MATTEL, INC.

In 1945, Elliot and Ruth Handler, along with a friend, Harold Matson, founded a small toy company, which they operated out of the Handlers' garage. Within a few months, Matson decided to pursue other interests and left Mattel, Inc., to the Handlers. For the next decade, the husband-and-wife team worked long and hard hours struggling to make their small company a success. Elliot Handler, an artist, designed the toys the company produced, while Ruth Handler managed the company's business affairs, concentrating much of her time on finding sales outlets for their products. By 1955, the net worth of Mattel was a little more than $500,000. That year, Ruth Handler decided to take a daring step to expand the size of the company. Her plan was to advertise Mattel's toys on the popular children's television program, *The Mickey Mouse Club*. The cost of the advertising campaign was several hundred thousand dollars and if unsuccessful could have bankrupted the small company; however, Ruth Handler's gamble paid off handsomely. Within a few months, Mattel's sales orders increased dramatically, and the company was on its way to establishing itself as a major player in the highly competitive toy industry.

In 1959, Ruth Handler took a second gamble by introducing a full-figured, teenage doll named after her daughter Barbara. Industry experts maintained that the doll would not appeal to its target market of three- to eleven-year-old girls. The experts were wrong; the Barbie doll was an instant success, with more than 350,000 sold the first year it was on the market. By Barbie's thirtieth birthday, more than 500 million of the dolls had been sold. The Barbie product line, which eventually included her friend Ken, named after the Handlers' son, accounted for nearly one-half of Mattel's revenues by 1990.

Ruth Handler, the youngest of ten children of Polish immigrants, was never modest about explaining the success of Mattel. During an interview, she once noted matter-of-factly that she was "a marketing genius." A short and intensely competitive woman, Ruth Handler hated failure and refused to accept it. During the early 1970s, however, she and her company encountered a set of circumstances that would eventually take Mattel to the verge of bankruptcy.

TRYING TIMES AT MATTEL

By 1971, Mattel was recognized by financial analysts as one of the premier growth companies in the United States. In that year, the company reported pretax profits of $34 million on sales approaching $275 million. Investors were so infatuated by the company and its prospects that Mattel common stock traded on the New York Stock Exchange at an enormous price-earnings ratio, often exceeding 50 to 1. The Handlers and other key Mattel executives became fabulously wealthy as a result. By 1971 the Mattel stock controlled by Elliot and Ruth Handler had a market value approaching $300 million.

Despite the record earnings reported by Mattel for each successive year from 1967 through 1971, the company was beginning to experience serious problems by the early 1970s. Many of these problems could be traced to the Handlers' decision in the late 1960s to hire Seymour Rosenberg as the company's executive vice-president and chief financial officer. Rosenberg, formerly with Litton Industries, had earned a reputation for his skill in identifying and acquiring underperforming companies and making them financial successes. Shortly after joining Mattel, he convinced the Handlers to diversify into a number of industries and to completely overhaul the organizational structure of Mattel, breaking its operations down into numerous decentralized divisions. Unfortunately, four of the six companies acquired by Mattel on the recommendation of Rosenberg proved to be very poor investments, and his decentralization plan increased the operating costs of the company tremendously.

Besides the problems created by Rosenberg, who was dismissed by the Handlers in late 1972, Mattel encountered a series of largely uncontrollable circumstances in the early 1970s that damaged the company's profitability. First, one of the company's large warehouses in Mexicali, Mexico, was destroyed by fire in 1970. Then, the following year, a dockworkers' strike prevented the company from receiving any toy shipments from its large Hong Kong plant. Finally, the recession of the early 1970s cut significantly into the company's sales. These factors caused Mattel to register a loss of approximately $30 million in 1972.

A large banking syndicate that had significant loans outstanding to Mattel was instrumental in convincing the Handlers to dismiss Rosenberg. When another Mattel vice-president, Albert Spear, was promoted to executive vice-president and assumed control of Mattel's operations in 1973, he was shocked to learn that the company was facing a financial crisis. Shortly before Spear accepted his new position, Mattel had issued a press release stating that the company had undergone a dramatic turnaround in fiscal 1973 compared with fiscal 1972. However, an intensive study of Mattel's financial records by Spear disclosed that the company had actually realized a huge loss in fiscal 1973—larger than the loss reported the prior year. When Spear released this information to the public, panicked investors reacted immediately by dumping their Mattel stock. Spear's disclosures also resulted in five class action lawsuits being filed against Mattel and its executives by angry stockholders and spurred the Securities and Exchange Commission (SEC) to begin an investigation of the company's financial affairs.

In October 1975, Elliot and Ruth Handler resigned their positions with Mattel. One month later, the outside directors on the Mattel board released a five-hundred page report that detailed a massive earnings manipulation scheme masterminded by the company's executive officers. According to the report, the Handlers and other key Mattel officials issued "financial statements that were deliberately false and misleading" to give an illusion of continued spectacular growth.[1] The lengthy report also contained a discussion of the audits of Mattel by Arthur Andersen during the period in which the company's earnings were being manipulated. This review, performed by Price Waterhouse, was very critical of the Arthur Andersen audits: "In general, Price Waterhouse concluded that Arthur Andersen's audit procedures and tests weren't as comprehensive as they should have been in many areas and that certain information contained in the accountant's working papers should have been further pursued. If this had been done, the report said it could have led to the discovery of irregularities in the fiscal 1971 and 1972 financial statements."[2]

In March 1976, a federal judge approved an out-of-court settlement to the class action lawsuits filed by Mattel's stockholders. The $30 million settlement required multimillion-dollar payments by several former executives of Mattel, principally the Handlers and Rosenberg, as well as even larger payments by the insurance companies of these executives. The only defendant that refused to participate in the settlement was Arthur Andersen, which maintained that it was not responsible for the huge losses suffered by Mattel's stockholders following the disclosure of the earnings manipulation scheme. Nevertheless, in April 1977, Arthur Andersen agreed to make a cash payment of approximately $900,000 to the Mattel stockholders in return for the latter's dropping all civil claims against the accounting firm.

In February 1978, Ruth Handler, Seymour Rosenberg, and four other former Mattel executives were indicted by a federal grand jury on charges of falsifying the financial statements of Mattel for the period 1969 to 1974. In responding to the indictment, Ruth Handler proclaimed her innocence and maintained that she was "deeply offended" by the charges. Later that year, however, Handler submitted a plea of no contest to each of the ten counts of fraud filed against her. The plea bargain agreement that was approved by a federal judge allowed Handler to escape a prison sentence but required her to perform 2,500 hours of community service and to pay a $57,000 fine. A similar plea bargain arrangement was made with Rosenberg in the fall of 1978.[3]

ALLEGED DEFICIENCIES IN ARTHUR ANDERSEN'S AUDITS OF MATTEL

In June 1981, the SEC released the results of its lengthy investigation of Mattel's fraudulent earnings manipulation scheme and its report on the independent

---

1. R. Lindsey, "A Million-Dollar Business from a Mastectomy," *New York Times*, 19 June 1988, F3.

2. S. Sansweet, "Mattel Ex-Aides Tried Cover-Up, Report Asserts," *Wall Street Journal*, 4 November 1975, 10.

3. Elliot Handler was never indicted for criminal fraud. The federal grand jury that investigated the Mattel earnings manipulation scheme apparently concluded that he was not involved in the fraud.

audits of Mattel performed by Arthur Andersen. In that report, Arthur Andersen was criticized for numerous alleged auditing deficiencies, primarily in its fiscal 1971 and 1972 audits of Mattel. In particular, the SEC identified several alleged auditing errors or oversights that prevented Arthur Andersen from discovering the systematic methods employed by Mattel management to manipulate the company's reported operating results. These illicit methods were used by Mattel's executives to allow them to meet predefined earnings goals they had established for each fiscal year.

Improper Sales Cutoff at Year End

For fiscal year 1971, which ended January 30, 1971, Mattel management was facing the unpleasant prospect of informing stockholders that the company had failed for the first time in several years to post record sales and earnings. To increase the company's reported earnings, Mattel's top executives instituted in January 1971 what became known as the "bill and hold" program. Mattel used this program to overstate its fiscal 1971 sales by almost $15 million and its pretax earnings by approximately $8 million. In simple terms, the bill and hold program involved billing customers for future sales and then recording the sales immediately. The SEC identified the following six reasons why the bill and hold sales should not have been recorded by Mattel in January 1971:

1. The merchandise was not shipped as of January 30, 1971.
2. The customer did not have to make any payments until the goods were accepted and received by him.
3. The merchandise was not physically segregated from Mattel's inventory nor labeled as the property of the customer.
4. The customer could cancel the order without penalty at any time prior to his receipt and acceptance of the merchandise.
5. The risks of ownership remained with Mattel, including the risk of loss due to damage, theft or destruction of the merchandise.
6. In many instances, the invoices were prepared without prior consultation with, or participation by, the customer as to the content of the order.[4]

To provide documentary support for the bill and hold sales, Mattel prepared customer order forms, sales invoices, and bills of lading. Bills of lading normally required the signature of both a Mattel shipping employee and a representative of the common carrier transporting the goods. However, for the bogus bills of lading, Mattel shipping employees signed for both themselves and the common carriers.

The magnitude of the bill and hold program created tremendous confusion for Mattel accounting personnel. When the bill and hold sales were recorded in January 1971, the inventory quantities for the items allegedly sold were adjusted downward even though the goods were not segregated from the remaining inventory items. When the bill and hold goods were actually shipped, weeks or even months later, Mattel's inventory records became laced with errors resulting from employees' recording the shipments a second time in the inventory records.

---

4. This information was taken from Securities and Exchange Commission, *Accounting Series Release No. 292*, 22 June 1981. All subsequent quotations, unless indicated otherwise, are reprinted from this source.

The end result was that Mattel's inventory records were unreliable. To eliminate the inventory control problems created by the bill and hold sales, Mattel executives were forced to reverse those sales in fiscal 1972. The first reversing entry was booked in May 1971 and involved $12 million in sales; approximately one-half of this total was bill and hold sales recorded in fiscal 1971, and the other one-half was bill and hold sales recorded near the end of the first quarter of fiscal 1972. This reversing entry created another problem: the net sales for May 1971 was suddenly a negative figure.

Mattel executives decided to book a fictitious $11 million sale in May to conceal the large impact of the reversing entry on the recorded sales for that month. This fictitious transaction was recorded only in the general ledger, not in the accounts receivable subsidiary ledger, meaning that there was an unreconciled difference of $11 million between the two accounting records.

In August 1971, Mattel reversed the approximately $7 million of remaining bill and hold sales recorded in fiscal 1971. Then, in September, a month in which Mattel typically experienced a very high volume of sales, company management reversed the fictitious $11 million general ledger sales entry recorded in May of that year. This entry eliminated the large difference between the balance of the general ledger controlling account for receivables and the balance of the accounts receivable subsidiary ledger. The net effect of this series of bogus entries and correcting entries was that earnings and sales for fiscal 1972 were understated by approximately the same amounts that those items were overstated for fiscal 1971.

The SEC was very concerned by the alleged failure of Arthur Andersen to discover the bill and hold program initiated by Mattel in 1971. Arthur Andersen representatives maintained that their personnel were not aware of the fraudulent scheme until Mattel executives publicly disclosed its existence in 1974. However, the SEC pointed to a significant amount of evidence collected by Arthur Andersen during the 1971 and 1972 audits of Mattel that possibly should have resulted in the discovery of the bill and hold sales. First, several of the accounts receivable confirmations mailed by Arthur Andersen during the 1971 audit were returned with discrepancies noted by Mattel's customers—discrepancies caused by bill and hold sales that had been charged improperly to the customers' accounts as of January 30, 1971. In resolving these discrepancies, the Arthur Andersen auditors obtained copies of the bills of lading for the disputed charges to determine whether the goods had actually been shipped as of January 30, 1971. The SEC pointed out that all of these bills of lading were clearly marked "bill and hold" but that the Arthur Andersen auditors apparently never asked client personnel to explain the accounting significance of that term.[5]

Likewise, the Arthur Andersen auditors apparently failed to notice that the bills of lading they obtained to clear the confirmation discrepancies conspicuously lacked the required routing or delivery instructions. Finally, the auditors also failed to recognize that both of the two required signatures on the bogus bills of lading were those of Mattel employees rather than one being the signature of a common carrier representative and the other being that of a Mattel employee. Despite these apparent problems, the auditors cleared the confirmation discrepancies caused by the bill and hold sales with the following tickmark

5. However, an Arthur Andersen manager who reviewed the accounts receivable workpapers wrote a review comment addressed to an audit senior: "What does 'Bill and Hold' mean?" Unfortunately, this review comment was apparently never cleared by the audit senior.

explanation: "Traced to Mattel invoice and bill of lading noting agreement of amount and that shipment made prior to 1/30/71."

Besides the alleged deficiencies in Arthur Andersen's confirmation procedures, the SEC contended that the audit firm had made a number of other serious oversights while auditing Mattel's sales and accounts receivable. First, the SEC noted that Arthur Andersen's year-end sales cutoff test failed to disclose the financial irregularities resulting from Mattel's bill and hold program. Arthur Andersen personnel selected eighty-two large invoices for inclusion in this test, twenty-six of which were bill and hold invoices. Despite the phrase "bill and hold" written distinctly on the face of each of these invoices and the earlier noted problems with the related bills of lading, Arthur Andersen failed to recognize that these twenty-six sales were fictitious.

During the internal control phase of the fiscal 1972 Mattel audit, Arthur Andersen selected the month of August 1971 to perform its tests of controls for the sales cycle. Ironically, August was the month in which one of the large reversing entries was made by Mattel to eliminate a portion of the bill and hold sales recorded in January 1971. This reversing entry of nearly $7 million caused the total of August's general ledger sales to be that much less than the corresponding sales figure reported for that month by a supplementary ledger maintained by Mattel, the sales invoice register. The Arthur Andersen staff person who discovered this problem wrote the following explanation for this difference in the audit workpapers—an explanation given to him by a Mattel employee: "This amount is an offset to sales due to 'invoicing errors' uncovered by client when comparing computer prepared invoices to bills of lading. Client errors such as items not being shipped and wrong amount are the types found. At this time client does not know whether credit memos were issued or not. May create a cutoff problem for accounts receivable at year-end." To his credit, the Arthur Andersen senior who reviewed this explanation noted that it was unsatisfactory and wrote the staff person the following note: "Need a better explanation. This looks like a big problem." The SEC, however, could find no evidence in the audit workpapers that the problem had been further investigated.

Finally, the SEC criticized Arthur Andersen for not utilizing analytical procedures to evaluate the overall reasonableness of Mattel's monthly sales. If such tests had been performed, the Mattel auditors would have discovered that the client's monthly sales varied dramatically from 1970 through 1972. This volatility was largely a result of the errors introduced into the accounting records by the bill and hold program and the subsequent errors created when the bill and hold sales were reversed.

Intentional Understatement of Inventory Obsolescence Reserve

The SEC ruled that Mattel's management intentionally understated the company's reserve for inventory obsolescence by approximately $5 million for the 1971 and 1972 fiscal years. As noted by the SEC, inventory obsolescence has historically been a major problem for the large toy manufacturers, given the inherent difficulty of predicting children's taste in toys. In fiscal 1971, Mattel executives were faced with a huge and unexpected inventory buildup of the Hot Wheels toy, which had been one of the company's best-selling products in the previous few years. In 1972,

Mattel was forced to dispose of approximately 5.6 million of the Hot Wheels toys by selling them to a large oil company at a loss of more than $11 million.

In arriving at its year-end reserve for obsolete inventory, Mattel prepared weekly sales forecasts for the next several months for each toy that was potentially an "excess inventory" item. A reserve for obsolescence was then calculated for those toys for which expected sales in the following months were less than the year-end inventory. In 1971 and 1972, the SEC found that Mattel inflated the projected future sales of several excess inventory items to justify not recording a reserve for obsolescence for those toys. When auditing the reserve for inventory obsolescence, Arthur Andersen personnel compared the weekly sales forecasts prepared for the excess inventory toys to the actual sales realized by those toys in the first several weeks of the new fiscal year. For eight of the toys selected for testing, five had no recorded sales in the first several weeks of the new year, and three others actually had negative net sales during that time. Unfortunately, Arthur Andersen apparently failed to investigate this issue sufficiently and, as a result, did not discover the fraudulent understatement of Mattel's reserve for inventory obsolescence.

Overstatement of Deferred Tooling Costs

For each new toy Mattel produces, the company incurs significant "tooling" costs during the developmental phase of the product. These costs include expenditures related to producing the molds and die casts needed for the new product and the expenditures required to establish the production line for the product. Mattel's tooling costs are deferred in an asset account and amortized over the estimated useful life of the new toy. The proportion of the tooling costs amortized each year for a given toy is equal to the ratio of that year's sales for the toy to the total expected sales over the life of the toy. From 1970 through 1972, Mattel executives manipulated the company's deferred tooling costs to overstate Mattel's reported earnings. As was the case with the reserve for inventory obsolescence and other key financial statement amounts, Mattel executives established a "target" figure each year for the amount of deferred tooling costs to be amortized. In 1971, for example, the amortization of deferred tooling costs was understated by approximately $3.7 million. According to the SEC, the manipulation of the deferred tooling costs in 1971 was accomplished by the following means:

1. By reallocating tooling costs from various products with low forecasted sales to those with sizable forecasted sales.
2. By adjusting the ratio of various products' current sales to their forecasted sales.
3. By deferring all tooling costs incurred during the last three months of the year.
4. By deferring certain tooling costs twice.

Arthur Andersen's audit of Mattel's deferred tooling costs for 1971 consisted of obtaining and reviewing client-prepared schedules of these costs by product and then testing the propriety of the amounts for a small number of the products that had large deferrals. The most important of these audit tests were simple comparisons of forecasted sales to actual current year sales to determine that the amount of tooling costs amortized during the year under audit was reasonable. The SEC charged that Arthur Andersen's audit programs for 1971 and 1972 failed to provide for a sufficient investigation of the large increase in Mattel's deferred tooling costs in each of those years. The SEC implied that more extensive and rigorous audit tests were required, given the magnitude of the deferred tooling costs and the inherently subjective nature of that account.

Arthur Andersen did uncover at least two instances of material overstatements of Mattel's deferred tooling costs. Arthur Andersen refused to accept certain of the revised sales forecasts that Mattel used to justify reducing the amount of deferred tooling costs written off for several products. In 1971, for example, Arthur Andersen's workpapers documented a $2 million overstatement of deferred tooling costs resulting from improper revisions of certain products' expected lifetime sales. However, Mattel adjusted the account balance by only $1.4 million. According to the SEC, the 1971 audit workpapers of Arthur Andersen did not disclose how that figure was determined, nor did the workpapers provide any evidence suggesting that the $1.4 million adjustment was sufficient to correct the noted problem.

Mattel's auditors also discovered during the 1972 audit that more than $1.2 million in tooling costs had been deferred twice. This discovery was made by a senior member of the Arthur Andersen engagement team, who then wrote a review comment instructing a subordinate to make sure that the proper adjusting entry was recorded. In responding to the review comment, the subordinate subsequently noted, "Tooling write-off adjusted for this fact." However, the SEC determined that the adjustment was never made, nor was the error apparently subjected to any further investigation by the auditors.

Underpayment of Royalties

Mattel acquired the production rights to its popular Hot Wheels product from the man who invented that toy. The contract between Mattel and the inventor called for this individual to begin receiving significant royalties on Hot Wheels sales when the product reached the break-even point. In 1970, the break-even point for the Hot Wheels toy was reached; however, to avoid paying royalties to the inventor, Mattel management fabricated an additional $4.4 million in expenses allegedly related to that product. This amount consisted primarily of bogus advertising expenses and increases in the operating losses incurred by the product in the first few years following its introduction. Because of these fraudulent expenses, Mattel avoided paying the inventor nearly $2 million in royalties that he had rightfully earned from 1970 through 1972.

The SEC charged that Arthur Andersen failed to adequately investigate the contractual arrangement between the inventor and Mattel and the potential financial statement implications of violations of that contract. In particular, Arthur Andersen apparently did not investigate the additional $4.4 million in expenses added in 1970 to the schedule that summarized the operating results of the Hot Wheels product—expenses later proved to be fictitious. Additionally, the auditors failed to obtain a copy of a computer-generated royalties report that disclosed the proper amount of royalties due the inventor.

Improper Computation of Business Interruption Insurance Claim

Mattel's large warehouse in Mexicali, Mexico, that was destroyed by a fire in September 1970 was fully insured, as were its contents. The company's insurance policy also included a business interruption clause providing up to $10 million in coverage for revenues lost as a result of destruction of the facility. In its financial statements for the fiscal year ended January 30, 1971, Mattel included a $10 million receivable from its insurance company for a business interruption insurance claim. That figure was accepted by Arthur Andersen; however, the SEC charged that neither Mattel nor Arthur Andersen should have expected the insurance company to pay the full amount of the claim. The federal agency argued that the method used by Mattel to compute the amount recoverable from the insurance company, a method approved by Arthur Andersen, was not credible. In fact, Mattel did not receive any payment from its insurance company until 1977 and then was paid only $4.4 million.

ADDITIONAL SEC CRITICISM OF ARTHUR ANDERSEN'S MATTEL AUDITS

In addition to the five specific areas of the Mattel audits for which Arthur Andersen was criticized by the SEC, the federal agency also chastised the audit firm for other, more general deficiencies in those audits. First, the SEC criticized the Arthur Andersen auditors for repeatedly failing to sufficiently investigate the suspicious transactions and documents coming to their attention. An example noted earlier was the failure of the auditors to determine the significance of the phrase "bill and hold." Second, the SEC argued that Arthur Andersen failed to "apply industry knowledge" during the course of the Mattel audits. For example, if Arthur Andersen had been closely following its client's sales markets, the firm would likely have recognized that the large inventory of the Hot Wheels toy at the end of 1970 required a significant write-down, given the inability of retailers to sell their own inventories of that product. In commenting on this point, the SEC made the following remarks: "Auditors must acquire and apply sufficient knowledge of their clients' industries to enable them to intelligently audit their business operations and to evaluate the client's explanations of those operations."

The SEC also criticized Arthur Andersen for being overly willing to accept client representations as audit evidence "with little or no verification or documentation." As an example, the SEC noted the audit firm's acceptance of the spurious explanation given for the large discrepancy between the sales reported for August 1971 by the general ledger controlling account and the sales invoice register. Finally, the SEC contended that during the Mattel audits, the senior members of the Arthur Andersen engagement team had exhibited "insufficient control, coordination, and supervision." In particular, the SEC was concerned that Arthur Andersen's audit review process had failed to ensure that important problems discovered by staff auditors during the course of the Mattel audits were resolved satisfactorily.

EPILOGUE

Under the leadership of new management, Mattel slowly recovered from its nearly disastrous experiences of the early 1970s. By 1994, Mattel overtook Hasbro

EXHIBIT 1
**Measures Taken by
Arthur Andersen to
Strengthen Its Audit
Process Following the
Mattel Audits**

- **Consultation within the Firm.** In 1978, the firm's policies on intra-firm consultation regarding complex or unusual transactions were formalized and restated in a single source providing concise guidelines on specific practice problems where consultation is appropriate.
- **Rotation of Audit Partners**. In 1976, Arthur Andersen voluntarily adopted a policy requiring rotation of audit engagement partners every five years. A similar rule was adopted by the SEC Practice Section of the AICPA in 1977.
- **Second Partner Reviews.** In 1975, Arthur Andersen began requiring an extensive review of audit reports and supporting materials by a second partner not engaged in the audit. A similar requirement was subsequently adopted by the SEC Practice Section of the AICPA.
- **Personnel Training Programs.** In the early 1970s, Arthur Andersen opened a large training facility in St. Charles, Illinois, on a former college campus. This facility is used on a continuing basis to provide training for Arthur Andersen partners and professional employees.
- **Updating of Practice and Procedure Manuals.** Arthur Andersen updated all of its major practice and procedure manuals to provide a set of readily accessible guidelines to firm policy on financial reporting issues, accounting principles, auditing procedures, and ethical issues.
- **Public Review Board.** In 1974, Arthur Andersen established a Public Review Board, an independent body comprised of individuals from business, the profession and government. The Board establishes its own program for reviewing the professional operations of the firm and has in each year of its existence focused on a different area of the firm's practice.

as the nation's largest toy maker. In that year, the company had total revenues of approximately $3 billion, one-third of which were attributable to the Barbie product line. Ruth Handler also staged a dramatic comeback following her traumatic experiences of the early 1970s. After her forced retirement from Mattel, she founded a company, Ruthton Corporation, that manufactures prosthetic devices for women who, like herself, have undergone mastectomies. Although a small company with a relatively small market, Ruthton Corporation quickly established itself and within a few years was reporting annual sales of several million dollars. Additionally, in 1989, Ruth and Elliot Handler were recognized for their contributions to the toy industry by being inducted into the industry's hall of fame.

In 1981, the SEC censured Arthur Andersen for its alleged deficient audits of Mattel, Inc. The SEC apparently chose only to censure Arthur Andersen because the audit firm demonstrated that it had undertaken significant corrective measures to prevent the recurrence of the problems that had arisen during the Mattel audits. Exhibit 1 contains the list of these corrective measures that was appended to the SEC enforcement release in which Arthur Andersen was censured.

QUESTIONS

1. Identify the key variables that influenced the level of inherent risk Arthur Andersen faced during the 1971 and 1972 audits of Mattel.

2. The SEC noted six reasons why the bill and hold sales recorded by Mattel did not qualify as consummated sales transactions. Identify and discuss the general conditions for recognizing revenue from sales transactions. Also, identify circumstances in which revenues may be recognized on sales transactions even though these conditions are not met.

3. Identify and discuss the principal audit objectives associated with the performance of year-end sales cutoff tests. In general, is it appropriate to perform these tests at an interim date? Why or why not?

4. *SAS No. 31,* "Evidential Matter," identifies five key management assertions that underlie a set of financial statements. Identify the management assertions that would have been of primary concern to Arthur Andersen regarding the following items: the reserve for inventory obsolescence, royalty expense, and the receivable recorded by Mattel for the business interruption insurance claim. Why is it important for an auditor to identify the underlying management assertions for each major account of the client?

5. In at least two instances, key issues raised as a result of the review of Mattel's workpapers by Arthur Andersen personnel were not resolved satisfactorily prior to the completion of the audit. Which member of the audit engagement team has the primary responsibility to ensure that such issues are properly resolved and documented in the audit workpapers? Justify your answer.

6. Assume that Arthur Andersen had compared Mattel's monthly sales during the early 1970s with the comparable monthly sales figures of prior years. What additional audit procedures should Arthur Andersen have performed once it discovered the extreme volatility in these monthly sales figures?

7. Arthur Andersen proposed a $2 million adjusting entry to the deferred tooling costs account during its 1971 audit of Mattel. However, Mattel adjusted the balance of that account by only $1.4 million. Identify the conditions under which Arthur Andersen would have been justified in accepting this smaller adjusting entry.

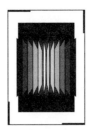

CASE 1.2
ESM GOVERNMENT SECURITIES, INC.

Jose Gomez achieved his long-sought goal of becoming a partner in Alexander Grant & Company on August 1, 1979. Only thirty-one years old, the outgoing and charming Gomez was recognized by his fellow partners as an individual who would almost certainly rise to the upper management ranks of Alexander Grant during his career. Gomez's bright future with Grant, the tenth largest CPA firm in the United States at the time, seemed all the more obvious when he was named the managing partner of the firm's Fort Lauderdale office while he was still in his early thirties. Unfortunately for Gomez, his potential was never realized. In March 1987, Gomez began serving a twelve-year term in a federal prison in Tallahassee, Florida, after pleading guilty to forgery and fraud charges.

Ironically, Gomez's fate was sealed just a few days following his promotion to partner. During a lunch with Alan Novick, an officer of his largest audit client, Gomez was startled by Novick's admission that the client's audited financial statements of the prior two years contained material errors. The client, ESM Government Securities, Inc., a Fort Lauderdale brokerage firm specializing in government securities, had several million dollars in losses that Novick had concealed from Gomez and his subordinates on the ESM audit team. Because the unqualified opinions issued on the ESM financial statements for 1977 and 1978 had been personally authorized by Gomez, Novick warned him that the disclosure of the material errors could jeopardize his career with Alexander Grant. According to Gomez, Novick repeatedly goaded him with comments such as, "It's going to look terrible for you . . . and you just got promoted to partner."[1] Novick maintained that his firm could recoup the losses that had been concealed from Alexander Grant if Gomez would not withdraw the audit reports issued on the misstated 1977 and 1978 financial statements. If Gomez insisted on

---

1. M. Brannigan, "Auditor's Downfall Shows a Man Caught in Trap of His Own Making," *Wall Street Journal*, 4 March 1987, 33.

withdrawing the audit reports, Novick warned him that ESM would fail and that a number of parties would suffer as a result, including the customers of ESM and Gomez. Eventually, Gomez capitulated to Novick's arguments.[2]

At the time Novick admitted that ESM's financial condition had been misrepresented, he was apparently aware that Gomez was experiencing considerable financial problems. Although Gomez was earning a sizable salary as a partner of a major CPA firm, that salary was not sufficient to support the affluent life-style he had adopted. After Gomez agreed to remain silent regarding the ESM fraud, Novick offered to help relieve Gomez's financial problems. In November 1979, Novick issued a $20,000 check to Gomez to cover past due credit card payments. The following year, after Gomez reportedly complained to Novick that his financial condition had worsened again, Novick provided an additional $60,000. Court records document that over the course of the seven-year ESM fraud, Gomez received approximately $200,000 from ESM officials.

If Gomez actually believed at the time, as he alleges, that ignoring the fraudulent misrepresentations in the ESM financial statements was the best alternative for all parties concerned, he was wrong. The relatively small unreported losses in the 1977 and 1978 ESM financial statements would grow to collective losses of more than $300 million by the spring of 1985. Unlike most financial scandals, which adversely affect the stockholders and creditors of one or a few companies, the ESM scandal triggered a series of events that would eventually rock both the national and international financial markets.

ESM's largest customer, Home State Savings, was an Ohio bank that was owed approximately $145 million by ESM when the latter ceased operations in March 1985. Home State Savings happened to be the largest of the more than seventy banks in Ohio whose deposits were not insured by the Federal Deposit Insurance Corporation. These banks had formed their own private deposit insurance fund into which each paid annual premiums. When Home State collapsed following the closure of ESM, panic-stricken depositors triggered runs on the other privately insured Ohio banks. Within a matter of days, the governor of Ohio decided to close all of the state's privately insured banks while state and federal regulatory authorities worked around the clock to prevent the economic fallout from the ESM scandal from spreading further. The closure of the Ohio banks and a growing loss of consumer confidence in the government securities market destabilized all of the nation's capital markets. At the peak of the crisis, the U.S. dollar plunged 14 percent in value in the international markets in one day as foreign investors became concerned that the entire U.S. banking system might be jeopardized.

The impact of the ESM scandal was not restricted to the state of Ohio or the financial markets. Besides Home State Savings, the major customers of ESM were municipalities nationwide, which collectively were owed more than $100 million by the government securities dealer. When the news of the ESM insolvency broke, the credit ratings of these municipalities plummeted, and many were forced to take immediate and drastic measures to remain solvent. One example

---

2. These are Gomez's personal recollections of his involvement in the ESM scandal. Former colleagues at Alexander Grant maintain that Gomez's account of his involvement with Novick is not totally accurate. For instance, certain of Gomez's former colleagues charge that he was aware of the ESM fraud prior to 1979.

was the city of Beaumont, Texas, which was forced to lay off approximately 15 percent of its municipal employees following the closure of ESM.

Possibly the most victimized parties in the ESM fraud were Gomez's colleagues, his fellow partners at Alexander Grant. A proud and respected firm nationwide, Alexander Grant suddenly became the focus of intense scrutiny and adverse publicity. The poor judgment of one partner cost the firm much of the credibility and prestige it had earned over its sixty-year history. To date, Alexander Grant, its successor firm, Grant Thornton, and the company that provided malpractice insurance for Alexander Grant have absorbed total legal judgments and out-of-court settlements of $175 million stemming from the ESM debacle.

HISTORY OF ESM GOVERNMENT SECURITIES

Ronnie Ewton, Bobby Seneca, and George Mead founded ESM Government Securities, Inc., in November 1975 with a total capitalization of $75,000. The principal line of business of the firm was buying and selling for customer accounts debt securities issued by the federal government and its various agencies. Ewton, who had a long and checkered career with a number of brokerage firms, was the principal executive of ESM. Ewton hired a close friend, Steve Arky, to serve as the firm's legal counsel and Alan Novick, a Wall Street investment banker who was later to corrupt Jose Gomez, to be the firm's principal securities trader.[3]

In the mid-1970s, the U.S. government securities market was subject to very little regulatory oversight although it was, and still is today, the largest securities market in the world. The average daily dollar volume of U.S. treasury bills, notes, and bonds is typically twenty to thirty times larger than the daily sales volume of the New York Stock Exchange. Despite the enormous size of the government securities market, most private investors know very little about it. Until the mid-1970s, large brokerage firms accounted for nearly all of the daily sales volume in government securities. However, the tremendous growth in the national debt during the Carter and Reagan administrations required the U.S. Treasury Department to begin working with so-called secondary dealers to raise the funds necessary to operate the federal government. These secondary dealers are generally small brokerage houses that deal almost exclusively in the trading of federal debt securities for the accounts of small to moderately sized banks and municipalities. Prior to legislation enacted in the late 1980s, these small government securities brokers were subject only to the regulatory oversight of state securities commissions, which tend to be severely underfunded and relatively ineffective as a result.

One of the most intriguing aspects of the government securities markets is the tremendous amount of leverage available to investors. Margin requirements in securities transactions of publicly owned firms typically average 50 percent, meaning that an investor must put up at least one dollar for every two dollars in stock purchased. In the government securities market, the federal government,

---

3. For an excellent and comprehensive history of the ESM scandal, see: D. L. Maggin, *Bankers, Builders, Knaves and Thieves* (Chicago: Contemporary Books, 1989).

because of the huge amount of funds it must raise, has established much more liberal margin requirements. For instance, to purchase $1,000,000 of government securities, an investor may be required to come up with as little as $10,000, or 1 percent of the total cost of those securities. Because the market value of government securities may move 2 to 3 percent in any one day in response to fractional changes in market interest rates, an investor could easily experience a 200 to 300 percent one-day rate of return, positive or negative, on an initial investment.

The majority of the transactions in which ESM engaged were repurchase agreements, more commonly known as "repos." In a repo transaction, a government securities dealer sells a customer a large block of federal securities and then simultaneously pledges to repurchase the securities at a later date at an agreed-upon price. The brokerage firm selling the securities hopes that their value will rise over the period of the repurchase agreement, which may be as short as twelve hours (overnight) or as long as twelve months. In substance, a repo transaction is a short-term loan from the customer to the securities dealer. ESM also engaged in a limited number of "reverse repos," in which it purchased government securities from a customer who simultaneously agreed to repurchase the securities at a later date at a predetermined price. In these transactions, ESM was essentially loaning funds to the other party to the transaction.

In repo transactions, it is critical that the purchaser either take physical possession of the government securities or have a bonded third party assume physical possession. If the purchaser does not take physical possession of the securities, an unscrupulous broker could sell them to another customer. Unfortunately, many of the banks and municipalities with which ESM did business were relatively unfamiliar with the government securities market. As a result, these customers naively relied on ESM to retain the securities or asked the brokerage firm to transfer the securities to a segregated account with a trust company for the term of the repurchase agreement. Even when instructed to transfer customer securities to a trust company, ESM often retained the securities or transferred them to a nonsegregated trust account, which allowed ESM officials to use the securities for whatever purpose they chose.

ESM, like many government securities dealers, also engaged in purely speculative transactions on its own behalf, transactions in which such dealers attempt to predict and profit from future changes in open market interest rates. Soon after joining ESM, Novick convinced Ewton and other ESM executives that he could earn millions of dollars in profits for ESM in speculative trades by utilizing the considerable leverage afforded by the small margin requirements in the government securities market. Unfortunately, Novick was less than proficient in predicting the future movement of interest rates. Over a short period in 1980, Novick lost more than $80 million when interest rates leaped dramatically a few weeks after he had gambled that they would fall.

The trading losses incurred by Novick in 1980, when coupled with the much smaller pre-1980 trading losses he had rung up, easily wiped out the equity of the three owners of ESM. At this point, the ESM officers could either publicly admit that their firm was bankrupt or employ on a much larger scale a practice they had begun a few years earlier: using (stealing) customer securities for their own benefit. Sadly, Ewton and his colleagues chose the latter alternative. Even though ESM was insolvent by 1980, the firm was able to remain in operation for several more years because of the huge sums of cash it acquired in repo transactions with customers. An accountant hired to reconstruct the history of the seven-year ESM scandal noted that cash flow, not profit, was the lifeblood of ESM: "The name of the game was cash flow. It had nothing to do with profit. As long as there was an ability to deliver enough cash, then whether or not the transactions made money was not relevant."[4] Of course, ESM could sell the same block of federal securities to several different customers, since the majority of its clients did not insist on taking physical possession of the securities. The positive cash flow that ESM was able to maintain because of such fraudulent practices allowed Novick to continue "playing the market" in an increasingly desperate effort to recoup the millions he had gambled away on earlier trades.

ESM's Bookkeeping Scam

One of the most problematic aspects of the ESM fraud for Alan Novick, its principal architect, was how to conceal his firm's insolvent condition from the Alexander Grant audit team that annually examined ESM's financial records. Novick had developed this scheme prior to the time he informed Gomez of ESM's unreported losses in 1977 and 1978. ESM Government Securities was actually one of several companies that Ewton and his associates had formed. The other companies were shells with no express business purpose and were not audited by Alexander Grant. Novick used these nonoperating entities to hide the huge trading losses of ESM.

Novick devised a bookkeeping scheme to transfer trading losses incurred by ESM to an affiliated company under the ESM corporate umbrella. For each repo or reverse repo that ESM engaged in, Novick would record a "mirror" intercompany transaction. If the actual transaction with a customer was a repo, then the mirror transaction would be a reverse repo, and vice versa. By covering both sides of each transaction, Novick could close out the "losing" side to the unaudited affiliate and close out the profitable side to ESM, ensuring that the latter appeared to be profitable. After this scam had gone on for several years, the cumulative trading losses transferred to the unaudited affiliate resulted in a huge receivable owed to ESM by the affiliate. This huge receivable did not appear explicitly on ESM's annual balance sheet.[5] The only reference to the mirror transactions was an oblique description of them in the footnotes accompanying the annual balance sheet. In 1984, the reference to these transactions was included in footnote D (see Exhibit 1).

Novick also used the unaudited affiliate to conceal the theft of ESM funds that he and his colleagues diverted for their own personal use or diverted to co-conspirators who were officers or employees of major customers of ESM. Many of these co-conspirators established personal trading accounts with ESM, into which Novick dumped millions of dollars of profits from repo and reverse

---

4. Unless noted otherwise, this and subsequent quotations were taken from the following source: U.S. Congress, House, Subcommittee on Oversight and Investigations of the Committee on Energy and Commerce, *SEC and Corporate Audits, Part 2* (Washington, D.C.: U.S. Government Printing Office, 1985).

5. Like many financial institutions, ESM prepared and issued only a balance sheet. In fact, ESM was not required by any regulatory body to issue a balance sheet but chose to do so apparently because many of its customers requested an audited balance sheet before they would transact business with the firm.

EXHIBIT 1
ESM's 1984 Balance Sheet and Accompanying Footnotes

ESM Government Securities, Inc.
(a wholly-owned subsidiary of ESM Group, Inc.)
STATEMENT OF FINANCIAL CONDITION
December 31, 1984

ASSETS

Cash	$ 421,000
Deposits with clearing organizations and others (note B)	182,000
Receivable from brokers and dealers (note C)	3,643,000
Receivable from customers (note C)	73,050,000
Securities purchased under agreement to resell (notes A and D)	2,945,953,000
Accrued Interest	406,000
Securities purchased not sold—at market (note A)	26,059,000
Due from parent	2,550,000
Other	61,000
	$3,052,325,000

LIABILITIES AND STOCKHOLDERS' EQUITY

Short-term bank loans (note E)	$ 47,258,000
Payable to brokers and dealers (note C)	12,266,000
Payable to customers	9,304,000
Securities sold under agreement to repurchase (notes A and D)	2,945,953,000
Accounts payable and accrued expenses	799,000
Commitment and contingencies (notes F and G)	
Stockholders' Equity	
Common stock—authorized, issued and outstanding	
1,000 shares at $1.00	1,000
Additional contributed capital	4,160,000
Retained earnings	32,584,000
	$3,052,325,000

The accompanying notes are an integral part of this statement.

NOTES TO STATEMENT OF FINANCIAL CONDITION
December 31, 1984

NOTE A—SIGNIFICANT ACCOUNTING POLICIES
A summary of the significant accounting policies applied in the preparation of the financial statements follows.

Security Transactions.   Security transactions are recorded on a settlement date basis, generally the first business day following the transaction date.

Purchases of securities under agreements to resell and sales of securities under agreements to repurchase are considered financing transactions and represent the amount of purchases and sales which will be resold or reacquired at amounts specified in the respective agreements.

---

repo transactions. In return, when ESM had a sudden need for additional government securities, these individuals would supply ESM with securities from their own firms' vaults.[6] Over the course of the ESM scam, Novick, his colleagues, and their co-conspirators were the beneficiaries of more than

---

6. These securities were allegedly collateral for loans that ESM had made earlier to these customers. Court records, however, document that these loans were grossly overcollateralized and that the true purpose of these transfers of securities was simply to perpetuate the ESM fraud.

NOTE A—SIGNIFICANT ACCOUNTING POLICIES—Continued

Securities Purchases, Not Sold. Securities inventory, which consists of marketable federal government or government agency securities, is carried at market value.

Furniture and Equipment. Furniture and equipment are stated at cost. Depreciation is provided in amounts sufficient to relate the cost of depreciable assets to operations over their estimated service lives, principally on a straight-line basis over 5 years.

Income Taxes. The company participates in the filing of a consolidated income tax return with its parent. Any tax liability of the affiliated group is allocated to each member company based on its contribution to taxable income.

NOTE B—DEPOSITS WITH CLEARING ORGANIZATIONS AND OTHERS

The company has deposits of cash and securities with commodity brokers to meet margin requirements. The company also has cash escrow deposits with its securities clearing agent.

NOTE C—BROKER, DEALER AND CUSTOMER ACCOUNTS

Receivables from brokers, dealers and customers at December 31, 1984, include outstanding securities failed to deliver. Payables to brokers, dealers and customers at December 31, 1984, include outstanding securities failed to receive. "Fails," all of which have been outstanding less than 30 days, represent the contract value of securities which have not been received or delivered by settlement date. Fails to receive and fails to deliver from brokers and customers were $7,291,426 and $9,993,081 respectively at December 31, 1984.

NOTE D—SECURITY TRANSACTIONS

The company entered into repurchase and resale agreements with customers whereby specific securities are sold or purchased for short durations of time. These agreements cover securities, the rights to which are usually acquired through similar purchase/resale agreements. The company has agreements with an affiliated company for securities purchased under agreements to resell amounting to approximately $1,621,481,000 and securities sold under agreements to repurchase amounting to approximately $1,324,472,000 at December 31, 1984. Accrued interest receivable from and payable to the affiliated company at year end were $11,174,000 and $64,410,000 respectively.

NOTE E—SHORT-TERM BANK LOANS

Short-term bank loans at December 31, 1984 are collateralized by securities purchased not sold.

NOTE F—RELATED PARTY TRANSACTIONS

Certain common expenses paid by the parent company, including depreciation, are allocated to the subsidiary companies based on transaction volume. The company paid a dividend of $10,000,000 to its parent company as of December 31, 1984. The company occupies premises leased by the parent company from a partnership of which one of the officers is a partner. Rent expense paid the partnership amounted to $112,000 for the year ended December 31, 1984 (note G).

NOTE G—COMMITMENTS

The company conducts its operations in leased facilities under noncancellable operating leases expiring at various dates through 2010. The minimum lease payment for one location has been calculated based on current transaction volume (note F) under a 30 year lease. The minimum rental commitments under the operating lease are as follows:

Year ended December 31,	
1985	$ 162,900
1986	162,900
1987	141,900
1988	112,400
1989	112,400
1990 and thereafter	2,332,400
	$3,024,900

Rental expense charged to operations approximated $137,000 for the year ended December 31, 1984.

EXHIBIT 1—Cont'd
ESM's 1984 Balance Sheet and Accompanying Footnotes

$100,000,000 of ESM funds, which essentially were stolen from the banks and municipalities that were ESM's major customers. When these defalcations were added to the trading losses incurred by Novick and to the other investment losses of ESM, the net deficit for the corporate ESM group exceeded $300 million by the spring of 1985.

Two events in late 1984 eventually proved to be the downfall of ESM. First, Novick collapsed and died at his desk of a massive heart attack in November 1984. Novick was in his early forties at the time of his death but had been under immense stress for several years, since he had been responsible for the day-to-day operations of the covert aspects of the ESM scam. Ewton and Steve Arky, ESM's legal counsel, attempted to persuade Gomez to leave Alexander Grant and assume Novick's position, but Gomez refused. Apparently concerned that the increasingly nervous Gomez might blow the whistle on the entire operation, Ewton transferred $100,000 to Gomez's personal ESM account to keep him on board. Second, a major customer demanded in late 1984 that ESM turn over the securities the customer had purchased in a long-term repo transaction—securities that ESM no longer had. Although ESM stalled the customer for months, eventually Ewton realized that the ESM fraud would soon be exposed, resigned from the firm, and retained the services of a criminal defense attorney.

Audit Issues Raised by the ESM Debacle

On February 28, 1985, Alexander Grant issued its final opinion on the financial statements of ESM Government Securities (see Exhibit 2). Less than twenty-four hours later, after Gomez admitted his involvement in the ESM scam to fellow partners, Alexander Grant hastily announced that it had withdrawn the unqualified opinion, stating that the opinion could no longer be relied upon. After learning of Grant's withdrawal of its audit report, an attorney for Home State Savings (which was owed approximately $145,000,000 by ESM) flew to Fort Lauderdale and demanded that ESM officials explain why the audit report had been rescinded. By this point, Ewton was nowhere to be found. Two of his subordinates referred the Home State attorney to an attorney that ESM had retained a few weeks earlier, following the resignation of Steve Arky. The two attorneys then contacted a local accountant and asked the latter to meet them at ESM headquarters the following morning. By midmorning on March 2, 1985, only two hours after the accountant first obtained the ESM records, he informed the attorneys that ESM was insolvent by at least $200 million.

The congressional subcommittee that investigated the ESM scandal was shocked that such a massive fraud could be detected in a matter of hours, when Alexander Grant had failed to detect the scam over a period of seven years. Members of the subcommittee insisted that at least some of Gomez's forty colleagues and subordinates who worked on the ESM audit engagements must have been aware of the fraudulent scheme; however, no other Alexander Grant auditors were ever criminally indicted in the case.[7] In a subsequent civil suit,

---

7. However, one individual on the tax staff of Alexander Grant did notice a payment in the ESM records that had been made to Gomez. Rather than bringing this matter to the attention of other partners, this individual took it directly to Gomez. Apparently, Gomez was able to fabricate an explanation for the payment that satisfied the individual.

[Note: This audit report appeared on the letterhead of Alexander Grant & Company.]

Board of Directors
ESM Government Securities, Inc.

We have examined the statement of financial condition of ESM Government Securities, Inc. (a Florida corporation and wholly-owned subsidiary of ESM Group, Inc.) as of December 31, 1984. Our examination was made in accordance with generally accepted auditing standards and, accordingly, included such tests of the accounting records and such other auditing procedures as we considered necessary in the circumstances.

In our opinion, the statement referred to above presents fairly the financial condition of ESM Government Securities, Inc. at December 31, 1984 in conformity with generally accepted accounting principles applied on a basis consistent with that of the preceding year.

Alexander Grant & Company

[signed]

Fort Lauderdale, Florida

January 30, 1985

**EXHIBIT 2
Alexander Grant's Audit
Report on ESM's 1984
Balance Sheet**

Gomez testified that little effort had been required on his part to divert the attention of his subordinates away from the fraudulent sections of the ESM financial records: "I thought about when my own audit people would come up with questions that I wouldn't be able to answer without forcing me to lie extensively. That never happened."[8]

The accountant who uncovered the ESM fraud on March 2, 1985, did not unravel the thousands of intercompany transactions that Novick had used to conceal the firm's trading losses and defalcations by employees. Instead, the accountant happened to compare the firm's audited balance sheets with the corporate tax returns filed for the ESM consolidated entity. Because the ESM executives did not want to pay federal taxes on the profitable securities trades diverted to ESM Government Securities, they had instructed the firm's tax accountant from Alexander Grant to prepare a consolidated tax return for the ESM corporate group. Over the period of the fraud, these corporate tax returns clearly demonstrated that the collective ESM operation was consistently losing tens of millions of dollars each year. An attorney in the law firm appointed as ESM's receiver noted that the scam was immediately obvious when the tax returns and audited balance sheets were compared: "It's incredible because it's so plain. It did not take detective work to find this. You just compare the reported balance sheets and the tax returns and you see the whole thing."[9]

The congressional subcommittee queried expert witnesses in the ESM hearings at length regarding the complex maze of intercompany transactions that Novick used to conceal the huge ESM deficits. The subcommittee members were particularly concerned that Alexander Grant had apparently failed to audit these transactions thoroughly.

MR. TEW [ATTORNEY FOR ESM RECEIVER]: ... it is critical that auditors inspect interrelated or affiliated transactions, because [in such cases] the client is

8. Maggin, *Bankers, Builders, Knaves and Thieves*, 215.

9. J. Sterngold, "ESM's Auditor Is Sued," *New York Times*, 16 March 1985, 30.

booking entries with itself. If you can book an entry with yourself, you can commit a massive fraud.

CONGRESSMAN DINGELL: And control both entries?

MR. TEW: Yes, sir. You have it on both sides. You can do what you want. If this company [ESM Government Securities] lost money on a term repo, they would record a reverse repo or a mirror transaction, and move the loss up to the parent company.

Another insightful question posed by the congressional subcommittee dealt with why neither ESM's auditors nor auditors of ESM's clients discovered the constant shortage of securities that was one result of Novick's fraudulent scheme. It seemed apparent to members of the subcommittee that the most basic audit procedures should have uncovered this shortage.

MR. TEW: . . . the first thing you do, one of the first and simplest things, is to do a box count of the securities or confirm that the actual securities are in the possession of the custodian.

CONGRESSMAN DINGELL: To make sure these securities and assets are a) what they purport to be; and b) are physically in the place that they are supposed to be; and c) are in the custody of the people in whose custody they are supposed to be. Isn't that right?

MR. TEW: Correct on all counts. The fundamental confirmation technique is to cover all the issues you just raised.

Auditors of major customers of ESM testified that they had performed confirmation procedures. Unfortunately, in most cases, they had directed their confirmations to Jose Gomez. This testimony incensed Representative Ron Wyden, who was the most severe critic of the auditors involved in the ESM case:

> The auditors tell us that they had no choice but to rely on second-party confirmations—in this case, the word of Mr. Gomez—that the collateral for these large loans did exist and did adequately secure their clients' interest. What disturbs me is that the system literally breeds this kind of buck-passing. If the auditors went as far as the system and the rules of their profession require in confirming the collateral, any reasonable person would conclude that once again the auditing system has failed . . . it is my view that the only watchdogs throughout this sorry spectacle were either asleep, forgot how to bark, or were taking handouts from the burglars.

Several of the congressmen were also confused as to why the audit review process of Alexander Grant had failed to uncover the fraud. In particular, representatives of Alexander Grant were questioned regarding the failure of their firm's review process to disclose the obvious contradiction in the ESM financial statements and the ESM tax returns.

CONGRESSMAN LUKEN: What is your [review] system?

MR. KLECKNER [managing partner of Grant Thornton, the successor firm to Alexander Grant & Company]: Every report that is issued by an office is required to receive what we call a basic review within that office. In certain circumstances, the report is required to receive what we call an in-depth review, and in other circumstances, a report is required to receive what we call a technical review, which normally involves people from outside that office.

CONGRESSMAN LUKEN: Would you say that the review system has broken down rather badly here since you say that Mr. Gomez passed the review system?

MR. KLECKNER: I think it's a key question.

CONGRESSMAN SIKORSKI: Can rendering an inaccurate audit opinion be the fault of only one person under your firm's quality control procedure?

MR. KLECKNER: I think it really depends upon the degree and the nature of the manipulation that was taking place.

CONGRESSMAN SIKORSKI: Well, your system allows that manipulation.

MR. KLECKNER: The system is based on a fundamental assumption. The fundamental assumption is that the audit partner is honest.

CONGRESSMAN SIKORSKI: That's right. What kind of system do you have set up to catch dishonest people?

MR. KLECKNER: I would have to admit that I don't think our system starts out to try to question the honesty and integrity of each partner.

In a subsequent court case, testimony obtained by a plaintiff attorney further disparaged the audit review process of Alexander Grant: "Garcia-Pedrosa [plaintiff counsel] got a review partner to admit that he only made cursory investigations of Gomez's ESM workpapers from 1977 to 1982. And there was no refutation of Jose Gomez's testimony that another review partner said, 'I don't understand this s——, so please tell me it's okay and I'll sign it.' "[10]

Congressman John Dingell, the chairman of the congressional subcommittee that investigated the ESM fraud, asked the accountant hired by the firm's receiver to identify the key red flags that should have alerted Alexander Grant auditors that something was wrong at ESM. The first warning signal was the magnitude of the intercompany transactions taking place between ESM and its affiliates. Even more important than the size of these transactions was the lack of an underlying business purpose for them. The inability of the Alexander Grant auditors to follow these huge and suspicious intercompany transactions from "cradle to grave," since the other party to the transactions was an unaudited affiliate of ESM, could easily have been considered a material limitation on the scope of the ESM audits. Ironically, the intercompany scheme utilized by Novick to hide the ESM losses was very similar to the bookkeeping scams used in several classic audit failures in the past, including Continental Vending, Equity Funding, and Drysdale Securities.

Another warning signal that should have raised questions in the minds of Alexander Grant auditors was the exorbitant life-styles that the officers of ESM adopted and flaunted over the short history of their firm. As an example, Exhibit 3 lists the personal assets of Ewton that a bankruptcy judge froze following the collapse of ESM.

Possibly the most important red flag of all was the personal background of ESM's chief executive, Ronnie Ewton. A thorough background investigation of Ewton would have disclosed a number of suspicious incidents in his past. In 1973, Ewton had been censured by the National Association of Securities Dealers, and two of his associates in a pre-ESM brokerage firm had been convicted of

10. Maggin, *Bankers, Builders, Knaves and Thieves*, 215.

Asset	Estimated Value (net of any mortgage balance)
Residence in Boca Raton, Fla.	$1,650,000
Residence in Greenwich, Conn.	330,000
5,600–acre horse farm in Aiken, S.C.	Unknown
Polo pony stable and 17 horses	700,000
House and two vacant lots in Boone, N.C.	Unknown
Boat slip in Key Largo, Fla.	Unknown
House and 57 acres in Aiken, S.C.	Unknown
One-fifteenth ownership interest in Hounds Lake Country Club in Aiken, S.C.	Unknown
Five lots in Elk River Country Club in Linville, N.C.	Unknown
One Aston Martin Laconda (automobile)	151,000
One 1984 Chevrolet Corvette	20,000
One Mercedes–Benz, one Cadillac, one Toyota, and several jeeps and trucks	Unknown
70–foot yacht	1,350,000
Partnership interest in horse-breeding operation	Unknown
Account with Provident Securities	400,000
Letter of credit held by Provident Bank	200,000
Partnership interest in 5,600 acres of property in Jasper, Tenn.	Unknown
Partnership interest in Colee Hammock Building	200,000
Mortgages receivable	1,995,279
Partnership interest in Tampa Bay Bandits professional sports franchise	Unknown
Partnership interest in S–J Minerals Partnership	Unknown
Numerous partnership interests in oil and gas ventures and coal-mining projects	Unknown

falsifying financial records and having used customer securities as collateral on personal loans. In the twelve months prior to forming ESM, Ewton had been employed for a short time by three different brokerage firms, two of which had bilked investors out of millions of dollars. In each case, Ewton escaped relatively unscathed, although several of his associates received jail terms. Finally, in the early months of ESM's existence, prior to the firm's hiring Alexander Grant, Ewton had been investigated by the Securities and Exchange Commission (SEC). Although the SEC had no direct regulatory oversight over ESM, it brought a suit against the firm that charged that Ewton had attempted to swindle an SEC-registered bank holding company. Ironically, the SEC investigator filed the following report regarding his investigation of ESM: "The staff believes that it may have uncovered the tip of an iceberg involving the fraudulent trading of Ginnie Mae's and other securities issued by the United States and its agencies."[11] Unfortunately for the future customers of ESM, Steve Arky, ESM's

---

11. Ibid., 75.

skillful legal counsel, was able to thwart the SEC charges, and once again, Ewton escaped unscathed.[12]

EPILOGUE

The principal conspirators in the ESM scandal were convicted of various crimes and sentenced to jail. Ewton, for example, received a twenty-four-year sentence and will apparently be required to serve fifteen years before he is eligible for parole. Three months following the collapse of ESM, Steve Arky committed suicide. Several months later, the accountant who had maintained the fraudulent books of ESM's bogus affiliate for Alan Novick also committed suicide after being convicted and sentenced to prison.

Shortly after the ESM scandal began grabbing nationwide headlines, the firm of Alexander Grant & Company changed its name to Grant Thornton. In a negotiated settlement with the Florida Board of Accountancy in 1985, Grant agreed to a sixty-day suspension on accepting any new clients and to submit to a peer review by a CPA firm selected by the state board. Prior to the ESM debacle, Grant's malpractice insurance provided for $195 million in coverage with a deductible of $500,000. The new insurance contract obtained by Grant following the ESM case reportedly had a deductible of $3 million. Another apparent consequence of the ESM case for Grant was the closure of approximately 20 percent of its offices.

QUESTIONS

1. In an interview with the *Wall Street Journal* following his admission of involvement in the ESM fraud, Jose Gomez reported that individuals recently promoted to partner in a major CPA firm are subject to considerable pressure from their superiors to attract and retain clients. What measures should audit firms take to ensure that such pressure does not become dysfunctional, as it did in the case of Jose Gomez?

2. Note A to the 1984 audited balance sheet of ESM (see Exhibit 1) discusses the consolidated tax return filed for the composite ESM corporate group. What responsibility, if any, do auditors have to review a client's corporate tax return? If tax and audit services are provided to a given client by a CPA firm, what responsibility, if any, does the tax practitioner have to communicate to the audit team any problematic information discovered during the preparation of the tax return?

---

12. The legal expertise of Steve Arky and his firm was required on a number of occasions to bail ESM out of desperate straits. In 1980, Bobby Seneca, one of the co-founders of ESM, was sued for divorce by his wife. To avoid a large divorce settlement, Seneca provided ESM's financial records, both those of ESM and those of the firm's affiliates, to the judge presiding over the divorce trial. Of course, the composite corporate records clearly demonstrated that ESM was bankrupt. However, Steve Arky's law firm was able to convince the judge that the insolvency of ESM should be kept confidential following the trial, ostensibly to allow the firm to liquidate in an orderly manner.

3. During his testimony before the congressional subcommittee, the managing partner of Grant Thornton pointed out that the audit review process of the firm is based on the fundamental assumption that the engagement audit partner is honest. Should CPA firms rethink their basic quality control strategies, given what happened in the ESM case?

4. When Alexander Grant was informed of the ESM fraud by Gomez, the firm immediately withdrew the audit opinion that had been issued on the December 31, 1984, ESM balance sheet. Was this the appropriate course of action to take in this set of circumstances? Did Alexander Grant have a responsibility to take any other actions?

5. During the congressional hearings in the ESM case, the auditors of customers of ESM were queried regarding the confirmation procedures they used in connection with their clients' transactions with ESM. What would be the key objective or objectives of an auditor's confirmation procedures when a client has engaged in (a) material repo transactions with a government securities broker, and (b) material reverse repo transactions with a government securities broker?

6. Following his death, Steve Arky's law firm was sued by the ESM receiver on the grounds that Arky had an obligation to inform Alexander Grant that ESM was insolvent. Which party to this suit do you believe prevailed, and why?

7. Because of the concept of joint and several liability, individual partners are personally responsible for the malfeasance of any and all of their fellow partners. Is it appropriate for society to impose joint and several liability on the partners of huge professional firms? Why or why not?

8. Congressional testimony disclosed that ESM officers had several million dollars in outstanding loans from ESM. These loans were not shown separately on the 1984 ESM balance sheet. Do technical standards require that such loans be reported separately in a client's financial statements? If so, why?

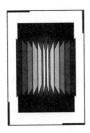

CASE 1.3
UNITED STATES SURGICAL CORPORATION

Leon Hirsch founded United States Surgical Corporation (USSC) in 1964 with very little capital, four employees, and one product: an awkward and clumsy-appearing surgical stapling device. In his mid-thirties at the time and lacking a college degree, Hirsch had already tried a number of lines of business, including frozen foods, dry cleaning, and advertising, each with little success. In fact, the dry cleaning venture had ended in bankruptcy. Consequently, few of Hirsch's friends and family members believed that USSC would become a viable entity. Despite the long odds against him, by 1980 Hirsch had built the Connecticut-based USSC into a large and profitable public company whose stock was traded on a national exchange. More important, the surgical stapler that Hirsch invented revolutionized surgery techniques in the United States and abroad.

During the early years of its existence, USSC dominated the small surgical stapling industry that Hirsch had founded in the mid-1960s. By 1980, however, several companies were beginning to encroach on USSC's market. USSC's principal competitor at the time was a company owned by Alan Blackman, a former associate of Hirsch, who allegedly had reverse-engineered USSC's products in foreign countries and then marketed them in those countries, as well as in the United States.

Beginning in 1980, USSC began an aggressive counterattack to repel Blackman's intrusion into its markets. First, USSC adopted a worldwide litigation strategy to contest Blackman's right to manufacture and market his competing products. Second, the company engaged in a large research and development program to create a line of new products technologically superior to those being manufactured by Blackman. Each of these activities involved multimillion-dollar commitments on the part of USSC—commitments that threatened the profitable earnings trend of the company and, as a result, the ability of Hirsch to raise additional capital to finance his expansionist policy.

Hirsch was successful in overcoming the major challenges facing his company in the early 1980s. USSC maintained its dominant position in the surgical stapling industry while continuing to post record levels of profits and sales. However, the rapid growth in sales and profits experienced by the company during the late 1970s and early 1980s spurred the Securities and Exchange Commission (SEC) to begin an investigation of USSC's financial affairs. In 1983, following the public disclosure by the SEC of several allegations of misconduct on the part of USSC officers, Ernst & Whinney resigned as the company's audit firm and withdrew the unqualified audit opinions it had issued on the 1980 and 1981 USSC financial statements. In 1985, the SEC issued a report on its lengthy investigation of USSC. The SEC ruled that the company had used a "variety of manipulative devices to overstate its earnings in its 1980 and 1981 financial statements."[1] (Exhibit 1 contains USSC's original balance sheets and income statements for the period 1979 to 1981.)

To settle the SEC charges, USSC officials agreed to reduce their company's previously reported earnings by $26 million. Additionally, senior executives of USSC were required to return to the company large bonuses they had been paid as a result of the inflated profits. Hirsch alone was required to repay more than $300,000 to USSC. Following the signing of the agreement with the SEC, Hirsch reported that the criticism of his company and his management decisions was undeserved. Hirsch implied that cost considerations were the key motivation for his agreeing to the SEC-imposed sanctions: "It was our opinion that the settlement [with the SEC] was preferable to long, costly and time-consuming litigation."[2]

USSC's Abusive Accounting Practices

The SEC enforcement release that disclosed the key findings of the federal agency's investigation of USSC charged the company with several abusive accounting and financial reporting practices. The focal point of the SEC investigation was an elaborate plan that USSC executives had developed and carried out to charge inventoriable production costs to a long-term asset account, molds and dies. This scheme, which required the cooperation of several of USSC's vendors, was deliberately concealed from the company's audit firm, Ernst & Whinney.[3]

The SEC investigation also disclosed that USSC had a policy of recording inventory shipments to its sales force as consummated sales transactions. Until the mid-1970s, USSC had marketed its products through a network of independent dealers. Historically, inventory shipments to these dealers had been treated as arm's length transactions and thus reportable as revenue. By 1980, however, nearly all of the company's products were marketed by a sales staff consisting of full-time employees working on a commission basis. Everyone on the sales staff maintained an inventory of USSC products, which they transported from client

---

1. This and subsequent quotations, unless indicated otherwise, were taken from Securities and Exchange Commission, *Accounting and Auditing Enforcement Release No. 109A*, 6 August, 1986.

2. K. B. Noble, "U.S. Surgical Settlement to Restate Earnings," *New York Times*, 28 February 1984, B2.

3. A subsequent section of this case discusses the details of this scheme, including the measures that USSC executives took to conceal it from Ernst & Whinney.

U.S. Surgical Corporation Consolidated Balance Sheets 1979–1981 (000s omitted)			
		December 31,	
	1981	1980	1979
Current Assets			
Cash	$ 426	$ 1,243	$ 596
Receivables (net)	36,670	30,475	22,557
Inventories			
Finished Goods	29,216	9,860	5,685
Work in Process	5,105	2,667	1,153
Raw Materials	20,948	18,806	7,365
	55,269	31,333	14,203
Other Current Assets	7,914	1,567	1,820
Total Current Assets	100,279	64,618	39,176
Property, Plant, and Equipment			
Land	2,502	2,371	1,027
Buildings	32,416	18,511	13,019
Molds and Dies	32,082	15,963	8,777
Machinery and Equipment	40,227	23,762	12,362
	107,227	60,607	35,185
Allowance for Depreciation	(14,953)	(9,964)	(6,340)
	92,274	50,643	28,845
Other Assets	14,786	3,842	2,499
Total Assets	$207,339	$119,103	$70,520
Current Liabilities			
Accounts Payable	$ 12,278	$ 6,951	$ 6,271
Notes Payable	—	—	1,596
Income Taxes Payable	—	1,685	—
Current Portion of Long-term Debt	724	666	401
Accrued Expenses	5,673	5,130	5,145
Total Current Liabilities	18,675	14,432	13,413
Long-term Debt	80,642	47,569	33,497
Deferred Income Taxes	7,466	2,956	1,384
Stockholders' Equity:			
Common Stock	1,081	930	379
Additional Paid-in Capital	72,594	34,932	10,736
Retained Earnings	32,665	20,881	13,189
Translation Allowance	(1,086)	—	—
Deferred Compensation—			
from Issuance of Restricted Stock	(4,698)	(2,597)	(2,078)
Total Stockholders' Equity	100,556	54,146	22,226
Total Liabilities and Stockholders' Equity	$207,339	$119,103	70,520

EXHIBIT 1
United States Surgical Corporation's 1979–1981 Financial Statements

to client. When a shipment was made to a salesperson, USSC recorded the inventory as having been sold, even though employees could return unsold items for full credit. Allegedly, USSC's management ordered that excessive amounts of inventory be shipped to salespeople to overstate the company's

EXHIBIT 1—Cont'd
United States Surgical Corporation's 1979–1981 Financial Statements

U.S. Surgical Corporation Consolidated Income Statements 1979–1981 (000s omitted)			
	December 31,		
	1981	1980	1979
Net Sales	$ 111,800	$ 86,214	$ 60,876
Costs and Expenses			
Cost of Products Sold	47,983	32,300	25,659
Selling, General, and Administrative*	45,015	37,740	23,935
Interest	5,898	4,063	3,403
	98,896	74,103	52,997
Income Before Income Taxes	12,904	12,111	7,879
Income Taxes:			
Federal and Foreign	795	3,406	2,279
State and Local	325	820	471
	1,120	4,226	2,750
Net Income	$ 11,784	$ 7,885	$ 5,129
Net Income per common share and common share equivalent	$1.13	$.89	$.68
Average number of common shares and common share equivalents outstanding			
1981	10,403,392		
1980		8,816,986	
1979			7,555,710

*Included in these amounts are the following research and development expenses: 1981—$1,337, 1980—$3,020, 1979—$2,289.

recorded profits. A former sales manager of the company testified that such excess shipments to sales staff were common: "It was nothing to come home and find $3,000 worth of product sitting in a box on your front porch from UPS and a note saying, 'We thought you needed a little more product.' "[4] According to the SEC, USSC's 1980 and 1981 pretax profits were overstated by $1,150,000 and $750,000, respectively, as a result of the company's policy of recognizing inventory shipments to its sales staff as consummated sales transactions.

Another charge leveled at USSC by the SEC's enforcement release was that the company had abused the accounting rule that permits the capitalization of legal expenses incurred to develop and successfully defend a patent. In 1980, USSC capitalized less than $1 million in litigation expenses incurred to defend its patents; the following year, that figure leaped to $5.8 million. The SEC investigation disclosed that a significant portion of the 1981 litigation expenses was incurred in Australian lawsuits filed against Alan Blackman and his company. However, USSC did not have any registered patents in Australia, meaning that the Australian legal expenses should not have been deferred in an asset account but instead immediately charged to operations. The SEC did find that approximately $3.7 million of the 1981 litigation expenses had been incurred by USSC to defend its U.S. patents. However, USSC had chosen to amortize these costs over

4. N. R. Kleinfeld, "U.S. Surgical's Checkered History," *New York Times*, 13 May 1984, F4.

a ten-year period even though the seventeen-year legal life of most of the patents in question would expire in 1983 or 1984.

Many of USSC's surgical tools were not sold, but rather leased, to customers. The cost of each of these assets was recorded in a subsidiary fixed asset ledger, leased and loaned assets. The SEC discovered that although USSC periodically retired such assets from use and removed them from the sub-ledger, the costs associated with these retired assets were not removed from the sub-ledger but instead debited to the accounts of other assets still in service. Additionally, in 1981, USSC inflated the balance sheet values of several fixed assets by arbitrarily extending their useful lives and by establishing salvage values for the first time for many of these same assets.

ALLEGATIONS OF AUDIT DEFICIENCIES

The SEC's investigation of USSC resulted in the identification of a number of alleged deficiencies in Ernst & Whinney's audits of the company. The SEC was particularly critical of Ernst & Whinney's 1981 audit of USSC. The enforcement release issued by the SEC maintained that Ernst & Whinney had failed to make proper use of analytical procedures in planning the 1981 USSC audit. Ernst & Whinney apparently failed to consider the important implications for its 1981 audit of several material increases and decreases in certain USSC account balances between December 31, 1980, and December 31, 1981. For example, the balance of the asset account molds and dies increased by more than 100 percent from the end of 1980 to the end of 1981. According to the SEC, "This unusually large increase should have caused the auditors to scrutinize carefully the nature and source of the additions, and whether certain costs were properly identified and capitalized under GAAP." Likewise, there was a greater than 50 percent decrease in research and development expenses included in USSC's 1981 income statement compared with the prior year's income statement. This decrease occurred even though USSC was engaged in a large product development campaign in 1981.

Ernst & Whinney apparently also failed to recognize the implications for its 1981 audit of the significant increase in the amount of litigation expense capitalized in USSC's patents account. (USSC included the patents account in noncurrent "Other Assets" on its balance sheet. See Exhibit 1.) According to the SEC, the increase in deferred litigation expenses between 1980 and 1981, when coupled with material changes in other key account balances, should have placed Ernst & Whinney on alert that the 1981 USSC audit would have a higher-than-normal degree of risk associated with it: "The heightened audit attention was particularly important since the aggregate effect of the changes was material to Surgical's 1981 financial statements, the changes ... all had the effect of increasing income, and there were extraordinarily large additions to the affected accounts."

Another risk factor Ernst & Whinney should have considered when planning the 1981 USSC audit was the incentive that USSC officials had to present their company as favorably as possible to security analysts, given the company's need to raise additional capital to finance the expansion of its product line. A former vice-president of USSC reported that Hirsch often made extensive commitments to security analysts regarding the company's sales and profits for future periods.[5] In that individual's opinion, many of the abusive practices of USSC were a direct consequence of Hirsch's efforts to deliver the promised sales and earnings figures. Finally, a bonus plan for management tied to reported profits provided an additional economic incentive for USSC officials to misrepresent their company's financial condition: "Surgical's executive officers could earn bonuses ranging from 15% to 75% of their base salaries, if the earnings per share growth ranged from 15% to 30% over the previous year. Management therefore had powerful personal incentives to keep the earnings per share high."

The SEC ruled that Ernst & Whinney had made three critical errors when considering the question of whether USSC should be allowed to record shipments of inventory to sales employees as valid sales transactions. First, the SEC pointed out that Ernst & Whinney failed to recognize that there is a strong presumption that "sales" of inventory to employees are not arm's length transactions: "Because the potential for abuse is so great when a 'sale' transaction is between a company and its employee, the presumption is that no 'true' sale has taken place." Second, the SEC maintained that USSC's repurchase of significant amounts of inventory from its salespeople during 1981 should have alerted Ernst & Whinney that the original "sales" to these employees were not bona fide transactions. This oversight by Ernst & Whinney was particularly troublesome to the SEC because these repurchases were clearly documented in the audit firm's 1980 and 1981 workpapers. Finally, Ernst & Whinney was criticized for failing to corroborate a client executive's assertion that USSC was not obligated to repurchase inventory from employees who resigned or were terminated. According to the SEC, Ernst & Whinney's 1981 audit program included a procedure to obtain and review a copy of the standard employment contract signed by USSC's sales employees and to incorporate that contract in the "permanent" workpaper file. Although the Ernst & Whinney audit program indicated that this procedure had been completed, there was no evidence to this effect in the firm's 1981 workpapers. The SEC ruled that if Ernst & Whinney had obtained and reviewed a copy of the employment contract, the auditors would have confirmed that USSC not only had a policy of repurchasing inventory from former employees but actually had a contractual obligation to do so.

The SEC's harshest criticism of Ernst & Whinney was reserved for the CPA firm's failure to prevent USSC from capitalizing a material amount of production expenses in the asset account molds and dies. The SEC found that during the last few months of 1980, USSC began systematically charging inventoriable production costs to that noncurrent asset account, resulting in a significant overstatement of assets and an understatement of cost of goods sold. Although company executives used a number of methods to conceal this illicit scheme, the most common technique was simply to instruct the company's vendors who did most of the production work on USSC's products to describe generic production costs as capitalizable expenses on the invoices submitted for payment to USSC. One of USSC's primary vendors was Lacey Manufacturing Company, a division of Barden Corporation, which also happened to be an audit client of Ernst & Whinney. In late 1980, USSC officials instructed Barden Corporation to begin using the phrase "tooling modifications" to describe the work performed for USSC by Lacey Manufacturing. Previously, these invoices had described the

---

5. Ibid.

work on USSC contracts as being generic production costs. This change in the description of the incurred costs was critical, since all tooling costs for new or redesigned products were capitalizable expenditures.

CHRONOLOGY OF USSC–ERNST & WHINNEY DISAGREEMENT REGARDING CAPITALIZATION OF ALLEGED TOOLING COSTS

For many years, accounting educators have maintained that the quality of audits is sometimes impaired by the imbalance of power in the auditor-client relationship.[6] Critics suggest that because client executives retain and compensate their company's independent auditors, auditors may capitulate to the demands of client executives when a technical dispute arises during the course of an audit. The series of events that resulted in Ernst & Whinney's agreeing to allow USSC to capitalize the disputed tooling costs provides a classic example of an audit conflict situation in which an audit firm eventually acquiesced to an overbearing client. The following are the key events in the USSC–Ernst & Whinney dispute regarding the alleged tooling costs:

1/27/82   The Ernst & Whinney audit team completes its fieldwork on the USSC engagement.

2/2/82   Paul Yamont, senior vice-president and treasurer of Barden Corporation, makes an unsolicited telephone call to William Burke, the Ernst & Whinney audit engagement partner on the Barden audit. Yamont informs Burke that Barden accountants have discovered numerous USSC purchase orders and corresponding Barden invoices that do not accurately describe the work that Lacey Manufacturing (a division of Barden Corporation) has been performing for USSC. According to Yamont, these invoices and purchase orders, totaling approximately $1 million, indicate that the Lacey work for USSC has been for "tooling modifications" when, in fact, Lacey has simply been producing and assembling products for USSC. Burke immediately visits Barden to discuss this issue with Yamont.

2/3/82   Ernst & Whinney approves the issuance of a press release by USSC management that reports the company's sales and earnings for 1981. (At this point, Michael Hope, the USSC audit engagement partner, is unaware of the problem brought to William Burke's attention by Paul Yamont.)

2/5/82   Burke again visits Yamont to discuss the alleged mislabeled invoices.

2/8/82   The board of directors of the Barden Corporation votes to retain Ernst & Whinney to formally investigate the mislabeled invoices.

2/10/82   Burke contacts Norman Strauss, regional director of accounting and auditing for Ernst & Whinney's New York region, and informs him of Yamont's concerns. Strauss immediately informs Bruce Dixon, Ernst & Whinney partner in charge of the New York region, of the Barden situation. Shortly

6. A. Goldman and B. Barlev, "The Auditor-Firm Conflict of Interests: Its Implications for Independence," *Accounting Review* 49 (October 1974): 707–18; D. R. Nichols and K. Price, "The Auditor-Firm Conflict: An Analysis Using Concepts of Exchange Theory," *Accounting Review* 51 (April 1976): 335–46; M. C. Knapp and B. H. Ward, "An Integrative Analysis of Audit Conflict: Sources, Consequences and Resolution," *Advances in Accounting* 4 (1987): 267–86.

thereafter, Dixon calls Hope and instructs him not to sign off on the USSC audit until the questionable invoice charges have been fully investigated. Dixon also informs Robert Neary, the chief technical partner for Ernst & Whinney, of the problem.

2/13/82   Burke sends an Ernst & Whinney audit manager to Barden Corporation to investigate the invoices and purchase orders in question.

2/15/82   Burke joins the Ernst & Whinney audit manager at Barden Corporation to tour the Lacey Manufacturing facility and to discuss the questionable invoices and purchase orders with Robert More, the Lacey general manager. More informs Burke that nearly all of the invoiced charges being reviewed were for generic production work performed for USSC rather than for tooling modifications.

2/18/82   Burke meets with the Barden board of directors and reports that the results of the Ernst & Whinney investigation demonstrate that the USSC purchase orders and the corresponding Barden invoices misrepresent the nature of the work performed by Lacey Manufacturing for USSC. The chairman of Barden's board of directors then reports that an independent investigation by an outside law firm has yielded the same conclusion. The Barden directors vote to require that all future work performed for USSC be properly described in invoices submitted for payment to the company.

2/20/82   Hope and Dixon are unsure how to proceed on the USSC audit, given the (approxi-   results of Burke's investigation. Because of confidentiality concerns, Hope mately)   cannot raise the issue directly with USSC officers. Barden officers are concerned that if USSC perceives that Barden has brought the problem to the attention of Ernst & Whinney, USSC may terminate its relationship with Barden. Finally, Hope and Dixon decide to send a confirmation letter to Yamont and More that asks them to confirm that the disputed $1 million in charges were for tooling modifications. (Hope and Dixon realize that Yamont and More will not sign the confirmation letter.)

2/25/82   Yamont contacts Hope and informs him that he cannot sign the confirmation letter since he is aware that the disputed charges are not for tooling modifications.

   Following the refusal of Yamont and subsequently, More to sign the confirmation letter, Ernst & Whinney officials discuss the problem with the management of both USSC and Barden. Eventually, top executives of each company agree to allow auditors from the two Ernst & Whinney audit teams to have mutual access to their company's accounting records.

3/3/82   Hope meets with top USSC executives and asks them to relate their understanding of the costs incurred by Lacey Manufacturing on behalf of USSC. The USSC officials inform Hope that in early 1981, they had instructed More, the Lacey general manager, to make certain tooling changes that would result in improved efficiency in the production of USSC products. The executives then provided an elaborate and confusing explanation as to why the tooling modifications were charged out on a per-unit basis. (Earlier, Ernst & Whinney representatives had noted that the disputed costs were billed to USSC based upon the number of units of product manufactured by Lacey. Intuitively, costs associated with tooling modifications should have been billed in one lump sum or in installments. The fact that the costs were billed on a per-unit basis suggested that they were production costs.)

Hope asks USSC's controller for purchase orders that the company had placed with outside contractors other than Barden (Lacey). Hope is looking for evidence of additional mislabeled costs. In the files that Hope is allowed to review, he finds charges billed to USSC that are similar to the disputed tooling modification costs appearing on purchase orders for goods from Barden. USSC officials assure Hope that the costs incurred on USSC's behalf by these vendors were, in fact, for tooling modifications.

3/5/82   Hope and Burke meet with senior USSC executives and More of Lacey Manufacturing. In More's presence, one of the USSC executives again explains that the disputed costs were for tooling changes requested by USSC in early 1981. Following the individual's explanation, More indicates that he agrees with that characterization of the costs. (More had previously maintained that the disputed amounts were production, not tooling, costs. More justifies his change in opinion by stating that earlier he "hadn't thought it through.")

3/10/82   Hope and Burke tour the Lacey Manufacturing facility to obtain a better understanding of the firm's production process. More is asked to act as a guide for the Ernst & Whinney partners on the tour. Shortly before the tour is scheduled to begin, a senior executive with USSC arrives unexpectedly at Lacey and asks permission to accompany the others on the tour. During the tour, More explains that production personnel charge their time to either tooling jobs or production jobs. He also notes that personnel often inadvertently charge tooling costs to production jobs.

3/11/82   During a conference call involving Hope, Burke, top technical partners of Ernst & Whinney, and the CPA firm's internal and external legal counsel, Hope explains the additional audit procedures that were performed to analyze the disputed tooling costs. He then reports his conclusion that the disputed costs were for tooling modifications, not generic production work, and the other Ernst & Whinney personnel agree.

3/14/82 (approximately)   To support the conclusion that the disputed costs were for tooling modifications, Hope is instructed to obtain a signed confirmation letter from Yamont of Barden Corporation to that effect. When asked to sign the letter, Yamont refuses, as he had done before in late February.

3/15/82   Hope decides not to investigate further the questionable tooling costs that he had discovered on March 3—tooling costs charged to USSC by vendors other than Lacey Manufacturing. Regarding these items, Hope makes the following entry in the USSC workpapers: "Discussed with [other audit partner] on 3/15/82. Although explanations are incomplete, amounts are immaterial."

3/16/82   More signs the Ernst & Whinney confirmation letter regarding the tooling modification costs that Yamont had refused to sign.

3/17/82   Hope signs Ernst & Whinney's unqualified audit report for USSC's 1981 financial statements, which are issued shortly thereafter.

The SEC's investigation of USSC's 1981 financial statements and Ernst & Whinney's 1981 audit of USSC disclosed that Hope and the other Ernst & Whinney auditors had been lied to extensively by USSC officials. The disputed tooling costs were, in fact, generic production costs. The mislabeled purchase orders and invoices that Ernst & Whinney had discovered were actually a part of a massive fraudulent scheme that USSC had concocted to make legitimate production expenses appear to be capitalizable tooling costs. Apparently, the scheme was initiated in 1980, when USSC executives attempted to force several of the company's vendors to take back a significant amount of inventory that had been rendered obsolete by technological changes. When the vendors refused, the USSC executives devised a "compromise" in which they would inflate the amount of future purchase orders for production work to include the cost of the obsolete inventory and then label these purchase orders as being for tooling modifications rather than for production expenses. The USSC executives also instructed the vendors to describe these amounts on subsequent invoices as charges for tooling modifications. Although this scheme forced USSC to pay for the obsolete inventory, the firm benefited, since the cost of that inventory was not written off immediately as expense but rather capitalized in the molds and dies account and depreciated over several years.[7]

The SEC censured Hope, even though its investigation demonstrated that he had been lied to repeatedly by USSC officials.[8] The SEC ruled that Ernst & Whinney, and Hope in particular, had sufficient opportunity to discover, and should have discovered, that USSC executives were engaging in a massive fraud to misrepresent their firm's financial condition and results of operations:

> The auditors failed to design proper audit procedures, test critical assertions, resolve material conflicts in the audit evidence, and reconcile with the other evidence what they should have recognized were implausible client representations, in violation of GAAS. The bulk of the evidence available to the auditors was so inconsistent with their client's position that the auditors should have realized the [disputed] billings were not properly capitalizable as tooling and that Surgical's representations were false and not made in good faith.

EPILOGUE

USSC and Leon Hirsch recovered from their problems of the early 1980s. Impressive growth rates in revenues and earnings sent USSC's stock price spiraling upward by the end of the decade. Leon Hirsch's personal fortunes also blossomed. In 1991, Hirsch was the third highest paid executive in the nation, earning more than $23 million.[9] However, bad times revisited both USSC and Hirsch. From a high of $134 per share in 1992, USSC's stock plummeted to less than $20 per share in early 1994. Disappointing earnings and a loss of market share were responsible for the collapse of USSC's stock. In June 1994, the *Wall*

---

7. In some instances, the SEC found that USSC and its vendors simply fabricated phony purchase orders and invoices for tooling modifications to "convert" the obsolete inventory costs to capitalizable expenses.

8. In addition to the penalties imposed on USSC and Michael Hope, the SEC filed a civil complaint against Barden Corporation and Robert More. The SEC alleged that Barden and More "provided substantial cooperation and assistance in furthering and concealing [fraudulent] practices" that USSC employed to misrepresent its financial condition and results of operations. Barden and More settled the SEC complaint without admitting guilt or denying any wrongdoing by agreeing to abide by a court order that prohibited them from engaging in any future violations of the federal securities laws.

9. "Executive Pay at New Highs," *New York Times*, 11 May 1992, D5.

Street Journal reported in a series of articles that two of Leon Hirsch's former housekeepers were threatening to sue him for more than $20 million. One of these individuals eventually filed suit against Hirsch, alleging that he had sexually assaulted her.[10] Hirsch denied the allegations. When the revelations were reported, the company's stock price rallied on speculation that Hirsch would be forced to step down as chief executive.[11]

QUESTIONS

1. Identify audit procedures that, if employed by Ernst & Whinney during the 1981 USSC audit, might have detected the overstatement of the leased and loaned assets account that resulted from the improper accounting for asset retirements.

2. In 1981, USSC extended the useful lives of several of its fixed assets and adopted salvage values for many of these same assets that previously had not been assigned salvage values. Are these changes permissible under generally accepted accounting principles? Assuming that these changes had a material effect on USSC's financial condition and results of operations, how should they have been disclosed in the company's financial statements? How should these changes have affected Ernst & Whinney's 1981 audit opinion? (Assume that the current audit reporting standards were in effect at the time.)

3. Prepare common-sized financial statements for USSC for the period 1979 to 1981. Also, compute key liquidity, solvency, activity, and profitability ratios for 1980 and 1981. Given these data, identify what you believe were the high-risk financial statement line items for the 1981 USSC audit.

4. What factors in the auditor-client relationship create a power imbalance in favor of the client? Discuss measures that the profession could take to mitigate the negative consequences of this power imbalance.

5. Regarding the dispute over the alleged tooling/production costs incurred for USSC by Barden, identify (a) the evidence Hope collected that supported the USSC point of view that the costs were for tooling modifications and (b) the evidence that supported the position that the costs were generic production expenses. What do generally accepted auditing standards suggest are the key evaluative criteria that an auditor should consider when assessing audit evidence? Given these criteria, do you believe Hope was justified in deciding that the costs were for tooling modifications? Why or why not?

6. In your opinion, did Hope satisfactorily consider the possibility that there were additional suspicious tooling charges being paid and recorded by USSC? If not, what additional steps should he have taken to further explore this possibility? If Hope believed that there was some likelihood that his client had engaged in an illegal act, what additional audit procedures, if any, would have been appropriate?

---

10. "U.S. Surgical, Officer Sued by Housekeeper Alleging Sex Assault," *Wall Street Journal,* 17 June 1994, A6.

11. J. J. Keller, "U.S. Surgical Paid Woman Planning Suit, Lawyer Says," *Wall Street Journal,* 14 June 1994, A6.

7. When a CPA firm has two audit clients that transact business with each other, should the two audit teams be allowed to share information regarding their clients, since such sharing of data might result in the auditors' obtaining a more accurate picture of each client's financial condition? Discuss the advantages and disadvantages of amending the client confidentiality rule to allow communication between audit teams under such circumstances.

CASE 1.4
ZZZZ BEST COMPANY, INC.

On May 19, 1987, a short article in the *Wall Street Journal* reported that ZZZZ Best Company, Inc., of Reseda, California, had signed a contract for a $13.8 million insurance restoration project. This project was the most recent of a series of large restoration jobs obtained by ZZZZ Best (pronounced "zee best") Company. Located in the San Fernando Valley of southern California, ZZZZ Best had begun operations in the fall of 1982 as a small, door-to-door carpet cleaning operation. Under the direction of Barry Minkow, the ambitious sixteen-year-old who founded the company and initially operated it out of his parents' garage, ZZZZ Best experienced explosive growth in both revenues and profits during the first several years of its existence. In the three-year period from 1984 to 1987, the company's net income surged from less than $200,000 to more than $5 million on revenues of $50 million.

When ZZZZ Best went public in 1986, Minkow and several of his close associates became multimillionaires overnight. By the late spring of 1987, Minkow's stock in the company had a market value exceeding $100 million, and the total market value of ZZZZ Best surpassed $200 million. Minkow's charm and entrepreneurial genius made him a sought-after commodity on the television talk show circuit and caused the print and visual media to tout him as an example of what America's youth could attain if they would only apply themselves. During an appearance on *The Oprah Winfrey Show* in April 1987, Minkow exhorted his peers with evangelistic zeal to "Think big, be big" and encouraged them to adopt his personal motto, "The sky is the limit."

Less than two years after his appearance on *The Oprah Winfrey Show,* Barry Minkow began serving a twenty-five-year prison sentence. Tried and convicted on fifty-seven counts of securities fraud, Minkow had been exposed as a fast-talking con artist who bilked his closest friends and Wall Street out of millions of dollars. Federal prosecutors estimate that, at a minimum, Minkow cost investors and creditors $100 million. The company that Minkow founded was, in fact, an elaborate Ponzi scheme. The reported profits of the firm were nonexistent and the huge restoration contracts, imaginary. As one journalist reported, rather than building a corporation, Minkow constructed a hologram of a corporation. In July 1987, just three months after the company's stock had reached a market value of $220 million, an auction of its assets netted only $62,000.

Unlike most financial frauds, the ZZZZ Best scam was perpetrated under the watchful eye of the Securities and Exchange Commission (SEC). The scrutiny of the SEC, one of the largest Wall Street brokerage houses, a large and reputable West Coast law firm that served as the company's general counsel, and an international public accounting firm had failed to expose Minkow's daring scheme. It was the persistence of an indignant homemaker who had been defrauded of a few hundred dollars by ZZZZ Best that was ultimately responsible for exposing Minkow's fraud.

How a teenage flimflam artist could make a mockery of the complex regulatory structure that oversees the U.S. securities markets was the central question posed by a congressional subcommittee that investigated the ZZZZ Best debacle. Representative John D. Dingell, chairman of the U.S. House Committee on Energy and Commerce, pointed out, "The ZZZZ Best prospectus told the public that revenues and earnings from insurance restoration contracts were skyrocketing but did not reveal that the contracts were completely fictitious. Where were the independent auditors and the others that are paid to alert the public to fraud and deceit?"[1] Like many other daring financial frauds, the ZZZZ Best scandal caused Congress to reexamine and modify the maze of rules that regulate financial reporting and serve as the foundation of the U.S. system of corporate oversight. However, Daniel Akst, a *Wall Street Journal* reporter who played a large role in exposing Minkow, suggests that another ZZZZ Best is inevitable: "Changing the accounting rules and securities laws will help, but every now and then a Barry Minkow will come along, and ZZZZ Best will happen again. Such frauds are in the natural order of things, I suspect, as old and enduring as human needs."[2]

THE EARLY HISTORY OF ZZZZ BEST COMPANY

Barry Minkow was introduced to the carpet cleaning industry at the age of twelve by his mother, who helped make ends meet by working as a telephone solicitor for a small carpet cleaning firm. Although certainly the great majority of companies in the carpet cleaning industry are legitimate, the nature of the business attracts a disproportionate number of seedy characters. There are essentially no barriers to entry: no licensing requirements, no apprenticeships to be served, and only a minimal amount of start-up capital needed. A sixteen-year-old youth with a driver's license can easily become what industry insiders refer to as a "rug sucker," which is exactly what Minkow did when he founded ZZZZ Best Company.

---

1. This and all subsequent quotations, unless indicated otherwise, were taken from the following source: U.S. Congress, House, Subcommittee on Oversight and Investigations of the Committee on Energy and Commerce, *Failure of ZZZZ Best Co.* (Washington, D.C.: U.S. Government Printing Office, 1988).

2. D. Akst, *Wonder Boy, Barry Minkow—The Kid Who Swindled Wall Street* (New York: Scribner, 1990), 271.

Minkow quickly recognized that carpet cleaning was a difficult way to earn a livelihood. The ease of entry into the field meant that cutthroat competition was prevalent within the industry. Customer complaints, bad checks, and nagging vendors demanding payment complicated the young entrepreneur's life immensely. Within months of striking out on his own, Minkow faced the ultimate nemesis of the small businessperson: a shortage of working capital. Because of his age and the fact that ZZZZ Best was only marginally profitable, local banks refused to loan him money. Ever resourceful, the brassy teenager came up with his own innovative ways to finance his business: check kiting, credit card forgeries, and the staging of thefts to bilk his insurance company. Minkow's age and personal charm allowed him to escape relatively unscathed from his early brushes with the law that were a result of his creative financing methods. The ease with which the "system" could be beaten encouraged him to exploit it on a broader scale.

Throughout his short business career, Minkow realized the benefits of having an extensive social network of friends and acquaintances. It was through acquaintances made at a health club that he was finally able to significantly expand his horizons. Soon after becoming a friend of Tom Padgett, an insurance claims adjuster, Minkow devised a scheme to exploit that friendship. Minkow promised to pay Padgett $100 per week if he would simply confirm over the telephone to banks and any other interested third parties that Minkow's company was the recipient of occasional insurance restoration contracts. Ostensibly, these contracts had been obtained by Minkow to clean and do minor remodeling work on properties damaged by fire, storms, or other catastrophes. The gullible Padgett was led to believe that the sole purpose of such confirmations was to allow Minkow to circumvent much of the bureaucratic red tape in the insurance industry.

From this beginning, the ZZZZ Best fraud blossomed. Initially, the insurance restoration work, which was totally fictitious, was a small sideline that Minkow used to generate paper profits and revenues to convince bankers to loan him money. Minkow's phony financial statements served their purpose, and he expanded his operations by opening several carpet cleaning outlets across the San Fernando Valley. Apparently, Minkow soon realized that there was no need to tie his future to the cutthroat carpet cleaning industry when he could literally dictate the size and profitability of his insurance restoration "business." Within a short period of time, insurance restoration, rather than carpet cleaning, became the major source of revenue appearing on the ZZZZ Best income statements.

Minkow's "The sky is the limit" philosophy drove him to be even more innovative. The charming young entrepreneur began using his phony financial statements to entice wealthy individuals in his ever-expanding social network to invest in ZZZZ Best. Eventually, Minkow realized that the ultimate scam would be to take his company public, a move that would allow him to tap the bank accounts of investors nationwide.

GOING PUBLIC WITH ZZZZ BEST

The decision to take ZZZZ Best public meant that Minkow no longer was able to completely control his firm's financial disclosures. Registering with the SEC required auditors, investment bankers, and outside attorneys to peruse the ZZZZ Best financial statements. Federal securities laws impose a due diligence obligation on these parties; that is, under the federal securities laws, parties associated with a securities registration statement must attempt to determine that the information therein is materially accurate. ZZZZ Best was first subjected to a full-scope independent audit of its financial statements for the twelve months ended April 30, 1986. George Greenspan, the sole practitioner who performed that audit, confirmed the existence of ZZZZ Best's major insurance restoration contracts by contacting Tom Padgett, the principal officer of Interstate Appraisal Services, which reportedly contracted the jobs out to ZZZZ Best. By this time, Padgett was an active and willing participant in Minkow's fraudulent schemes. Minkow had established Interstate Appraisal Services and Assured Property Management for the sole purpose of generating fake insurance restoration contracts for ZZZZ Best.

According to Greenspan's testimony before the congressional subcommittee that investigated the ZZZZ Best scandal, he not only confirmed the existence of the insurance restoration jobs but also obtained and reviewed copies of all key documents regarding those jobs. In addition, Greenspan performed various analytical procedures to determine that the company's key financial ratios were in line with industry averages. However, Greenspan did not inspect any of the insurance restoration sites. The congressional subcommittee was surprised, if not alarmed, that he had not personally visited at least a few of the job sites.

CONGRESSMAN LENT: Mr. Greenspan, I am interested in the SEC Form S-1 that ZZZZ Best Company filed with the SEC. . . . You say in that report that you made your examination in accordance with generally accepted auditing standards and accordingly included such tests of the accounting records and other auditing procedures as we consider necessary in the circumstances. . . . You don't say in that statement that you made any personal on-site inspections.

MR. GREENSPAN: It's not required. Sometimes you do; sometimes you don't. I was satisfied that these jobs existed and I was satisfied from at least six different sources, including payment for the job. What could you want better than that?

CONGRESSMAN LENT: Your position is that you are an honest and reputable accountant.

MR. GREENSPAN: Yes, sir.

CONGRESSMAN LENT: You were as much a victim as some of the investors in this company?

MR. GREENSPAN: I was a victim all right. . . . I am as much aghast as anyone. And every night I sit down and say, why didn't I detect this damned fraud.

RETENTION OF ERNST & WHINNEY BY ZZZZ BEST

Shortly after Greenspan completed his audit of ZZZZ Best's April 30, 1986, financial statements, he was informed by Minkow that Ernst & Whinney would be retained to perform the following year's audit. Apparently, ZZZZ Best's investment broker requested that Minkow obtain a Big Eight accounting firm to enhance the credibility of the company's financial statements. About the same time, and for the same reason, Minkow retained a high-profile Los Angeles law firm to represent ZZZZ Best as its legal counsel.

The congressional subcommittee asked Greenspan what information he provided to Ernst & Whinney regarding his former client. In particular, the subcommittee was interested in whether Greenspan had discussed the insurance restoration contracts with the new auditors.

CONGRESSMAN WYDEN: Mr. Greenspan, in September 1986, Ernst & Whinney came on as the new independent accountant for ZZZZ Best. What did you communicate to Ernst & Whinney with respect to the restoration contracts?

MR. GREENSPAN: Nothing. I did—there was nothing because they never got in touch with me. It's protocol for the new accountant to get in touch with the old accountant. They never got in touch with me, and it's still a mystery to me.

Representatives of Ernst & Whinney later testified that they did, in fact, communicate with Greenspan prior to accepting ZZZZ Best as an audit client. However, Ernst & Whinney's testimony did not disclose the nature or content of that communication, and Greenspan was not recalled to rebut Ernst & Whinney's testimony on this issue.

Exhibit 1 shows the engagement letter signed by Ernst & Whinney and Barry Minkow in September 1986. The engagement letter outlined four services that the audit firm intended to provide ZZZZ Best: a review of the company's financial statements for the three-month period ending July 31, 1986; assistance in the preparation of a registration statement to be filed with the SEC; a comfort letter to be submitted to ZZZZ Best's underwriters; and a full-scope audit for the fiscal year ending April 30, 1987. Ernst & Whinney completed the review, provided the comfort letter to ZZZZ Best's underwriters, and apparently assisted the company in preparing the registration statement for the SEC; however, Ernst & Whinney never completed the 1987 audit. The audit firm resigned on June 2, 1987, amid growing concerns that ZZZZ Best's financial statements were grossly misstated.

Ernst & Whinney representatives who appeared before the congressional subcommittee investigating the ZZZZ Best debacle were questioned at length regarding the bogus insurance restoration contracts—contracts that accounted for 90 percent of ZZZZ Best's reported profits. The congressional testimony disclosed that Ernst & Whinney repeatedly insisted on visiting several of the largest of these contract sites, and that Minkow and his associates attempted to discourage such visits. Eventually, Minkow realized that the auditors would not relent and agreed to allow them to visit certain of the restoration sites, knowing full well that none of the sites actually existed.

To convince Ernst & Whinney that the insurance restoration contracts actually existed, Minkow and his associates devised a series of sting operations. In the late fall of 1986, Larry Gray, the engagement audit partner for ZZZZ Best, insisted on visiting a restoration site in Sacramento on which ZZZZ Best had reported obtaining a multimillion-dollar contract. Two of Minkow's co-conspirators were sent to Sacramento to find a large building under construction or renovation that would provide a plausible site for a restoration contract. Gray had visited Sacramento weeks earlier to search for the site that Minkow had refused to divulge. As chance would have it, the building chosen by the ZZZZ Best co-conspirators was the same one Gray had identified as the most likely site of the insurance restoration job.

September 12, 1986

Mr. Barry Minkow
Chairman of the Board
ZZZZ Best Co., Inc.
7040 Darby Avenue
Reseda, California

Dear Mr. Minkow:

This letter is to confirm our understanding regarding our engagement as independent accountants of ZZZZ BEST CO., INC. (the Company) and the nature and limitations of the services we will provide.

We will perform the following services:

1. We will review the balance sheet of the Company as of July 31, 1986, and the related statements of income, retained earnings, and changes in financial position for the three months then ended, in accordance with standards established by the American Institute of Certified Public Accountants. We will not perform an audit of such financial statements, the objective of which is the expressing of an opinion regarding the financial statements taken as a whole, and, accordingly, we will not express an opinion on them. Our report on the financial statements is presently expected to read as follows:

   "We have made a review of the condensed consolidated balance sheet of ZZZZ BEST CO., INC. and subsidiaries as of July 31, 1986, and the related condensed consolidated statements of income and changes in financial position for the three-month period ended July 31, 1986, in accordance with standards established by the American Institute of Certified Public Accountants. A review of the condensed consolidated financial statements for the comparative period of the prior year was not made.

   A review of financial information consists principally of obtaining an understanding of the system for the preparation of interim financial information, applying analytical review procedures to financial data, and making inquiries of persons responsible for financial and accounting matters.

   It is substantially less in scope than an examination in accordance with generally accepted auditing standards, which will be performed for the full year with the objective of expressing an opinion regarding the financial statements taken as a whole. Accordingly, we do not express such an opinion.

   Based on our review, we are not aware of any material modifications that should be made to the condensed consolidated interim financial statements referred to above for them to be in conformity with generally accepted accounting principles."

Our engagement cannot be relied upon to disclose errors, irregularities, or illegal acts, including fraud or defalcations, that may exist. However, we will inform you of any such matters that come to our attention.

2. We will assist in the preparation of a Registration Statement (Form S-1) under the Securities Act of 1933 including advice and counsel in conforming the financial statements and related information to Regulation S-X.
3. We will assist in resolving the accounting and financial reporting questions which will arise as a part of the preparation of the Registration Statement referred to above.
4. We will prepare a letter for the underwriters, if required (i.e., a Comfort Letter), bearing in mind the limited nature of the work we have done with respect to the financial data.
5. We will examine the consolidated financial statements of the Company as of April 30, 1987, and for the year then ended and issue our report in accordance with generally accepted auditing standards approved by the American Institute of Certified Public Accountants. These standards contemplate, among other things, that (1) we will study and evaluate the Company's internal control system as a basis for reliance on the accounting records and for determining the extent of our audit tests; and (2) that we will be able to obtain sufficient evidential matter to afford a reasonable basis for our opinion on the financial statements. However, it should be understood that our reports will necessarily be governed by the findings developed in the course of our examination and that we could be required, depending upon the circumstances, to modify our reporting from the typical unqualified opinion. We will advise you, as our examination progresses, if any developments indicate that we will be unable to express an unqualified opinion. Because our examination will be performed generally on a test basis, it will not necessarily disclose irregularities, if any, that may exist. However, we will promptly report to you any irregularities which our examination does disclose.

EXHIBIT 1
Ernst & Whinney's ZZZZ Best Engagement Letter

EXHIBIT 1—Cont'd
Ernst & Whinney's ZZZZ Best Engagement Letter

Our fees will be derived from our customary rates for the various personnel involved plus out-of-pocket expenses. Certain factors can have an effect on the time incurred in the conduct of our work. Among these are the general condition of the accounting records, the amount of assistance received from your personnel in the accumulation of data, the size and transaction volume of business, any significant financial reporting issues that arise in connection with the SEC's review of the S-1, as well as unforeseen circumstances. Based upon our current understanding of the situation, the amount of our proposed billing for the various services which we will be providing are estimated to be:

Review of the July 31, 1986 financial statements	$5,000–	$ 7,500
Assistance in the preparation of the Registration Statement	8,000–	30,000
Comfort Letter	4,000–	6,000
Audit of financial statements as of April 30, 1987	24,000–	29,000

We will invoice you each month for the time charges and expenses incurred in the previous month and such invoices are due and payable upon presentation.

Larry D. Gray, Partner, is the Client Service Executive assigned to the engagement. Peter Griffith, Audit Manager, and Michael McCormick, Tax Manager, have also been assigned.

We greatly appreciate your engagement of our firm; if you have any questions, we shall be pleased to discuss them with you. Please indicate your acceptance of the above arrangements by signing and returning the enclosed copy. This letter constitutes the full understanding of the terms of our engagement.

Very truly yours,

ERNST & WHINNEY

By Larry D. Gray, Partner

ACCEPTED:

ZZZZ BEST CO., INC

Barry J. Minkow, Chairman of the Board

(signed)

9–16–86

Two of Minkow's confederates, while posing as leasing agents of a property management firm, convinced the supervisor of the construction site to provide the keys to the building one weekend on the pretext that a large prospective tenant wished to tour the facility. Prior to the arrival of Larry Gray and an attorney representing ZZZZ Best's law firm, Minkow's subordinates visited the site and placed placards on the walls at conspicuous locations indicating that ZZZZ Best was the contractor for the building renovation. No details were overlooked by the ZZZZ Best conspirators; they even paid the building's security officer to greet the visitors and demonstrate that he was aware in advance of their tour of the site and its purpose. Although the building had not been damaged and instead was simply in the process of being completed, the sting operation went off as planned. Exhibit 2 contains the memorandum Gray wrote describing his tour of the building—a memorandum that was included in Ernst & Whinney's ZZZZ Best workpapers.

Congressional investigators quizzed Gray regarding the measures he took to confirm that ZZZZ Best actually had a restoration contract on the Sacramento

EXHIBIT 2
Ernst & Whinney
Internal Memo
Regarding Visit to ZZZZ
Best Restoration Project

TO: ZZZZ Best Co., Inc. File

FROM: Larry D. Gray

RE: Visit to Sacramento Job

At our request, the Company arranged for a tour of the job site in Sacramento on November 23rd [1986]. The site (not previously identified for us because of the confidentiality agreement with their customer) had been informally visited by me on October 27. I knew approximately where the job was, and was able to identify it through the construction activity going on.

On November 23, Mark Morse accompanied Mark Moskowitz of Hughes Hubbard & Reed and myself to Sacramento. We visited first the offices of the Building Manager, Mark Roddy of Assured Property Management, Inc. Roddy was hired by the insurance company (at Tom Padgett's suggestion according to Morse) to oversee the renovation activities and the leasing of the space. Roddy accompanied us to the building site.

We were informed that the damage occurred from the water storage on the roof of the building. The storage was for the sprinkler systems, but the water was somehow released in total, causing construction damage to floors 17 and 18, primarily in bathrooms which were directly under the water holding tower, then the water spread out and flooded floors 16 down through about 5 or 6, where it started to spread out even further and be held in pools.

We toured floor 17 briefly (it is currently occupied by a law firm) then visited floor 12 (which had a considerable amount of unoccupied space) and floor 7. Morse pointed out to us the carpet, painting and clean up work which had been ZZZZ Best's responsibility. We noted some work not done in some other areas (and in unoccupied tenant space). But per Mark, this was not ZZZZ Best's responsibility, rather was work being undertaken by tenants for their own purposes.

Per Morse (and Roddy) ZZZZ Best's work is substantially complete and has passed final inspection. Final sign-off is expected shortly, with final payment due to ZZZZ Best in early December.

Morse was well versed in the building history and in the work scope for ZZZZ Best. The tour was beneficial in gaining insight as to the scope of the damage that had occurred and the type of work that the Company can do.

building. They were particularly concerned that he never discovered that the building had not suffered several million dollars in damages a few months earlier, as claimed by ZZZZ Best personnel.

CONGRESSMAN LENT: ... did you check the building permit or construction permit?

MR. GRAY: No, sir. That wouldn't be necessary to accomplish what I was setting out to accomplish.

CONGRESSMAN LENT: And you did not check with the building's owners to see if an insurance claim had been filed?

MR. GRAY: Same answer. It wasn't necessary. I had seen the paperwork internally of our client, the support for a great amount of detail. So, I had no need to ask—to pursue that.

CONGRESSMAN LENT: You understand that what you saw was not anything that was real in any sense of the word? ... You are saying you were duped, are you not?

MR. GRAY: Absolutely.

Congressional testimony disclosed that one of the visitations by Ernst & Whinney forced ZZZZ Best to lease a partially completed building and to hire subcontractors to do a considerable amount of work on the site. In total, ZZZZ Best reportedly spent several million dollars for the sole purpose of deceiving its auditors.

The success of the bogus site visitations was due in large part to Minkow's insistence that Ernst & Whinney and ZZZZ Best's law firm sign confidentiality agreements before the visits were made. A copy of one such agreement is shown in Exhibit 3. Members of the congressional subcommittee were particularly concerned by the following stipulation of the confidentiality agreement: "We will not make any follow-up telephone calls to any contractors, insurance companies, the building owner, or other individuals involved in the restoration contract." Unfortunately, such stipulations effectively precluded the auditors and attorneys from corroborating the insurance restoration contracts with independent third parties.

RESIGNATION OF ERNST & WHINNEY

Ernst & Whinney resigned as ZZZZ Best's auditor on June 2, 1987, following a series of disturbing events that caused the firm to question the integrity of Minkow and his associates. First, Ernst & Whinney was alarmed by a *Los Angeles Times* article in mid-May 1987 that revealed Minkow had been involved in a string of credit card forgeries as a teenager. Second, on May 28, 1987, ZZZZ Best issued a press release, without consulting or notifying Ernst & Whinney, that reported record profits and revenues. Ostensibly, the purpose of this press release was to restore investors' confidence in the company—confidence that had been shaken by the damaging *Los Angeles Times* story. Third, and probably most important, on May 29, Ernst & Whinney auditors discovered evidence supporting allegations made several weeks earlier by a third party informant that ZZZZ Best's insurance restoration business was fictitious. The informant had contacted Ernst & Whinney in April 1987 and asked for $25,000 in exchange for information that would prove that one of the firm's clients was engaging in a massive fraud. Ernst & Whinney refused to pay the sum, and the individual recanted shortly thereafter, but not until the firm determined that the allegations were in regard to ZZZZ Best. (Congressional testimony disclosed that the individual recanted because of a bribe paid to him by Minkow.) Despite the recantation, Ernst & Whinney took the allegations to Minkow and ZZZZ Best's board of directors, at which point Minkow denied ever knowing the individual who had made the allegations. On May 29, 1987, however, Ernst & Whinney auditors discovered a number of canceled checks that Minkow had personally written to the informant several months earlier.

Because ZZZZ Best was a public company, the resignation of its independent auditor was required to be reported to the SEC in an 8-K filing. One purpose of this requirement is to alert investors and creditors of the circumstances that may have led to the change in auditors. At the time, SEC registrants were allowed fifteen days to file the 8-K auditor change announcement. After waiting the maximum permissible time, ZZZZ Best reported the change in auditors but, in spite of Ernst & Whinney's insistence, made no mention in the 8-K of the allegations of fraud that had been subsequently recanted. The SEC's rules that were in effect at the time also required a former audit firm to file an exhibit letter

EXHIBIT 3
Ernst & Whinney's
Confidentiality
Agreement with ZZZZ
Best Regarding Visits to
Restoration Projects

Mr. Barry Minkow, President
ZZZZ Best Co., Inc.
7040 Darby Avenue
Reseda, California

Dear Barry:

In connection with the proposed public offering (the Offering) of Units consisting of common stock and warrants of ZZZZ Best Co., Inc. (the Company), we have requested a tour of the site of the Company's insurance restoration project in Sacramento, California, Contract No. 18886. Subject to the representations and warranties below, the Company has agreed to arrange such a tour, which will be conducted by a representative of Assured Property Management Inc. (the Representative), which company is unaffiliated with Interstate Appraisal Services. The undersigned, personally and on behalf of Ernst & Whinney, hereby represents and warrants that:

1. We will not disclose the location of such building, or any other information with respect to the project or the building, to any third parties or to any other members or employees of our firm;
2. We will not make any follow-up telephone calls to any contractors, insurance companies, the building owner, or other individuals involved in the restoration project;
3. We will obey all on-site safety and other rules and regulations established by the Company, Interstate Appraisal Services and the Representative;
4. The undersigned will be the only representative of this Firm present on the tour.

This Confidentiality Letter is also being furnished for the benefit of Interstate Appraisal Services, to the same extent as if it were furnished directly to such company.

to a former client's 8-K commenting on the 8-K's accuracy and completeness. Former audit firms were given thirty days to file the exhibit letter, which was the length of time Ernst & Whinney waited before submitting its exhibit letter to the SEC. In that letter, Ernst & Whinney reported its concern regarding the earlier allegations that certain of ZZZZ Best's insurance contracts were fraudulent.

The congressional subcommittee was alarmed that forty-five days passed before the charges of fraudulent misrepresentations in ZZZZ Best's financial statements were disclosed to the public. By the time Ernst & Whinney's exhibit letter was released to the public, ZZZZ Best had filed for protection from its creditors under Chapter 11 of the federal bankruptcy code. During the period of time that elapsed between Ernst & Whinney's resignation and its filing of the 8-K exhibit letter, ZZZZ Best obtained significant financing from a number of parties, including $1 million from a close friend of Minkow's. These parties never recovered the funds invested in, or loaned to, ZZZZ Best. As a direct result of the ZZZZ Best debacle, the SEC subsequently shortened the length of time that registrants and their former auditors may wait before filing the required auditor change documents.

The congressional subcommittee also quizzed Ernst & Whinney representatives regarding the information they disclosed to Price Waterhouse, the audit firm hired by Minkow to replace Ernst & Whinney.[3] Congressman Wyden was concerned that Price Waterhouse had not received all relevant information that Ernst & Whinney had in its possession regarding its former client.

---

3. Price Waterhouse never issued an audit report on ZZZZ Best's financial statements because the company was liquidated less than two months after the new audit firm was retained.

CONGRESSMAN WYDEN: I am going to insert into the record at this point a memo entitled "Discussion with successor auditor," written by Mr. Gray and dated June 9, 1987. Regarding a June 4 meeting, Mr. Gray, with Dan Lyle of Price Waterhouse concerning the integrity of ZZZZ Best's management, you stated that you had no reportable disagreements and no reservations about management integrity pending the results of a board of directors' investigation. Then you went on to say that you resigned because, and I quote here: "We came to a conclusion that we didn't want to become associated with the financial statements."
Is that correct?

MR. GRAY: That is correct.

MR. WYDEN: . . . Mr. Gray, you told the committee staff on May 29, 1987, that when you uncovered evidence to support allegations of fraud that you decided to pack up your workpapers and leave the ZZZZ Best audit site. How did your leaving without telling anybody except the ZZZZ Best management and board of directors the reasons for leaving help the public and investors?

Ernst & Whinney's reluctance to disclose its reservations regarding Minkow's integrity quite possibly stemmed from concern that such disclosures might result in Minkow suing the accounting firm.[4]

A final twist to the ZZZZ Best scandal was an anonymous letter received by Ernst & Whinney exactly one week after the firm resigned as ZZZZ Best's auditors. On that date, no one other than Ernst & Whinney and ZZZZ Best's officers was aware of the firm's resignation. The letter, shown in Exhibit 4, detailed a number of allegations suggesting that the ZZZZ Best financial statements were fraudulent. According to the congressional testimony, Ernst & Whinney forwarded this letter to the SEC on June 17, 1987.

COLLAPSE OF **ZZZZ** BEST

When the extremely negative and revealing article regarding Minkow appeared in the *Los Angeles Times* in mid-May 1987, the collapse of ZZZZ Best was probably inevitable. Several years earlier, a homemaker had fallen victim to Minkow's credit card forgeries. Minkow had added a fraudulent charge to the credit charge slip the woman had used to make a payment on her account. Despite her persistence, Minkow avoided repaying the small amount. The woman never forgot the insult and industriously tracked down, and kept a record of, the individuals who had been similarly harmed by Minkow. At the urging of this individual, a reporter for the *Los Angeles Times* investigated her allegations. The woman's diary eventually became the basis for the *Los Angeles Times* article that, for the first time, cast doubt on the integrity of the "boy wonder" who was the talk of Wall Street.

The newspaper article triggered a chain of events that quickly spelled the end of ZZZZ Best. First, a small brokerage firm specializing in newly registered companies with suspicious earnings histories began short-selling ZZZZ Best stock, forcing the stock's price into a tailspin. Second, Ernst & Whinney, ZZZZ

---

4. For a discussion of this issue and related issues, see M. C. Knapp and F. M. Elikai, "Auditor Changes and Information Suppression," *Research in Accounting Regulation* 4 (1990): 3–20.

EXHIBIT 4
Anonymous Letter
Received by Ernst &
Whinney Regarding
ZZZZ Best

June 9, 1987

Mr. Guy Wilson
Ernst & Whinney
515 South Flower
Los Angeles, California 90021

Dear Mr. Wilson:

I am an individual having certain confidential information regarding the financial condition of
ZZZZ Best Co., Inc. I have read the prospectus and your Review Report dated October 3, 1986
and recognize you have not done an examination in accordance with generally accepted auditing standards, but that such audit will be forthcoming by you.

I wish to make you aware of the following material facts which require you to confirm or disaf-
firm:

1. The electric generators which appear on the balance sheet under Note 6 as being
   purchased for $1,970,000 were purchased for scrap for less than $100,000 thru
   intermediaries of ZZZZ Best and resold to ZZZZ Best at the inflated value. The sole
   purpose was to boost the assets on the balance sheet. These generators have never been
   used and have no utility to the company.
2. Note 5 of the balance sheet discusses joint ventures and two restoration contracts. These
   contracts are fictitious as are the bookkeeping entries to support their validity. Interstate
   Appraisal Service [sic] did not let such contracts although they confirm their existence. The
   same is true for the alleged $7,000,000 Sacramento contract and the $40–100 million
   contracts with Interstate.
3. Further, checks made and passed between ZZZZ Best, its joint ventures and some of its
   vendors are no more than transactions among conspirators to support the validity of these
   restoration contracts.
4. Earnings reported by ZZZZ Best are being reported as Billings in excess of costs and
   estimated earnings on restoration contracts. These contracts do not exist nor do the
   earnings. This can be confirmed directly by contacting the alleged insurance carriers as
   well as physical inspections as to the existence and extent of the contracts.
5. Billings and Earnings for 1985 and 1986 were fabricated by the company before being
   presented to other accountants for certification.

Confirmation of these allegations can be accomplished by a careful due diligence. Such due
diligence on your behalf is imperative for your protection.

Very truly yours,

B. Cautious

(signed)

Best's law firm, and ZZZZ Best's brokers began giving more credence to the
allegations and rumors of financial wrongdoing by Minkow and his associates.
Third, and most important, the article panicked Minkow and compelled him to
make a number of daring moves that cost him even more credibility. The most
critical mistake was his issuance of the May 28, 1987, press release that boldly
reported record profits and revenues for his firm.

Epilogue

Among the parties most criticized for their roles in the ZZZZ Best scandal was
Ernst & Whinney. Included in the congressional testimony into the ZZZZ Best

fraud was a list of ten "red flags" that the audit firm had allegedly overlooked while examining ZZZZ Best's financial statements (see Exhibit 5). In testifying before the subcommittee, Leroy Gardner, the West Coast director of accounting and auditing for Ernst & Whinney, maintained that when all the facts were revealed, his firm would be totally vindicated.

> The ZZZZ Best situation proves at least one thing: a well-orchestrated fraud will often succeed even against careful, honest, hard-working people.... The facts that have begun to emerge establish that Minkow along with confederates both inside and outside ZZZZ Best went to extraordinary lengths to deceive Ernst & Whinney. For example, Thomas Padgett, an alleged conspirator, revealed in a recent televised interview that Minkow spent $4 million to deceive Ernst & Whinney during a visit to one of ZZZZ Best's job sites.... Ernst & Whinney never misled investors about the reliability of ZZZZ Best's financial statements. Ernst & Whinney never even issued an audit opinion for ZZZZ Best.... We are not part of the problem in this case. We were part of the solution.

In one of the largest civil suits stemming from the ZZZZ Best insolvency, Ernst & Whinney was found not liable to a large California bank that had extended ZZZZ Best a loan of several million dollars in 1986. The bank alleged that in granting the loan, it had relied upon the review report issued by Ernst & Whinney on ZZZZ Best's financial statements for the three-month period ending July 31, 1986. However, an appellate judge ruled that the bank was not justified in relying on the review report since Ernst & Whinney had expressly stated in the report that it was not issuing an opinion on the ZZZZ Best financial statements: "Ernst, because it issued only a review report, specifically declined to express an opinion on ZZZZ Best's financial statements. The report expressly disclaimed any right to rely on its content."[5]

In December 1994, Barry Minkow was released from prison. Minkow earned the reduction in his twenty-five year prison sentence for "good behavior and efforts to improve himself.[6] "These efforts included earning by correspondence bachelor's and master's degrees in religion from Liberty University, the university founded by Jerry Falwell. After completing those degrees, Minkow began working on a doctorate in theology through the correspondence program of the University of South Africa. After being released from prison, Minkow informed talk-show host Tom Snyder that he planned to enter the ministry. Minkow also disclosed that he was writing his autobiography entitled *"Clean Sweep."*

QUESTIONS

1. Ernst & Whinney never issued an audit opinion on the financial statements of ZZZZ Best; however, Ernst & Whinney did issue a review report on the company's quarterly statements for the three months ending July 31, 1986. How does a review differ from an audit, particularly in terms of the level of assurance implied by the auditor's report?

2. *Statement on Auditing Standards No. 31*, "Evidential Matter," identifies five key management assertions that underlie a set of financial statements. In the case of

---

5. "Ernst & Young Not Liable in ZZZZ Best Case," *Journal of Accountancy* 172 (July 1991): 22.

6. M. Matzer, "Barry Minkow," *Forbes*, 15 August 1994, 134.

EXHIBIT 5
Ten Red Flags that ZZZZ Best's Auditors Allegedly Overlooked

1. The amounts called for by the insurance restoration contracts were unrealistically large.
2. The number of multimillion dollar insurance restoration contracts reportedly obtained by ZZZZ Best was in excess of the total number available nationwide during the relevant time period.
3. The purported contracts failed to identify the insureds, the insurance companies or the locations of the jobs.
4. The contracts consisted of a single page which failed to contain details and specifications of the work to be done, such as the square yardage of carpet to be replaced, which were usual and customary in the restoration business.
5. Virtually all of the insurance restoration contracts were with the same party.
6. A large proportion of the ZZZZ Best insurance restoration contracts occurred immediately, and opportunistically, prior to a planned offering of stock.
7. The purported contracts provided for payments to ZZZZ Best or Minkow alone rather than to the insured or jointly with ZZZZ Best and the insured, contrary to the practice of the industry.
8. The purported contracts provided for payments by the insurance adjustor contrary to normal practice in the industry under which payments are customarily made by the insurance company directly to its insured or jointly to its insured and the restorer.
9. ZZZZ Best's purported gross profit margins for its restoration business were greatly in excess of the normal profit margins for the restoration industry.
10. The internal controls at ZZZZ Best were grossly inadequate.

ZZZZ Best, the existence assertion was particularly critical with respect to the insurance restoration contracts. ZZZZ Best's auditors, George Greenspan and Ernst & Whinney, obtained third party confirmations to support the contracts, reviewed all available documentation, performed analytical procedures to evaluate the reasonableness of the revenues recorded on the contracts, and visited selected restoration sites. Comment on the limitations of the evidence that these procedures provide regarding the management assertion of existence.

3. In addition to existence, what other management assertion or assertions should ZZZZ Best's auditors have considered corroborating regarding the insurance restoration contracts? What audit procedures would have been appropriate to substantiate these assertions?

4. In testimony before Congress, Greenspan reported that one means he used to substantiate the insurance restoration contracts was to verify that his client actually received payment on those jobs. How can such apparently reliable evidence lead an auditor to an improper conclusion?

5. *Statement on Auditing Standards No. 7,* "Communications between Predecessor and Successor Auditors," outlines the communications that should take place between the two audit firms involved in a change of auditors. Briefly summarize the nature of these communications and the auditor (predecessor or successor) who has the responsibility to initiate them. In the ZZZZ Best case, were the requirements of *Statement on Auditing Standards No. 7* complied with by Greenspan, Ernst & Whinney, and Price Waterhouse?

6. Did the confidentiality agreement that Minkow required Ernst & Whinney to sign improperly limit the scope of the ZZZZ Best audit? Why or why not? Discuss general circumstances under which confidentiality concerns on the part of a client may properly affect audit planning decisions. At what point would these limitations be so significant as to affect the type of audit opinion issued?

7. What procedures, if any, do professional standards require auditors to perform when reviewing a client's preaudit but post-year-end earnings press release?

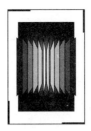

CASE 1.5

LINCOLN SAVINGS AND LOAN ASSOCIATION

In 1978, Charles Keating, Jr., founded American Continental Corporation (ACC) in Ohio. Six years later, ACC acquired Lincoln Savings and Loan Association, which was headquartered in Phoenix, Arizona, although its principal operations were in California. In his application to purchase Lincoln, Keating pledged to regulatory authorities that he would retain the Lincoln management team, not use brokered deposits to expand the size of the savings and loan, and continue residential home loans as Lincoln's principal line of business. Shortly after gaining control of Lincoln, Keating replaced the management team; began accepting large deposits from money brokers, which allowed him to nearly triple the size of the savings and loan in two years; and shifted the focus of Lincoln's lending activity from residential mortgage loans to land development projects.

On April 14, 1989, the Federal Home Loan Bank Board (FHLBB) seized control of Lincoln Savings and Loan, alleging that it was dissipating its assets by operating in an unsafe and unsound manner. On that date, Lincoln's balance sheet reported total assets of $5.3 billion, only 2.3 percent of which were investments in residential mortgage loans. Nearly two-thirds of Lincoln's asset portfolio was invested directly or indirectly in high-risk land ventures and other commercial development projects. At the time, federal authorities estimated that the closure of Lincoln Savings and Loan would eventually cost U.S. taxpayers at least $2 billion.

The hearings into the collapse of Lincoln Savings and Loan focused national attention on the methods that Keating and his associates had used to circumvent banking laws, on disclosures that five U.S. senators had intervened on Keating's behalf with federal banking regulators, and on the failure of Lincoln's independent auditors to expose allegedly fraudulent real estate transactions that allowed the savings and loan to report millions of dollars of nonexistent profits. In summarizing the Lincoln debacle, U.S. Representative Jim Leach laid the blame for the costly savings and loan failure on a number of parties, including Lincoln's auditors and the accounting profession as a whole.

I am stunned. As I look at these transactions, I am stunned at the conclusions of an independent auditing firm. I am stunned at the result. And let me just tell you, I think that this whole circumstance of a potential $2.5 billion cost to the United States taxpayers is a scandal for the United States Congress. It is a scandal for the Texas and California legislatures. It is a scandal for the Reagan administration regulators. And it is a scandal for the accounting profession.[1]

CREATIVE ACCOUNTING, INFLUENCE PEDDLING, AND OTHER ABUSES AT LINCOLN SAVINGS AND LOAN

Representative Henry Gonzalez, chairman of the U.S. House Committee on Banking, Finance, and Urban Affairs, charged that over the five years Charles Keating owned Lincoln, he employed a number of accounting schemes to divert the savings and loan's federally insured deposits into ACC's treasury. Keating was aware that he would be permitted to withdraw funds from Lincoln and invest them in ACC or use them for other purposes only to the extent that Lincoln reported after-tax profits. Consequently, he and his associates wove together complex real estate transactions involving Lincoln, ACC, and related third parties to manufacture paper profits for Lincoln. Kenneth Leventhal & Company, a CPA firm retained by regulatory authorities to investigate Lincoln's accounting for its real estate transactions, used a few simple examples to explain how these schemes worked. Exhibit 1 contains a portion of the expert testimony of the Leventhal firm before Representative Gonzalez's committee, which sponsored the lengthy congressional investigation of Lincoln Savings and Loan.

One of the most scrutinized of Lincoln's multimillion-dollar real estate deals was the large Hidden Valley transaction that took place in the spring of 1987. On March 30, 1987, Lincoln loaned $19.6 million to E. C. Garcia & Company. On that same day, Ernie Garcia, a close friend of Keating and the owner and operator of the land development company bearing his name, extended a $3.5 million loan to Wescon, a mortgage real estate concern owned by a friend of Garcia's, Fernando Acosta. The following day, Wescon purchased 1,000 acres of unimproved desert land in central Arizona from Lincoln for $14 million, nearly twice the value established for the land by an independent appraiser one week earlier. Acosta used the loan from Garcia as the down payment on the tract of land and signed a nonrecourse note for the balance. Lincoln recorded a profit of $11.1 million on the transaction—profit that was never realized, since neither Acosta nor Garcia paid the nonrecourse note.

Neither Acosta nor Garcia apparently ever intended to pay off the note. Garcia later testified that he agreed to become involved in the deceptive Hidden Valley transaction only because he wanted the $19.6 million loan from Lincoln.[2] Recognizing a profit on the Hidden Valley transaction would have openly violated financial accounting standards if Garcia had acquired the property

---

1. This and all subsequent quotations, unless indicated otherwise, were taken from the following source: U.S. Congress, House, Committee on Banking, Finance and Urban Affairs. *Investigation of Lincoln Savings and Loan Association, Part 4* (Washington, D.C.: U.S. Government Printing Office, 1990).

2. K. Kerwin and C. Yang, "Everything Was Fine until I Met Charlie: The Rise and Stumble of Whiz Kid and Keating Crony Ernie Garcia," *Business Week,* 12 March 1990, 44, 46.

> To illustrate the accounting concepts Lincoln used, let me give you a few simple, hypothetical examples. Suppose you own a house that you paid $100,000 for, and against which you still owe $60,000. Now, suppose you could not find a buyer for your house. Therefore, you go out and find an individual who agrees to pay you the $200,000 you want for your house, but is only willing to give you one dollar in cash and a non-recourse note for the balance of $199,999. A non-recourse note means that you cannot get at him personally. If he defaults on the note, your only recourse is to take the house back.
>
> So now you have one dollar in your pocket, and a note for the rest. You very likely have not parted company with your house in this situation, because your so-called buyer may be unable to pay you, or he may simply decide that he does not want to pay you. Economically, he has an option to stick to the deal if the price of the house appreciates, or he can walk away from it if it does not. That is not a sale.
>
> Now suppose you have the same house again. Your next-door neighbor has a different house, but it is worth the same as yours, and has the same outstanding mortgage balance. You then swap houses and mortgages with your neighbor.
>
> You now have a house which is different, but very similar to the one that you did have. I think that you will agree, there is no profit realized on this exchange. By the accounting theory that Lincoln appears to have followed, you would be able to record a $100,000 profit, the difference between what you originally paid for your house and what you think your neighbor's house is worth.
>
> Really, it could have been more, if you could have found an appraiser to tell you that your neighbor's house was worth $300,000. And it could have been still more if you and your neighbor had simply chosen to agree upon a stated price which was even in excess of these amounts.
>
> As you can see, all sales of real estate are not created equal. Over the years, accountants have had to wrestle with what is economically a sale and what is not. The economic substance of a transaction should of course be the controlling consideration.

EXHIBIT 1
Congressional Testimony of Kenneth Leventhal & Company Regarding Lincoln's Real Estate Transactions

directly from Lincoln and used funds loaned to him by the savings and loan for his down payment. Acosta eventually admitted that his company, which prior to the Hidden Valley transaction had total assets of $87,000 and a net worth of only $30,000, was only a "straw buyer." In a *Los Angeles Times* article, Acosta reported that his company "was too small to buy the property and that he signed the documents without reading them to help his friend, Ernie Garcia."[3] Exhibit 2 contains a letter that a worried Acosta wrote to Garcia in 1988 regarding the Hidden Valley transaction. In that letter, Acosta encourages Garcia to assume title to the property so that Acosta can take it off his company's books.

Methods such as those used in the Hidden Valley transaction were repeated by Keating and his associates in dozens of real estate transactions to generate enormous capital gains for Lincoln. In 1986 and 1987 alone, Lincoln recognized in excess of $135 million in profits by employing such schemes, an amount representing more than one-half of the savings and loan's total reported profits for that two-year period. The gains recorded by Lincoln on its real estate transactions allowed ACC to withdraw huge sums of cash from the savings and loan—funds that were actually federally insured deposits. When the "purchasers" of these tracts of land defaulted on their nonrecourse notes, Lincoln was forced to recognize losses—losses that could only be offset by additional "profitable" real estate transactions. This recurring cycle of events ensured that Lincoln would eventually fail. However, since the Federal Savings and Loan Insurance Corporation (FSLIC) was guaranteeing the liabilities of Lincoln (that is, its deposits), and since ACC had relatively little equity capital invested in

---

3. J. Granelli, "Firm Says It Was a 'Straw Man' in Lincoln Deal," *Los Angeles Times*, 3 January 1990, D1, D13.

EXHIBIT 2
Letter from Wescon to
Ernie Garcia Regarding
Hidden Valley
Acquisition

[This letter was addressed to Mr. E. C. Garcia, E. C. Garcia and Company, Inc., and appeared on Wescon letterhead.]

Re: Hidden Valley Project/Property

Dear Ernie:

The time when we should have been out of this project is well past.

For various reasons, our discomfort with continuation in the project is growing. Particularly of late, we have been concerned with how to report this to the IRS. We are convinced that all we can do is report as if the corporation were not the true/beneficial owner, but merely the nominal title holder, which is consistent with the facts and the reality of the situation. Correspondingly, it seems you should have, and report, the real tax burdens and benefits arising from this property.

Also, we are increasingly uncomfortable with showing this property on our company's financial statements (and explaining why it is there). We absolutely need to extract this item.

In order to expedite relief for us on this matter, in line with your repeated assurances, please arrange for the transfer of this property to its rightful owner as soon as possible.

Sincerely,

FRA/Wescon

Fernando R. Acosta

Lincoln, Keating was apparently not overly concerned by the inevitable demise of his company's savings and loan subsidiary.

Members of Representative Gonzalez's congressional committee were appalled by Lincoln's convoluted and contrived real estate transactions. One of the Leventhal partners who testified before the congressional committee summarized his firm's report on Lincoln's accounting schemes in the following manner:

> Seldom in our experience have we encountered a more egregious example of misapplication of generally accepted accounting principles. This association [Lincoln] was made to function as an engine, designed to funnel insured deposits to its parent in tax allocation payments and dividends. To do this, it had to generate reportable earnings. It created profits by making loans. Many of these loans were bad. Lincoln was manufacturing profits by giving money away.

Charles Keating was criticized not only for employing creative accounting techniques but for a number of other abusive practices as well. In 1979, Keating signed a consent decree with the Securities and Exchange Commission (SEC) to settle conflict of interest charges the agency had filed against him. After acquiring Lincoln, Keating appointed his son, Charles Keating III, who was only in his mid-twenties, president of the savings and loan at a salary of approximately $1 million. At the time, his son's only prior work experience was reportedly as a busperson in a country club restaurant. Later, the younger Keating would testify that he did not understand the nature of many of the transactions he approved.

The elder Keating's gaudy life-style and ostentatious spending habits were legendary. Unfortunately, many of the outrageous expenses rung up by Keating were paid for, in part, by U.S. taxpayers, since the expenditures were pawned off as business expenses of Lincoln. For example, in a 1987 dinner hosted by Keating at an upscale Washington, D.C., restaurant, the bill for the evening came to just slightly less than $2,500. One of the guests at that dinner was a former SEC commissioner. In another incident, after inadvertently scuffing a secretary's $30 shoes, Keating wrote her a check for $5,000 to replace them—and the rest of her wardrobe as well, apparently. Safaris, vacations in European castles, numerous trips to the south of France, and lavish parties for relatives and government officials were among the other Keating excesses that have been documented by federal and state investigators.

The most serious charges leveled at Keating involved allegations of influence peddling. Keating contributed heavily to the election campaigns of five prominent senators, including John Glenn and Alan Cranston. These five senators, who became known as the Keating Five, met with federal banking regulators and allegedly lobbied for favorable treatment for Lincoln Savings and Loan. The key issue in these lobbying efforts was the so-called direct investment rule adopted by the FHLBB in 1985. This rule limited the amount that savings and loans could invest directly in subsidiaries, development projects, and other commercial ventures to 10 percent of their total assets. Because such investments were central to Lincoln's operations, the direct investment rule imposed severe restrictions on Keating—restrictions that he repeatedly ignored.

In 1986, a close associate of Keating's was appointed to fill an unexpired term on the FHLBB. Shortly thereafter, this individual proposed an amendment to the direct investment rule that would have exempted Lincoln from its requirements. The amendment failed to be seconded and, consequently, was never adopted. Congressional testimony also disclosed that Keating loaned $250,000, with very favorable payback terms, to a former SEC commissioner, who then lobbied the SEC on behalf of Lincoln. Keating also hired Alan Greenspan to represent Lincoln before the FHLBB shortly before Greenspan was appointed to the powerful position of chairman of the Federal Reserve Board. In a legal brief submitted to the FHLBB, Greenspan reported that Lincoln's management team was "seasoned and expert" and that the savings and loan was a "financially strong" institution.

Keating failed to be concerned by the charges of influence peddling leveled against him. In responding to these charges, Keating made the following remarks during a press conference: "One question, among the many raised in recent weeks, has to do with whether my financial support in any way influenced several political figures to take up my cause. I want to say in the most forceful way I can: I certainly hope so."[4]

Keating was eventually indicted on racketeering charges and sued by the Resolution Trust Corporation, the federal agency created to manage the savings and loan crisis, for insider dealing, illegal loans, sham real estate and tax transactions, and the fraudulent sale of Lincoln securities.

AUDIT HISTORY OF LINCOLN SAVINGS AND LOAN

Arthur Andersen served as the independent auditor of Lincoln Savings and Loan until 1985, when it resigned "to lessen its exposure to liability from savings and loan audits," according to a *New York Times* article.[5] That same article describes

---

4. D. J. Jefferson, "Keating of American Continental Corp. Comes Out Fighting," *Wall Street Journal*, 18 April 1989, B2.

5. E. N. Berg, "The Lapses by Lincoln's Auditors," *New York Times*, 28 December 1989, D1, D6.

the very competitive nature of the Phoenix audit market during the mid-1980s, when Lincoln was seeking a replacement auditor. Because of the large size of the Lincoln audit, several audit firms sought the engagement, including Arthur Young & Company.[6] Arthur Young's bid to obtain the Lincoln audit was quite possibly motivated by the significant loss of clients that firm experienced from 1978 to 1984. During that time, Arthur Young suffered a net loss of sixty-three clients, which was among the highest of the Big Eight firms.[7] Over the next five years, an intense marketing effort by Arthur Young resulted in a net increase of one hundred clients nationwide for the firm, among the highest net increase for Big Eight firms during that period. A question raised by critics of the accounting profession is whether the highly competitive nature of the audit market has induced some audit firms to accept high-risk clients in exchange for large audit fees: "The savings industry crisis has revived questions repeatedly raised in the past about the profession's independence in auditing big corporate clients: whether the accounts need more controls and whether some firms are willing to sanction questionable financial statements in exchange for high fees, a practice called 'bottom fishing.' "[8]

Prior to pursuing Lincoln as an audit client, Jack Atchison, an Arthur Young partner in Phoenix, contacted the former Lincoln engagement partner at Arthur Andersen and made the standard inquiries recommended by *Statement on Auditing Standards No. 7*, "Communications between Predecessor and Successor Auditors." The Arthur Andersen partner reported that he had no reason to question the integrity of Lincoln's management and that no major disagreements preceded the resignation of his firm as Lincoln's auditor. At the time of Arthur Andersen's resignation, however, Lincoln was undergoing an intensive examination by FHLBB auditors, who were raising serious questions regarding Lincoln's financial records. Arthur Young was not informed of this investigation by Arthur Andersen. Years later, Arthur Andersen partners denied that they were aware of the examination when they resigned from the audit.

Shortly after accepting Lincoln as an audit client, Arthur Young became aware of the FHLBB audit. Among the most serious charges of the FHLBB auditors was that Lincoln had provided interest-free loans to ACC—a violation of federal banking laws—and had falsified loan documents. Three years later, officials from the Office of Thrift Supervision testified before Congress that Arthur Andersen and Lincoln employees had engaged in so-called file-stuffing—charges that resulted in an inquiry by the Federal Bureau of Investigation and an investigation by the Justice Department.[9] Arthur Andersen officials denied involvement in any illegal activities but did disclose that personnel from their firm had worked

---

6. Arthur Andersen and, subsequently, Arthur Young audited both ACC and Lincoln, a wholly owned subsidiary of ACC. However, the Lincoln audit was much more complex and apparently required much more time to complete than the ACC audit. Reportedly, the ACC/Lincoln audit accounted for one-fifth of the annual audit revenues of Arthur Young's Phoenix office during 1986 and 1987.

7. L. Berton, "Spotlight on Arthur Young Is Likely to Intensify as Lincoln Hearings Resume," *Wall Street Journal*, 21 November 1989, A20.

8. N. C. Nash, "Auditors of Lincoln on the Spot," *New York Times*, 14 November 1989, D1, D19.

9. P. Thomas and B. Jackson, "Regulators Cite Delays and Phone Bugs in Examination, Seizure of Lincoln S&L," *Wall Street Journal*, 27 October 1989, A4; Berg, "Lapses by Lincoln's Auditors," D1, D6.

"under the direction of client [Lincoln] personnel to assist them in organizing certain [loan] files."[10] Later, a representative of Lincoln admitted that "memorialization" had been used in connection with certain loan files but that such a practice was common in the industry.

The congressional testimony of several Arthur Young representatives revealed that the 1986 and 1987 Lincoln audits were very complex engagements. William Gladstone, the co-managing partner of Ernst & Young (the firm formed by the 1989 merger of Ernst & Whinney and Arthur Young), testified that the 1987 audit required 30,000 labor hours to complete. Despite concerns being raised by regulatory authorities, in both 1986 and 1987, Arthur Young rendered an unqualified opinion on Lincoln's financial statements. Critics contend that these clean opinions allowed Lincoln to continue engaging in illicit activities. Of particular concern to congressional investigators was that during this time Keating and his associates marketed high-yield junk bonds of ACC in the lobbies of Lincoln's numerous branches. The sale of these bonds, which were destined to become totally worthless following the demise of Lincoln, raised more than $250 million for ACC. The large marketing campaign for the bonds was targeted at retired individuals, many, if not most, of whom were reportedly led to believe that the bonds were federally insured, since they were being sold on the premises of a savings and loan.

When called to testify before the U.S. House committee, SEC Commissioner Richard Breeden was asked to explain why his agency did not force ACC to stop selling the high-yield corporate bonds in Lincoln's branches.

CONGRESSMAN HUBBARD: Didn't the SEC have not one, not two, but actually three or more opportunities to stop the sale of the ACC subordinated debt?

COMMISSIONER BREEDEN: We did not have any opportunity—the only way in which the SEC can stop the sale of securities is if we are able to prove those securities are being distributed based on false and misleading information. And we have to prove that in court. We cannot have reasons to be concerned about it, we cannot have suspicions, we cannot just have cause to be concerned; we have to be able to prove that in court.

And remember that this is a situation in which one of the Big Eight accounting firms is certifying that these accounts comply fully with generally accepted accounting principles, without caveat or limitation in any way. That is an important factor in that kind of decision. [Emphasis added.]

Following the completion of the 1987 Lincoln audit, the engagement audit partner, Jack Atchison, resigned from Arthur Young and accepted a position with ACC. Exhibit 3 contains the memorandum Atchison wrote to William Gladstone, who at the time was the managing partner of Arthur Young, to inform him of the resignation. Gladstone later testified that Atchison was earning approximately $225,000 as a partner with Arthur Young before his resignation. ACC records showed that Atchison's new position came with an annual salary of approximately $930,000.

The congressional investigators were alarmed by the close relationship that Atchison developed with Keating prior to resigning from Arthur Young. Testimony before the congressional committee disclosed that Atchison had written

10. Thomas and Jackson, "Regulators Cite Delays and Phone Bugs," A4.

EXHIBIT 3
Memorandum From Jack
Atchison to William
Gladstone

[This memorandum appeared on Arthur Young letterhead.]

TO: Office of Chairman   FROM: Phoenix Office
       William L. Gladstone   Jack D. Atchison
       Hugh Grant, West Regional Office
       Al Boos, Phoenix Office

SUBJECT:

Several weeks ago, Charles H. Keating Jr., Chairman of American Continental Corporation, asked me to consider joining his company at a senior executive level. Because we were in the process of conducting an audit, I informed Mr. Keating that any discussions regarding future employment would have to await the conclusion of the audit. I also informed Hugh Grant of Mr. Keating's overtures to me.

Knowing Mr. Keating would raise the subject again at the conclusion of the audit, I began to seriously consider the possibility of leaving Arthur Young to join American Continental. Arthur Young has been my professional home for over 24 years, providing a comfortable source of income and rewarding professional environment. My closest personal friends are also my partners. To even consider no longer being a part of Arthur Young was difficult and traumatic, since serving as a partner in Arthur Young has been my single professional goal since 1962.

On April 8, and 11, 1988, I had discussions with Mr. Keating wherein he presented an employment offer which was very rewarding economically and very challenging professionally. His offer addressed all of my economic, job security and position description requirements and concerns. American Continental offers some unique challenges and potential rewards not presently available in Arthur Young. It also presents some risks not present in the Arthur Young environment.

Based on American Continental's offer and my perception of the future there, I have decided to accept their offer and seek to withdraw from the Arthur Young partnership at the earliest possible date. Since American Continental is an SEC client and active issuer of securities requiring registration, and Arthur Young's consent to the use of its report is needed in such filings, an expedited withdrawal arrangement would protect against any real or apparent conflicts of interest between Arthur Young and American Continental.

several letters to banking regulators and U.S. senators vigorously supporting the activities of Keating and Lincoln while he was serving as the engagement partner on the Lincoln audit: "Atchison seemed to drop the auditor's traditional stance of independence by repeatedly defending the practices of Lincoln and its corporate parent to Congress and federal regulators. ... Since when does the outside accountant—the public watchdog—become a proponent of the client's affairs?"[11]

Congressman Gonzalez's committee also questioned Arthur Young representatives regarding Atchison's relationship with the Arthur Young audit team after he joined ACC. The congressmen were concerned that Atchison may have been in a position to improperly influence the auditors he had supervised just weeks earlier.

CONGRESSMAN LEHMAN: Did anyone at AY have any contact with Mr. Atchison after he left and went to work for Lincoln?

MR. GLADSTONE: Yes, sir.

CONGRESSMAN LEHMAN: In the course of the audit?

MR. GLADSTONE: Yes.

CONGRESSMAN LEHMAN: So he went from one side of the table to the other for $700,000 more?

---

11. Berg, "Lapses by Lincoln's Auditors," D1, D6.

MR. GLADSTONE: That is what happened.

CONGRESSMAN LEHMAN: And he—just tell me what his role was in the audits . . . when he was on the other side of the table.

MR. GLADSTONE: He was a senior vice president for American Continental when he joined them in May 1988.

CONGRESSMAN LEHMAN: Did the job he had there have anything to do with interfacing with the auditors?

MR. GLADSTONE: To some extent, yes.

CONGRESSMAN LEHMAN: What does "to some extent" mean?

MR. GLADSTONE: On major accounting issues that were discussed in the Form 8-K, we did have conversations with Jack Atchison.

CONGRESSMAN LEHMAN: So he was the person Mr. Keating had to interface with you in major decisions?

MR. GLADSTONE: Him, and other officers of American Continental.

During the summer of 1988, the relationship between officers of Lincoln and the Arthur Young audit team gradually soured. Janice Vincent, who became the engagement partner on the Lincoln audit following Atchison's resignation, testified that disagreements arose with client management that summer over the proper accounting treatment for several large real estate transactions engaged in by Lincoln. The most serious disagreement stemmed from a proposed exchange of assets between Lincoln and another corporation—a transaction for which Lincoln intended to record a $50 million profit. Lincoln management insisted that the exchange involved dissimilar assets, whereas Vincent maintained that the transaction involved the exchange of similar assets and, consequently, that the gain on the transaction could not be recognized. Vincent described during the congressional hearings how this dispute and related disputes eventually led to the resignation of Arthur Young as Lincoln's auditor: "These disagreements created an adversarial relationship between members of Arthur Young's audit team and American Continental officials, which resulted in Mr. Keating requesting a meeting with Bill Gladstone. . . . While in New York at that meeting, Mr. Keating turned to me at one point and said, 'Lady, you have just lost a job.' That did not happen. Rather, he had lost an accounting firm."

Following the resignation of Arthur Young as ACC's and Lincoln's audit firm in October 1988, Keating retained Touche Ross to audit Lincoln's 1988 financial statements. Unfortunately for Touche Ross, it became ensnared, along with Arthur Andersen and Arthur Young, in the web of litigation following the collapse of Lincoln. In particular, Touche Ross was named in a large lawsuit filed by the purchasers of the ACC bonds that were sold through Lincoln's branches. The suit alleged that had Touche Ross not accepted Lincoln as an audit client, ACC's ability to sell the bonds would have been diminished significantly.

CRITICISM OF ARTHUR YOUNG FOLLOWING THE LINCOLN COLLAPSE

Arthur Young and its successor, Ernst & Young, were criticized by a number of parties for the former's role in the Lincoln Savings and Loan debacle. One of the most common criticisms was that Arthur Young was too quick to accept documentary evidence provided by Lincoln employees in support of the savings and loan's large real estate transactions. During the congressional hearings into the collapse of Lincoln, William Gladstone commented on the appraisals that Arthur Young obtained to support these transactions: "All appraisals of land [owned by Lincoln] were done by appraisers hired by the company, and we had to rely on them." Certainly, these appraisals were relevant evidence to be used in auditing Lincoln's real estate transactions. However, if Arthur Young had retained independent appraisals of such properties, the resulting audit evidence would have been relevant, as well as less subject to bias than appraisals prepared at the request of Lincoln management.[12]

During the congressional hearings, one of the most vocal critics of Arthur Young was the newly appointed SEC commissioner, Richard Breeden. Commissioner Breeden was particularly critical of Arthur Young for its failure, or alleged failure, to cooperate with an SEC investigation into Lincoln's affairs.

COMMISSIONER BREEDEN: We subpoenaed the accountants [Arthur Young] to provide all of their work papers and their back-up.

CONGRESSMAN HUBBARD: Do you know if they were forthcoming and helpful in helping you resolve some of these questions, or helping the SEC resolve some of these questions?

COMMISSIONER BREEDEN: No. I would characterize them as very unhelpful, very unforthcoming, and very resistant to cooperate in any way, shape or form.

Earlier, Commissioner Breeden had testified that many of the subpoenaed documents that Arthur Young eventually produced were illegible or obscured: "The firm [Arthur Young] ultimately, after much discussion, produced legible copies of the documents, but not before the Commission [SEC] was forced to prepare court enforcement requests to overcome Arthur Young's uncooperative stance. Unfortunately, a substantial amount of staff time and resources was devoted unnecessarily to overcoming this resistance to the Commission's subpoenas."

When given an opportunity to respond to Commissioner Breeden's charges, William Gladstone maintained that the delays in providing the SEC with the requested documents were not intentional: "We did not stonewall the SEC. There are Arizona state privilege statutes and ethics rules which prohibit our producing our work papers without a client consent. . . . I also take issue with the allegation that we obliterated some papers. . . . The SEC itself requires a confidentiality stamp on all papers on which confidentiality was requested."

The most stinging criticism of Arthur Young during the congressional hearings stemmed from the results of the Kenneth Leventhal & Company investigation into Lincoln's accounting for its major real estate transactions. Although the Leventhal report served as the basis for much of the criticism directed at Arthur Young, the report did not mention Arthur Young or, in any way, explicitly criticize the audits that firm performed for Lincoln. Nevertheless, since Arthur Young had issued unqualified opinions on the Lincoln financial statements, the

---

12. Quite possibly, Arthur Young did obtain independent appraisals in certain cases, although Gladstone's testimony suggests otherwise.

Leventhal report was seen by many parties, including officials of Ernst & Young, as an indictment of the quality of the Arthur Young audits.

The key finding of the Leventhal report was that Lincoln had repeatedly violated the fundamental "substance-over-form" rule by engaging in "accounting-driven" deals among related parties to manufacture illusory profits. Ernst & Young representatives contested this conclusion by pointing out that the Leventhal investigative team reviewed only fifteen of the hundreds of real estate transactions that Lincoln engaged in during Arthur Young's tenure. The Ernst & Young representatives were particularly upset that, based upon a review of these fifteen transactions, the Leventhal investigators implied that none of Lincoln's major real estate transactions were accounted for properly. In Leventhal's defense, a congressman pointed out that the fifteen transactions examined by Leventhal were all very large, accounting collectively for one-half of Lincoln's pretax profits during 1986 and 1987.

During the course of the congressional hearings, the debate over the Leventhal report often became very heated. William Gladstone was extremely critical of the report, stating that it was gratuitous; contained broad, sweeping generalizations; in certain cases was "flatly wrong"; and in his opinion, was unprofessional. In responding to these charges, Congressman Leach questioned the professionalism of Gladstone's firm.

CONGRESSMAN LEACH: [addressing William Gladstone] I am going to be very frank with you, that I am not impressed with the professional ethics of your firm vis-a-vis the United States Congress. Several days ago, my office was contacted by your firm, and asked if we would be interested in questions to ask of Leventhal. We said, "Surely." The questions you provided were of an offensive nature. They were to request of Leventhal how much they were paid, implying that perhaps based upon their payment from the U.S. Government that their decisions as CPAs would be biased. I consider that to be very offensive.

Now, in addition, one of the questions that was suggested I might ask of the Leventhal firm was: Could it be that their firm is biased because a partner in their firm did not make partner in your firm?

I consider that exceedingly unprofessional. Would you care to respond to that?

MR. GLADSTONE: I do not know who contacted you, and I certainly do not know how the questions were raised.

Later in the hearings, the individual who had submitted the questions to Congressman Leach's office was identified as an Ernst & Young employee.

Congressman Leach also took issue with the contention of Ernst & Young representatives that Leventhal's report contained angry and vengeful comments regarding their firm.

CONGRESSMAN LEACH: I read that report very carefully, and I found no angry, vengeful sweeping statements. But I did find a conclusion that Arthur Young had erred rather grievously.

In any regard, what we are looking at is an issue that is anything but an accounting kind of debate. One of the techniques of Lincoln vis-a-vis the U.S. Government was to attack the opposition. You are employing the same tactics toward Leventhal. . . . I think that is unprofessional, unethical, and, based upon a very careful reading of their statement, irresponsible.

Now, I would like to ask you if you would care to apologize to the Leventhal firm.

MR. GLADSTONE: First, Mr. Leach, I stated in my opening remarks that I believed that their report was general and sweeping and unprofessional, because what I would call unprofessional about it is the statement that looking at 15 transactions, that therefore they would conclude that nothing Lincoln did had the substance—

CONGRESSMAN LEACH: I have carefully read their report, and they note that they have just been allowed to look at 15 transactions. They could not go into more detail, but they were saying that ACC batted 15 for 15, that all 15 transactions were unusual, perplexing, and in their judgment in each case breached ethical standards in terms of generally accepted accounting principles.

Your firm in effect is saying, "We think that there may be some legal liabilities. Therefore, we are going to stonewall, and we are going to defend each and every one of these transactions."

I believe that you are one of the great firms in the history of accounting. But I also believe that big and great people and institutions can sometimes err. And it is better to acknowledge error than to put one's head in the sand.

I think before our committee you have rather righteously done that.

EPILOGUE

Anthony Elliot, a widower and retired accountant in his eighties, was one of thousands of elderly Californians who had invested heavily in the junk bonds of Lincoln Savings and Loan's parent company, ACC. Elliot had invested practically all of his life savings, approximately $200,000, in the ACC bonds. Like many of his friends who had also purchased the bonds—which they, along with Elliot, believed were federally insured—Elliot was forced to scrape by each month on his small Social Security check after ACC defaulted on the bonds. On Thanksgiving Day 1990, Elliot slashed his wrists and bled to death in his bathtub. In a suicide note, he remarked that there was "nothing left for me."[13] Elliot's story is just one of many personal tragedies that has resulted from the Lincoln Savings and Loan scandal.

By late 1993, the estimated losses resulting from the demise of Lincoln Savings and Loan had risen to $3.4 billion, making it the most costly savings and loan failure in U.S. history. In March 1991, after posting huge losses—approximately $1 billion in 1989 alone—most of the remaining assets of Lincoln were sold to another financial institution by the Resolution Trust Corporation, which had been operating the savings and loan for more than a year. One month later, Lincoln's parent company, ACC, filed for protection from its creditors under the federal bankruptcy laws.

In late 1992, Ernst & Young agreed to pay $400 million to settle four lawsuits filed against it by the federal government. These suits stemmed from allegedly negligent audits performed by Ernst & Young for four savings and loans, including Lincoln Savings & Loan. In a similar settlement reported in 1993,

---

13. M. Connelly, "Victim of S&L Loss Kills Self," *Los Angeles Times*, 29 November 1990, B1.

Arthur Andersen agreed to pay $85 million to the federal government to settle lawsuits resulting from the firm's allegedly negligent audits of five savings and loans, including Lincoln. Finally, although Touche Ross was the auditor of Lincoln for only five months, that firm's successor, Deloitte & Touche, paid nearly $8 million to the federal government to settle charges filed against it for Touche Ross's role in the Lincoln debacle.

In April 1991, Ernst & Young agreed to pay the California State Board of Accountancy $1.5 million to settle the allegations of negligence that the state agency had filed against the firm in connection with Arthur Young's audits of Lincoln. A spokesman for the firm noted that the settlement was made to "avoid protracted and costly litigation" and did not involve the "admission of any fault by the firm or any partner."[14] In August 1994, Arthur Andersen agreed to pay $1.7 million to the California State Board of Accountancy for its alleged negligent audits of Lincoln. As a part of this settlement, Andersen personnel were also required to perform 10,000 hours of community service. Like Ernst & Young, Andersen denied any wrongdoing when its settlement with the California State Board was announced.

In October 1990, Ernie Garcia pleaded guilty to fraud for his role in the Hidden Valley real estate transaction. One stipulation of his plea bargain agreement with federal prosecutors was that he would assist them in their investigation of Charles Keating, Jr.'s, role in the Hidden Valley transaction and other similar transactions. In March 1991, the Lincoln executive who was responsible for managing the sale of ACC's junk bonds through Lincoln's branches pleaded guilty to eight state and federal fraud charges that he had misled the investors who purchased those bonds. Two years later, Charles Keating III was sentenced to eight years in prison after being convicted of fraud and conspiracy charges. In a California jury trial presided over by Judge Lance Ito, Charles Keating, Jr., was convicted in 1991 on seventeen counts of securities fraud for his role in marketing ACC's junk bonds. While serving a ten-year prison term for that conviction, Keating was convicted of similar fraud charges by a federal jury and sentenced to an additional twelve years in prison. By 1994, Keating had been ordered by various courts to pay restitution of more than $5 billion to thousands of victims of Lincoln and ACC. Unfortunately for those victims, Keating maintains that he is destitute.

In 1992, Janice Vincent was elected president of the California Society of Certified Public Accountants. Vincent was the first woman to hold that position. Finally, in early 1995, Jack D. Atchison published a book entitled "Legal Extortion" (CharBro Books, Inc., 1995). This book relates Atchison's view of the Lincoln Savings and Loan debacle. In a marketing brochure for this book, Atchison had the following to say regarding Charles Keating, Jr.: "This is a story which should shock and dismay all citizens. If a person of Keating's wealth and social status can be so completely destroyed by the zealous, misguided, and immensely powerful bureaucrats who inhabit the halls of government, no citizen in this land is safe. God forbid, someday you could find yourself in Keating's shoes. Then, you, too, could be the victim of *Legal Extortion*."

---

14. "E&Y Pays $1.5M in Lincoln Failure," *Accounting Today*, 13 May 1991, 1, 25.

QUESTIONS

1. Arthur Young has been criticized for failing to ensure that the substance-over-form rule was followed by Lincoln in accounting for its large real estate transactions. Briefly describe the substance-over-form rule and exactly what it requires. Which party—a firm's independent auditors or its financial accountants—is primarily responsible for ensuring compliance with that rule? If auditors are not primarily responsible for ensuring compliance with the substance-over-form rule, what are their responsibilities when that rule has been violated by a client?

2. Explain how the acceptance of large, high-risk audit clients for relatively high audit fees may threaten the de facto and perceived independence of an audit firm. Under what circumstances should such prospective clients be avoided?

3. How is an auditor's examination affected when a client has engaged in significant transactions with related parties? What measures would an auditor generally take to determine that such transactions have been properly recorded by the client?

4. According to *Statement on Auditing Standards No. 55*, "Consideration of the Internal Control Structure in a Financial Statement Audit," an auditor should review a client's "control environment." Define *control environment*. What weaknesses, if any, were evident in Lincoln's control environment?

5. What was the significance of the fact that Lincoln received nonrecourse notes rather than recourse notes as payment or partial payment on many of the properties it sold?

6. *Statement on Auditing Standards No. 31*, "Evidential Matter," identifies five key management assertions that underlie a set of financial statements. In the case of the Hidden Valley transaction, what were the key assertions that Arthur Young should have attempted to substantiate? What procedures should Arthur Young have used for this purpose, and what types of evidence should have been collected?

7. Do you believe that Jack Atchison's close relationship with Lincoln and Charles Keating prior to his leaving Arthur Young was proper? Why or why not? After joining Lincoln's parent company, ACC, should Atchison have been involved in the independent audits of Lincoln and ACC? Again, support your answer.

8. Does the AICPA Code of Professional Conduct discuss the collegial responsibilities of CPA firms? In your opinion, were representatives of either Ernst & Young or Kenneth Leventhal & Company unprofessional in this regard during the course of their congressional testimony?

9. What responsibility does an auditor have to uncover fraud perpetrated by client management? Discuss factors that mitigate this responsibility and factors that compound it. Relate this discussion to Arthur Young's audits of Lincoln.

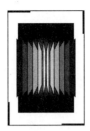

CASE 1.6
CRAZY EDDIE, INC.

In 1969, Eddie Antar, a twenty-one-year-old high school dropout from Brooklyn, opened a consumer electronics store with 150 square feet of floor space in New York City.[1] Despite this modest beginning, Antar would eventually dominate the retail consumer electronics market in the New York City metropolitan area. By 1987, Antar's firm, Crazy Eddie, Inc., had forty-three retail outlets, sales exceeding $350 million, and outstanding stock with a collective market value of $600 million. Antar personally realized more than $70 million from the sale of Crazy Eddie stock during his tenure as the chief executive of the company.

A classic rags-to-riches story became a spectacular business failure in the late 1980s when Crazy Eddie collapsed following allegations of extensive financial wrongdoing on the part of Antar and his associates. Shortly after a hostile takeover of the company in November 1987, the firm's new owners discovered that Crazy Eddie's inventory had been overstated by more than $65 million. This huge inventory shortage had been concealed from the public in registration statements filed with the Securities and Exchange Commission (SEC). Subsequent investigations by regulatory authorities would demonstrate that Crazy Eddie's profits had been intentionally overstated by Eddie Antar with the help of several subordinates.[2]

---

1. This case was co-authored by Carol Knapp, assistant professor at the University of Nevada Las Vegas.

2. The facts of this case were drawn from numerous articles published over a period of several years, including several SEC releases. The *New York Times* and *Wall Street Journal,* in particular, followed closely and reported upon the lengthy saga of Crazy Eddie and its founder, Eddie Antar. One of the more comprehensive investigative reports regarding the history of Crazy Eddie, Inc., is the following article: G. Belsky and P. Furman, "Calculated Madness: The Rise and Fall of Crazy Eddie Antar," *Crain's New York Business,* 5 June 1989, 21–33. This article provided much of the background information regarding Eddie Antar that was included in this case.

EDDIE ANTAR: THE MAN BEHIND THE LEGEND

Eddie Antar was born into a large, closely knit Syrian family in 1947. After dropping out of high school at the age of sixteen, Eddie began peddling television sets in his Brooklyn neighborhood. Within a few years, Antar and one of his cousins scraped together enough cash to open an electronics store near Coney Island. It was at this tiny store that Antar acquired the nickname "Crazy Eddie." Whenever a customer would attempt to leave the store empty-handed, Eddie would block the store's exit, sometimes locking the door until the individual agreed to buy something. To entice a reluctant customer to make a purchase, Antar would first determine which product the customer was considering and then would lower the price until the customer finally capitulated.

Antar became well known in his neighborhood not only for his unusual sales tactics but also for his unconventional, if not asocial, behavior. A bodybuilder and fitness fanatic, he typically came to work in exercise togs, accompanied by a menacing German shepherd. His quick temper caused repeated problems with vendors, competitors, and subordinates. Antar's most distinctive trait was his inability to trust anyone outside of his large extended family. In later years when he needed someone to serve in an executive capacity in his company, Antar nearly always tapped a family member, although the individual seldom had the appropriate training or experience for the position. Eventually, Antar's father, sister, two brothers, uncle, brother-in-law, and several cousins would assume leadership positions with Crazy Eddie, while more than one dozen other relatives would hold minor positions with the firm.

CRAZY EDDIE'S FORMULA FOR SUCCESS

In the early 1980s, sales in the consumer electronics industry exploded, doubling in the four-year period from 1981 to 1984 alone. As the public's demand for electronic products grew at an ever-increasing pace, Antar converted his Crazy Eddie stores into consumer electronics supermarkets. The shelves of Crazy Eddie's retail outlets were stocked with every electronic gadget Antar could find and with as many different brands of those products as he could obtain. By 1987, the company had seven distinct product lines. The following are those product lines and the percentage of sales they accounted for in the company's 1987 income statement.

Televisions	53%
Audio and audio systems	15%
Portable and personal electronics	10%
Car stereos	5%
Accessories and tapes	4%
Computers and games	3%
Miscellaneous items—including microwaves, air conditioners, and small appliances	10%
Total	100%

Antar encouraged his salespeople to supplement each store's retail profits by pressuring customers to buy extended product warranties. Many, if not most, of the repair costs that Crazy Eddie paid under these warranties were recovered by the company from manufacturers that had issued factory warranties on the products. As a result, the company realized a 100 percent profit margin on much of its warranty revenue.

As his firm grew rapidly during the late 1970s and early 1980s, Antar began extracting large price concessions from his suppliers. His ability to purchase electronic products in large quantities and at cut-rate prices enabled him to become a "transhipper" or secondary supplier of these goods to smaller consumer electronics retailers in the New York City area. Although manufacturers frowned on this practice and often threatened to stop selling to him, Antar continually increased the scale of his transhipping operation.

The most important ingredient in Antar's marketing strategy was large-scale advertising. Antar created an advertising "umbrella" over his company's principal retail market that included the densely populated area within a 150-mile radius of New York City. Antar blanketed this region with raucous, sometimes annoying, but always memorable radio and television commercials. In 1972, Antar hired a local radio personality and part-time actor known as Doctor Jerry to serve as Crazy Eddie's advertising spokesman. Over the fifteen years that the bug-eyed Doctor Jerry hawked products for Crazy Eddie, he became more recognizable, according to one survey, than Ed Koch, the longtime mayor of New York City. Doctor Jerry's series of ear-piercing television commercials that featured him screaming "Crazy Eddie—His prices are insane!" brought the company national notoriety when they were parodied by Dan Akroyd on *Saturday Night Live.*

The focal theme of Crazy Eddie's advertising campaigns was the discounting policy of the company. The company promised to refund the difference between the selling price of a product and any lower price for that same item that a customer found within thirty days of the purchase date. Despite the advertising barrage that was intended to convince the public that Crazy Eddie was a deep-discounter, the company's prices on most products were in line with those of its major competitors. Customers who were attracted to Crazy Eddie outlets by "advertised specials" were often diverted by the company's sales staff to a higher quality and higher profit margin product.

CRAZY EDDIE GOES PUBLIC

In 1983, Antar decided to sell stock in Crazy Eddie to raise capital to finance his aggressive expansion program. The initial public offering of Crazy Eddie's stock was delayed for more than a year when the underwriting firm Antar retained to market the stock discovered that the company's financial records were in disarray. Among the problems uncovered by the underwriter were extensive related party transactions, interest-free loans to employees, and highly speculative investments unrelated to the company's principal line of business. The underwriting firm was also disturbed to find that nearly all of the firm's key executives were members of the Antar family. Certain of these individuals, including Eddie's wife and mother, were being paid salaries approaching $100,000 for little or no work.

To prepare the company for its initial public stock offering, the underwriter encouraged Antar, Crazy Eddie's chairman of the board and president, to put the company's accounting records and financial affairs into good order. Antar was strongly urged by the underwriter to retain a chief financial officer who had experience with a public company and who was not a member of the Antar family. The underwriter was concerned that investors would question the competence of Crazy Eddie's executives, since many of those individuals, principally those who were Antar's relatives, appeared to be unqualified for the positions they held. Despite the underwriter's concern, Antar hired one of his cousins, Sam E. Antar—who became known within the company as "Sam the CPA" to distinguish him from Eddie's father of the same name—to serve as Crazy Eddie's chief financial officer.

The sale of Crazy Eddie's stock to the public was a tremendous success. Because the initial public offering was oversubscribed, the company's underwriter obtained permission from the SEC to sell 200,000 more shares than originally planned. Following the public offering, Antar strived to convince the investment community, particularly financial analysts, that his firm was financially strong and well managed. At every opportunity, Antar painted a picture of continued growth and increased market share for Crazy Eddie.

One tactic Antar used to convince financial analysts that the company had a rosy future was to invite them to one of his most successful stores and demonstrate in person his uncanny ability to "close" sales. Such tactics worked to perfection as analysts from the most prominent investment firms wrote glowing reports regarding Crazy Eddie's management team and the company's bright prospects for the future. One analyst wrote, "Crazy Eddie is a disciplined, competently organized firm with a sophisticated management and a well-trained, dedicated staff."[3] Another analyst wrote that Antar is a "brilliant merchant surrounded by a deeply dedicated organization eager to create an important retail business."[4] Because of such reports and continued strong operating results, as shown in the company's financial statements for 1984–1987 included in Exhibits 1 and 2, the price of Crazy Eddie's stock skyrocketed. Investors who purchased the company's stock in the initial public offering realized as much as a 1000 percent increase in the value of their investments.

CRAZY EDDIE GOES . . . BUST

Despite Crazy Eddie's impressive operating results during the mid-1980s and the company's stock being one of the hottest investments on Wall Street, all was not well within the firm. By 1986 the company was in deep trouble. By the latter part of that year, the boom days for the consumer electronics industry had ended. Although sales of consumer electronics were still increasing, the rate of

3. J. E. Tannenbaum, "How Mounting Woes at Crazy Eddie Sank a Turnaround Effort," *Wall Street Journal,* 10 July 1989, A1, A4.

4. G. Belsky and P. Furman, "Calculated Madness: The Rise and Fall of Crazy Eddie Antar," *Crain's New York Business,* 5 June 1989, 26.

EXHIBIT 1
1984–1987 Balance Sheets of Crazy Eddie

Crazy Eddie, Inc. Balance Sheets (000's omitted)				
	March 1, 1987	*March 2, 1986*	*March 3, 1985*	*May 31, 1984*
Current assets				
Cash	$ 9,347	$ 13,296	$22,273	$ 1,375
Short-term investments	121,957	26,840	—	—
Receivables	10,846	2,246	2,740	2,604
Merchandise inventories	109,072	59,864	26,543	23,343
Prepaid expenses	10,639	2,363	645	514
Total current assets	$261,861	104,609	52,201	27,836
Restricted cash	—	3,356	7,058	—
Due from affiliates	—	—	—	5,739
Property, plant and equipment	26,401	7,172	3,696	1,845
Construction in process	—	6,253	1,154	—
Other assets	6,596	5,560	1,419	1,149
Total assets	$294,858	$126,950	$65,528	$36,569
Current liabilities				
Accounts payable	$ 50,022	$ 51,723	23,078	$20,106
Notes payable	—	—	—	2,900
Short-term debt	49,571	2,254	423	124
Unearned revenue	3,641	3,696	1,173	764
Accrued expenses	5,593	17,126	8,733	6,078
Total current liabilities	$108,827	74,799	33,407	29,972
Long-term debt	8,459	7,701	7,625	46
Convertible subordinated debentures	80,975	—	—	—
Unearned revenue	3,337	1,829	635	327
Stockholders' equity				
Common stock	313	280	134	50
Additional paid-in capital	57,678	17,668	12,298	574
Retained earnings	35,269	24,673	11,429	5,600
Total stockholders' equity	$ 93,260	42,621	23,861	6,224
Total liabilities and stockholders' equity	$294,858	$126,950	$65,528	$36,569

growth had tapered off considerably compared to the dramatic growth rates realized by the industry during the early 1980s. Additionally, by this point, the consumer electronics industry was saturated with retailers, particularly in major metropolitan areas such as New York City, the home base of Crazy Eddie. Increased competition meant smaller profit margins for Crazy Eddie and diminished Antar's ability to extract sweetheart deals from his suppliers.

In addition to the problems posed by the increasingly competitive nature of the retail consumer electronics industry, Crazy Eddie was facing a corporate

EXHIBIT 2
1984–1987 Income Statements of Crazy Eddie

Crazy Eddie, Inc. Income Statements (000's omitted)				
	Year Ended March 1, 1987	Year Ended March 2, 1986	Nine Months Ended March 3, 1985	Year Ended May 31, 1984
Net sales	$ 352,523	$ 262,268	$ 136,319	$ 137,285
Cost of goods sold	(272,255)	(194,371)	(103,421)	(106,934)
Gross profit	$ 80,268	67,897	32,898	30,351
Selling, general and administrative expense	(61,341)	(42,975)	(20,508)	(22,560)
Interest and other income	7,403	3,210	1,211	706
Interest expense	(5,233)	(820)	(438)	(522)
Income before taxes	21,097	27,312	13,163	7,975
Pension contribution	(500)	(800)	(600)	—
Income taxes	(10,001)	(13,268)	(6,734)	(4,202)
Net income	$10,596	$13,244	$5,829	$3,773
Net income per share	$.34	$.48	$.24	$.18

meltdown by the late 1980s. The tripling of the company's annual sales volume between 1984 and 1987 and the more complex responsibilities associated with managing a public company imposed a huge administrative burden on Crazy Eddie's executives. Complicating matters was the fact that Antar's inner circle of relatives, who had served as his principal advisers during the first fifteen years of his company's existence, had disintegrated by 1986, leaving him to run the firm largely on his own. Antar personally forced or coerced many of his relatives to leave the firm after they sided with his former wife in a bitter and highly publicized divorce. Even as Crazy Eddie's internal affairs spiraled into chaos and the firm lurched toward financial disaster, the company's stock was still being touted by Wall Street as a can't-miss investment.

In late 1986, Eddie Antar resigned as company president although he retained the title of chairman of the board. Shortly thereafter, he simply dropped out of sight. By that time, Antar had already realized more than $50 million from the sale of Crazy Eddie stock. In the absence of Antar, Crazy Eddie's financial condition worsened rapidly. Poor operating results reported in early 1987 for the fourth quarter of that fiscal year sent the company's stock price into a tailspin from which it never recovered. In November 1987, a takeover group headed by two prominent financiers gained control of the company. A companywide physical inventory taken by the new owners disclosed the $65 million shortage of inventory, an amount that easily negated the total profits that had been reported by Crazy Eddie since it went public in 1984. It was this shortage that would eventually plunge Crazy Eddie into bankruptcy and send regulatory authorities in pursuit of Eddie Antar for an explanation.

Charges of Accounting Irregularities

Extensive investigations of Crazy Eddie's financial records by the new owners and regulatory authorities resulted in numerous fraud charges being leveled against Eddie Antar and his former associates. According to the SEC, after Crazy Eddie went public in 1984, Eddie Antar was preoccupied with ensuring that the company's stock price continued to rise. To accomplish this objective, Antar realized that Crazy Eddie had to keep posting impressive operating results. The SEC reported that within the first six months after the company went public, Antar ordered a subordinate to overstate inventory by $2 million, resulting in the firm's gross profit being overstated by the same amount. The following year, Antar ordered year-end inventory to be overstated by $9 million and accounts payable to be understated by $3 million. Court records document that Crazy Eddie employees overstated year-end inventory by preparing inventory count sheets for items that did not exist. To overstate accounts payable, bogus debit memos were prepared and entered in the company's accounting records.

As the economic fortunes of Crazy Eddie began to decline in the late 1980s, Antar became more desperate in his efforts to enhance the company's reported revenues and profits. Company employees were ordered to include in inventory consigned merchandise and goods that were being returned to suppliers. Another fraudulent tactic to overstate inventory involved transhipping transactions, the large volume wholesale transactions between Crazy Eddie and many of its smaller competitors.

Antar realized that a key statistic financial analysts follow for retailers is the annual percentage change in "same store" sales. Any decline in this percentage is seen as a negative signal of a retailer's future prospects. As the retail consumer electronics industry became increasingly crowded, the revenues of Crazy Eddie's individual stores began to decline, although the firm's total revenues continued to climb due to several new stores being opened each year. To remedy the drop in same store sales, Antar instructed his employees to record selected transhipping transactions as retail sales of specific stores. For instance, if 100 microwaves costing $180 each were sold to another retailer at a per unit price of $200, the $20,000 in sales would be recorded as if they were retail sales with a normal gross profit margin of 30 to 50 percent—meaning that inventory would not be credited for the total number of microwaves actually sold. This practice killed two birds with the proverbial stone. Same store sales were inflated for selected operating units, and inventory was overstated with a corresponding increase in gross profit from sales.

Where Were the Auditors?

When the scale of the Crazy Eddie fraud was revealed to the public, the question on the minds of many investors, creditors, and other interested parties was, "Where were the auditors?" when all this chicanery was going on. Four different accounting firms audited Crazy Eddie's financial statements over its turbulent history. Crazy Eddie's first accounting firm, a local firm, was dismissed by Antar before he took the company public. The underwriting firm that managed Crazy Eddie's initial public stock offering urged Antar to retain a more prestigious accounting firm to increase the public's confidence in the company's audited financial statements. As a result, Antar retained Main Hurdman to serve as Crazy Eddie's audit firm. Main Hurdman had a nationwide accounting practice with several prominent clients in the consumer electronics industry. In the mid-1980s, Peat Marwick became Crazy Eddie's audit firm when it merged with Main Hurdman. Following the corporate takeover of Crazy Eddie in 1987, Peat Marwick was replaced by Touche Ross.

Much of the criticism stemming from the Crazy Eddie scandal was directed toward Main Hurdman and its successor, Peat Marwick. For example, published reports suggested that the audit fee charged Crazy Eddie by Main Hurdman was unreasonably low. In one year, the accounting firm reportedly charged Crazy Eddie only $85,000 for a full-scope independent audit—an audit of a firm that had several hundred million dollars of revenues. A leading critic of major accounting firms suggested that Main Hurdman had "lowballed" to obtain the Crazy Eddie audit, realizing that it could make up for any lost audit revenue by selling the company consulting services.

> In one year, Main Hurdman charged only $85,000 to do a complete audit of Crazy Eddie—a business with hundreds of millions of dollars in reported revenues, dozens of retail stores, and two large warehouses. At the very same time that Main Hurdman was charging the bargain basement price of $85,000 for supposedly conducting an audit, its consulting division was charging Crazy Eddie millions of dollars to computerize Crazy Eddie's inventory system.[5]

This same individual questioned Main Hurdman's ability to objectively audit an inventory system that it had effectively developed. Main Hurdman's independence was also questioned because many of Crazy Eddie's accountants were former members of that accounting firm. Critics charge that a company that hires one of its former auditors can more easily conceal fraudulent activities during the course of subsequent audits. The reasoning here is that the former auditor will help his or her new employer undermine those subsequent audits. Crazy Eddie's hiring several of its former independent auditors was not unusual; auditors commonly accept positions with former clients when they leave public accounting. Many accounting firms help arrange such "placements," a practice that has been widely criticized.

> You would think that if an auditor wanted to leave a public accounting firm, he or she would be discouraged from going to work for clients they had audited. Instead, just the opposite is true with big accounting firms encouraging their personnel to work for clients in the apparent belief that it helps cement the accountant-client relationship.[6]

Most of the criticism directed at Crazy Eddie's auditors stemmed from their failure to uncover the huge overstatement of the company's inventory and the related understatement of accounts payable. Third parties who filed suit against the auditors charged them with "aiding and abetting" the fraud by failing to

---

5. M. I. Weiss, "Auditors: Be Watchdogs, Not Just Bean Counters," *Accounting Today*, 15 November 1993, 41.

6. Ibid., 42.

properly investigate numerous suspicious circumstances. Of particular concern were several reported instances in which the auditors requested client documents, only to be told that those documents had been lost or inadvertently destroyed.

In Peat Marwick and Main Hurdman's defense, Antar and his associates engaged in a large-scale plan to deceive the auditors. For example, after discovering which inventory sites the auditors would be visiting at year-end, Antar would have sufficient inventory shipped to those stores or warehouses to conceal any shortages. Likewise, Crazy Eddie personnel systematically destroyed incriminating documentation to conceal the inventory shortages from the auditors. Antar also ordered his employees to stop using the sophisticated, computer-based inventory system designed by Main Hurdman. Instead, the accounting personnel were required to return to an archaic manual inventory system previously used by the company. The absence of a computer-based inventory system made it much more difficult for the auditors to determine exactly how much inventory the firm had at any point in time.

A particularly disturbing aspect of the Crazy Eddie scandal was the involvement of several key accounting employees in the various fraudulent schemes. Among the parties who were charged with participating directly in the fraud or being aware of it was the director of the internal audit staff, the acting controller, and the director of accounts payable. Past experience has proven repeatedly that a fraud involving the collusion of numerous client executives, particularly key accounting personnel, is extremely difficult for auditors to uncover.

EPILOGUE

In June 1989, Crazy Eddie lost its line of credit and was forced to file a Chapter 11 bankruptcy petition. Later that same year, the company closed its remaining stores and liquidated its assets because it could not obtain credit from its vendors. Meanwhile, Eddie Antar was named as a defendant in several lawsuits, including a large civil suit filed by the SEC and a criminal indictment filed by a U.S. district attorney. In January 1990, Antar was ordered by a federal judge to repatriate $52 million that he had transferred to foreign bank accounts in 1987. The following month, federal marshals began searching for Antar after he failed to appear in federal court for a hearing in which he was to account for the funds transferred to overseas bank accounts. After finally surrendering to federal marshals, Antar appeared in court and was found in contempt and released on his own recognizance. Shortly thereafter, he became a fugitive, eluding federal authorities for more than two years despite reported sightings of him in Brooklyn, South America, and Jerusalem.

On June 25, 1992, Eddie Antar was arrested by Israeli police. At the time, Antar was living in a small town outside Tel Aviv and posing as an Israeli citizen, David Jacob Levi Cohen. On December 31, 1992, Antar's attorney announced that an extradition agreement had been reached with the U.S. Justice Department and Israeli authorities. After being extradited, Antar was convicted in July 1993 on seventeen counts of financial fraud including racketeering, conspiracy, and mail fraud. In May 1994, Antar was sentenced to twelve and one-half years in federal prison and ordered to pay restitution of $121 million to former stockholders and creditors. Several of Antar's former associates have also been convicted or have pleaded guilty to fraud charges, including Crazy Eddie's former chief financial officer, Sam E. Antar.

To date, more than $50 million has been recovered from Antar, including funds discovered in bank accounts in Israel, Great Britain, Switzerland, and Liechtenstein. Federal authorities believe they may be able to recover additional funds that are still concealed in secret bank accounts around the world.

In March 1993, a $42 million settlement was announced for dozens of lawsuits filed against Crazy Eddie. Although the contributions of the various defendants to the settlement pool were not disclosed, among those defendants were Peat Marwick and the local accounting firm used by Crazy Eddie before the company went public.

In April 1995, a federal appeals court overturned the seventeen-count fraud conviction of Eddie Antar. The appeals court ruled that the judge who presided over Antar's trial had been biased against him. The appeals court ordered that a new trial be held for Antar under a different judge.

QUESTIONS

1. Compute key ratios and other financial measures for Crazy Eddie during the period 1984–1987. Identify and briefly explain the red flags in Crazy Eddie's financial statements which suggested that the firm posed a higher-than-normal level of audit risk.

2. Identify specific audit procedures that might have resulted in the detection of the following accounting irregularities perpetrated by Crazy Eddie personnel: (a) the falsification of inventory count sheets, (b) the bogus debit memos for accounts payable, (c) the recording of transhipping transactions as retail sales, and (d) the inclusion of consigned merchandise in year-end inventory.

3. The retail consumer electronics industry was undergoing rapid and dramatic changes during the 1980s. Discuss how changes in an audit client's industry should affect audit planning decisions. Relate this discussion to Crazy Eddie.

4. Explain what is implied by the term *lowballing* in an audit context. How can this practice potentially affect the quality of independent audit services?

5. Assume that you were a member of the Crazy Eddie audit engagement team in 1986. You were assigned to test the client's year-end inventory cutoff procedures. You selected thirty invoices entered in the accounting records near year-end—fifteen in the few days prior to the client's fiscal year-end and fifteen in the first few days of the new year. Assume that client personnel were unable to locate ten of these invoices. What course of action would have been appropriate at this point and why?

6. Should companies be allowed to hire individuals who formerly served as their independent auditors? Discuss the pros and cons of such a policy.

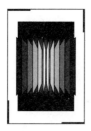

Case 1.7
Penn Square Bank

At 7:05 P.M. on July 5, 1982, a squad of bank examiners from the Federal Deposit Insurance Corporation (FDIC) locked the doors of the Penn Square Bank of Oklahoma City, Oklahoma. Thus ended the legacy of a small shopping center bank that grew from total assets of $29 million in 1974, when it was acquired by the flamboyant B. P. "Beep" Jennings, to total assets of more than $500 million at the time of its closing. The more than $1.5 billion in losses suffered by Penn Square, its affiliated banks, uninsured depositors, and the FDIC insurance fund made this bank failure the most costly in U.S. history at the time. The deluge of lawsuits subsequent to the closing of Penn Square ensnared a wide range of parties, including the former bank's directors and officers; money brokers that funneled huge sums of depositors' funds into the bank; correspondent banks of the failed institution; and the bank's audit firm, Peat, Marwick, Mitchell & Company.

Peat Marwick became an easy target of third parties who were attempting to assign the burden of responsibility for the bank's collapse. The federal banking agencies, Penn Square's sister banks, the money brokers who had been Penn Square's primary source of deposits, and even the U.S. House of Representatives, which investigated the bank's failure, pointed accusatory fingers in the direction of Peat Marwick. Representative Fernand St Germain, chairman of the U.S. House Committee on Banking, Finance, and Urban Affairs, was particularly critical of Peat Marwick's role in the Penn Square debacle. At one point in the hearings, a Peat Marwick partner explained that his firm's audit report was intended only for the bank's directors, implying that external parties had not and should not have relied on Peat Marwick's unqualified opinion issued on Penn Square's 1981 financial statements three months prior to the bank's demise. The partner's caveat provoked an indignant response from Representative St Germain: "You are not aware of the fact that the people at Penn Square dealing with brokers gave your reports . . . to people, credit unions, S&Ls around this nation who put enormous sums of money into this institution based on your audit reports, since that was all that was available. . . . Did it come as a complete and total surprise to you, like the fact that when you get to be 10 years old you find out there is no Santa Claus?"[1]

Peat, Marwick, Mitchell & Company endured considerable criticism for its role in the Penn Square saga. This client relationship, which lasted only seven months, proved to be not only one of the shortest for Peat Marwick but also one of the most costly.

The History of Penn Square

Penn Square Bank was incorporated in 1960 and during its entire twenty-two-year existence was located in a shopping mall in a northwest Oklahoma City neighborhood. For many years, the bank's primary customers were the small businesses in the mall and residents of the surrounding community. The role of the bank changed rapidly, however, after being acquired by Jennings in 1974. Under the ownership of Jennings, the bank became caught up in the Oklahoma oil boom of the late 1970s and went on a lending spree to oil and gas speculators—a spree that resulted in the bank's doubling its total assets every two years from 1976 to 1982. When closed by the FDIC, oil and gas loans accounted for over 80 percent of the bank's assets.

Penn Square's explosive growth was engineered primarily by one individual, William Patterson, who was hired by Jennings as a favor to a family friend shortly after Jennings acquired the bank. Patterson, then in his mid-twenties, was given a job as a loan officer even though he had only limited prior lending experience. Within eighteen months, the affable and ambitious Patterson was managing the bank's oil and gas loan portfolio and had become the protégé and most trusted ally of Jennings. Patterson quickly became well known in the Oklahoma City banking community for his idiosyncracies, which included wearing a Mickey Mouse hat while doing business with prospective clients and drinking beer from his cowboy boots at swank Oklahoma City watering holes.

To finance its rapid growth, Penn Square was forced to continually expand its deposit base. The bank attracted a significant amount of deposits in a short period of time by offering interest rate premiums on "jumbo" certificates of deposit (CDs) that were 25 to 150 basis points above prevailing market rates. Even though the bank grew at a phenomenal rate under the guidance of Jennings and Patterson, Penn Square was still only a medium-sized bank when it failed. In terms of total assets, Penn Square ranked, at the time of its closing, as only the seventh largest bank ever closed by the FDIC. Consequently, the failure of the Oklahoma City bank was noteworthy not because of its size but rather because some of the nation's largest banks had become involved in the speculative oil and gas lending activities of Penn Square's energy division.

In the late 1970s, Patterson became so successful in attracting oil and gas ventures to Penn Square that his bank, because of its limited size, was unable to fund the loans requested by many prospective customers. At that point, Patter-

---

1. This and all subsequent quotations were taken from the following source: U.S. Congress, House, Committee on Banking, Finance, and Urban Affairs, *Penn Square Bank Failure, Part 1* (Washington, D.C.: U.S. Government Printing Office, 1982).

son convinced several major metropolitan banks to help finance the largest of these oil and gas ventures. Penn Square would arrange the lending "syndicates" for these ventures and perform all necessary administrative functions, such as obtaining appraisals and engineering estimates of oil reserves. In some cases, Penn Square served strictly as an intermediary in these loans. Rather than assuming an equity interest in these "100 percent participations," Penn Square was simply paid a fee for its services by the banks actually providing the loans. Seattle First National Bank, Continental Illinois, and Chase Manhattan were among the metropolitan banks that financed numerous large oil and gas ventures with the assistance of Penn Square. Continental Illinois alone provided over $1 billion to Penn Square customers, and Chase Manhattan provided more than $200 million.

As a result of President Jimmy Carter's energy conservation policies and massive overproduction by the Organization of Petroleum Exporting Countries (OPEC), oil and gas prices began plummeting in 1980. Many, if not most, of the Penn Square–backed exploration ventures were aimed at recovering oil and gas from the deepest reservoirs. These reservoirs had not been tapped prior to the 1970s oil boom, because low prices made it economically infeasible to extract the oil from them. As the price of crude oil suddenly dropped several dollars per barrel, these ventures quickly became unprofitable.

By early 1980, the Office of the Comptroller of the Currency (OCC) had turned a wary eye in the direction of Penn Square. The large profits, booming loan volume, and unheard-of growth rates had caused the OCC to become suspicious. An investigation by OCC federal bank examiners in that year uncovered many violations of banking laws by Penn Square, including insufficient liquidity, inadequate capital, and poor loan documentation. Later that year, the OCC forced the bank's directors to sign an "administrative agreement" promising to undertake remedial measures to correct these problems. Actions taken by Penn Square in response to the OCC order included the hiring of a new president, Eldon Beller, a banker with strong credentials in the Oklahoma City business community, as well as the hiring of several other key executive officers who had considerable banking experience. Additionally, loan review and documentation procedures were tightened and codified, and the reserves for loan losses were increased 100 percent over the previous year.

The measures taken by Penn Square resulted in a more positive evaluation of the bank's condition by federal bank examiners in the fall of 1981. However, shortly after the examiners left the bank, the oil glut worsened, forcing increasing numbers of small exploration companies—the backbone of Penn Square's clientele—out of business. Critics allege that Penn Square, faced with the need for steady growth to continue attracting large investors and participant banks, returned to its former ways. In the last seven months of its existence, Penn Square loaned more than $1 billion to oil and gas speculators, by direct loans or indirectly through participation deals, eclipsing even its own pre-1980 frantic lending pace.

By the time federal examiners returned to Penn Square in the spring of 1982, the condition of the bank had deteriorated alarmingly. Penn Square was in such poor condition in the last few weeks before its closing that the Federal Reserve was forced to extend the bank several million dollars in emergency loans to keep it solvent. Finally, in July 1982, the OCC concluded that Penn Square was beyond rescue and ordered the FDIC to shut down the bank and serve as its receiver.

EXHIBIT 1
Arthur Young's 1980
Penn Square Audit
Option

The Board of Directors
First Penn Corporation

We have examined the accompanying balance sheets (company and consolidated) of First Penn Corporation at December 31, 1980 and 1979, and the related statements (company and consolidated) of income, stockholders' equity, and changes in financial position for the years then ended. Except as stated in the following paragraph, our examinations were made in accordance with generally accepted auditing standards and, accordingly, included such tests of the accounting records and such other auditing procedures as we considered necessary in the circumstances.

We were unable to satisfy ourselves as to the adequacy of the reserve for possible loan losses at December 31, 1980, due to the lack of supporting documentation of collateral values of certain loans.

In our opinion, except for the effects of such adjustments, if any, on the 1980 financial statements (company and consolidated) as might have been determined to be necessary had we been able to satisfy ourselves as to the adequacy of the reserve for possible loan losses, the statements mentioned above present fairly the financial position (company and consolidated) of First Penn Corporation at December 31, 1980 and 1979, and the results of operations (company and consolidated) and the changes in financial position (company and consolidated) for the years then ended, in conformity with generally accepted accounting principles applied on a consistent basis during the period.

Arthur Young & Company
March 13, 1981

DISMISSAL OF ARTHUR YOUNG BY PENN SQUARE

The Oklahoma City office of Arthur Young & Company audited Penn Square's annual financial statements from 1976 through 1980. Beginning with the fiscal year ending December 31, 1979, Penn Square Bank became a wholly owned subsidiary of the newly formed bank holding company First Penn Corporation. Nevertheless, the de facto audit client remained Penn Square Bank. For the years ending December 31, 1976, through December 31, 1979, the bank received unqualified opinions from Arthur Young. In 1980, however, the Arthur Young auditors issued a qualified opinion on Penn Square's financial statements (shown in Exhibit 1), which stated that the auditors were unable to satisfy themselves "as to the adequacy of the reserve for possible loan losses."

In the fall of 1982, during the Penn Square congressional hearings, Harold Russell, managing partner of the Oklahoma City office of Arthur Young, was asked to discuss the problems that his firm had encountered during its 1980 audit of Penn Square. Russell reported that the bank's loan documentation practices had deteriorated between 1979 and 1980. In particular, Arthur Young found that many loans did not have current engineering reports documenting oil reserves, and others had engineering reports that did not include an opinion of the engineer or did not list the assumptions that the engineer had used in estimating the reserves. When asked if these problems had been discussed with bank management, Russell replied affirmatively and noted that Jennings was "not pleased" with the audit firm's decision to qualify its opinion. Without prior warning, Jennings informed Russell in late November 1981 that the bank had decided to retain the firm of Peat, Marwick, Mitchell & Company to audit its 1981 financial statements. Although media reports implied that Arthur Young had been dismissed because of the qualified opinion, Penn Square officials repeatedly denied that was the case.[2]

The congressional investigative committee that sponsored the Penn Square hearings was very interested in determining why Peat Marwick was selected as the bank's new auditor following the dismissal of Arthur Young. Jim Blanton, the managing partner of Peat Marwick's Oklahoma City office, informed the committee that several members of his firm were well acquainted with top executives of Penn Square prior to his firm's being selected as the bank's new auditor. Blanton suggested that these relationships were responsible, at least in part, for Penn Square's decision to retain Peat Marwick as its new audit firm in the fall of 1981.

Under further questioning by the committee, Blanton disclosed that a number of Peat Marwick's Oklahoma City partners had previously obtained more than $2 million in loans and a $1 million line of credit from Penn Square. These loans presented the audit firm with an independence "problem" that had to be resolved before the bank could be accepted as a client. The agreement reached between the two parties was that Penn Square would "fully participate out" the loans and the line of credit to other banks. Even though these participations were intended to be nonrecourse transactions, on July 1, 1982—just four days prior to the bank's closing—Peat Marwick learned that one of the loans had been repurchased by Penn Square. Peat Marwick officials noted that this repurchase had been done without their knowledge and that it was "completely contrary to our prior understanding with the bank."

THE 1981 PEAT MARWICK AUDIT

Jim Blanton submitted to the congressional investigative committee a detailed memorandum that discussed, among other items, his firm's 1981 audit of Penn Square. Apparently, the focal point of the 1981 audit was the bank's allowance for possible loan losses. Blanton noted that the balance of that account at December 31, 1981, was more than twice that of December 31, 1980, and that Penn Square had written off $4.8 million in loans in 1981, compared with just slightly more than $600,000 in 1980. Nevertheless, as demonstrated by Penn Square's December 31, 1981, balance sheet (which is reproduced in Exhibit 2), the allowance for possible loan losses at the end of 1981 was a very modest 1.5 percent of the bank's total loans. (Exhibit 3 presents note 4 to the 1981 Penn Square balance sheet which summarized the activity in the allowance for possible loan losses account for 1980 and 1981.)

Blanton reported that his firm paid particular attention during the 1981 audit of Penn Square to the $15 million in problem loans that had resulted in the

2. Peat Marwick officials testified that their firm made the standard inquiries of Arthur Young that are required by *Statement on Auditing Standards No. 7*, "Communications between Predecessor and Successor Auditors." Arthur Young responded to these inquiries by stating that its relationship with Penn Square Bank had been "free of significant problems." However, Arthur Young did bring to Peat Marwick's attention the qualified opinion that it had issued on Penn Square's 1980 financial statements.

EXHIBIT 2
Penn Square's 1981
Balance Sheet

PENN SQUARE BANK, N.A.
(A Wholly-owned Subsidiary of First Penn Corporation)

Assets	December 31,	
	1981	1980
Cash, time deposits and due from banks	$ 87,465,338	$ 59,625,519
Investments securities (note 2):		
U.S. Treasury securities	13,123,075	10,992,420
Obligations of state and political subdivisions	34,362,974	31,334,926
Loans (notes 3 and 4)	277,407,896	203,437,140
Less:		
Unearned discount	2,171,330	1,537,889
Allowance for possible loan losses	4,141,447	2,004,587
Loans, net	271,095,119	199,894,664
Federal funds sold	53,000,000	16,000,000
Bank premises, property and equipment, net (note 5)	3,877,929	2,481,667
Accrued interest receivable	20,495,932	7,372,553
Other assets (note 9)	1,704,004	762,888
	$485,124,371	$328,464,637
Liabilities and Stockholder's Equity		
Deposits:		
Demand	232,636,575	142,624,714
Savings and NOW accounts	18,223,800	13,341,126
Time (note 6)	196,817,006	144,822,794
Total deposits	447,677,381	300,788,634
Loans sold under agreements to repurchase	—	2,795,561
Federal funds purchased	900,000	650,000
Accrued interest and other liabilities (note 9)	4,949,589	3,808,039
Total liabilities	453,526,970	308,042,234
Stockholder's equity:		
Common stock	1,000,000	1,000,000
Surplus	18,000,000	10,500,000
Undivided profits	12,597,401	8,922,403
Total stockholder's equity	31,597,401	20,422,403
Commitments and contingent liabilities (note 12)		
	$485,124,371	$328,464,637

See accompanying notes to financial statements.

Arthur Young qualification. By the end of 1981, many of those loans had been repaid by the borrowers, according to Blanton. For the problem loans that were still outstanding as of December 31, 1981, Blanton reported that the documentation concerns raised by Arthur Young had been adequately addressed by the establishment of a credit review department and by other remedial measures undertaken by the bank. In support of this contention, Blanton referred to the OCC's October 1981 examination, which commended the bank's directors for the improvement in Penn Square's administrative and operating policies.

The results of the 1981 Penn Square audit apparently left little doubt in the minds of the Peat Marwick auditors that the bank's financial statements were fairly stated. The Peat Marwick workpapers contained a lengthy memorandum

A summary of transactions in the allowance for possible loan losses is as follows:

	1981	1980
Balance at beginning of year	$ 2,004,587	$1,002,097
Recoveries credited to the allowance	629,417	212,061
Provision charged to expense	6,343,000	1,407,830
	8,977,004	2,621,988
Less loans charged off	(4,835,557)	(617,401)
Balance at end of year	$ 4,141,447	$2,004,587

Management's judgment as to the level of future losses on existing loans involves the consideration and related effect of current and anticipated economic conditions on specific borrowers, an evaluation of the existing relationship among loans, examinations by regulatory authorities and management's internal review of the loan portfolio. In determining the collectibility of certain loans, management also considers the fair value of the underlying collateral.

During 1981, the Bank formed a loan review function and adopted a formalized approach to the evaluation and documentation of credit risks within the loan portfolio. The conclusions reached from this systematic analysis of the loans are translated on a quarterly basis to adjustments, if any, which are deemed necessary to maintain the allowance for possible loan losses at an adequate level. Also during 1981, the Bank significantly improved its documentation of the loan files with respect to credit and collateral information.

It should be understood that estimates of future loan losses involve an exercise of judgment. It is the judgment of management that the allowance is adequate at both December 31, 1981 and 1980.

EXHIBIT 3
Note 4 to Penn Square's 1981 Balance Sheet: Allowance for Possible Loan Losses

written by Dean York, the partner in charge of the Penn Square engagement; that memorandum outlined the sensitive nature of the audit and the reasons leading York to conclude that the unqualified opinion, shown in Exhibit 4, was appropriate.[3] According to Peat Marwick's congressional testimony, the specific wording of the firm's opinion on Penn Square's 1981 financial statements was reviewed and approved by several senior partners in the firm, including Blanton.

Although testimony of the Peat Marwick partners supported the firm's decision to accept Penn Square's 1981 allowance for possible loan losses, congressional investigators were not convinced that the bank's balance sheet fairly presented its financial condition at the time. For instance, Congressman Doug Barnard noted that Penn Square had reserved a much smaller percentage of specifically identified problem loans than was normal, according to statistics made available by the federal bank agencies. In rebuttal, York stated that loan review "is a highly judgmental area, and there are different rules of thumb used."

---

3. Most of York's memo consisted of an explanation of how Penn Square's loan documentation problems, which were responsible for Arthur Young's qualified opinion on the bank's prior year financial statements, had been resolved. York's memo also suggested, however, that he was concerned with the significant increase in the provision for uncollectible loans and the implications of this increase for the bank's financial health. For instance, near the end of the memo he remarked, "As a result of our review and tests . . . I believe that we can give an opinion on the 1981 results of operations." This latter statement seems to suggest that Peat Marwick may have considered issuing a disclaimer of opinion on the bank's financial statements, given its deteriorating financial condition.

**EXHIBIT 4
Peat Marwick's 1981
Penn Square Audit
Opinion**

The Board of Directors and Stockholders
First Penn Corporation

We have examined the consolidated and parent-only financial statements of First Penn Corporation and subsidiaries and the consolidated balance sheet of Penn Square Bank, N.A., and subsidiary as listed in the accompanying index. Our examination was made in accordance with generally accepted auditing standards, and accordingly included such tests of the accounting records and such other auditing procedures as we considered necessary in the circumstances. The financial statements for the year ended December 31, 1980, for First Penn Corporation as listed in the accompanying index, which are included for comparative purposes, were examined by other auditors whose report, dated March 13, 1981, was qualified because they were unable to satisfy themselves as to the adequacy of the allowance for possible loan losses due to the lack of supporting documentation of collateral values of certain loans. As described in note 4 to the accompanying financial statements, the subsidiary bank, during 1981, formalized its approach to the evaluation of credit risks within the loan portfolio and documentation of the loan files with respect to credit and collateral information. The consolidated balance sheet for Penn Square Bank, N.A., and subsidiary as of December 31, 1980, which is included for comparative purposes, was included in the consolidated balance sheet of First Penn Corporation but was not presented separately and, therefore, not covered by the aforementioned auditors' report dated March 13, 1981.

In our opinion, the aforementioned financial statements present fairly the consolidated and parent-only financial position of First Penn Corporation and subsidiaries at December 31, 1981, the results of their operations and the changes in their financial position for the year then ended, and the consolidated financial position of Penn Square Bank, N.A., and subsidiary at December 31, 1981, in conformity with generally accepted accounting principles applied on a basis consistent with that of the preceding year.

Peat, Marwick, Mitchell & Co.
March 19, 1982

The congressional investigators also focused considerable attention on the "management letter" that Peat Marwick provided to the Penn Square directors upon completion of the audit. That letter was critical of several facets of Penn Square's internal accounting controls. The investigators were confused as to why these problems had not been mentioned in the audit report. At one point in the hearings, Congressman George Wortley asked Blanton whether the internal controls of the bank were "adequate."

MR. BLANTON: No, sir. We don't believe they were adequate.

CONGRESSMAN WORTLEY: Well, did you criticize them in the public statement?

MR. BLANTON: No, sir.

CONGRESSMAN WORTLEY: You only criticized them in the management letter?

MR. BLANTON: That is correct.

CONGRESSMAN WORTLEY: Do you think that is fair to the public? And is that a custom of the profession?

MR. BLANTON: I am not sure that I can determine what is fair or unfair to the public. I can say that it is a normal procedure to issue a management letter, and that we do not address in the financial statements or in footnotes all of the problems of a client.

CONGRESSMAN WORTLEY: Well, do you not feel that you have a responsibility to someone other than your client, in this case Penn Square? Is the whole purpose of an audit not to make certain that things are verified and the public is adequately informed of it, and shareholders and investors and depositors?

A final facet of the 1981 Penn Square audit that the congressional investigative committee scrutinized intently was communications that occurred during that audit between Penn Square's auditors and auditors from the same firm who examined Chase Manhattan's financial statements. The congressional committee was concerned that Chase Manhattan, as a result of those communications, had become aware of banking law violations by Penn Square, as well as the deteriorating financial condition of the bank. Such knowledge could have been used by Chase to recover funds that it had made available to Penn Square. Subsequent to the hearings, Chase was sued by the FDIC for an alleged improper withdrawal of funds from Penn Square a few days before the bank's closing.

The Peat Marwick partners denied that the communications between the Oklahoma City and New York City offices of their firm had provided Chase Manhattan with inside information concerning the condition of Penn Square. Congressman Ed Weber pursued this issue by asking Blanton whether independent auditors are required to protect the confidentiality of sensitive information they obtain from clients.

MR. BLANTON: That is correct.

CONGRESSMAN WEBER: And the thing that clouds the issue here is that we may be dealing in an area of civil fraud or actual illegality, and the question is at that point, do you maintain the confidentiality of those potential violations of law from other people who may be affected by that information? [Pause.]

CONGRESSMAN WEBER: Can you answer?

MR. BLANTON: I am thinking. I really do not know the answer to that question. It obviously has been the subject of much debate among accountants.

CONGRESSMAN WEBER: You are in a situation of a conflict of interest. You are representing two clients who have conflicting interests. The interest of one client is to keep the information totally confidential. The interest of the other client, of course, is to be informed.

MR. BLANTON: I think that I can safely say that it is our firm policy that we do not ever discuss the condition of one client with another client.

PENN SQUARE—AN AUDIT FAILURE?

The evidence introduced into the congressional testimony that was most damaging to the credibility of the Peat Marwick audit was an OCC report that labeled the firm's 1982 audit "unacceptable." That report, dated March 31, 1982, stated:

> The unqualified opinion [issued by Peat Marwick] was rendered despite the identification of excess collateral exceptions, discovery of incidences where the bank was making payments of principal and interest to the correspondent banks on certain

participations without first receiving payment from the borrowers, and acceptance of a reserve for possible loan losses which was deemed inadequate by the examiners during their review of the loan portfolio.

Congressman Weber noted that the results of the spring 1982 OCC audit—performed almost simultaneously with that of Peat Marwick—uncovered "serious problems." Unfortunately, the Peat Marwick audit team did not have access to the results of the OCC audit, nor did the independent auditors' own examination lead them to conclude that the problems were as severe as later noted in the OCC report. As is the case in any audit of a sizable client, Peat Marwick was forced to arrive at a decision on the Penn Square financial statements based largely on evidence collected via random test checks. Such economic constraints are normally not present in audits performed by federal bank examiners.

The testimony of the Peat Marwick partners suggests that the audit firm may have overrelied on the controls implemented by the bank as a result of the 1980 OCC order. In addition, Peat Marwick may have been lulled into a false sense of security by the favorable report issued on Penn Square by the OCC examiners who visited the bank in the fall of 1981. In retrospect, it appears that the new controls implemented by the bank in 1980 were only temporarily effective.

At least one definitive conclusion can be drawn from analyzing the autopsy of the Peat Marwick audit: the alleged Penn Square audit failure would not have occurred had oil prices continued their upward surge. As noted by one of the congressional investigators, Penn Square was a "house of cards" built on the assumption of continually escalating oil prices. Because of the Penn Square debacle, audit firms will look more warily upon prospective clients whose future operating results are more dependent on exogenous variables than on the decisions of a prudent, disciplined management team.

EPILOGUE

In the spring of 1985, William Patterson was acquitted on twenty-six counts of bank fraud in a criminal lawsuit filed against him in a federal court in Oklahoma City. Three years later, twelve similar criminal complaints were dropped when a mistrial was declared in a criminal lawsuit brought against Patterson in a federal court in Chicago. Finally, in July 1988, in a plea bargain agreement with federal prosecutors, Patterson pleaded guilty to misapplication of bank funds and was sentenced to two years in federal prison. In 1984, a colleague of Patterson's at Penn Square pleaded guilty to bank fraud charges and was sentenced to a thirty-month prison sentence.

By the early 1990s, well over $1 billion in civil lawsuits had been filed against Peat Marwick for its involvement with Penn Square Bank. Apparently nearly all of these lawsuits were settled privately out of court. The FDIC sued Peat Marwick for $90 million and reportedly collected approximately one-half of that amount from the audit firm in a confidential settlement. In August 1994, Peat Marwick agreed to pay $186 million to settle numerous lawsuits filed by the federal government in connection with the firm's allegedly negligent audits of several banks and savings and loans. Similar settlements were paid by other Big

Six accounting firms. For example, Ernst & Young paid $400 million to settle claims filed against it by the federal government. The U.S. Justice Department also filed suit against twelve Peat Marwick employees or former employees, alleging, among other charges, that these individuals were guilty of conflict of interest with respect to Penn Square. Apparently, the charges against these individuals were settled privately as well.

In October 1993, the FDIC office in Oklahoma City that had been established to manage the liquidation of Penn Square Bank was finally closed—after eleven years. Arriving at a reliable estimate of the total losses stemming from the bank's collapse is a difficult, if not impossible, task. However, by the early 1990s, most estimates put these losses in excess of $2 billion. Among the parties hardest hit were credit unions that had purchased jumbo CDs from Penn Square Bank. Approximately forty credit unions lost more than $110 million on these CDs.

With the advent of the banking and savings and loan crises of the 1980s, the auditing profession took a number of steps to assist auditors in developing more effective audit strategies for financial institutions. One of the most important of these measures was the publication of a monograph entitled *Auditing the Allowance for Credit Losses of Banks* (New York: AICPA, 1986). This publication is designed to help auditors corroborate the material accuracy of the allowance for credit losses or bad loans, which is typically the most problematic account to audit in banking and savings and loan engagements.

QUESTIONS

1. What characteristic of the Penn Square loan portfolio caused the business risk of this bank to be much higher than it would have been otherwise? Which component of audit risk, as discussed in *Statement on Auditing Standards No. 47*, "Audit Risk and Materiality in Conducting an Audit," is affected by a client's business risk? Demonstrate with a numerical example how the relative business risk of an audit client affects the degree of audit risk that an audit firm faces.

2. Are an audit firm's professional responsibilities affected when it succeeds a firm that issued a qualified opinion on the given client's prior financial statements? Why or why not? What has the auditing profession done, if anything, to minimize "opinion shopping" by audit clients?

3. Did the Penn Square loans to the Peat Marwick partners present the audit firm with an apparent or de facto independence problem? Identify the conditions, if any, under which it would not have been necessary for the loans to have been sold by Penn Square.

4. Discuss an auditor's reporting responsibilities when significant problems are discovered in a client's internal control structure. Should independent auditors report on the quality or adequacy of a client's internal controls to financial statement users?

5. One of the Peat Marwick partners implied that his firm's audit report was intended only for the benefit of the bank's board of directors. Under common law, were any other parties justified in relying on Peat Marwick's audit report? Penn Square Bank and the holding company of which it was a subsidiary were privately owned. Does this fact change your answer?

6. Would Peat Marwick have violated the profession's ethical standards if its New York City office had informed Chase Manhattan that Penn Square had violated certain banking laws? What if the New York City office had informed Chase Manhattan that Penn Square was apparently on the verge of bankruptcy?

7. Peat Marwick was criticized after the fact for failing to warn those parties relying on Penn Square's 1981 financial statements that the bank was in danger of failing. Under present auditing standards, what responsibility, if any, do auditors have to forewarn financial statement users of companies that are in danger of failing?

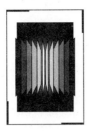

CASE 1.8
IFG LEASING

In 1974, Inter-Regional Financial Group, Inc. (IFG), a financial services company based in Minneapolis, purchased a small leasing company located in Great Falls, Montana. Even though the leasing company, which became known as IFG Leasing, was a wholly owned subsidiary of IFG, it was required to file periodic financial statements with the Securities and Exchange Commission (SEC) because it had publicly traded debt securities. IFG Leasing's sole line of business was the writing of "small ticket" leases. Small ticket leases typically have terms of three to five years and involve assets such as farm equipment, office furniture, and construction equipment with costs ranging from $2,000 to $100,000. IFG Leasing rapidly expanded its scope of operations and significantly increased its market share in the small ticket leasing industry following its acquisition by IFG. In 1974, IFG Leasing had thirty employees and $20 million in lease receivables, the company's principal asset.[1] Seven years later, IFG Leasing had more than four hundred employees in ten branch offices located across the country and nearly $400 million in lease receivables outstanding, which represented 35 percent of the consolidated assets of IFG.

Most of IFG Leasing's phenomenal growth occurred between 1979 and 1981, when the company's lease receivables increased nearly 120 percent. The company's growth rate over that two-year period is even more dramatic when one considers that interest rates in the U.S. economy reached their all-time high during that time frame. In December 1980, the prime rate peaked at 21.5 percent, at which time the effective interest rate on the leases signed by most of IFG Leasing's customers was approximately 26 percent. The rapid growth experienced by IFG Leasing during this troubled economic period was primarily due to an aggressive marketing strategy adopted by its management team. In the late 1970s, a large proportion of the company's clientele was companies and individuals who were unable to obtain asset financing from other sources: "[IFG] Leasing enjoyed rapid growth by effectively becoming a 'lender of last resort,' lending to lessees who for a variety of reasons could not obtain financing

---

1. By 1981, lease receivables accounted for 96 percent of IFG Leasing's total assets.

elsewhere. . . . In short, Leasing fueled its growth with a substantial amount of 'bad' credit risks."[2]

By late 1981, the aggressive marketing policy of IFG Leasing began to manifest itself in a rapidly increasing delinquency rate on its lease receivables.[3] Internal reports prepared by IFG Leasing at the time demonstrated that approximately 15 percent of the company's lease portfolio was ninety days or more delinquent, while the industry norm was only 1.2 percent. The company's soaring delinquency rate in the early 1980s created a severe cash flow problem for IFG Leasing. Most of the equipment and other assets the company purchased for leasing purposes were financed by short-term loans that were secured by the leased assets. IFG Leasing used the funds provided by its customers' monthly lease payments to service these loans. However, as its delinquency rate rose steadily, the company was forced to seek emergency cash infusions from its parent company and other IFG subsidiaries. Finally, in July 1983, IFG Leasing discontinued leasing equipment and focused its efforts exclusively on collecting its outstanding lease receivables.

ACCOUNTING AND CONTROL PROBLEMS AT IFG LEASING

An SEC investigation of IFG Leasing in 1988 disclosed that the company had used a number of illicit means in the early 1980s to mask its deteriorating financial condition. Apparently, company executives were attempting to conceal IFG Leasing's true financial condition from the banks that supplied the company with funds for additional equipment purchases and with the lines of credit that IFG Leasing used for working capital purposes. The SEC charged that IFG Leasing consistently reported an insufficient allowance for uncollectible lease receivables in its periodic financial statements. The company's policy was to record a fixed percentage of lease receivables generated in each accounting period as a charge to bad debt expense and a credit to the allowance for uncollectible lease receivables. In 1981, this percentage was increased from 1.5 to 2 percent and then to 3 percent the following year. Although the accounting method used by the company to estimate bad debts was considered acceptable by the SEC, the federal agency maintained that company management should have recognized that the fixed percentages used in estimating bad debts were much too small. By September 1982, more than 20 percent of the company's receivables was more than ninety days delinquent.

---

2. This and all subsequent quotations are taken from Securities and Exchange Commission, *Accounting and Auditing Enforcement Release No. 200,* 23 September 1988.

3. When IFG Leasing recorded a lease, it debited lease receivables for the total amount of the payments to be received from the lessee over the term of the lease and credited the appropriate asset account. The difference between the aggregate lease payments and the cost of the leased asset was credited to a deferred income account. The credit to deferred income, however, was reduced by any residual value the asset was expected to have at the end of the lease term. Income on the leases was recorded at a decreasing rate over the lease term, with a significant amount of the gross profit on each lease "front-ended" on the date the lease was signed. The SEC noted that this "front-ending" of lease income was a "very aggressive" accounting method compared with the income recognition methods used by other small-ticket lessors.

Surprisingly, the SEC investigation disclosed that no specific individual in the company had been assigned ultimate responsibility for evaluating the adequacy of the allowance for uncollectible lease receivables.

> [IFG] Leasing's CEO testified that he relied on the company's CAO (chief accounting officer) to review the allowance. . . . The CAO testified that he relied on the CEO and the collections department to determine the adequacy of the allowance, and counted on Touche Ross [the company's auditors] to corroborate its adequacy. The collections manager testified that he relied on the CAO to review the adequacy of the allowance. . . . IFG [the parent company] senior management testified that they relied on IFG Leasing and Touche Ross to assess the allowance's adequacy.

A direct consequence of this lack of control over the allowance for uncollectible lease receivables was a material understatement of that account for financial reporting purposes.

The SEC also pointed out a number of other major deficiencies in IFG Leasing's internal control structure. For instance, the company had no systematic procedure for repossessing assets leased to individuals who were significantly past due on their lease payments. As a result, in many cases, delinquent lessees continued to use leased equipment indefinitely. A lack of sufficient storage space and the absence of a reliable system to monitor its asset inventory prevented the company from providing effective safeguards over the equipment that was repossessed from delinquent lessees. The SEC's investigation also disclosed that the company's leasing policies were often violated. Personnel in branch offices would frequently change the terms of leases without obtaining proper authorization for such changes. The SEC suggested that such violations of company policies may have been a consequence of the use of "performance-based" compensation schemes by IFG Leasing. Finally, the SEC expressed concern that the operations of IFG Leasing were dominated by one individual, the founder and chief executive officer (CEO) of the company.

As noted earlier, the increasing rate of delinquencies in its lease receivables portfolio presented major problems for IFG Leasing by the early 1980s. Most of the loan agreements signed by the company when acquiring equipment included a clause that made the loan immediately due and payable if the lessee of the equipment was ninety days or more past due in its payments. Another common clause was that a loan became immediately due and payable if IFG Leasing's ninety-day delinquencies exceeded 6 percent of its total outstanding lease receivables. In 1980, to conceal the company's high delinquency rate, a member of IFG Leasing's senior management began altering aging summaries of the company's lease receivables—summaries provided to lending institutions and incorporated as exhibits in periodic registration statements filed with the SEC. Exhibit 1 lists the ninety-day delinquencies that IFG Leasing reported publicly and the comparable delinquencies reflected by its internal accounting records.

The SEC charged that the misleading aging summaries not only obscured the collectibility of the company's lease receivables but also caused its overall financial statements to be materially distorted: "As a result, investors and creditors had no indication of [IFG] Leasing's critically deteriorating financial condition."

The irregularities in the aging summaries were eventually discovered by several lower-level employees of IFG Leasing, who then reported the problem to

EXHIBIT 1
IFG Leasing's Publicly Reported and Internally Reported Delinquent Receivables, 1980–1982

	Publicly Reported		Internally Reported	
Date	90-Day Delinquencies	% of Lease Receivables	90-Day Delinquencies	% of Lease Receivables
Dec. 1980	$ 6,800,000	2.5	$31,000,000	11.5
Dec. 1981	16,200,000	4.3	57,300,000	15.3
Mar. 1982	25,700,000	6.4	63,700,000	15.9
Jun. 1982	31,700,000	7.5	83,400,000	19.5
Sep. 1982	33,900,000	7.7	89,300,000	20.2

company executives. In early 1981, the company's chief accounting officer, along with other company officials, brought the misleading aging summaries to the attention of IFG Leasing's CEO. The CEO refused to correct the aging summaries, alleging that the company's accounting system could not be relied upon to generate accurate estimates of receivables delinquencies. In addition, the CEO reportedly threatened to fire any officer who disclosed the internally generated loan delinquency figures to anyone outside the company. Finally, in September 1982, when the delinquencies had become so large as to be totally unmanageable, the chief accounting officer of IFG Leasing reported the problem to IFG headquarters in Minneapolis. Despite objections by IFG Leasing's CEO, IFG executives forced the subsidiary to record a $17 million increase in its allowance for uncollectible leases in the fourth quarter of 1982. Six months later, IFG ordered the subsidiary to discontinue writing new leases and instead concentrate its efforts on collecting its outstanding lease receivables.

1980 TOUCHE ROSS AUDIT OF IFG LEASING

During the interim tests-of-controls phase of the 1980 audit of IFG Leasing by Touche Ross & Company, the auditors discovered that the company's aging summaries of lease receivables were inaccurate. In particular, these audit tests demonstrated that numerous delinquent lease receivables were excluded from the aging summaries that the company intended to include in the annual 10-K statement to be filed with the SEC. Further tests also demonstrated that the company's delinquencies exceeded 6 percent of total lease receivables, causing IFG Leasing to be in violation of a key loan agreement covenant. The Touche Ross audit engagement partner informed client management that an unqualified audit opinion could not be issued unless a waiver of the violated loan covenant was obtained. Client officials obtained the requested waiver prior to the issuance of the company's 1980 10-K; however, they failed to make the necessary corrections in the aging summaries of lease receivables that were eventually included in the 10-K.

Later in the 1980 audit, a junior auditor also discovered that the aging summaries were materially in error. The junior auditor carefully noted in her audit workpapers that a significant number of delinquent lease receivables were excluded from those summaries. When these workpapers were reviewed by the audit engagement partner, he instructed the junior auditor to erase all references she had made in the workpapers to the omitted delinquencies: "At first hesitant, the junior complied after being assured that Touche would recommend clarifying language reflecting the omissions that would accompany the aging tables appearing on the Form 10-K." The aging summaries were never corrected, however, nor was any narrative added to the 10-K to explain the omitted delinquent lease receivables. After the 10-K was filed with the SEC, the junior auditor realized that the changes she suggested had not been made. She subsequently testified that she did not pursue the matter any further at that point because she believed the audit engagement partner had resolved the issue somehow with client officials.

1981 TOUCHE ROSS AUDIT OF IFG LEASING

The SEC was extremely critical of the 1981 audit of IFG Leasing by Touche Ross. In particular, the federal agency charged that the audit for that year was "inadequately planned and supervised." The SEC alleged that the planning decisions made during preparation for the 1981 audit failed to take into account a number of key audit risk factors and noted that the audit program for that year "was in large part carried over from prior audits." The following are condensed summaries of several of the SEC's principal criticisms of the Touche Ross audit plan for 1981:

1. Touche Ross failed to test IFG Leasing's internal accounting controls over delinquent accounts. Because the audit plan failed to test whether the accounting system accurately aged delinquent accounts, the auditors had no way of knowing whether the aging summaries they received from the client were accurate.

2. The Touche Ross audit plan called for testing of only a small proportion (8 percent) of the client's outstanding lease receivables. By focusing almost exclusively on lease receivables that were in excess of $50,000 and 120 days delinquent, Touche Ross overlooked a significant portion of receivables that were uncollectible.

3. Although the audit plan called for a review of the client's write-off policy for bad debts, it failed to require the field auditors to determine whether the policy was actually being followed. In fact, the policy was not being followed. IFG Leasing was actually using a "budget" system to write off bad debts, a system that resulted at any point in time in a significant backlog of uncollectible receivables that had not been charged to the allowance account. According to the SEC, some of these uncollectible accounts had been carried on the company's books for several years.

4. Despite the complexity of the IFG Leasing audit and the inordinately high risks that the client posed, the individuals assigned to the 1981 engagement were almost totally unfamiliar with the client and the leasing industry. The chief accounting officer of the company subsequently testified that the Touche Ross audits were historically performed by inexperienced auditors with little or no exposure to the leasing industry.

The junior auditor assigned to the allowance for uncollectible lease receivables during the 1981 IFG Leasing engagement began his audit of that account by obtaining a computer run from the client that allegedly included all accounts that exceeded $50,000 and were more than 120 days delinquent. The auditor failed, however, to test the run to determine whether it actually included all accounts meeting those criteria, which it did not. Later in the audit, when the senior supervising this individual recognized that the completeness of the computer run had not been questioned, she performed a limited test to determine whether the run included any of the client's designated "problem" accounts. The problem accounts were a relatively small subset of delinquent receivables, many of which were in litigation or arbitration. When the senior recognized several of the problem accounts in the computer run, she apparently concluded that the run listed all delinquent accounts satisfying the audit scope and performed no further tests of the run's completeness.

Shortly after obtaining the computer run of delinquent accounts, the junior auditor realized that he could not complete the required audit procedures on all of those accounts in the amount of time budgeted for that segment of the audit. With the senior's approval, the junior selected 171 of the 264 accounts listed in the delinquency run for testing. The primary audit procedure used to test the collectibility of the delinquent accounts involved simply reviewing those accounts with the client's collections manager. However, the managers of IFG Leasing's branch offices, not the collections manager, were primarily responsible for overseeing collection activities related to delinquent accounts. The collections manager was generally unfamiliar with the ability and/or incentive of delinquent customers to pay their outstanding balances. As a result, the SEC maintained that the Touche Ross audit program was deficient, since it did not contain provisions for corroborating representations made by the collections manager with other forms of audit evidence.[4]

The audit program for the delinquent accounts also required the junior auditor to obtain written representations from the client's attorneys regarding many of the problem accounts selected for testing. In particular, IFG Leasing's attorneys were asked to comment on losses the company could expect on lease receivables in litigation or arbitration. However, all of the attorneys' responses to the Touche Ross inquiries were dated after the conclusion of the audit fieldwork. The earliest response received was March 8, 1982, nearly two weeks after Touche Ross had issued an unqualified opinion on IFG Leasing's 1981 financial statements. The attorneys' written responses identified numerous delinquent leases not included in the delinquency run obtained by the junior auditor that were in excess of $50,000 and more than 120 days past due. In addition, in many cases the attorneys provided higher estimates of projected losses on the problem accounts than the estimates derived by the junior auditor.

The SEC criticized the method Touche Ross used to arrive at an independent estimate of the allowance for uncollectible lease receivables. The junior auditor used three criteria that he developed on his own for estimating the amount that IFG Leasing would likely fail to collect on any given delinquent account. For instance, if an account was in litigation, the junior auditor estimated that the client would eventually recover an amount equal to 50 percent of the cost of the

---

4. According to the SEC, the junior auditor was not adequately apprised by the engagement audit partner of the problems that Touche Ross had encountered in prior audits of the allowance account. If the junior auditor had been adequately informed of these problems, he may have scrutinized the account more closely during the 1981 audit.

leased asset. Prior experience demonstrated, however, that IFG Leasing was fortunate in such cases to recoup 20 percent of the original cost of a repossessed asset. Additionally, the junior auditor failed to apply the 50 percent rule consistently. IFG Leasing's collections manager apparently convinced the junior auditor that a recovery percentage substantially greater than 50 percent should be used in many of these cases. If the 50 percent rule had been consistently applied, the junior auditor's estimate of the allowance account would have been nearly $600,000 higher.

On the accounts for which the customer had made a verbal commitment to pay the past due balance, the junior auditor provided for a reserve of 10 percent. Regarding this rule of thumb, the SEC stated, "The workpapers indicate no basis to assume that a mere promise to pay from a severely delinquent lessee provides any reliable indication of collectibility." Finally, the junior auditor provided no estimated reserve for the delinquent accounts on which a payment of any size had been received in the prior thirty days. Again, the SEC took issue with the validity of this criterion. Many of the accounts in this latter category were delinquent on their monthly payments by more than a year, even though they had made a nominal payment to IFG Leasing in the prior thirty days.

The junior auditor's crude analysis suggested that the allowance for uncollectible receivables was almost $4 million understated. After reviewing this individual's workpapers, the audit engagement partner informed the junior auditor that the assumptions used in arriving at the independent estimate of the allowance were "too conservative." The partner instructed the junior auditor to reach a more "realistic" estimate of the allowance by "re-reviewing" the large delinquent accounts for which a significant reserve had been established. According to the SEC, during this further review of these accounts, the junior auditor failed to examine any additional documentation regarding their collectibility. Apparently, the only additional audit procedure performed by the junior auditor was another inquiry of the collections manager regarding these accounts. Based upon this cursory additional audit procedure, the junior auditor significantly reduced his estimate of the allowance for uncollectible lease receivables. The SEC noted that the Touche Ross workpapers provided no support for the changes made by the junior auditor in his original estimate: "In fact, the workpapers contain no evidence to support the reductions. Thus there is no basis for the junior auditor's statement that his revised estimates were 'more realistic.'"

After adjusting his initial estimate of the allowance account, the junior auditor noted that his figures showed a $1.2 million "cushion" remaining in the client's balance for that account. That is, after subtracting his estimated bad debt reserve for the accounts included in the delinquency run from the balance of the client's allowance account, more than a million dollars remained in that account to provide a reserve for any nondelinquent accounts that might prove to be uncollectible.[5] However, these nondelinquent accounts totaled more than $340

---

5. The junior auditor's estimate was significantly understated in the first place since millions of dollars of delinquent accounts were not included in the delinquency computer run. The SEC pointed out that the omission of numerous past due receivables from the computer run could have been discovered quite easily by totaling the dollar value of the accounts listed on the run and then subtracting that total from gross lease receivables. This latter difference would not have agreed with the total of the nondelinquent accounts reported in the company's records.

million, meaning that the remaining allowance provided for a default rate on these receivables of only one-third of 1 percent. The SEC maintained that the Touche Ross auditors should have realized that percentage was much too low. In fact, the true balance of the allowance account was much smaller than reported by the company, since a large backlog of delinquent receivables known to be uncollectible was being gradually written off against the allowance via the so-called budget method. That is, to minimize the impact on the allowance account, company executives permitted only a certain "budgeted" amount of accounts recognized as uncollectible to be written off each month.

1982 TOUCHE ROSS AUDIT OF IFG LEASING

In September 1982, the chief accounting officer of IFG Leasing informed IFG executives that the subsidiary had almost $90 million in accounts that were ninety days or more past due.[6] The IFG executives were alarmed by that figure and instructed Touche Ross to begin the 1982 IFG Leasing audit as quickly as possible and to take a "hard look" at the adequacy of the allowance for uncollectible lease receivables. The engagement audit partner was also apparently alarmed by the magnitude of the delinquent accounts reported by IFG Leasing. As a result, the audit partner developed a much more intensive audit plan to be used for the allowance account during the 1982 audit compared with the audit plans used for that account in prior years.

The first change the audit partner made in the audit plan was to assign an auditor with five years of experience to the allowance for uncollectible lease receivables. Second, the partner modified the audit scope for testing delinquent lease receivables by requiring that all individual receivables in excess of $50,000 and ninety days or more past due be tested. Additionally, the estimated uncollectible percentage for the delinquent accounts exceeding $50,000 was projected to the delinquent accounts with balances of less than $50,000 in arriving at a total estimated allowance for uncollectible receivables. In prior audits, the smaller accounts had simply been ignored. Touche Ross also applied an expected bad debt percentage of 2 percent to all nondelinquent accounts. Finally, a number of the mechanical oversights that occurred during the prior year's audit of the allowance account were corrected during the 1982 engagement. For instance, the delinquency run was clerically tested to ensure that it was complete, and representations from the client's legal counsel regarding the collectibility of problem accounts were obtained on a timely basis.

When the senior auditor assigned to the allowance for uncollectible lease receivables completed her audit procedures, she recommended that a large increase be made to the allowance. After her work was reviewed by the audit partner and discussed with the chief financial officer of IFG, the latter two individuals agreed that an adjustment of $17 million, which was much smaller than the adjustment proposed by the senior, would be made to increase the

---

6. Late in the fall of 1982, IFG Leasing modified the payment terms of many of its delinquent accounts. The new payment terms for these "restructured" lease receivables allowed the company to remove them from delinquency status. As a result, the company reduced the total of its delinquent accounts by approximately $43 million.

balance of the allowance account.[7] The SEC apparently never contested the adequacy of that adjustment but did adamantly contend that the adjustment should have been treated for accounting purposes as a prior period adjustment, since it amounted to the correction of an error made in an earlier year:

> Where, as here, the adjustment to the estimate results from the oversight or misuse of facts that existed at the time the financial statements were prepared, that adjustment must be accounted for as the correction of an error. In attributing the entire $17 million adjustment to 1982, [IFG] Leasing materially understated its 1982 income, overstated its 1981 income, as well as understated its 1981 allowance, all in violation of GAAP.

The SEC also criticized Touche Ross for not contesting the accounting treatment given to the adjustment by IFG Leasing. The SEC pointed out that the 1982 Touche Ross workpapers specifically stated that the adjustment was attributable to events occurring in 1982 rather than to "problems that existed at the end of 1981 that went undetected." Given the circumstances, the SEC believed this conclusion was highly suspect. At the very least, the SEC alleged, the Touche Ross auditors had a responsibility to further investigate the possibility that the large adjustment related, at least partially, to years prior to 1982.

EPILOGUE

In June 1983, IFG Leasing recorded an additional $25 million increase in its allowance for uncollectible lease receivables. Three years later, the SEC issued a permanent injunction against IFG, IFG Leasing, and three executives of the companies as a result of the materially false and misleading aging summaries for lease receivables that were included in registration statements filed with the federal agency. The injunction permanently enjoined the parties from further violations of the reporting and antifraud stipulations of the federal securities laws. Also in 1986, IFG filed suit against Touche Ross, alleging that the CPA firm was negligent in its audits of IFG Leasing. No public comment regarding the resolution of that lawsuit could be found. Finally, in 1988, the SEC censured the Touche Ross audit partner who supervised the 1980 through 1982 audits of IFG Leasing.

QUESTIONS

1. Identify the alternative accounting methods that IFG Leasing could have used to estimate its allowance for uncollectible lease receivables. Which of these methods would have been preferable, given the circumstances? Was the "budget" method of writing off uncollectible receivables against the allowance account an acceptable accounting method?

---

7. The SEC's enforcement release does not disclose the actual amount of the senior auditor's original proposed adjustment. The release simply states that it was "significantly" greater than the amount eventually agreed to by IFG management.

2. The aging tables included in IFG Leasing's 10-K registration statements were considered to be "other information," according to the auditing profession's technical standards. What responsibilities do auditors have to attest to the material accuracy of "other information" included in an annual report or registration statement that contains audited financial statements?

3. Did the junior auditor who discovered during the course of the 1980 audit that the aging tables were materially in error fulfill her professional responsibility to follow up on the resolution of that problem? Why or why not?

4. Identify the key factors that influenced the level of inherent risk for the 1980 through 1982 IFG Leasing audits. How should these factors have influenced the nature, extent, and timing of the audit procedures performed by Touche Ross?

5. During the 1981 audit, client representations were the principal type of evidence that was collected to support the balance of the allowance account. Identify the limitations of using client representations as audit evidence. What are the other basic types of audit evidence? Which, if any, of these additional types of audit evidence should the junior auditor have considered collecting during his examination of the allowance account?

6. Apparently, the hours budgeted for the audit of the allowance for uncollectible lease receivables account during the 1981 IFG Leasing engagement restricted the scope of the audit procedures performed on that account. Should time budgets be allowed to restrict the scope of independent audits? Why or why not?

7. Identify the factors that determine whether adjusting journal entries, such as the $17 million adjustment made to the allowance account as a result of the 1982 audit, should be treated as prior period adjustments or changes in accounting estimates. Do you believe the SEC was correct in asserting that the $17 million adjustment should have been recorded as a prior period adjustment? Explain.

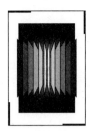

CASE 1.9
THE FUND OF FUNDS, LTD.

Bernie Cornfeld founded Investors Overseas Services (IOS) in 1956 with an initial investment of $300. Cornfeld, who was twenty-nine years old at the time, recognized that the large contingent of U.S. troops stationed in post–World War II Europe collectively had a huge amount of funds to invest but very few investment opportunities. Consequently, Cornfeld, through IOS, created eleven specialized mutual funds in which members of the U.S. military could invest as little as $25 per month. One of the most successful of these funds was The Fund of Funds, Ltd., an open-ended mutual fund that initially invested only in U.S.-based mutual funds. Eventually this fund alone would grow to almost $500 million.

Cornfeld was born in Turkey and trained as a social worker while in his early twenties, before he became intrigued by the world of finance. Five feet five inches tall and shy by nature because of a speech impediment, the ambitious and industrious Cornfeld rose from total obscurity at the time he founded IOS to international fame and an estimated net worth of $200 million only a decade later. At the height of IOS's financial success, Cornfeld lived in a castle in France; dated actress Victoria Principal; and could count as friends a number of international jet-setters, including his best friend, the acclaimed designer Oleg Cassini.

The Securities and Exchange Commission (SEC) disrupted the idyllic life-style of Cornfeld in the mid-1960s, when it conducted a lengthy investigation of IOS's financial affairs. As the IOS mutual funds, Fund of Funds in particular, grew dramatically in size during the early 1960s, the SEC became increasingly alarmed about the IOS portfolio managers' ability to influence the U.S. stock markets. By 1965, it was not unusual for IOS transactions to account for 5 percent of the daily volume of activity on the New York Stock Exchange. The SEC was concerned that within a few years, the IOS portfolio managers would have the ability to manipulate the market for their own benefit. Even more troubling to the SEC was the difficulty of imposing regulatory oversight on IOS, since the firm's corporate headquarters was in Geneva, Switzerland. After a two-year investigation, the SEC and Cornfeld finally reached an agreement in 1967. The SEC would drop its

101

investigation of IOS in exchange for Cornfeld's agreeing to abide by all SEC regulations and pledging not to allow IOS to obtain a controlling interest in any U.S. company.

One of Bernie Cornfeld's contemporaries in the international investment community of the 1960s was John McCandish King, a Denver-based speculator in the oil and gas industry. Although Cornfeld and King were the same age and both rose from obscurity to tremendous wealth in a short period of time, there were also striking contrasts between the two men. At six feet three inches, the 250-pound King towered over the diminutive Cornfeld. A high school dropout, the brash and often arrogant King was known for his expensive taste in cowboy boots, his ten-gallon cowboy hats, his three thousand pairs of cuff links, and his stretch limousine that sported a custom-designed sunroof to accommodate his zealous interest in hunting. While still in his twenties, King became renowned for his seemingly innate ability to discover oil. In 1952, King invested $1,500, approximately one-half of his net worth at the time, in an oil-drilling venture in Oklahoma. A string of wildcat wells that he struck in that venture allowed him to form King Resources, which soon became one of the nation's largest and most profitable independent oil companies. By the mid-1960s, *Forbes* estimated that King was worth at least $300 million and well on his way to achieving his personal goal of becoming a billionaire.

In early 1968, Cornfeld was seeking to diversify the investment portfolio of Fund of Funds. A mutual acquaintance of King and Cornfeld arranged for a meeting in April 1968 between the two prominent multimillionaires in Acapulco, Mexico, to discuss the possibility of Fund of Funds investing in oil and natural gas properties owned by King Resources. Cornfeld invited King to make a presentation during the Fund of Funds board of directors meeting being held in Acapulco. Following that presentation, Cornfeld and King reached an agreement. Fund of Funds would establish a natural resources proprietary account (NRPA) for investments in oil and gas properties to be purchased from King Resources. Although a formal contractual agreement was never signed between the two parties, the minutes of the Fund of Funds board of directors meeting clearly specified the intended relationship between the two companies: "The role of King Resources with respect to the contemplated Natural Resources Proprietary Account would be that of a vendor of properties to the proprietary account, with such properties to be sold on an arm's length basis at prices no less favorable to the proprietary account than the prices charged by King to its 200-odd industrial and other purchasers."[1] Subsequently, a Fund of Funds executive testified that an implicit part of the agreement was that King Resources would sell the natural resource properties to Fund of Funds at cost, including administrative expenses incurred to acquire the properties, plus a reasonable markup. Apparently, this markup percentage was supposed to approximate 7 to 8 percent in most cases.

Initially, Cornfeld agreed to purchase $10 million of oil and gas properties from the large portfolio of such investments that King Resources maintained. By the end of 1969, however, the overbearing King had convinced Fund of Funds' officers to purchase more than $100 million of oil and gas properties from his

---

1. Unless indicated otherwise, this and all subsequent quotations were taken from the following court opinion: The Fund of Funds, Limited v. Arthur Andersen & Co., 545 F. Supp. 1314 (1982).

company. Unfortunately for Fund of Funds shareholders, King did not honor his obligations under the Acapulco agreement he had negotiated with Cornfeld. Court records documented that King would often buy relatively inexpensive oil and gas properties and then immediately sell these same properties to Fund of Funds at grossly inflated prices, sometimes approaching 3,000 percent of the original cost to King Resources.

Within a few years, falling stock prices and the weight of the poor investments made for Fund of Funds by King forced the huge mutual fund into bankruptcy. One of the principal defendants in the massive tangle of civil lawsuits filed as a result of the Fund of Funds insolvency was the public accounting firm of Arthur Andersen, which had served as the auditor of both Fund of Funds and King Resources. Arthur Andersen was sued by John Orr, a Touche Ross partner who had been appointed to serve as the bankruptcy trustee of Fund of Funds, for allegedly failing to disclose to the officers of the mutual fund that they were being defrauded by King Resources. When the verdict in the ensuing trial was handed down, Arthur Andersen would become the victim of the largest court-ordered judgment ever imposed on a public accounting firm at the time.

ARTHUR ANDERSEN'S DUAL RELATIONSHIP WITH FUND OF FUNDS AND KING RESOURCES

Three of Arthur Andersen's offices were involved in the CPA firm's annual audits of Fund of Funds. The Geneva office coordinated the audits of all the IOS mutual funds and apparently paid particular attention to the Fund of Funds audit, given the size, prominence, and complexity of that fund. The New York City office had primary responsibility for the performance of the Fund of Funds audit and issued the audit report on the mutual fund's annual financial statements. Finally, the Denver office played a critical role in the Fund of Funds audit. Each year, personnel from that office, at the request of the New York City engagement audit partner, performed extensive audit procedures to corroborate the material accuracy of the year-end balance of the NRPA. The Denver office also audited King Resources, which was headquartered in Denver. The partner in charge of the King Resources audit and the principal manager assigned to that audit were also responsible for supervising the audit of the NRPA segment of the Fund of Funds.

A key issue in the suit filed against Arthur Andersen by the Fund of Funds bankruptcy trustee was the extent to which the CPA firm was aware of the excessive prices Fund of Funds was paying for the properties it purchased from King Resources—prices established by John King or by one of his associates. Court testimony clearly demonstrated that Arthur Andersen personnel in the Denver office were aware that King Resources essentially managed the NRPA for Fund of Funds. The Arthur Andersen workpapers specifically noted that King Resources had "carte blanche authority to buy oil and gas properties" for the NRPA. The Denver office of Arthur Andersen also had complete access to King Resources data that documented the cost of the properties sold to Fund of Funds and the profit margins on these sales.

A closely related issue in the Fund of Funds civil suit was exactly when Arthur Andersen personnel obtained information suggesting that the mutual fund was being charged excessive prices for oil and gas properties acquired from King Resources. Because the audit report for the 1968 Fund of Funds financial statements was filed by Arthur Andersen on February 5, 1969, the court was particularly interested in determining what the CPA firm knew by that date about the pricing structure King Resources had established for its sales transactions with Fund of Funds.

A final issue addressed at length in the Fund of Funds civil suit was Arthur Andersen's awareness of, and involvement in, several so-called revaluation transactions arranged by King Resources for Fund of Funds. Because Fund of Funds was an open-ended mutual fund, it was required to revalue its entire portfolio every day. On a daily basis, Fund of Funds established a market value for each of its investments, including its natural resource properties, and then divided this collective market value by the number of outstanding mutual fund shares. This "net asset value" (NAV) was then used as the basis for distributing proceeds to shareholders electing to redeem their shares. The illiquid nature of the natural resource investments complicated the computation of a daily NAV for the Fund of Funds portfolio. To facilitate this process, King Resources would periodically authorize the sale of a portion of certain natural resource properties owned by Fund of Funds to establish a fair market value for the residual portions of these properties retained by the mutual fund. Alternatively, King Resources would sell a portion of its own equity interest in these properties to establish a fair market value for investments of Fund of Funds.[2]

Evidence presented during the Fund of Funds trial demonstrated that many of the revaluation transactions arranged by King Resources were fraudulent. For instance, in at least two cases, King Resources identified a third party that would agree to buy a small portion of either Fund of Funds' or King Resources' interest in an oil and gas property at a price far in excess of the property's fair market value. However, unknown to Fund of Funds' officials, King Resources made secret "side agreements" with the purchasers of these properties that effectively insured the latter from any loss in these transactions. Because of these side agreements, the revaluation transactions were not arm's length transactions and, consequently, were not a valid basis for establishing a fair market value for the properties in question. Apparently, King Resources arranged these fraudulent revaluation transactions to convince Fund of Funds' executives that the natural resource investments were profitable. Since these transactions grossly inflated the NAV of Fund of Funds shares, the investors who redeemed their shares following these transactions profited greatly, to the detriment of investors who chose to retain their shares indefinitely.

Arthur Andersen's 1968 and 1969 Audits of Fund of Funds

Court records in the Fund of Funds trial documented that Arthur Andersen considered the IOS and Fund of Funds audits to be high-risk engagements. The highest-risk areas in the 1968 and 1969 Fund of Funds audits were the large

---

2. King Resources retained a 12.5 percent equity interest in most of the natural resource properties it sold to Fund of Funds.

investments in natural resource properties. In the 1968 Fund of Funds workpapers, Arthur Andersen noted that it was quite unusual that "in each and every natural resource transaction, the interest purchased [by Fund of Funds] was a portion of an interest previously or contemporaneously owned by a member of the King group." The court records also noted that Arthur Andersen had "repeated serious difficulties with King as a client at least since 1961" and had expressed concern regarding several of King's questionable business practices. These prior difficulties with John King, at the very least, placed Arthur Andersen on notice that the Fund of Funds–King Resources transactions needed to be scrutinized closely.

During the 1968 Fund of Funds audit, Arthur Andersen personnel in the Denver office performed a detailed analysis of the pricing structure that King Resources was using in establishing the selling prices for its natural resource properties. This analysis demonstrated that King Resources was charging Fund of Funds significantly higher prices than it was charging its other customers. Arthur Andersen documented the following gross profit percentages for five of the sales made by King Resources to Fund of Funds: 98.6, 98.7, 56.7, 58, and 85.6 percent. These gross profit percentages appeared particularly excessive, since most of the properties had been owned a relatively short period of time by King Resources before being sold to Fund of Funds. The court reached the following conclusion regarding Arthur Andersen's knowledge of the prices charged Fund of Funds by King Resources: "It is reasonable to find that AA knew what FOF paid for the [natural resource] interests purchased in 1968, that AA knew what King Resources paid for them, and that AA knew King Resources' profits [on these transactions] prior to February 5, 1969, when the FOF audit report was filed."

Although Arthur Andersen clearly had knowledge of the excessive prices charged by King Resources to Fund of Funds, there was a lengthy debate during the trial regarding whether that information could and should have been used in connection with the Fund of Funds audit. The key issue in this debate was whether the client confidentiality rule precluded Arthur Andersen from using the price data obtained from King Resources to audit Fund of Funds' natural resource investments. Clouding this issue was the close linkage of the Fund of Funds and King Resources audits: "The NRPA audit was performed by using the records of King Resources, and sometimes AA staffers would work on the King Resources and NRPA audits contemporaneously. Thus, AA's understanding of the ongoing business relationship between FOF and the King group can be determined from documents found in the AA files for King Resources or NRPA and from testimony regarding the actual conduct of the audits."

Another critical issue addressed by Arthur Andersen during the Fund of Funds audits was the validity of the revaluation transactions. In December 1968, John King arranged for Fund of Funds to sell 10 percent of a natural resource property to Fox-Raff, a Seattle brokerage firm that was also an audit client of Arthur Andersen. This sale allowed Fund of Funds to recognize an increase in the value of its investment portfolio of approximately $900,000. Arthur Andersen questioned this transaction, since the property had been owned a very short time by Fund of Funds and since there were no new geological data suggesting that the property was worth more than Fund of Funds had paid for it. Arthur Andersen also doubted whether the sale of a 10 percent interest in the property was sufficient to recognize an increase in the value of the remaining 90 percent

EXHIBIT 1
Key Parties and Events
in the Fund of Funds
Case

Blakely-Wolcott transaction.   A transaction that involved the sale of an oil and gas property by King Resources to a third party in 1966. Arthur Andersen subsequently discovered that John King had negotiated an undisclosed and illicit "side agreement" with the purchaser of the property that invalidated the sale as an arm's length transaction. This fact was significant because it cast doubt on the integrity of the audit evidence collected by Arthur Andersen from John King to support Fund of Funds' 1969 financial statements.

Phil Carr.   An Arthur Andersen partner assigned to the firm's Denver office. Carr supervised both the King Resources audit and the audit of Fund of Funds' NRPA account.

Bernie Cornfeld.   The founder of Investors Overseas Services.

Fox-Raff transaction.   A transaction that involved the sale of a small portion of an oil and gas property owned by Fund of Funds to a Seattle brokerage firm. The transaction was negotiated by John King and was intended to establish a fair market value for the portion of the property retained by Fund of Funds. Arthur Andersen discovered, after the fact, that King had a "side agreement" with the brokerage firm.

Investors Overseas Services (IOS).   An investment company founded by Bernie Cornfeld in 1956. One of the many mutual funds managed by IOS was The Fund of Funds, Ltd.

John McCandish King.   The founder and principal owner of King Resources.

King Resources.   An investment company specializing in natural resource properties. King Resources sold Fund of Funds more than $100 million of oil and gas properties during the late 1960s.

John Mecom.   An investor who purchased a small percentage of a large Arctic oil and gas property from King Resources. This transaction allowed Fund of Funds to increase the value of its residual interest in the property by $119 million.

John Orr.   A Touche Ross partner who was appointed the bankruptcy trustee for Fund of Funds.

John Robinson.   A New York partner with Arthur Andersen who served as the audit engagement partner for Fund of Funds.

interest retained by Fund of Funds. It was later discovered that John King had a "side agreement" with Fox-Raff. King had provided Fox-Raff with the required down payment for the purchase transaction and relieved the brokerage firm of any commitment to pay the balance of the purchase price. (Because of the complexity of this case, Exhibit 1 provides a glossary of the principal parties involved, as well as a summary of certain of the key events.)

In January 1969, Phil Carr, the Arthur Andersen partner in the Denver office who was responsible for both the King Resources audit and the audit of Fund of Funds' NRPA investments, discovered that the Fox-Raff transaction was not a bona fide sale. Carr passed this information on to John Robinson of the New York City office of Arthur Andersen, who was the engagement audit partner for Fund of Funds. According to court records, the Fox-Raff transaction was ultimately discussed at the "very highest partnership level" within Arthur Andersen. For undisclosed reasons, the CPA firm chose not to inform Fund of Funds' executives that the Fox-Raff sale was something less than a legitimate arm's length transaction. Instead, John Robinson decided that the revaluation of the Fund of Funds assets due to the Fox-Raff transaction had not materially affected the mutual fund's NAV. Shortly thereafter, on February 5, 1969, Arthur Andersen issued an unqualified opinion on the December 31, 1968, financial statements of Fund of Funds.

During the planning phase for the 1969 audit of Fund of Funds, Phil Carr decided to develop a set of guidelines to be used in auditing subsequent revaluation transactions engaged in by Fund of Funds. Carr's decision to develop these guidelines was apparently spurred by the questions raised regarding the Fox-Raff transaction during the prior year's audit. Carr's decision was also at least partly a consequence of the Denver office's being assigned a greater degree of responsibility in 1969 for the Fund of Funds audit. Court testimony disclosed that during the 1969 audit of the large mutual fund, the Denver office of Arthur Andersen assumed "full audit responsibility for the investment [NRPA] account both as to cost and market value." During the 1968 audit, Phil Carr had perceived the Denver office's role in the Fund of Funds engagement as simply collecting information regarding the mutual fund's natural resource investments for the New York City audit team. The higher level of responsibility assigned to his audit team for the risky Fund of Funds audit troubled Carr. Also troubling to him was a stern warning he had been given by the IOS audit engagement partner in Geneva. That individual had informed him that it would not be appropriate to simply disclose the valuation method used by Fund of Funds for its natural resource properties if such disclosure "does not fairly present the facts."

In November 1969, Carr drafted a memo discussing the guidelines that Arthur Andersen would follow in reviewing subsequent Fund of Funds revaluation transactions. The memorandum, reproduced in Exhibit 2, was reviewed, and apparently approved, by the regional director of Arthur Andersen's West Coast audit practice and by an executive partner in the firm's headquarters office in Chicago. A copy of the memo was also given to a Fund of Funds officer.

In late 1969, King Resources began searching for a third party to purchase a portion of its interest in a large natural resource property in the Arctic. The majority interest in this property had been sold previously by King Resources to Fund of Funds, and there was a need for a revaluation transaction to establish a fair market value for the mutual fund's interest in the property. The King Resources personnel arranging the transaction were aware of the Arthur Andersen memo and apparently attempted to structure the transaction so that it would satisfy the memo's key stipulations. Eventually, King Resources arranged for a sale of slightly less than 10 percent of the Arctic property to John Mecom, the principal owner of U.S. Oil of Louisiana, also an audit client of Arthur Andersen. At the time, it was widely known that Mecom was experiencing serious financial difficulties. In February 1968, the managing partner of Arthur Andersen had met with Mecom and John King for the purpose of helping Mecom resolve his financial problems.

The sale of the partial interest in the Arctic property to Mecom allowed Fund of Funds to recognize a more than 25 percent increase in the value of its investment portfolio—an increase of approximately $119 million in total. However, unknown to Arthur Andersen, John King had made a side agreement with Mecom that was very similar to the agreement he had arranged with the Fox-Raff brokerage firm during the prior year. Because of this side agreement, the Mecom transaction was not a valid arm's length sale, and thus not a proper basis for increasing the value of Fund of Funds' remaining interest in the Arctic property.

Phil Carr was alarmed when he realized how large an impact the Arctic revaluation transaction would have on the market value of the Fund of Funds portfolio. According to court records, Carr informed the regional director of

EXHIBIT 2
Arthur Andersen Memo
Dictating Conditions for
Recognizing Increases
in the Value of Natural
Resource Properties of
Fund of Funds

November 7, 1969

Any significant increase in the value of natural resource properties over original cost to FOF must, for audit purposes, be supported by either:

1) An appraisal report rendered by a competent, independent expert, or
2) an arm's length sale of a sufficiently large portion of a property to establish a proportionate value for the portion retained.

Item 2 above is where we currently are not in clear agreement with the client. King Resources Company has been informed by FOF (purportedly Ed Cowett, Executive Vice President) that sale of a 10% interest in a property would be sufficient for FOF's purposes in ascribing a proportionate value to the 90% retained. This procedure was first used at December 31, 1968, when King Resources Company arranged, on behalf of FOF, for the sale of a 10% interest in an oil and gas drilling prospect and certain uranium claims and leases to Fox-Raff Inc., a Seattle brokerage firm affiliate.

Since our responsibilities here in Denver with respect to the December 31, 1968, FOF audit consisted only of determining the basis on which King Resources determined the valuations (not auditing such values), we discussed this transaction with John Robinson and Nick Constantakis in New York but left any final audit decision up to them. It is our understanding that the King Resources valuations determined by the 10% sale were allowed to stand in the final FOF audit report.

On the question of what constitutes adequate sales data for valuation purposes (i.e., the 10% question), we have proposed the following to King Resources:

1) No unrealized appreciation would be allowed on sales of relatively small percentages of properties to private investors or others who do not have the necessary expertise to determine a realistic fair market value. By "relatively small," we envision approximately 50% as being a minimum level in this type of sale to establish proportionate values for the remaining interests. This would preclude any unrealized appreciation on sales such as the December, 1968, sale to Fox-Raff, Inc. since it could not be reasonably sustained that a brokerage firm has the expertise necessary to evaluate primarily undeveloped resource interests.
2) Appreciation would be allowed if supported by arm's length sales to knowledgeable outside parties. For example, if King Resources sold a 25% interest in the Arctic permits to Texaco or another major oil company, we believe it would be appropriate to ascribe proportionate value to the 75% retained. Just where to draw the line on the percentage has not been clearly established. We feel 10% would be a bare minimum and would like to see a higher number.

Drafted by: Phil Carr, Partner,
Denver Office of AA & Co.

Arthur Andersen's West Coast audit practice that the Denver office's review of the revaluation transaction did not provide sufficient evidence to support the increased market value ascribed to Fund of Funds' residual interest in the Arctic property. The regional director supported Carr's conclusion.

Carr went on to argue that Arthur Andersen's headquarters office in Chicago should have the final responsibility for approving the valuation of Fund of Funds' natural resource investments. These investments were discussed at length by top partners of Arthur Andersen, the focus of this discussion being whether it was possible to reach an audit conclusion regarding the fair market value of the investments. The IOS audit engagement partner in Geneva was very concerned with the possibility of Fund of Funds' receiving a qualified audit opinion. That

EXHIBIT 3
Arthur Andersen's Audit
Opinion on Fund of
Funds' 1969 Financial
Statements

To the Shareholders and Board of Directors,
The Fund of Funds, Limited:

We have examined the consolidated statements of net assets and investments of The Fund of Funds, Limited (an Ontario, Canada, corporation) and subsidiary as of December 31, 1969, and the related consolidated statements of fund operations and changes in net assets for the year then ended. Our examination was made in accordance with generally accepted auditing standards, and accordingly included such tests of the accounting records and such other auditing procedures as we considered necessary in the circumstances. Investments owned by the Fund at December 31, 1969, were confirmed directly to us by the custodian or brokers. The position of investments sold short was confirmed directly to us by the custodian or brokers. Consistent with past practice, certain investments, in the absence of quoted market prices, have been valued by the Board of Directors as indicated in Note 9. These valuations have been reviewed by us to ascertain that they have been determined on the bases described, but since we are not competent to appraise these investments we do not express an opinion as to such valuations.

In our opinion, subject to the effect of certain investment valuations referred to in the preceding paragraph, the above-mentioned financial statements present fairly the financial position of The Fund of Funds, Limited and subsidiary as of December 31, 1969, and the results of their operations and the changes in their net assets for the year then ended, in conformity with generally accepted accounting principles applied on a basis consistent with that of the preceding year.

individual remarked that a qualification would cause an "explosion" at Fund of Funds. Nevertheless, the qualified audit report shown in Exhibit 3 was eventually agreed upon by Arthur Andersen personnel and was issued on the December 31, 1969, financial statements of Fund of Funds.

A key issue that the judge in the Fund of Funds trial considered when evaluating Arthur Andersen's conduct in reviewing the 1969 Arctic revaluation transaction was the CPA firm's awareness of what became known as the Blakely-Wolcott transaction—a transaction that accounted for nearly 40 percent of King Resources' net income in 1966. The Blakely-Wolcott transaction involved another sale of an oil and gas property by King Resources, in which John King had negotiated an illicit and undisclosed side agreement with the purchaser of the property. Although this transaction was similar to the Fox-Raff and Mecom transactions, it did not involve either Fund of Funds or IOS. The audit workpapers for the 1966 King Resources audit documented that Arthur Andersen was aware that the transaction was suspicious in nature. In fact, the workpapers noted that the Blakely-Wolcott transaction was a "borderline case of simply writing up property." Despite the concern expressed by certain Arthur Andersen personnel assigned to the 1966 King Resources audit, the firm accepted King Resources' accounting for the transaction. This decision was made only after the firm had obtained a representation letter from John King in which he essentially denied the existence of any side agreements in connection with the Blakely-Wolcott sale: "King had signed a representation letter in 1967 that all transactions of King Resources and its officers were arm's length and that King Resources' officers and key employees had no material direct or indirect participation in outside business enterprises purchasing or selling to King Resources."

In early 1970, prior to signing off on the 1969 Fund of Funds audit, the Denver office of Arthur Andersen discovered that the Blakely-Wolcott transaction was fraudulent and, as a result, that the 1967 representation letter obtained from John

King was blatantly misleading. This discovery cast doubt on the integrity of all of the audit evidence collected from King Resources to support the 1969 Fund of Funds financial statements, particularly the evidence used to corroborate the large increase in the reported fair market value of the mutual fund's investment in the Arctic property. Despite the new information regarding the Blakely-Wolcott transaction, the court noted that Arthur Andersen continued to rely on audit evidence collected from John King and King Resources in connection with the 1969 audit of Fund of Funds.

> AA's audit thus continued after the December 1969 Arctic revaluation and after AA knew about Blakely-Wolcott. AA sought and obtained representation letters from King and [an associate] that the Arctic sale was bona fide. Although AA obtained representation letters from Mecom and [an associate] confirming the terms of the express purchase [Arctic] agreement, no inquiry was made of Mecom concerning side agreements as was made to King Resources.

Prior to the issuing of an audit opinion on Fund of Funds' 1969 financial statements, a *Wall Street Journal* article caused Arthur Andersen personnel to suspect that the Mecom transaction involved an undisclosed side agreement. At this point, King Resources was asked again to confirm, and did reconfirm, the nature of the transaction as disclosed to Arthur Andersen initially.

THE FUND OF FUNDS, LIMITED V.
ARTHUR ANDERSEN & CO.: ALLEGATIONS AND COURT RULINGS

In the civil suit brought by the Fund of Funds bankruptcy trustee against Arthur Andersen, the principal allegation was that the CPA firm had allowed Fund of Funds to be defrauded by King Resources. In particular, the trustee alleged that Arthur Andersen had failed to disclose to Fund of Funds' executives the cost and price data that the auditors from the firm's Denver office had collected from King Resources. Regarding the large Arctic revaluation transaction, the trustee alleged that Arthur Andersen had failed to disclose to Fund of Funds its suspicions that the sale was fraudulent and that the terms of the sale did not satisfy the guidelines developed by Arthur Andersen to approve such transactions. Executives of Fund of Funds maintained that they would not have used the partial sale of King Resources' interest in the Arctic oil and gas property to revalue their firm's investment in that property if Arthur Andersen had disclosed its concerns regarding the validity of that transaction. Finally, the Fund of Funds trustee alleged that Arthur Andersen had breached its contractual obligation to disclose to the mutual fund's officers irregularities discovered during the course of the audit. An excerpt from the engagement letter obtained for the Fund of Funds audit is shown in Exhibit 4. As indicated in the final paragraph of that excerpt, Arthur Andersen had expressly agreed to disclose any irregularities discovered during the course of its audit to Fund of Funds' officers.

Attorneys for Arthur Andersen responded to each allegation leveled at their firm by the Fund of Funds bankruptcy trustee. First, regarding the decision not to disclose King Resources' price and cost data to Fund of Funds, Arthur Andersen argued that such disclosure would have been a violation of the client confiden-

Our audit work on companies for which we are responsible will consist of examination of the respective balance sheets and statements of net assets and investments as of December 31, 1968, and the related statements of income, surplus and changes in net assets for the year then ending in order to enable us to express an opinion on the financial position and the results of their operations. These examinations will be made in accordance with generally accepted auditing standards and will include all auditing standards and will include all auditing procedures which we consider necessary in the circumstances. These procedures will include, among other things, review and tests of the accounting procedures and internal controls, tests of documentary evidence supporting the transactions recorded in the accounts and direct confirmation of certain assets and liabilities by correspondence with selected customers, creditors, legal counsel, banks, etc.

While certain types of defalcations and similar irregularities may be disclosed by this kind of an examination, it is not designed for that purpose and will not involve the audit of a sufficiently large portion of the total transactions to afford assurances that any defalcations and irregularities will be uncovered. Generally, primary reliance for such disclosure is placed on a company's system of internal control and effective supervision of its accounts and procedures. *Of course, any irregularities coming to our attention would be reported to you immediately.* [Emphasis added by court.]

EXHIBIT 4
Excerpt from 1968 Engagement Letter Obtained by Arthur Andersen from IOS and Fund of Funds

tiality rule.[3] Second, Arthur Andersen maintained that Fund of Funds' board of directors had the primary responsibility for ratifying the partial sale of the Arctic property by King Resources as a proper basis for revaluing the mutual fund's investment in that property. In this same vein, Arthur Andersen contended that there was no available evidence prior to that transaction, and very little afterwards, that suggested it was fraudulent. Arthur Andersen also argued that the plaintiff had not proved that the revaluation transaction resulted in a material overstatement in the value of the portion of the Arctic property owned by Fund of Funds. Finally, Arthur Andersen asserted that none of the transactions or activities discovered during the course of the Fund of Funds audits qualified as "irregularities" and thus were not subject to being reported to client management.

Regarding the excessive prices charged by King Resources to Fund of Funds, the court concluded that Arthur Andersen should have disclosed that information to Fund of Funds' executives. The court found that Arthur Andersen had actual knowledge that Fund of Funds was being defrauded by King Resources; it further found that the failure of Arthur Andersen to disclose this information caused Fund of Funds' financial statements to be misleading: "AA's failure to clarify the parties' differing conceptions of the relationship and the pricing arrangement materially affected the fair presentation of FOF's financial condition."

The court also ruled that Arthur Andersen had a responsibility to determine whether the Arctic sale was an arm's length transaction and whether that sale satisfied the guidelines established in November 1969 to approve revaluation transactions. The judge presiding over this case went on to state that Arthur Andersen had misled Fund of Funds because the audit engagement team had reason to doubt that the Arctic sale was an arm's length transaction.

---

3. Plaintiff legal counsel argued that Arthur Andersen, at the very least, had a responsibility to resign from the Fund of Funds engagement after discovering that King Resources was charging Fund of Funds exorbitant prices for the natural resource properties. Arthur Andersen's attorneys responded by asserting that even if their firm had resigned, Fund of Funds would not have benefited, since its management would still have been unaware of King Resources' pricing structure.

Moreover, AA knew all the facts which reasonably suggested that the methodology and result of the 1969 Arctic revaluation was a sham and yet AA persisted in the misleading and incomplete disclosures. . . . Although Fund of Funds management bears primary responsibility for business decisions, the auditor must inform the client when the basic terms of business dealings are so confused as to effectively prevent any conclusions as to the client's financial picture.

The court also found that the effect of the Arctic sale on the NAV of Fund of Funds was clearly material and, thus, had a "substantial likelihood" of influencing the investment decision of a reasonable investor. Because the civil suit was brought under the Securities and Exchange Act of 1934, Fund of Funds' attorneys had to prove that scienter, or intent to deceive, was present on the part of Arthur Andersen. The court ruled that Arthur Andersen exhibited such a reckless disregard for the truth that the scienter standard was satisfied.[4]

Regarding the breach of contract allegation, the court found that Arthur Andersen failed to satisfy its contractual commitment to disclose to Fund of Funds' officers any irregularities discovered during the course of the audit. In particular, the court concluded that the Arctic revaluation transaction was fraudulent and thus an irregularity that should have been disclosed to Fund of Funds' management. In ruling on this issue, the court emphasized the following three points: (1) Arthur Andersen knew, prior to issuing its audit opinion on the 1969 Fund of Funds financial statements, that John King had engaged in a similar fraudulent sale, that is, the Blakely-Wolcott transaction in 1966;[5] (2) Arthur Andersen knew that John Mecom did not have the financial wherewithal to buy a 10 percent interest in the Arctic property; and (3) Arthur Andersen failed to ask Mecom whether a side agreement with John King was a part of the Arctic transaction.

Two issues in the Fund of Funds case that had particularly important implications for the public accounting profession were the ruling made regarding the client confidentiality defense asserted by Arthur Andersen and the court's decision that the "subject to" qualification in the 1969 Fund of Funds audit opinion did not mitigate Arthur Andersen's legal liability. Regarding the first of these issues, Arthur Andersen's legal counsel argued that the client confidentiality rule precluded the accounting firm from disclosing to Fund of Funds the excessive prices King Resources was charging the mutual fund for the natural resource properties. However, the judge in the Fund of Funds case was unimpressed with this argument.

AA's invocation of the shield of client confidentiality conveniently disregards the fact that King Resources' and [an affiliated firm's] records were used for the NRPA audits and that on numerous occasions AA sought information about the King Resources/FOF relationship from the King group. Assuming that the duty of confidentiality applies in this instance . . . [the auditor] may: 1) strongly encourage one client to make

---

4. Another important issue in the Fund of Funds case was exactly what standards of conduct governed the performance of Arthur Andersen during its audits of the large mutual fund. According to the judge in this case, "GAAS were relevant to but not determinative of AA's duties of inquiry and disclosure."

5. Arthur Andersen had also seriously questioned the legitimacy of Fund of Funds' sale of a 10 percent interest in a natural resource property to the Fox-Raff brokerage firm in 1968—a transaction arranged by King Resources.

the necessary disclosure; 2) disclose that it has relevant information not available to the other client; or 3) resign from one account. AA did none of these.

Regarding Arthur Andersen's audit report on Fund of Funds' 1969 financial statements, the judge ruled that the "subject to" qualification did not sufficiently inform Fund of Funds' management of Arthur Andersen's concerns regarding the valuation of the natural resource properties: "The addition of the words 'subject to' in the 1969 FOF Annual Report was neither soon enough nor complete enough to avoid substantial damage to FOF."

Following an eight-week trial in the summer of 1981 and two weeks of deliberation, the Fund of Funds bankruptcy trustee was awarded an $80.7 million judgment against Arthur Andersen. That amount represented the largest court judgment ever imposed on a CPA firm at the time.

EPILOGUE

In July 1982, Judge Charles Stewart, who presided over the trial in the Fund of Funds case, reduced the damages awarded to Fund of Funds by approximately $10 million. Nevertheless, the still huge size of the judgment raised new concerns within the profession concerning the economic viability of CPA firms, particularly smaller national firms that would likely be forced into bankruptcy if required to pay such a large sum. Ironically, the Fund of Funds shareholders, who were the principal victims of the frauds that John King perpetrated, eventually recovered the majority of their losses. The Arthur Andersen judgment alone allowed them to recoup a significant portion of their original investments. However, the most significant recovery for the Fund of Funds shareholders resulted from the eventual discovery of oil on the large Arctic property that John King had pawned off on the mutual fund in 1969.[6]

John King was eventually convicted and sentenced to jail for the fraudulent transactions he arranged through King Resources. Likewise, Bernie Cornfeld served nearly one year in a Swiss prison after he was charged in a stock-swindling case brought against him by employees of IOS. In 1970, Cornfeld lost control of IOS to a prominent businessman and financier, Robert Vesco. Approximately three years later, the SEC filed suit against Vesco, charging him with stealing $224 million from the IOS funds. Shortly thereafter, Vesco fled the United States and became one of the most sought-after fugitives in U.S. history. At the present time, Vesco is allegedly living under the protection of Fidel Castro in Havana.

QUESTIONS

1. Was it appropriate for the Denver office of Arthur Andersen to audit King Resources and to be involved in the audit of Fund of Funds' NRPA investments?

---

6. Following the liquidation of Fund of Funds, its former shareholders were given shares of stock in a company that was formed to assume ownership of the Arctic property acquired from King Resources.

What were the advantages and disadvantages of this arrangement for Arthur Andersen?

2. According to the judge who presided over the trial in this case, Arthur Andersen could have chosen to resign from the Fund of Funds engagement when auditors from that firm discovered the excessive prices being charged the mutual fund by King Resources. Arthur Andersen contended that resigning at that point would not have benefited Fund of Funds. Do you agree? Why or why not? Does the Code of Professional Conduct adopted by the profession in 1988 recommend a course of action in this set of circumstances?

3. Do you believe that the decision rendered by the New York City audit partner regarding the Fox-Raff transaction was appropriate given the circumstances? What precedent, if any, did that decision establish for future audits of Fund of Funds?

4. Arthur Andersen contended during the Fund of Funds trial that the client's board of directors was primarily responsible for reviewing and eventually approving the revaluation transactions. Do you agree with this position? Why did the judge reject this argument?

5. During the 1966 audit of King Resources, Arthur Andersen placed significant reliance on the letter of representations signed by John King which indicated that the Blakely-Wolcott sale, as well as related sales, were arm's length transactions. What are the primary objectives an auditor hopes to accomplish by obtaining a letter of representations from client management? How competent is the audit evidence that is provided by a letter of representations?

6. The judge ruled in this case that the Arctic revaluation transaction involving Fund of Funds and John Mecom failed to comply with the guidelines specified in the Arthur Andersen memo for such transactions. Do you agree with the judge? Why or why not? What additional evidence could Arthur Andersen have obtained to assess the legitimacy of the Arctic revaluation transaction?

7. Briefly define *errors* and *irregularities* per *Statement on Auditing Standards No. 53,* "The Auditor's Responsibility to Detect and Report Errors and Irregularities." Do you agree with Arthur Andersen's contention that none of the King Resources transactions arranged for Fund of Funds were "irregularities"? Explain your answer.

8. Discuss the general elements of proof that a plaintiff must establish when bringing a suit under the Securities Exchange Act of 1934. Briefly discuss the evidence that Fund of Funds' attorneys likely presented to the court to establish each of these elements of proof.

9. The qualified audit opinion that Arthur Andersen issued on Fund of Funds' 1969 financial statements was criticized by the judge in this case as being "neither soon enough nor complete enough to avoid substantial damages to Fund of Funds." Draft an audit report that you believe would be appropriate for the 1969 Fund of Funds financial statements, given present audit reporting standards.

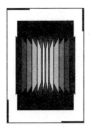

CASE 1.10

WEDTECH CORPORATION

In 1968 the federal government initiated what became known as the set-aside program to benefit small and economically disadvantaged minority-owned businesses.[1] Overseen by the Small Business Administration (SBA), the set-aside program was designed to allow such companies to obtain federal contracts without participating in a competitive bidding process. In the mid-1970s, Welbilt Electronic Die Corporation began applying for federal contracts under the set-aside program. Founded in 1965 by John Mariotta, a U.S. citizen of Puerto Rican descent, the small machine tooling company struggled to survive during the first several years of its existence. In 1970, Mariotta took on a new partner, Fred Neuberger, a Romanian citizen. Neuberger was given a one-third interest in the small company by Mariotta and charged with the responsibility of making it more profitable.

With Mariotta's assistance, Neuberger devised a strategy to assist Welbilt in obtaining federal contracts under the set-aside program. This strategy called for the company to develop an extensive network of "general allies," principally influential politicians, who would lobby SBA officials on behalf of Welbilt. During this time the SBA had become known as a federal agency that was susceptible to such lobbying efforts, since it was staffed largely by federal appointees who owed their jobs, and thus political favors, to the elected officials and bureaucrats who had secured their appointments. With the assistance of a public relations firm, Welbilt's new marketing strategy was implemented by a series of contributions to local politicians in the South Bronx area of New York City, where the company was located.

Welbilt was awarded its first contract from the SBA in 1979. In the years to follow, the company would become one of the largest participants in the set-aside program, garnering more than $250 million in federal contracts.[2] In

---

1. The author acknowledges the research assistance of Kimberly L. Cotton in developing this case.

2. Ironically, the eventual size and apparent profitability of Welbilt, later renamed Wedtech Corporation, nearly disqualified the company from participation in the SBA set-aside program. The financial success of Wedtech made it difficult for its officers to argue credibly that the company was "small and disadvantaged," which was a requirement for involvement in the program. After much prodding by the SBA, the company finally agreed to voluntarily withdraw from the set-aside program in April 1986.

EXHIBIT 1
Excerpt of a 1984
Speech by President
Ronald Reagan Praising
John Mariotta

> Real progress in this country can be traced to the work of conscientious and hardworking individuals. One such person is John Mariotta, who's providing jobs and training for the hardcore unemployed of the South Bronx. Born of Puerto Rican immigrants and having served in the United States Army, Mr. Mariotta has had all the ups and downs associated with entrepreneurship. And today, through Wedtech, he not only has built a successful corporation, he's helping hundreds of people who would otherwise be condemned to menial jobs or a life on the dole.
>
> And what gave Mr. Mariotta the courage to keep going when others quit? He tells us it was his faith in God. Now his faith has moved mountains, helping hundreds of people who'd almost given up hope. People like John Mariotta are heroes for the '80s.

1983, the company, renamed Wedtech Corporation by this time, went public shortly after receiving a $32 million contract to manufacture eleven thousand small engines for the U.S. Army. The public offering of Wedtech stock made Mariotta, Neuberger, and other company executives multimillionaires overnight.

The rapidly increasing revenues and profits of the company in the early 1980s, as shown in the following table, caught the attention of the investing public and Wall Street experts. In 1984, *Inc.* identified Wedtech as one of the one hundred fastest-growing small public companies in the United States and the third most profitable of that group. The impressive operating results of Wedtech, along with analysts' favorable projections for the company's future, caused an upward spiral in the price of its stock and allowed company executives to raise additional capital at will through a series of public securities offerings. As a result of Wedtech's apparent success, Mariotta and Neuberger became widely recognized as successful and innovative businessmen. In a speech in 1984, an excerpt of which is shown in Exhibit 1, President Ronald Reagan hailed Mariotta as one of the "heroes for the '80s" for his entrepreneurial skills and altruistic nature.

	1985	1984	1983	1982	1981
Revenues (in thousands)	$117,514	$72,367	$27,433	$20,492	$9,781
Earnings per share	$1.09	$.53	$.67	$.48	$(.16)

MASSIVE FRAUD AT WEDTECH EXPOSED

Unfortunately, Mariotta and Wedtech were not what they seemed. In August 1986, the Wedtech financial statements included in a registration statement filed with the Securities and Exchange Commission (SEC) reported a net worth of approximately $67 million for the company. The company actually had a negative net worth of approximately $100 million at the time. A series of investigations by federal regulatory authorities and criminal prosecutors would reveal that Wedtech executives had engaged in a massive fraud to grossly exaggerate the company's apparent financial condition, as well as its reported operating results. These same investigations also demonstrated that a large portion of the profits from the $250 million in federal contracts obtained by Wedtech had been diverted to company officers and used to pay bribes to the company's "general allies." Many of these allies, among them local politicians, a U.S. congressman, and officials of the Reagan administration, were subsequently convicted of various charges of fraud, conspiracy, and racketeering. An investigative report of a law firm retained by a congressional committee studying the Wedtech scandal succinctly summarized the nature of the huge fraud:

> As soon as we began to investigate the company's finances, we learned that its financial condition was dramatically different than the company's public disclosures. It appeared that the company had probably been insolvent for years. . . . [I]t was subsisting on money improperly obtained from public offerings of Wedtech securities and progress payments received from the Department of Defense. Members of its management had been misappropriating millions of dollars from the company for their personal benefit for years as well as creating a slush fund, used for the admitted bribery of city, state, and federal officials.[3]

A lengthy criminal trial and the congressional investigation in the wake of the Wedtech scandal demonstrated that the company was not recognized as a supplier of high-quality military parts, as claimed by Mariotta and his associates. Pentagon officials disclosed that the quality of Wedtech's products was often less than acceptable and that the company had a poor record of meeting contractually specified delivery dates. Despite its poor performance record, Wedtech continued to receive military contracts because of the bribes being paid government officials. Furthermore, Mariotta apparently was not the altruistic individual his supporters claimed he was. A former Wedtech accountant testified that after the company went public, Mariotta insisted on a huge salary increase. When the accountant pointed out that the stockholders might respond negatively to such a move, Mariotta allegedly retorted, "———— the stockholders. This is my company, and I'll take what I want to take."[4]

CRITICISM OF WEDTECH'S AUDITORS

The key question posed by congressional investigators of the Wedtech scandal was how the company had successfully concealed the massive fraud for so long, since its periodic financial statements were submitted to the SEC and came under the scrutiny of independent auditors and outside legal counsel. Critics of Wedtech's prestigious law firm and the company's international CPA firm maintained that these parties had provided Wedtech and its criminal element with a "veneer of respectability" that allowed the fraud to continue unabated for many years.[5] If the fraudulent activities that Wedtech's outside legal counsel and

---

3. U.S. Congress, Senate, Committee on Governmental Affairs, *Oversight of Federal Procurement Decisions on Wedtech* (Washington, D.C.: U.S. Government Printing Office, 1988), 163–64.

4. G. Lardner, "Wedtech Officials' Raids on Its Treasury Outlined," *Washington Post*, 3 June 1988, A3. Note: In August 1988, Mariotta was convicted on several charges of bribery, mail fraud, and income tax evasion. Prior to Mariotta's criminal trial, Neuberger and three other former Wedtech executives pleaded guilty to fraud charges filed against them. These individuals then testified as prosecution witnesses in Mariotta's trial.

5. P. Dwyer, "Wedtech: Where Fingers Are Pointing Now," *Business Week*, 5 October 1987, 34–35.

auditors discovered had been publicly disclosed, critics contend, the "whole scheme would have unraveled" well before it actually did in late 1986.[6]

The focal point of the criticism of Wedtech's independent auditors was their handling of nearly $5 million of forged invoices they discovered in 1982. Company officials forged these invoices to accelerate progress payments being made to Wedtech under a large, multiyear defense contract. The forgery also affected Wedtech's reported profits, since the company was using the percentage-of-completion method to account for profit recognized under its long-term contracts. The footnotes appended to Wedtech's 1985 financial statements explained how this method was applied by the company: "Revenue under U.S. government fixed-price contracts in process is recognized under the percentage-of-completion method of accounting whereunder the estimated revenue is measured by the percentage that costs incurred to date bears to the latest estimated total costs of the contract less revenue recognized in previous periods."[7] The fake invoices allowed the company to overstate the costs it had incurred to that point in time on its government contracts and thus recognize a larger portion of the unrealized profit on the contracts than was justified by their actual stage of completion. In fact, the total profit to be recognized under many of the contracts obtained by Wedtech was indeterminate when they were signed, since the federal agencies granting the contracts had an option to cancel them at any time. Because of these cancellation clauses, critics alleged that the use of the percentage-of-completion accounting method for Wedtech's federal contracts was inappropriate.

Representatives of KMG Main Hurdman, the company's audit firm until 1985, admitted discovering the forged invoices during their 1982 audit of Wedtech but alleged that they fulfilled their professional responsibilities by referring the matter to company executives and outside legal counsel. When outside legal counsel assured the auditors that the problem had been corrected, KMG Main Hurdman continued the audit and eventually issued an unqualified opinion on Wedtech's 1982 financial statements. In subsequent testimony before Congress, the law firm retained by Wedtech following the discovery of the fraud maintained that KMG Main Hurdman had a responsibility to report the irregularities directly to the SBA.

In 1983, the KMG Main Hurdman audit team discovered the large slush fund that Wedtech officials had established to disburse bribes to government officials and to be used for the personal benefit of company executives. According to a memo included in the audit firm's workpapers, the slush fund was simply a vehicle used "to divert money out of the company to the general use of its officers."[8] However, in a registration statement filed by Wedtech shortly after the discovery of the slush fund, no disclosures were made by the auditors or company management regarding its existence.

Two key members of the Wedtech audit team resigned from KMG Main Hurdman and accepted lucrative positions with Wedtech subsequent to the discovery of the forged invoices and slush fund. One of these individuals, Anthony Guaraglia, was eventually promoted to president of the company in

---

6. Ibid., 34.

7. 1985 Annual Report of Wedtech Corporation, p. 32.

8. Lardner, "Wedtech Officials' Raids," A3.

**EXHIBIT 2
Touche Ross Audit
Opinion on Wedtech's
1985 Financial
Statements**

1986. Apparently, Guaraglia used his accounting background to help Wedtech prepare false financial statements and to conceal the irregularities from third parties. In 1987, Guaraglia pleaded guilty to bribery and conspiracy charges and agreed to testify against other former Wedtech executives.

In September 1983, the audit partner in charge of the Wedtech engagement resigned from KMG Main Hurdman and accepted a position with the company. Subsequently, a U.S. district attorney charged that the former audit partner agreed to accept $1.5 million in Wedtech stock and a $900,000 low-interest loan from Wedtech before resigning from KMG Main Hurdman. Allegedly, these funds were payments made in exchange for the partner's remaining silent regarding the fraudulent Wedtech financial statements. The district attorney also disclosed that prior to resigning from KMG Main Hurdman, the partner had paid for air transportation for himself and two Wedtech executives to Japan. The purpose of the trip was to help Wedtech market a license it owned for a manufacturing process. Although the partner was later fully reimbursed by Wedtech, his initial payment of the airfare raised questions regarding his independence from the company.

In 1985, Wedtech executives dismissed KMG Main Hurdman and retained Touche Ross to serve as their company's independent audit firm. The unqualified opinion that Touche Ross issued on Wedtech's 1985 financial statements is shown in Exhibit 2. In August 1986, Wedtech issued $75 million of high-yield junk bonds shortly before reports began surfacing that company executives had bribed government officials to obtain defense contracts. In December 1986, following the resignation of Touche Ross and the cancellation of several of Wedtech's defense contracts by the federal government, the company was forced into Chapter 11 bankruptcy. Later, Touche Ross officials testified that they had relied "somewhat" on KMG Main Hurdman's prior audits of Wedtech in reaching their decision to issue an unqualified opinion on Wedtech's 1985 financial statements. The legal counsel of Touche Ross also testified that "KMG assured us there was no reason to doubt the integrity of Wedtech's management."[9]

In February 1992, a $77.5 million out-of-court settlement was announced to a large class action lawsuit filed by Wedtech's former stockholders and bondholders. Of the twenty-nine defendants named in the lawsuit, KPMG Peat Marwick, the successor firm of KMG Main Hurdman, and Deloitte Touche, the successor firm of Touche Ross, reportedly assumed responsibility for payment of most of the settlement. Another large civil lawsuit filed against the two accounting firms by the trust set up to liquidate Wedtech's assets was settled one week later for a reported $7 million. The individual amounts contributed by the two firms to that settlement were not disclosed.

WEDTECH: AN UNTIMELY SCANDAL FOR THE PUBLIC ACCOUNTING PROFESSION

The Wedtech scandal came at a point in time when the public accounting profession was under an intensive investigation by a subcommittee of the U.S. House of Representatives chaired by Representative John Dingell. Among the issues addressed by the Dingell subcommittee was the responsibility of independent auditors to discover and disclose management fraud. The Wedtech case provided Dingell's subcommittee with another in what, by then, was a long list of audits that had failed to result in the public disclosure of a financial fraud. At least partially in response to criticism of the public accounting profession's failure to reveal such frauds, the Auditing Standards Board adopted *Statement on Auditing Standards No. 53*, "Errors and Irregularities," which imposed more responsibility on auditors for discovering client fraud. Nevertheless, many critics of the profession do not believe that *SAS No. 53* is sufficient. Whether auditors will eventually be forced to accept even more responsibility for discovering client fraud is a question that may well depend on the frequency of occurrence of financial scandals similar to Wedtech.

QUESTIONS

1. Wedtech was criticized for using the percentage-of-completion method of accounting for its long-term contracts, since the profit to be recognized on those contracts was indeterminate at the time they were signed. What other method of accounting for these contracts would have been more appropriate, and why?

2. In your opinion, should KMG Main Hurdman have resigned from the Wedtech (Welbilt) audit in 1982 after discovering the forged invoices? Why or why not? Identify the general conditions under which it is appropriate for an audit firm to resign after discovering irregularities in a client's financial records.

9. L. Berton, "Wedtech Used Gimmickry, False Invoices to Thrive," *Wall Street Journal*, 23 February 1987, 6.

3. Regarding the forged invoices, did KMG Main Hurdman have a responsibility to report those invoices to the SBA, to other federal agencies or any other party? How should the discovery of the Wedtech slush fund in 1983 by KMG Main Hurdman have affected the audit firm's planning decisions for the 1983 Wedtech audit?

4. Assuming the former audit partner for Wedtech paid for the airfare of client executives on the business trip to Japan, would this payment be a violation of the AICPA Code of Professional Conduct? Why or why not? Does the fact that he was reimbursed by Wedtech affect your answer?

5. Touche Ross officials reported that their auditors relied "somewhat" on the prior audits of Wedtech by KMG Main Hurdman in issuing the unqualified opinion on Wedtech's 1985 financial statements. To what extent, if any, was Touche Ross justified in relying on KMG Main Hurdman's prior audits of Wedtech?

6. Touche Ross officials also testified that KMG Main Hurdman did not warn their firm that Wedtech's management lacked integrity when Touche Ross replaced KMG Main Hurdman as the company's audit firm in 1985. Did KMG Main Hurdman have a responsibility to inform Touche Ross of the forged invoices and slush fund discovered during the course of its earlier audits of Wedtech? Explain.

SECTION TWO
AUDITS OF HIGH-RISK ACCOUNTS AND INTERNAL CONTROL ISSUES

Case 2.1   Doughtie's Foods, Inc.

Case 2.2   Flight Transportation Corporation

Case 2.3   The Trolley Dodgers

Case 2.4   J. B. Hanauer & Co.

Case 2.5   Berkshire Hathaway, Inc.

Case 2.6   Giant Stores Corporation

Case 2.7   Howard Street Jewelers, Inc.

Case 2.8   E. F. Hutton & Company, Inc.

Case 2.9   J. B. Lippincott Company

Case 2.10   Porta-John Corporation

Case 2.11   Four Seasons Nursing Centers of America, Inc.

CASE 2.1
DOUGHTIE'S FOODS, INC.

In the late 1970s, William Nashwinter accepted a position as a salesman with Doughtie's Foods, Inc., a publicly owned food products company headquartered in Portsmouth, Virginia.[1] The ambitious young salesman impressed his superiors with his hard work and dedication and was soon promoted to general manager of the Gravins Division of Doughtie's, a promotion that nearly doubled his salary. The Gravins Division was essentially a large warehouse that wholesaled frozen food products to retail outlets on the East Coast.

Nashwinter quickly discovered that managing a large wholesale operation was much more complicated and stressful than working a sales route. Within a short time after accepting the promotion, he was being criticized by corporate headquarters for his division's poor performance. Eventually, after several rounds of scathing criticism for failing to meet what he perceived were unrealistic profit goals, Nashwinter decided to take matters into his own hands and began fabricating fictitious inventory on his monthly performance reports to headquarters. By inflating his monthly inventory balance, Nashwinter lowered his division's cost of goods sold and thus increased its gross profit.

Several years later, Nashwinter alleged that he had never intended to continue his scheme permanently. Instead, he saw his actions simply as a solution to a short-term problem: "I always had in the back of my mind that the division would make enough legitimate profit one day to justify the fake numbers."[2] Unfortunately for Nashwinter, the actual operating results of the Gravins Division continued to be disappointing. With each passing year, Nashwinter was forced to fabricate larger amounts of fictitious inventory to meet his profit goals. Finally, in 1982, Nashwinter admitted to a Doughtie's executive that he had been filing false inventory reports to corporate headquarters for several years. Nashwinter was fired almost immediately. Shortly thereafter, Price Waterhouse was

---

1. This case was developed primarily from Securities and Exchange Commission, *Accounting and Auditing Enforcement Release No. 30*, 21 May 1984.

2. R. L. Hudson, "SEC Charges Fudging of Corporate Figures Is a Growing Practice," *Wall Street Journal*, 2 June 1983, 1, 19.

retained by Doughtie's to determine the magnitude of the inventory errors that had been introduced into Gravins's accounting records and their effect on the firm's financial statements. The Price Waterhouse study disclosed that Doughtie's 1980 consolidated net income had been overstated by 15 percent as a result of Nashwinter's scheme, and the firm's 1981 net income had been overstated by 39 percent.[3]

The methods used by Nashwinter to misrepresent his division's inventory were quite simple. In 1980, he inflated Gravins's inventory by including three pages of fictitious inventory items in the count sheets that summarized the results of the division's annual physical inventory. Nashwinter also changed the unit of measure of many of the inventory items. For instance, rather than reporting fifteen single boxes of a given product, Nashwinter would change the inventory sheet so that it reported fifteen cases of the product. In 1981, after Doughtie's had acquired a computerized inventory system, Nashwinter simply input a large number of fictitious inventory items into Gravins's computerized inventory ledger.

In 1980 and 1981, Doughtie's was audited by the CPA firm of Goodman & Company. Thomas Wilson of Goodman & Company served as the audit manager on the 1980 audit and as the audit engagement partner the following year, after having been promoted to partner. In both years, Frank Pollard was the audit supervisor assigned to the Doughtie's engagement. Following the disclosure of Nashwinter's scheme to the Securities and Exchange Commission (SEC) by Doughtie's executives, the federal agency investigated the 1980 and 1981 audits of Doughtie's by Goodman & Company. The SEC criticized Wilson and Pollard for their role in those audits, particularly for their failure to rigorously audit the inventory accounts of Doughtie's. For several reasons, the SEC maintained that the inventory of Doughtie's should have been considered a high-risk account and thus subject to a higher-than-normal degree of scrutiny by Wilson and Pollard during the 1980 and 1981 audits of the company. First, inventory was the largest line item on the Doughtie's balance sheet, accounting for approximately 40 percent of the company's total assets. Second, Wilson and Pollard were aware that Doughtie's internal controls for inventory had a number of weaknesses, particularly within the Gravins Division, and that these weaknesses increased the likelihood that the company's inventory would be misstated. Finally, the SEC noted that Gravins's inventory balance was increasing at a very high rate during 1980 and 1981, which caused the division's inventory turnover rate to be abnormally low.

The SEC also criticized Wilson and Pollard for failing to pursue problems that they or their subordinates noted during the 1980 and 1981 audits of Gravins's inventory. Following the completion of the physical inventory for Gravins in 1980, Nashwinter forwarded the three fictitious inventory count sheets to Wilson and Pollard and alleged that the sheets had been overlooked by the audit team. After a brief review of these inventory sheets, Wilson and Pollard accepted them and included the items listed thereon in Gravins's inventory balance. Following the completion of the physical inventory for Gravins in 1981, the audit senior assigned to the Doughtie's engagement was unable to reconcile the quantities for numerous items listed on the inventory count sheets with the quantities shown on the computer printout of the details of Gravins's year-end inventory balance.

---

3. The reported earnings of Doughtie's for several earlier years were also distorted by Nashwinter's scheme, but Price Waterhouse was unable to determine the magnitude of those misstatements.

This individual notified Wilson of the problem and wrote Nashwinter a memo asking for an explanation. Wilson failed to follow up on the problem, and Nashwinter never responded to the memo. In his review of the senior's workpapers, Pollard either did not notice the numerous discrepancies between the count sheets and the computer listing of Gravins's inventory or chose not to investigate those discrepancies.

Nashwinter's testimony to the SEC regarding the work of the Goodman & Company auditors was not complimentary. Nashwinter testified that he often was forced to make up excuses to account for missing or misplaced inventory and that the auditors apparently never double-checked his explanations. He also testified that the auditors were lax when it came time to test-count inventory items in Gravins's blast freezer: "A lot of times the auditors didn't want to stay in the freezer. It was too cold."[4]

Epilogue

For their role in the Doughtie's case, Wilson and Pollard were required by the SEC to complete several professional education courses and to have the results of certain audits they supervised in the future subjected to peer reviews to determine that the appropriate audit procedures had been performed. The CPA firm of Goodman & Company was not sanctioned by the SEC, since Wilson and Pollard had failed to comply with the quality control standards established by that firm. In 1983, Doughtie's dismissed Goodman & Company and retained Price Waterhouse as its audit firm. To settle the charges filed against him by the SEC, William Nashwinter signed a consent decree in which he neither admitted nor denied the charges but agreed not to violate federal securities laws in the future. At last report, Nashwinter was employed by a competitor of Doughtie's.

Questions

1. What are the auditor's primary objectives when he or she is observing the client's annual physical inventory? Identify the key audit procedures that an auditor would typically perform during and after the client's physical inventory.

2. What audit procedure or procedures might have prevented Nashwinter from successfully overstating the 1980 physical inventory of the Gravins Division? What audit procedure or procedures might have prevented Nashwinter from successfully overstating the division's 1981 physical inventory?

3. In 1981, Gravins's inventory turnover was approximately one-half that of comparable divisions within the firm. How should this fact have affected the planning for the 1981 audit of Doughtie's? What audit procedures should Wilson and Pollard have performed to investigate this unusually low inventory turnover rate for the Gravins Division?

4. Nashwinter was apparently under considerable pressure to improve the operating results of his division. Discuss how this fact, if known to the auditors of Doughtie's, should have affected their assessment of audit risk for this client.

---

4. Hudson, "Fudging of Corporate Figures," 19.

CASE 2.2

FLIGHT TRANSPORTATION CORPORATION

In January 1982, Charles Aune picked up his phone and called the Federal Bureau of Investigation (FBI).[1] Aune informed the FBI of a large-scale fraud being perpetrated by his former employer. Until 1981, Aune had worked for Flight Transportation Corporation (FTC), an aviation company based in Eden Prairie, Minnesota. FTC's principal line of business was executive and group air charters. In 1980 and 1981, the rapidly growing company reported revenues of $8 million and $24.8 million, respectively. FTC's dramatic growth caught the attention of thousands of investors. These investors were particularly impressed by FTC's strong operating results in the face of a nationwide recession. Unfortunately for these investors, most of FTC's revenues were fabricated by its executives. Similarly, several million dollars of assets reported in the company's 1980 and 1981 balance sheets did not exist.

From 1979 through 1982, FTC executives used the company's bogus financial statements to raise more than $32 million of capital in three securities offerings to the public. Several million dollars of these funds were diverted by the executives for their personal use. For example, the company's president apparently financed his expensive hobby, collecting vintage cars, by tapping the company's bank accounts. In June 1982, FTC was preparing to sell an additional $24 million of securities. However, as a result of Aune's tip and a secret six-month investigation by the FBI, the Securities and Exchange Commission (SEC) shut down FTC's operations. A federal judge then appointed a receiver to take custody of the company's assets.

Over the next several months, press reports of the FTC fraud shocked investors who had purchased the company's securities on the basis of its impressive financial statements. Almost immediately, the underwriting firms that

1. Most of the facts of this case and the quotations, unless indicated otherwise, were drawn from the following source: Securities and Exchange Commission, *Accounting and Auditing Enforcement Release No. 81*, 5 December 1985.

had managed FTC's securities offerings came under fire. An executive of one of these firms responded to this criticism. "I don't see this as embarrassing to our firm at all. Underwriters aren't auditors."[2] Predictably, the press then turned to FTC's auditors, Fox & Company, for an explanation. John Harrington, a senior partner with Fox & Company, defended the 1980 and 1981 audits of FTC for which he had served as the audit engagement partner.

> We're not the guardians of the world. It's the con artists who should be punished. Besides, if we go into every client's office with our eyes wide open, saying, "there's a crime in here somewhere," nobody is going to hire us.[3]

Fox's 1980 Audit of FTC

The Minneapolis office of Fox & Company, the thirteenth-largest accounting firm in the nation at the time, acquired FTC as an audit client in March 1980. In prior years, the company had been audited by a sole practitioner. In addition to Harrington, the audit engagement team assigned to the 1980 and 1981 FTC audits included an audit manager, Gregory Arnott, and three staff auditors. The fieldwork in both audits was supervised by Arnott. The 1980 FTC audit was the first engagement on which Arnott had served as an audit manager, since he had been promoted to that position shortly before the audit began. In his previous eight years with Fox & Company, Arnott had been assigned to only one audit of a public company. Harrington had been a partner with Fox & Company since 1975 and had served for a time as the managing partner of the Minneapolis office. During the early 1980s, Harrington was in charge of the auditing practice of Fox's Minneapolis office and was responsible for reviewing and approving SEC registration statements filed by clients of that office.

Harrington and Arnott met with the top executives of FTC in early March 1980 and discussed the contractual details of the audit engagement. These details were documented in an engagement letter signed by Harrington and an FTC officer. At this meeting, the staffing of the 1980 audit and timing issues were also discussed. FTC's fiscal year ended on June 30. The company's president, William Rubin, insisted that the audited financial statements be ready for the printer by early August. Rubin wanted the audit completed quickly to expedite the filing of a registration statement with the SEC that would allow his firm to sell additional securities to the public.

Like most large accounting firms, Fox & Company used a risk assessment questionnaire during the planning phase of each audit engagement to document "special" audit risks. This questionnaire contained several inquiries regarding such high-risk items as related party transactions. When asked whether FTC had engaged in any related party transactions during fiscal 1980, FTC officials responded with a blunt no. However, shortly after the audit fieldwork began, a Fox auditor discovered that most of FTC's revenues resulted from a contractual arrangement with International Air Systems (IAS), a company owned and operated by William Rubin. Approximately two-thirds of FTC's 1980 consoli-

---

2. K. Johnson, "How High-flying Numbers Fooled the Experts," *New York Times*, 29 August 1982, sec. 3, 9.

3. Ibid. Note: Fox issued unqualified opinions on FTC's 1980 and 1981 financial statements.

> **A.** IAS shall provide FTC with large aircraft (727's and/or DC 8's) for charter to the Cayman Islands and Mexico.
> **B.** All revenues earned by FTC will be recorded by IAS during the term of the agreement and provided to FTC at the conclusion of all flights along with the gross or net profit to be paid. Gross profit will be earned and paid if sufficient volume is attained. If volume is not high enough, only net profit will be paid to FTC.
> **C.** This agreement covers the period from July 1, 1979, through June 30, 1980.
>
> Source: Securities and Exchange Commission, *Accounting and Auditing Enforcement Release No. 81*, 5 December 1985.

EXHIBIT 1
Alleged Contractual Agreement between FTC and IAS

dated revenues stemmed from more than one hundred air charters that had been flown on IAS aircraft. To the staff auditor's surprise, he could find almost no documentary support for the $5.2 million of these air charter revenues. There were no sales invoices, no entries in the sales journal, and no related expenses recorded for these revenues. The support for the revenues consisted almost entirely of handwritten entries made in FTC's general journal. Because of the revenues' unusual nature and lack of documentation, the staff auditor prepared a list of the air charter revenues, which he gave to Arnott.

Arnott immediately went to FTC's controller and asked for the documentation for the air charter revenues. The controller responded that the auditors would have to make arrangements with Rubin to obtain that documentation. Arnott then took the matter to Harrington, who contacted Rubin. After a brief conversation with Harrington, Rubin agreed to provide extensive documentation for the IAS-related revenues. This documentation was to include sales invoices, cash receipts and disbursements records, canceled checks, contracts, and computer runs listing the individual air charters. However, despite Rubin's interest in completing the audit as quickly as possible, he continually fabricated excuses to delay turning the documentation over to the auditors. Rubin's most frequent excuse for the delays was computer malfunctions.

With only a few days remaining to meet the audit deadline, Rubin finally provided the Fox auditors with evidence to support the IAS-related air charter revenues. This evidence consisted of two one-page documents. The first document was the brief and ambiguous one-page contract between IAS and FTC that is shown in Exhibit 1. The second document was a one-page statement reporting the number of charter flights flown for FTC on IAS aircraft and the resulting revenues for FTC. When the auditors balked at accepting this documentation, Rubin took Harrington aside and informed him that the air charter revenues were not FTC revenues at all. Instead, these revenues had been generated strictly by IAS, which, again, was owned and operated by Rubin. Rubin explained to Harrington that "he was bored, had plenty of money, and wanted to use IAS to help FTC get into the charter business." Consequently, Rubin had donated the more than $5 million of IAS air charter revenues to FTC.

Harrington accepted Rubin's explanation for the IAS revenues that were booked in FTC's accounting records. Rubin's explanation accounted for FTC's lack of documentation for those transactions. In a subsequent meeting, Harrington explained to Arnott the true nature of the air charter revenues. He also informed Arnott that, in his opinion, no further evidence would be needed to support those revenues. Arnott disagreed with Harrington initially but then changed his mind after the two men discussed the matter. Arnott eventually indicated in the 1980 audit workpapers that the $5.2 million of air charter revenues were "appropriately included" in FTC's 1980 financial statements.

During a subsequent SEC investigation, Arnott testified that he never believed sufficient competent audit evidence had been obtained to support the suspicious air charter revenues. An SEC representative then questioned Arnott regarding his knowledge of a Fox "disagreement procedure." This procedure or policy allowed subordinate members of an audit team to express their disagreement with a decision rendered on an audit engagement. This disagreement was to be documented in a written memorandum included in the audit workpapers. The disagreement memorandum effectively dissociated the individual from the decision. Arnott testified that he was aware of the disagreement procedure but did not take advantage of it for two reasons. First, he realized that as the audit engagement partner, Harrington would make the final decision in the matter. Second, he was worried that his job with Fox & Company might be jeopardized if he followed that procedure.

The SEC also quizzed Harrington regarding his discussion of the air charter revenues with Arnott. Harrington reported that he could not recall Arnott disagreeing with his decision that sufficient evidence had been collected to support the air charter revenues.

Fox's 1981 Audit of FTC

In July 1980, shortly after the beginning of FTC's 1981 fiscal year, the company established a subsidiary located in the Cayman Islands. The reported purpose of this subsidiary was to operate an air charter business. During fiscal 1981, FTC booked more than $13 million of nonexistent revenues through FTC Cayman Ltd., its Cayman Islands subsidiary. These revenues represented more than one-half of FTC's consolidated revenues for fiscal 1981. FTC's consolidated balance sheet as of June 30, 1981, the final day of the company's 1981 fiscal year, reported more than $6 million of receivables, land, and other assets related to FTC Cayman. Again, these assets did not exist or were not owned by FTC or its subsidiary.

In June 1981, Harrington and Arnott met with Rubin and other FTC officers in a planning conference for the 1981 audit. During this conference, Harrington and Arnott were informed that most of FTC's revenues had been generated by the company's new Cayman Islands subsidiary. They were also told by FTC's management that the documentation for these revenues was in the Cayman Islands but that this documentation would be brought to Minnesota during the audit. Again, Rubin wanted the audit completed as quickly as possible. The parties agreed that the fieldwork would be completed by July 31 and that the audit report would be signed by August 12.

When the 1981 audit began in early July, the only documentation made available to the Fox auditors for FTC Cayman was a trial balance and a computerized general ledger and general journal. On August 6, one week after the fieldwork was supposed to be finished and less than one week before the audit report was to be signed, the auditors were also given the fiscal 1981 bank statements for FTC Cayman. Except for a few other minor items, these bank statements were the only externally prepared documents provided to the Fox auditors to support the revenues of FTC Cayman. These bank statements were not obtained directly from the subsidiary's bank but instead were given to the Fox auditors by an FTC employee.

Rubin informed Harrington and Arnott that they could verify the subsidiary's revenues by reviewing the deposits reported in its bank statements during fiscal 1981. A member of the audit engagement team did just that. A reconciliation of the revenues reported by FTC Cayman and the deposits reflected in the subsidiary's 1981 bank statements resulted in a small, unlocated difference between the two amounts. Given this small difference, the auditors concluded that the subsidiary's 1981 revenues were materially accurate. In fact, the bank statements were forgeries.

The Fox auditors attempted to confirm $3 million of cash that FTC Cayman reportedly had on deposit in the Cayman Islands as of June 30, 1981. Throughout the audit, FTC executives tried to persuade the auditors that obtaining a confirmation for that cash balance would be difficult, given the bank secrecy laws in the Cayman Islands. The auditors mailed a confirmation to the subsidiary's Cayman Islands bank using an address supplied by FTC. That confirmation was never returned. Eventually, Harrington agreed to accept a confirmation of the year-end cash balance that an employee of the subsidiary had allegedly obtained from the Cayman Islands bank. This confirmation was forged by the FTC employee.

Harrington arranged to speak with an official of the Cayman Islands bank to obtain an oral confirmation of the year-end cash balance. Rubin invited Harrington to come to his office to obtain this confirmation over the telephone. After Rubin placed a call—allegedly to the bank—and had a brief conversation, he handed the telephone to Harrington. The individual at the other end of the line then confirmed that FTC's subsidiary had the reported amount of cash on deposit as of June 30, 1981.

The Fox auditors also attempted to confirm a $2 million receivable of FTC Cayman at the end of fiscal 1981. A confirmation for this amount was mailed to a tour group operator who allegedly organized most of the subsidiary's air charter flights. A confirmation was returned indicating that the receivable did exist in the correct amount. However, the confirmation returned was not the confirmation that had been mailed by the Fox auditors. The returned confirmation was a forgery that contained typographical errors not included in the original confirmation.

SANCTIONS IMPOSED ON HARRINGTON AND ARNOTT

In late 1985, following the SEC investigation of the 1980 and 1981 FTC audits, the federal agency sanctioned both John Harrington and Gregory Arnott. Harrington was permanently banned from practicing before the SEC. However, the SEC's disciplinary order allowed Harrington to apply for a repeal of this ban after five years. Arnott was suspended from practicing before the SEC for one year. In commenting on Arnott's role in the FTC audits, the SEC stressed the need for members of an audit engagement team to maintain an independent state of mind even if that means jeopardizing their jobs.

> Arnott engaged in unprofessional conduct by abdicating his role as an independent professional to the audit partner. He properly recognized that the audit evidence was

inadequate and took the appropriate step of informing the partner. However, he failed to act on his conviction and caused the workpapers to evidence incorrectly his agreement.

EPILOGUE

Following a series of highly publicized "problem" audits by Fox & Company, including the 1980 and 1981 FTC audits, the SEC prohibited the firm from accepting new SEC clients for a six-month period beginning in 1983. During this time, the SEC formed an independent committee to review Fox & Company's auditing practice. The purpose of this review was to recommend changes to improve Fox & Company's quality control procedures. In 1985, Fox & Company merged with Alexander Grant & Company. Shortly thereafter, Alexander Grant was renamed Grant Thornton.

In 1982, the SEC sanctioned William Rubin for his role in the fraudulent misrepresentation of FTC's financial statements. The SEC permanently enjoined Rubin from further violations of the federal securities laws. Eventually, the SEC, other federal agencies, and private plaintiffs recovered more than $45 million from FTC and its executives including almost $2 million from Rubin. These funds were distributed by FTC's court-appointed receiver to the company's bondholders, other creditors, and stockholders.

QUESTIONS

1. Assume the role of Gregory Arnott during the 1980 FTC audit and draft a memo to be included in the FTC workpapers. In this memo, express your disagreement with John Harrington's decision that sufficient competent evidence had been collected to support the suspicious air charter revenues.

2. Identify measures accounting firms could adopt to diminish the likelihood that auditors will capitulate to their superiors when technical disagreements arise during an audit.

3. Assume that you were the staff auditor who discovered the bogus air charter revenues during the 1980 audit. What responsibilities did you have with respect to these revenues? For example, did you have a responsibility to write a memo dissociating yourself from Harrington's decision regarding these revenues? Make any assumptions you believe are necessary to respond to this question.

4. Besides the related party transactions, what other "special" audit risks existed in the FTC audits? How should these factors have affected the planning decisions for these audits?

5. Identify specific measures that audit firms can take to ensure that client-imposed pressure does not adversely affect the quality of an independent audit.

6. In your opinion, what additional audit procedures should the Fox auditors have applied to the 1981 FTC Cayman revenues?

7. Briefly identify the deficiencies in the confirmation procedures used by the Fox auditors. How did these deficiencies affect the competence and sufficiency of the audit evidence yielded by these procedures?

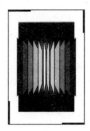

CASE 2.3
THE TROLLEY DODGERS

In 1890 the Brooklyn Trolley Dodgers professional baseball team joined the National League. Over the years that would follow, the Dodgers would have considerable difficulty competing with the other baseball teams in the New York City area, teams that generally were much better financed and, as a result, stocked with players of higher caliber. In 1958, after nearly seven decades of mostly frustration on and off the baseball field, the Dodgers shocked the sports world by moving to Los Angeles. Walter O'Malley, the flamboyant owner of the Dodgers at the time, saw an opportunity to introduce professional baseball to the rapidly growing population of the West Coast and, more important, an opportunity to make his team more profitable. As an inducement to the Dodgers, Los Angeles County purchased a goat farm located in Chavez Ravine, an area two miles northwest of downtown Los Angeles, and gave the property to O'Malley for the site of his new baseball stadium.

Since moving to Los Angeles, the Dodgers have been the envy of the baseball world: "In everything from profit to stadium maintenance . . . the Dodgers are the prototype of how a franchise should be run."[1] During the decade of the 1980s, the Dodgers were reportedly the most profitable franchise in baseball with a pretax profit margin approaching 25 percent in many years. By 1990, the franchise, still owned by the O'Malley family, was valued at an incredible $250 million. Peter O'Malley, the current Dodgers president, attributes the success of his organization to the experts he has retained in all functional areas: "I don't have to be an expert on taxes, split-fingered fastballs, or labor relations with our ushers. That talent is all available."[2]

Edward Campos, a longtime accountant for the Dodgers, was seemingly a perfect example of one of the experts in the Dodgers organization to whom Peter O'Malley alluded. Campos accepted a position with the Dodgers as a young man and by 1986, after almost two decades with the club, had worked his way up the

---

1. R. J. Harris "Forkball for Dodgers: Costs Up, Gate Off," *Wall Street Journal*, 31 August 1990, B1, B4.

2. Ibid., B1.

employment hierarchy to become the operations payroll chief, a job with considerable prestige in the organization. After taking charge of the payroll department, Campos designed and implemented a new payroll system, a system that reportedly only he fully understood. In fact, Campos controlled the system so completely that he personally filled out the weekly payroll cards for each of the four hundred employees of the Dodgers. Campos was known not only for his work ethic but also for his loyalty to the club and its owners: "The Dodgers trusted him, and when he was on vacation, he even came back and did the payroll."[3]

Unfortunately, the Dodgers' trust in Campos was misplaced. Over a period of several years, Campos embezzled several hundred thousand dollars from the Dodgers organization. According to court records, Campos padded the Dodgers' payroll by adding a number of fictitious employees to various departments in the organization. In addition, Campos inflated the number of hours worked by several employees and then split the resulting overpayments fifty-fifty with those individuals. The fraudulent scheme was finally discovered when Campos was unable to work for a period of time due to illness and his responsibilities were assumed temporarily by the Dodgers' controller. While completing the payroll one week, the controller noticed that several employees, including ushers, security guards, and ticket salespeople, were being paid unusual amounts. In some cases, employees earning $7 per hour were receiving weekly paychecks approaching $2,000. Following a criminal investigation and the filing of charges against Campos and his cohorts, all the individuals involved in the payroll fraud confessed.

After pleading guilty to embezzlement charges, Campos was sentenced to eight years in state prison and agreed to make restitution of approximately $132,000 to the Dodgers. Another of the conspirators also received a prison sentence, whereas the remaining individuals involved in the payroll scheme made restitution and were placed on probation.

QUESTIONS

1. What are the key objectives in the audit of a client's payroll transaction cycle? Comment on both objectives related to tests of controls and those related to substantive audit procedures.

2. What internal control weaknesses were evident in the Dodgers' payroll system?

3. What specific audit procedures might have led to the discovery of Campos's fraudulent scheme?

---

3. P. Feldman, "7 Accused of Embezzling $332,583 from Dodgers," *Los Angeles Times*, 17 September 1986, sec. 2, 1, 6.

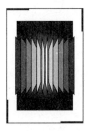

CASE 2.4
J. B. HANAUER & CO.

Pick up the financial statements of a brokerage firm and you will find a balance sheet that is quite different from the typical corporate balance sheet.[1] Take Quick & Reilly, for example, the large discount broker. In its 1994 balance sheet, Quick & Reilly reported total assets of almost $2.5 billion. Approximately 95 percent of those assets were "invested" in receivables from customers or other brokerage firms. Likewise, short-term payables tend to dominate the liability side of a brokerage firm's balance sheet. In 1994, Quick & Reilly reported $2.3 billion of liabilities, 94 percent of which was owed to customers and other brokerage firms. Clearly, confirmation procedures for receivables and payables are important audit tests for brokerage clients. So it was in the late 1970s and early 1980s for the annual audits of J. B. Hanauer & Co. Hanauer, a brokerage firm specializing in municipal securities, was headquartered in New Jersey but had several branch offices in Florida.

Stanley Goldberg supervised the annual audits of J. B. Hanauer & Co. for several years during the late 1970s and early 1980s. During this time, Goldberg was a partner with three different public accounting firms: J. K. Lasser & Co., Touche Ross & Co., and Richard A. Eisner & Co. Goldberg became a partner of Touche Ross following a merger between that firm and J. K. Lasser. As often happens, when Goldberg left Touche Ross to join Eisner, Hanauer's executives wanted Goldberg to continue supervising their annual audits. As a result, in 1980 these executives dismissed Touche Ross as their independent auditors and retained the Eisner firm.

ASSESSMENT OF HANAUER'S INTERNAL CONTROLS

Hanauer's fiscal year ended on March 31. Two to three months prior to that date, Goldberg would send a senior and two or more staff accountants to Hanauer's

1. This case was developed primarily from the following source: Securities and Exchange Commission, *Accounting and Auditing Enforcement Release No. 13*, 22 September 1983.

EXHIBIT 1
Selected Job
Responsibilities of
Hanauer's Sales Staff

- Opened customer accounts and obtained all required personal data such as addresses and credit references.
- Provided requested price quotations to customers.
- Accepted and processed customer purchase orders.
- Mailed or personally delivered customer confirmations.
- Obtained bearer (coupon) bonds from Hanauer's vault and delivered them to customers, often at locations other than Hanauer's offices.
- Received payment for securities from customers in currency, often at locations other than Hanauer's offices.
- Deposited cash received from customers in Hanauer's bank accounts.

offices to complete the internal control phase of the annual audit. Given the nature of the brokerage business, internal controls are extremely important. The large volume of cash and securities that exchange hands daily dictates that brokerage firms establish extensive and rigorous internal controls over their day-to-day operations.

During each audit of Hanauer, Goldberg's subordinates completed a lengthy internal control questionnaire covering all facets of Hanauer's internal control structure. Among the key issues documented in the internal control workpapers was the unusual scope of job responsibilities assigned to the brokerage firm's sales staff. Shown in Exhibit 1 are some of these responsibilities.

Apparently, Goldberg was uncomfortable with the extensive and unusual degree of authority granted the Hanauer's sales staff. Contributing to his concern was the fact that several officials of the brokerage firm had been censured by the Securities and Exchange Commission (SEC) in 1977 for engaging in improper securities transactions.[2] Goldberg's concern regarding the competence and integrity of these individuals was allayed somewhat by Hanauer's response to the SEC's sanctions. In a news release, the firm correctly pointed out that the individuals had not admitted to any of the charges. The news release also stated that the individuals had agreed to accept the SEC's penalties to avoid the costs associated with contesting the allegations in court.

Despite several questions regarding the reliability of Hanauer's internal controls, each year that Goldberg supervised the firm's independent audit, he concluded that there were no material weaknesses in its internal control structure. The Securities Exchange Act of 1934 required Goldberg to file reports to this effect with the SEC, since Hanauer was a "registered broker-dealer" under that federal law.

CUSTOMER ACCOUNT CONFIRMATION PROCEDURES

As suggested earlier, confirmation procedures are an extremely important and widely used method of collecting audit evidence for brokerage clients. In planning their confirmation procedures each year, Hanauer's auditors identified four groups of customer accounts. The accounts that were of primary concern

---

2. "J. B. Hanauer & Co., Officials Are Censured by SEC for Dealings," *Wall Street Journal*, 30 September 1977, 4.

	Number of Accounts Selected for Confirmation	Confirmations Not Mailed at Hanauer's Request	Dollar Value of Unmailed Confirmations as a Percentage of the Dollar Value of Accounts Selected for Confirmation
1978	227	45	18%
1979	145	36	25%
1980	216	36	26%

EXHIBIT 2
Selected Account Confirmation Data, 1978–1980 Audits of J. B. Hanauer & Co.

were those with "open" balances at the end of Hanauer's fiscal year. The open accounts with credit balances represented customers to whom Hanauer owed cash at year-end, while the open accounts with debit balances represented customers who owed cash to the brokerage firm. In 1978, Goldberg decided to send confirmations to all customers with open balances at year-end. In 1979 and 1980, confirmations were mailed to approximately 50 percent of these customers.

The third group of accounts included those with only securities balances at year-end. For the customers represented by these accounts, Hanauer was holding securities that had been purchased but not delivered. The fourth group of accounts included those that had neither an open balance nor a securities balance. Many of these accounts were inactive or dormant. Each year, Goldberg instructed his subordinates to mail confirmations to a small, randomly selected sample of these final two groups of accounts.

In 1978, a senior executive of Hanauer asked Goldberg not to send confirmations to certain accounts that had been selected for that purpose. The executive indicated that many of his firm's customers insisted that their account information be kept strictly confidential. When pressed to provide an explanation for this confidentiality, the executive responded that these customers wished to conceal the existence of their brokerage accounts from their spouses. Goldberg agreed to the client's request not to mail confirmations to certain accounts. Before mailing the confirmations for the 1978 audit, the senior assigned to the Hanauer audit engagement provided a Hanauer accountant with a list of the accounts selected for confirmation. The accountant then individually contacted the salespeople of Hanauer and asked them to check off the accounts that they did not want confirmed. This procedure was repeated during both the 1979 and 1980 Hanauer audits.

Exhibit 2 shows selected data regarding the confirmation procedures performed during the 1978–1980 Hanauer audits. The table indicates the number of accounts selected for confirmation each year, the number of confirmations not mailed at the request of Hanauer personnel, and the dollar value of the unmailed confirmations relative to the total dollar value of all the accounts selected for confirmation.

Goldberg instructed his subordinates to perform alternative audit procedures on those open accounts that the client did not want confirmed. These procedures consisted principally of determining that the year-end account balance was eventually "cleared" by a receipt from the customer or a disbursement to the customer. The auditors also occasionally checked the supporting documentation for these entries such as canceled checks. During at least one audit of Hanauer, Goldberg's subordinates attempted to determine whether there were any discernible differences in the accounts that the client allowed to be confirmed and those which it did not. Apparently, the senior and staff auditors assigned to the engagement performed this latter procedure on their own initiative. However, either no such differences were discovered or, if they were, they were not documented in the workpapers.

At the completion of each Hanauer audit for the period 1978–1980, Goldberg authorized the issuance of an unqualified audit opinion on the brokerage firm's financial statements. Again, because Hanauer was a registered broker-dealer under the Securities Exchange Act of 1934, these financial statements were filed with the SEC.

Money Laundering
Allegations Leveled Against Hanauer

In the early 1980s, a series of articles in several major newspapers revealed that J. B. Hanauer & Co. was under investigation by the U.S. Attorney's office, a federal grand jury, the Internal Revenue Service (IRS), and the SEC. The allegations against the firm centered on charges that Hanauer was involved in a "money laundering" operation. According to published reports, many Hanauer customers purchased large blocks of bearer (coupon) bonds under fictitious names. These transactions were made on a cash basis and involved covert exchanges of large bundles of cash between Hanauer representatives and the customers at such locations as restaurants, bars, and airport parking lots.

Under the Currency and Foreign Transactions Reporting Act, brokers, banks, and other financial institutions must report cash transactions exceeding $10,000 to the IRS. Hanauer's employees often avoided this requirement for the large cash transactions with certain customers by entering these transactions in the accounting records on a piecemeal basis. For example, a $45,000 cash receipt might be entered in $9,000 "chunks" over a period of five days. Likewise, to prevent Hanauer's banks from reporting these transactions to the IRS, these large cash receipts were deposited in amounts of less than $10,000.

The cash basis of transacting business provided Hanauer salespeople with the opportunity to take unfair advantage of their customers, which they apparently did. In one case, the SEC reported that a Hanauer salesman collected nearly $70,000 from a customer in payment for a purchase of municipal bonds. However, the bonds had cost less than $60,000. The difference between the cash collected from the customer and the cost of the bonds was pocketed by the Hanauer salesman. To prevent customers from discovering that they had been defrauded, Hanauer's sales representatives would destroy the customer transaction confirmations. Because many of the municipal securities Hanauer bought and sold were infrequently traded, customers often could not obtain independent confirmations of the prices they were being charged for these securities.

The SEC's investigation also revealed that Hanauer's salespeople had not complied with the firm's internal control policies regarding the recording of customer account information. The SEC confirmed that many of the accounts involving the confidential cash transactions were recorded under fictitious names. Additionally, all required information was not obtained for certain of these accounts. For example, several accounts established under fictitious names did not have information on file regarding the customer's bank references, home and business addresses, and telephone numbers. The SEC pointed out that the failure of Hanauer to identify the actual customers with whom it was transacting business posed serious financial risks for the firm. For example, investors who had access to market price quotations could simply refuse to consummate a transaction if the market price of the securities they had purchased, but not yet paid for, dropped significantly in the first few days following the transaction.

JUDGMENT DAY FOR HANAUER AND GOLDBERG

In early 1982, Hanauer's executives settled several charges filed against the firm by the SEC. Eighteen of the company's employees and officers were sanctioned by the SEC, including two executive officers who were barred indefinitely from working in the brokerage industry. Four of these individuals were among those censured by the SEC in 1977. The brokerage firm was also ordered to pay to the United States Treasury an amount equal to the fraudulent overcharges on the large customer cash transactions. Among other penalties imposed on the firm were restrictions on future expansion and the forfeiture of profits for a four-month period on new customer accounts. Finally, the SEC required Hanauer to retain a new accounting firm and to establish internal controls that would prevent future violations of federal securities laws. In responding to published reports of the SEC settlement, Hanauer's president stated that a key factor in the firm's decision to settle the case was to avoid the costs of fighting the charges in court.

Two years following the settlement with the SEC, Hanauer pleaded guilty to criminal charges of failing to comply with the requirements of the Currency and Foreign Transactions Reporting Act. In responding to this settlement, Hanauer's president noted that the failure to report the large cash transactions was a result of clerical oversights and that the firm pleaded guilty to the criminal charges to avoid the costs of future litigation. In September 1983, the SEC sanctioned Stanley Goldberg for his role in the Hanauer case. The SEC charged that Goldberg should have recognized that there were material weaknesses in his client's internal controls. Additionally, the SEC maintained that Goldberg should have recognized that the client had imposed material scope limitations on the annual audits by not allowing many customer accounts to be confirmed. The SEC was particularly concerned that Goldberg had not instructed his subordinates to apply more extensive alternative audit procedures to those accounts that the client did not want confirmed. Finally, the SEC pointed out that Goldberg never inquired of his subordinates regarding how many confirmations were not mailed at the client's request or the collective dollar value of those accounts. Surprisingly, this information was not compiled in a summary format in the Hanauer audit workpapers.

QUESTIONS

1. Identify several internal control risks faced by a brokerage firm. What specific risks existed in the internal control structure of Hanauer? Were these risks properly considered and investigated during the internal control phase of each Hanauer audit?

2. Identify the audit objectives that Hanauer's auditors hoped to accomplish as a result of their account confirmation procedures. In your response, consider each of the four types of account balances.

3. What additional alternative audit procedures do you believe the Hanauer auditors should have used for those accounts that the client did not want confirmed?

4. Define a material audit scope limitation in general terms. Do you agree with the SEC that Hanauer's management imposed a material scope limitation on the firm's annual audits?

5. Should an audit client be allowed to "follow" its engagement audit partner to another accounting firm? Discuss the issues raised by auditor changes made for this purpose.

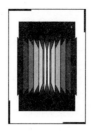

CASE 2.5
BERKSHIRE HATHAWAY, INC.

In 1983, GEICO, a large insurance company, announced plans to purchase several million shares of its outstanding common stock at a price of $60 per share. One of the largest stockholders of GEICO at the time was Berkshire Hathaway, Inc., an investment company. Executives of the two companies agreed that Berkshire would be allowed to tender approximately 350,000 of the shares it owned in GEICO so that the transaction could be treated as a proportionate redemption. In a proportionate redemption, the percentage equity interest of one company (the investor) in a second company (the investee) is maintained at the level that existed immediately prior to the redemption. For federal tax purposes, the total proceeds received by the investor company in a proportionate redemption are taxed as dividends by applying the effective intercorporate dividend tax rate, which was approximately 6.9 percent in 1983.

Berkshire also chose to treat the proceeds it received in the redemption of the GEICO stock as dividend income in its 1983 financial statements, a decision approved by Peat, Marwick, Mitchell & Company, Berkshire's audit firm. In 1984, another company in which Berkshire had a significant equity interest, General Foods, announced a stock buyback plan. Again, Berkshire was successful in structuring the sale of the stock to General Foods as a proportionate redemption, thus maintaining its percentage equity interest in that company at the level that existed prior to the buyback plan. Berkshire also opted to report the total proceeds received from General Foods as dividend income in its 1984 financial statements.

In late 1984, representatives of Peat Marwick contacted Berkshire executives and informed them that the proceeds of the General Foods stock redemption could not be treated as dividend income for financial reporting purposes. Instead, Peat Marwick maintained that the transaction had to be reported as a sale of stock with the difference between the selling price and cost shown as a capital gain on Berkshire's income statement. This latter treatment of the transaction with General Foods was less favorable for financial reporting purposes from the standpoint of Berkshire executives, since it did not allow the full amount of the proceeds received from General Foods to be treated as income.

Also upsetting to Berkshire executives was Peat Marwick's insistence that the investment company's 1983 financial statements be restated to reflect the GEICO stock redemption as a sale of stock rather than as a dividend distribution.

Warren Buffett, the chief executive officer of Berkshire Hathaway, discussed the GEICO and General Foods stock redemptions at length in his company's 1984 annual report.[1] Buffett was very vocal in disputing Peat Marwick's contention that the transactions should be treated as sales of stock and not as dividend distributions, and then explained why he eventually agreed to accept the audit firm's position:

> We disagree with [Peat Marwick's] position from both the viewpoint of economic substance and proper accounting. But, to avoid a qualified auditor's opinion, we have adopted Peat Marwick's 1984 view and restated 1983 accordingly. None of this, however, has any effect on intrinsic business value: our ownership interests in GEICO and General Foods, our cash, our taxes, and the market value and tax basis of our holdings all remain the same.[2]

The net effect of the change in the method used in accounting for the GEICO and General Foods transactions was an 8 percent reduction in Berkshire's 1984 net income and a 1 percent reduction in its 1983 net income after restatement.

In a *Wall Street Journal* article that disclosed the disagreement between Berkshire executives and Peat Marwick, the vice-chairman of Peat Marwick was asked to comment on the criticism of his firm by Buffett in Berkshire's 1984 annual report. The Peat Marwick vice-chairman simply noted, "It's the client's prerogative to disagree. Our report speaks for itself."[3] Another prerogative of an audit client is to change auditors. In 1985, Berkshire retained Touche Ross & Company to audit its financial statements. In the 8–K statement filed with the Securities and Exchange Commission to disclose the change in auditors, Berkshire reported that it was "dissatisfied" with the inconsistency of Peat Marwick regarding the proper accounting for the 1983 and 1984 stock redemptions.[4]

QUESTIONS

1. Warren Buffett invoked the substance-over-form rule to justify accounting for the GEICO and General Foods transactions as dividend distributions rather than as sales of stock. Buffett pointed out that the proportionate interest in those companies' undistributed earnings that had inured to Berkshire over the term it had owned stock in the two companies far exceeded the amount of funds Berkshire received in the stock redemptions. Buffett also observed that the

---

1. Warren Buffett gained control of Berkshire Hathaway in the mid-1960s and since that time has become recognized as one of the nation's shrewdest investors. Since Buffett assumed control of Berkshire, the investment company has realized an annual average rate of return on its stockholders' equity exceeding 20 percent. During that same time frame, Buffett has amassed a personal fortune estimated at nearly $2 billion.

2. 1984 Annual Report of Berkshire Hathaway Inc., 3.

3. L. Berton, "Billionaire Investor Loses Recent Battle with Auditor," *Wall Street Journal*, 26 April 1985, 18.

4. "Berkshire Hathaway Dismisses Its Auditor in Accounting Dispute," *Wall Street Journal*, 8 July 1985, 21.

Internal Revenue Service considers proportionate redemptions to be essentially equivalent to dividend distributions. Do you agree with Buffett that the substance of each of the proportionate redemptions was a dividend and not a sale of stock? Why or why not?

2. In deciding how to account for an unusual or unique transaction for financial reporting purposes, should one consider the position that the IRS has taken regarding the proper tax treatment of the transaction? Explain.

3. In 1983, Peat Marwick accepted Berkshire's decision to account for the GEICO transaction as a dividend distribution but then decided the following year that both the GEICO and General Foods transactions were, in fact, sales of stock. Did Peat Marwick have a right to change its position on the proper accounting for the stock redemptions? What factor or factors may have been responsible for Peat Marwick's decision to change its position regarding these transactions?

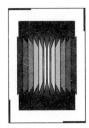

CASE 2.6

GIANT STORES CORPORATION

Following the end of World War II, large discount retail stores began appearing in the major cities of the northeastern United States and then quickly spread across the nation. Eventually, numerous mergers among discount retailers led to the formation of large retail chains that could offer even greater discounts to their customers because of the huge quantities in which they purchased goods and their ability to buy directly from manufacturers. These chains flourished for more than two decades with their low overhead cost structures and deep discount pricing strategies. By the early 1970s, though, many discount retailers began seeing their sales drop as the major department stores lured their customers away. Apparently, many customers of discount retailers became disenchanted with the no-frills marketing philosophy of those stores and began opting for the higher quality of products and better customer service available in department stores.

Giant Stores Corporation was one of the discount retailers that began experiencing financial problems in the early 1970s. Founded in 1959 and headquartered in Chelmsford, Massachusetts, Giant Stores realized dramatic sales growth during the 1960s and was operating 112 retail outlets by 1972. In that year, Giant Stores' executives were faced with a significant operating loss for the first time in the company's history. By manipulating the company's financial records, these executives converted a $2.5 million loss for 1972 into a $1.5 million profit and greatly enhanced key liquidity and activity ratios of Giant Stores. Eventually, four of the company's officials would be indicted for various fraud charges by a grand jury and would either plead guilty or be convicted of the charges in federal court.

ACCOUNTS PAYABLE IRREGULARITIES

One of the principal means the executives of Giant Stores used to misrepresent their company's financial condition was to understate, for financial reporting purposes, amounts owed to suppliers. Exhibit 1 summarizes the five major

EXHIBIT 1
Vendor Accounts
Payable Balances
Intentionally
Understated by Giant
Stores Executives

Vendor	Reduction in Accounts Payable Balance	Purported Reason for Reduction
Various	$300,000	Previously unrecorded advertising credits
Millbrook Distributors	257,000	Return of merchandise, volume discounts, and a concession to retain the Giant Stores account
Rozefsky, Inc.	130,000	Return of merchandise
Various (referred to as the Miller–Lesser credits by the SEC)	177,000	Overcharges on earlier invoices
HBA	162,000	Return of merchandise

fraudulent schemes that the four Giant Stores officials used to misrepresent the company's accounts payable for the fiscal year ending January 29, 1972. Also shown in Exhibit 1 are the dollar amounts that were involved in these schemes and the reasons given to Touche Ross, the audit firm of Giant Stores, for the adjustments used to distort the balances of individual payable accounts.

Advertising Credits

According to the results of an investigation by the Securities and Exchange Commission (SEC), the president and treasurer of Giant Stores ordered the head of the company's advertising department to fabricate at least $300,000 of fictitious advertising credits from suppliers (debits to accounts payable balances) for the fiscal year ending January 29, 1972. The advertising manager complied by preparing a fourteen-page memorandum listing alleged advertising credits extended to Giant Stores by approximately 1,100 of the company's suppliers. When questioned by Touche Ross auditors regarding the number and cumulative size of the advertising credits, client officials responded that the advertising department had simply been negligent in collecting the credits for several months.

To test the fourteen-page listing of advertising credits, Touche Ross mailed confirmations to four of the vendors included on the list and asked client personnel to provide supporting documentation for another twenty of the alleged credits. The SEC maintained that the audit procedures applied by Touche Ross to the advertising credits were inadequate for a number of reasons. First, the SEC alleged, the sample size of twenty-four items did not provide sufficient evidence to reach a conclusion regarding the material accuracy of the cumulative $300,000 in advertising credits. Second, Touche Ross reportedly failed to follow up on comments made by vendors who returned the accounts payable confirmations, comments suggesting that the purported credits were in error. Third, the SEC charged the auditors relied extensively on internal documentation to corroborate the additional twenty credits selected for testing from the detail listing. Given the suspicious nature and timing of the advertising credits, the SEC maintained that Touche Ross had a responsibility to obtain much more rigorous and extensive audit evidence to support the material accuracy of the client-prepared listing.

Millbrook Distributors

The chairman of the board of Giant Stores and the company's vice-president of finance produced twenty-eight fictitious credit memos to reduce the outstanding balance of Giant Stores' payable to Millbrook Distributors, a major supplier of health and beauty aids. When these memos came to the attention of Touche Ross, two staff auditors were eventually given three different explanations for the source of the credits. Originally, the staff auditors were told that the credits were for merchandise returns. Then they were told that the $257,000 debit to the Millbrook payable was a volume discount granted to Giant Stores. Finally, Giant's officers contended that the amount was a concession made by Millbrook to Giant Stores to induce the latter to retain Millbrook as a vendor. One of the staff auditors questioned the final explanation because the reduction in the payable seemed much too large a price for Millbrook to pay to retain Giant Stores as a customer, given the relatively modest volume of transactions between the two companies.[1]

Touche Ross personnel eventually requested that a top executive of Millbrook confirm the $257,000 concession supposedly granted to Giant Stores. In response to this request, Giant Stores' vice-president of finance placed a telephone call, in the presence of Touche Ross auditors, to an individual who was supposedly the president of Millbrook. After a short exchange, the vice-president handed the phone to one of the Touche Ross auditors. At this point, the individual on the other end of the line verbally confirmed the concession and agreed to send Touche Ross a written confirmation of the concession as well. A few days later, however, the vice-president of finance reported back to Touche Ross that the Millbrook president had changed his mind about signing the written confirmation. The individual was reportedly angry because the confirmation had not been delivered to him personally, as he had requested. At this point, the two staff auditors assigned to investigate the Millbrook credits wrote a memorandum, which they included in the Touche Ross workpapers, that questioned the validity of the credits. In spite of the position taken by the staff auditors, the partner in charge of the Giant Stores audit engagement subsequently decided that sufficient evidence had been collected to support the Millbrook credits and chose not to pursue the matter any further.

Rozefsky, Inc.

A $130,000 intentional understatement of the amount owed by Giant Stores to Rozefsky, Inc., another of the company's vendors, was accomplished by the posting of thirty-five false credit memos to the payable account of Rozefsky.[2] These credit memos were allegedly issued by this vendor for goods returned by

---

1. Giant Stores never contested the actual amount due Millbrook Distributors and eventually paid that amount, as well as the total amounts due other suppliers whose payable accounts were intentionally understated in Giant Stores' financial records.

2. The "credit" memos allegedly issued by Rozefsky were recorded as debits to that vendor's account in Giant Stores' accounts payable subsidiary ledger.

various retail outlets of Giant Stores. However, the SEC's subsequent investigation disclosed that many of these memos were issued to stores that did not even stock Rozefsky products. Additionally, the SEC discovered that the financial records of Rozefsky did not contain references to, or entries for, any of the thirty-five credit memos allegedly issued to Giant Stores. When a Touche Ross staff auditor was given copies of these credit memos, he noticed that a felt tip marker had been used to obscure a typed sentence on each of them. By holding the memos up to a light, he was able to read the obscured sentence: "Do not post until merchandise is received."[3] Ostensibly, this line informed a Giant Stores accounting clerk not to reduce the Rozefsky account balance for the invoiced goods until the cost of the goods was credited to the Rozefsky payable account. It would have appeared very suspicious if the debit for the alleged returned goods had been posted to the Rozefsky account prior to the goods' actually having been delivered and credited to the vendor's account.

After reviewing the credit memos, the Touche Ross staff auditor called an accounting officer of Rozefsky and inquired regarding the alleged merchandise returns. The Rozefsky official reported that none of the goods had been returned by Giant Stores. The staff auditor then informed the Touche Ross audit engagement partner of the memos and his conversation with the vendor. When apprised of the situation by the audit partner, Giant Stores' vice-president of finance responded that he had spoken with the Rozefsky official shortly after the staff auditor had contacted that individual. According to the vice-president of finance, the Rozefsky official indicated that the staff auditor had misinterpreted their conversation regarding the memos and then asserted that the memos actually were for returned goods. However, the vice-president insisted that the audit partner not contact the Rozefsky official to discuss the matter any further because of "pending litigation" between the two companies. Eventually, the audit partner accepted the client's explanation for the credit memos when he requested and received confirmation letters corroborating the merchandise returns from the managers of the Giant Stores who allegedly ordered and then returned the merchandise in question to Rozefsky.

Miller-Lesser Overcharges

Executives of Giant Stores pressured the merchandise managers (a Mr. Miller and a Mr. Lesser) of two of the company's largest departments to prepare a list of several hundred fictitious merchandise purchases on which Giant Stores had been supposedly overcharged by suppliers. These overcharges totaled approximately $177,000. Touche Ross's principal audit procedure for investigating these overcharges involved selecting random line items from the client-prepared list and then confirming the overcharges via telephone calls to the vendors.

> The procedure used in soliciting the fifteen telephone confirmations allowed Giant to communicate with the vendor first and to inform the vendor that Touche Ross would be calling them. Giant then placed a second call to reexplain the nature of the Touche Ross inquiry, after which the telephone was handed to the Touche Ross auditor. Only

---

3. This and all subsequent quotations are taken from Securities and Exchange Commission, *Accounting Series Release No. 153A*, 27 June 1979.

then was the Touche Ross auditor permitted to speak over the telephone to the vendor.

The results of this confirmation procedure and limited other audit tests apparently persuaded Touche Ross to accept the overcharges as valid reductions to the various payable accounts. The subsequent SEC investigation disclosed that, under similar circumstances, three suppliers of Giant Stores provided false confirmations to Touche Ross of credits allegedly due the company after apparently being convinced to do so by Giant Stores executives. Possibly, the confirmation tests applied to the Miller-Lesser overcharges were victimized by the same subterfuge.

HBA Credits

A final deliberate understatement of accounts payable involved a number of credit memos that Giant Stores recorded as a result of presumably returning $162,000 of health and beauty aid (HBA) products to manufacturers. Again, apparently none of these merchandise returns ever occurred. As in the case of the other fictitious entries to Giant Stores' accounts payable, the SEC criticized Touche Ross for failing to adequately investigate these items.

ADDITIONAL SEC CRITICISM OF THE 1972 TOUCHE ROSS AUDIT OF GIANT STORES

In addition to the specific charges that Touche Ross failed to thoroughly investigate the five major accounts payable irregularities perpetrated by Giant Stores, the SEC leveled a number of more general criticisms at the audit firm for its conduct during the 1972 Giant Stores audit. Of particular concern to the SEC was the extent of pressure that Touche Ross allowed Giant Stores executives to impose on members of the audit engagement team: "The audit was conducted under stressful conditions including a request from Giant to Touche Ross to fire [the audit engagement partner], a Giant executive's threat to throw one staff auditor off the premises and profane verbal abuse of a staff auditor from another Giant executive." At one point in the audit, the bullying tactics of the Giant Stores executives and the suspicious nature of many of the large year-end adjustments to accounts payable led one Touche Ross staff auditor to suggest that the client's officers were engaging in, and attempting to cover up, an accounting fraud. Unfortunately, the audit engagement partner chose to ignore the speculation of the staff auditor.

The SEC also contended that the Touche Ross audit engagement partner and a second partner who assisted in completing the audit were overly willing to compromise with client personnel on important technical disputes. According to the SEC, certain audit judgments were "arrived at through a trade-off and bargaining process not conducive to appropriate audit decisions." This bargaining process was particularly evident during a meeting between the two Touche Ross audit partners and Giant Stores executives that took place in April 1972, shortly before the completion of the audit. The purpose of this meeting was to determine the final disposition of several questionable items discovered during the course of the audit by the Touche Ross auditors. It was reported that "during this meeting, Giant personnel continuously calculated earnings per share on a pocket calculator. When the calculations reached Giant's reduced target earnings of $.83 per share, Giant ceased to be contentious."

COLLAPSE OF GIANT STORES

Giant Stores filed its annual form 10-K registration statement for the fiscal year ended January 29, 1972, with the SEC on April 28, 1972. Included in that 10-K was an unqualified audit opinion issued by Touche Ross on the Giant Stores financial statements. These same financial statements and the accompanying audit opinion were contained in a registration statement filed by Giant Stores with the SEC in August 1972, a registration statement used by the company to sell approximately $3 million of common stock. In addition, the financial statements were used to obtain $12 million in additional debt capital. In an April 1973 press release, the president of Giant Stores disclosed that the company had discovered potential bookkeeping errors that might affect the reported profits of the company for the prior year. Approximately one month later, Touche Ross withdrew the unqualified opinion it had issued the prior April on Giant Stores' financial statements for the fiscal year ended January 29, 1972. In August 1973, Giant Stores filed a bankruptcy petition with a federal district court in Boston and was eventually declared insolvent by that court approximately two years later.

The former president and vice-president of finance of Giant Stores were convicted in 1978 of conspiracy to file false financial statements with the SEC. Prior to those convictions, the former chairman and treasurer of Giant Stores pleaded guilty to similar charges. Each of the four individuals was fined and given jail terms ranging from six to eighteen months.

The SEC issued its final report on its lengthy investigation of the Giant Stores fraud in June 1979. As a result of that investigation, the SEC censured Touche Ross and prohibited the Giant Stores audit engagement partner from practicing before the federal agency for five months. The SEC also required Touche Ross to undergo an extensive review of its operating procedures by a panel of independent experts. Shown in Exhibit 2 are the specific Touche Ross operating procedures that the SEC required the independent panel to review.

QUESTIONS

1. In auditing accounts payable, which of the five management assertions identified by *Statement on Auditing Standards No. 31*, "Evidential Matter," is of primary concern to the auditor? Why?

2. The search for unrecorded liabilities is a common substantive test used at year-end to obtain evidence regarding the material accuracy of a client's current liabilities. Briefly explain the nature of the search for unrecorded liabilities and how this audit procedure might have resulted in the detection of the accounts payable understatement in Giant Stores' financial records.

1. Hiring practices for all professionals (partners and employees).
2. Training and continuing education of all professionals.
3. Promotion and compensation of all professionals.
4. Acceptance and retention of clients.
5. Setting and recovering audit engagement fees.
6. Allocation of professional responsibilities within the firm.
7. Professional staffing of offices.
8. Methods of maintaining professional independence.
9. Conduct of audit engagements.
    a. professional staffing and allocation of responsibilities.
    b. audit program and workpaper preparation and review.
    c. inter-office communications in the case of multi-office engagements.
    d. identification and resolution of problems during the course of the audit.
    e. independence.
    f. review of engagements.
    g. availability and application of industry expertise.
10. Formulating and communicating firm practices, procedures, and policies to professionals.
11. Procedures for creating and implementing quality controls.
12. Criteria and procedures followed in connection with analysis of potential merger or combination of practice candidates and with absorption of an acquired practice into that of Touche Ross.
13. Adequacy of corrective measures.

EXHIBIT 2
Touche Ross Operating Procedures that the SEC Required an Independent Panel to Review

3. Develop a statistical sampling plan that Touche Ross could have employed to test the material accuracy of the $300,000 total of the fourteen-page listing of purported advertising credits.

4. Discuss the validity of audit evidence collected via telephone confirmations. Under what general conditions is it permissible for auditors to accept telephone confirmations?

5. How does the nature of written accounts payable confirmation procedures differ from written accounts receivable confirmation procedures? Comment on both technical differences and differences in audit objectives between the two audit tests.

6. During the 1972 audit of Giant Stores, differences of opinion arose between the staff auditors assigned to that engagement and the partner in charge of the engagement regarding the material accuracy of certain of the client's outstanding payables. How should such differences of opinion between members of an audit engagement team be resolved? Was it appropriate for the staff auditors to include a memorandum in the audit workpapers that questioned the validity of the disputed payables?

CASE 2.7
HOWARD STREET JEWELERS, INC.

Lore Levi was worried as she sat and scanned the March 1983 bank statement for the Howard Street Jewelers.[1] For more than four decades, she and her husband, Julius, had owned and operated the small business. Certainly the business had experienced ups and downs before, but now, it seemed to be in a downward spiral from which it could not recover. In previous times when sales had slackened, the Levis had survived by cutting costs here and there. Now, however, despite several measures the Levis had taken to control costs, the cash position of the business continued to worsen steadily. If a turnaround did not occur soon, Mrs. Levi feared that she and her husband might be forced to sell or close their store.

Mrs. Levi had a theory regarding the financial problems of Howard Street Jewelers. On more than one occasion, she had wondered whether Betty the cashier, a trusted and reliable employee for nearly twenty years, might be stealing from the cash register. To Mrs. Levi, it was a logical assumption. Besides working as a part-time salesclerk, Betty handled all of the cash that came into the business and was also responsible for maintaining the cash receipts and sales records. If anybody had an opportunity to steal from the business, it was Betty.

Reluctantly, Mrs. Levi approached her husband about her theory. Mrs. Levi pointed out to Julius that Betty had unrestricted access to the cash receipts of the business. Additionally, over the previous few years, Betty had developed a taste for more expensive clothes and was taking more frequent and costly vacations than she had in the past. Julius paid little heed to his wife's speculation regarding Betty. To him, it was preposterous to even consider the possibility that Betty

---

1. Most of the facts of this case were reconstructed from information included in several legal opinions. Additional sources were the following two articles: *Securities Regulation and Law Report*, "Accounting & Disclosure: Accounting Briefs," Vol. 23, No. 21 (24 May 1991), 814; *Securities Regulation and Law Report*, "Accounting & Disclosure: Accounting Briefs," Vol. 24, No. 19 (8 May 1992), 708.

could be stealing from the business. Shortly thereafter, Mrs. Levi raised the subject with her son, Alvin, who worked side by side with his parents in the family business. Alvin responded similarly to his father and warned his mother that she was becoming paranoid.

Near the end of each year, the Levis met with their accountant to discuss various matters, principally taxation issues. The Levis placed a great deal of trust in the CPA who served as their accountant; for almost forty years he had given them good, professional advice on a wide range of accounting and business matters. It was only natural for Mrs. Levi to confide in the accountant about her suspicions regarding Betty the cashier. The accountant listened intently to Mrs. Levi and then commented that he had noticed occasional shortages in the cash receipts records that were larger than normal for a small retail business. Despite Julius's protestations that Betty could not be responsible for any cash shortages, the accountant encouraged the Levis to monitor the work of the cashier as closely as possible.

Embezzlements are typically discovered by luck rather than by design. So it was with the Howard Street Jewelers. In the spring of 1985, a customer approached the cash register and informed Alvin Levi that she wanted to make a payment on a layaway item. Alvin, who was working the cash register because it was Betty's day off, searched the file of layaway sales tickets and the daily sales records but was unable to find any trace of the customer's layaway purchase. Finally, he apologized and asked the customer to return the next day when Betty would be back at work.

The following day, Alvin informed Betty of his inability to find the layaway sales ticket. Betty expressed surprise and said she would search for the ticket herself. Within a few minutes, Betty approached Alvin, waving the layaway sales ticket in her hand. Alvin was stumped. He had searched the layaway sales file several times and simply could not accept Betty's explanation that the missing ticket had been there all along. Suspicious, as well, was the fact that the sale had not been recorded in the sales records—a simple oversight, Betty had explained. As Alvin walked away and returned to his work, a troubling and sickening sensation settled into the pit of his stomach. Over the next several weeks, as Alvin closely monitored the sales and cash receipts records, it became apparent that his mother had been right all along. Betty, the trusted, reliable, longtime cashier of the Howard Street Jewelers, was stealing from the business. The embezzlement loss suffered by Howard Street Jewelers over the term of Betty's employment was eventually estimated to be $350,000.

QUESTIONS

1. What internal control concepts did the Levis overlook or ignore? Explain.

2. When Mrs. Levi informed the CPA of her suspicions regarding Betty, what responsibilities, if any, did the CPA have to pursue this matter? In addition to preparing tax returns for the Howard Street Jewelers, alternately assume that the CPA: (a) was retained to provide an annual audit, (b) was retained to review the business's annual financial statements, and (c) was retained to compile the business's annual financial statements.

3. Assume that you have a small CPA firm and have been contacted by a husband and wife, Margie and Lou Ward, who are in the final stages of negotiating to purchase a local jewelry store. Lou will prepare jewelry settings, size jewelry for customers, and perform related tasks, while Margie will be the head salesclerk. The Wards intend to retain four of the current employees of the jewelry store—two salesclerks, a cashier, and a college student who cleans the store, runs errands, and does various other odd jobs. They inform you that the average inventory of the jewelry store is $100,000 and average annual sales are $400,000, 30 percent of which occur in the six weeks prior to Christmas.

The Wards are interested in retaining you as their accountant should they purchase the store. They know little about accounting and have no prior experience as business owners. They would require assistance in establishing an accounting system, monthly financial statements for internal use, annual financial statements to be submitted to their banker, and all necessary tax returns. Margie and Lou are particularly concerned with control issues, given the dollar value of inventory that will be continually on hand in the store and the significant amount of cash that will be processed daily.

You see this as an excellent opportunity to acquire a good client. However, you have not had a chance to prepare for your meeting with the Wards because they came in without an appointment. You do not want to ask them to come back later, since that may encourage them to check out your competitor across the street.

Required: Provide the Wards with an overview of the key internal control issues they will face in operating a jewelry store. In your overview, identify at least five specific internal control procedures that you believe they should implement if they acquire the store. You have never had a jewelry store as a client but you have several small retail clients. Attempt to impress the Wards with your understanding of internal control issues for small retail businesses.

CASE 2.8

E. F. HUTTON & COMPANY, INC.

Edward F. Hutton was born into a poor family in New York City in 1876. Fatherless at the age of ten and lacking a high school education, Hutton drifted from one job to another in New York City's financial district until his mid-twenties. When Hutton was twenty-seven, his personal fortunes took a turn for the better after he married the daughter of a well-to-do broker. With the financial backing of his father-in-law, Hutton founded a small brokerage firm, E. F. Hutton & Company, Inc., in 1904. Ever the opportunist, Hutton recognized the growth potential for his industry in California and opened a San Francisco office of his firm in 1905, becoming the first brokerage house with operations on both coasts and the first to have a private telegraph wire connecting New York City and San Francisco. With this communications link, Hutton's firm had the ability to complete bi-coastal securities transactions in a matter of three minutes.

Ironically, the devastating San Francisco earthquake of 1906 was largely responsible for the eventual financial success of E. F. Hutton & Company. Hutton's direct telegraph line to New York City was one of the few, and possibly the only, communication linkages to the East Coast immediately following the 1906 quake. Because no other brokerage firm on Wall Street was aware of the earthquake for several hours, the Hutton firm was able to use that short period of time to pile up significant trading profits for itself and its customers. Such ingenuity was cultivated and rewarded at E. F. Hutton & Company over its entire existence. Top management was disdainful of bureaucratic policies, centralized decision making, and organizational charts, all of which they believed stifled employee creativity. Instead, Hutton employees were encouraged to exercise their own judgment and to be innovative, particularly when it came to increasing the profitability of the brokerage firm.

E. F. Hutton & Company grew and prospered over the first three-quarters of the twentieth century. By the 1970s, Hutton was the second largest brokerage firm in the nation and had the industry's highest return on stockholders' equity. Unfortunately, the laissez-faire management style that contributed significantly to Hutton's success ultimately proved to be the firm's downfall. In the spring of 1985, the brokerage firm pleaded guilty to 2,000 counts of mail and wire fraud filed against it by the U.S. Justice Department. The fallout from this scandal eventually drove Hutton to the brink of insolvency before it was bought out in 1988 by Shearson Lehman Brothers, one of its major competitors.

The mail and wire fraud charges filed against Hutton were the culmination of an intensive, two-year investigation by the Justice Department. Hutton was charged with defrauding numerous banks with which it did business by maintaining a complex cash management system that allowed the firm to run huge negative balances in its operating bank accounts. These enormous cash overdrafts were essentially interest-free loans from Hutton's banks. The banks extending these "loans" either failed to uncover Hutton's scheme or were coerced into ignoring it by Hutton officials. In any case, the cash overdrafts allowed Hutton's branch managers to earn abnormally large amounts of interest profits, 10 percent of which went directly to the managers in the form of an annual bonus.

The disclosure of the Hutton scheme and the firm's subsequent guilty plea shocked the nation's financial community and the federal government. Justice Department officials alleged that Hutton's cash management practices, if used by a large number of corporations, would have threatened the nation's entire banking system, a conclusion that prompted a lengthy investigation of the Hutton scandal by the Subcommittee on Crime of the U.S. House of Representatives Committee on the Judiciary. Exactly who was responsible for the massive Hutton fraud and how it went undetected for so long were the key questions addressed by the subcommittee. Of particular interest to Congress was the failure of the Justice Department to indict any individual officer or employee of Hutton on fraud charges. Instead, the plea bargain agreement with the Justice Department simply allowed Hutton, as a firm, to plead guilty to the fraud charges and pay millions of dollars in restitution to the affected banks, as well as a multimillion-dollar fine.

The Subcommittee on Crime was frustrated repeatedly in its efforts to determine which Hutton officer or branch manager was responsible for conceiving the abusive cash management practices. The free-spirited corporate culture and loosely organized structure of the huge brokerage firm made it impossible to pinpoint responsibility for the fraud. Consequently, the objective of the congressional inquiry gradually evolved from determining who was responsible for the fraudulent scheme to determining the parties who were aware of the scheme yet failed to notify federal authorities. Eventually, the focus of the investigation settled on Hutton's independent auditors, Arthur Andersen & Company. Evidence presented before the investigative subcommittee demonstrated that Arthur Andersen auditors had questioned the legality of Hutton's cash management scheme years before the Justice Department began its probe. The subcommittee's subsequent grilling of Arthur Andersen representatives was intended to determine why the audit firm failed to take affirmative steps to convince Hutton officials to discontinue the fraudulent cash management methods.

Overview of Hutton's Cash Management System

Cash management became a popular topic in the 1970s in corporate boardrooms and MBA programs. During that decade, corporate managers came to realize that electronic technology provided them with the means to manage cash balances efficiently and profitably. Cash management models, similar to the economic order quantity model for investments in inventory, became widely used by corporations that had millions or even hundreds of millions of dollars flowing through their operating bank accounts daily. A key component of these models was the management of bank float, the amount of funds that a given entity has at any point in time in outstanding checks and in-transit deposits. A company benefits by decreasing the amount of bank float for its in-transit deposits and by lengthening the time required for its disbursement checks to work their way through the banking system.

In the mid-1970s, many firms in the cash-intensive brokerage industry began formalizing their cash management practices. For instance, to facilitate the timely clearing of customers' checks, brokerage firms opened bank accounts in the communities in which their retail offices were located. Conversely, to delay the clearing of their checks, brokerage firms established disbursement accounts in banks far removed from their retail offices. In fact, a consulting company specializing in cash management developed and marketed an optical scanning device that read zip codes on vendor invoices and then determined which disbursement bank of a given company would maximize the amount of time required for the payment on the invoice to clear the banking system.

Most cash management methods, including those just described, are clearly legal. However, innovative companies, such as E. F. Hutton, soon developed methods that abused the banking system. In the early 1980s, Bank of America discovered that its electronic processing equipment was rejecting a disproportionately large percentage of Hutton's checks. On average, Bank of America experienced a 1 percent rejection rate for checks processed by its electronic equipment, but the rate for Hutton's checks was nearly 50 percent. The rejection of a check by a bank's electronic scanning equipment forces bank personnel to process the check manually, thus adding, often significantly, to the amount of time required for the check to clear. Methods that can be used to cause a check to be rejected for automatic processing include tampering with the microencoding line (such as stapling the check at that point), bending the corners, and smearing a small quantity of a foreign substance on the check's surface (petroleum jelly is apparently the foreign substance of choice among tamperers). When the check-clearing problem at Bank of America was brought to the attention of Hutton executives, it was quickly resolved to the satisfaction of Bank of America and no criminal or civil actions were brought against Hutton as a result.

The Justice Department's investigation of Hutton's cash management practices focused principally on the brokerage firm's drawdown system. This system, originally developed with the cooperation and participation of several of Hutton's banks, allowed the firm to minimize its cash balances in noninterest-paying collection accounts maintained in communities in which Hutton's retail offices were located. Through a complex equation, each retail office of Hutton would estimate by 1 P.M. of each business day the dollar value of customer remittances that would be available by the end of that day in its local collection account. These funds would then be transferred by wire out of the collection account and into an interest-bearing regional clearing account.

Gradually, over a several-year period, many of Hutton's branch managers began abusing the drawdown system. Because the managers were paid 10 percent of the interest profits of their branch as a year-end bonus, they had an incentive to draw down excessive amounts in the local collection accounts. For instance, in one case, Hutton's drawdown equation indicated that $70,000 would be available for withdrawal at the end of a certain branch's business day. Instead of transferring out that amount, the branch manager transferred approximately $7 million to his regional clearing account. This practice resulted in huge cash overdrafts in the local Hutton bank accounts—overdrafts that in certain cases exceeded the entire capital of the affected banks.

Why banks would allow Hutton to continually overdraw their operating cash accounts was one of the key questions posed by the congressional subcommittee. First, Hutton apparently used the overdrafting scheme on a recurring basis only with its smaller banks, principally the banks that serviced Hutton's small to moderately sized retail offices. Second, although there were numerous cases of enormous overdrafts, most Hutton branch managers using the scheme were much more conservative. Finally, congressional testimony suggests that certain of the banks that were being abused by Hutton treated the cash overdrafts as a cost of doing business with the huge brokerage firm. Nevertheless, the investigation of the Justice Department disclosed that many of the affected banks were not aware that they were the victims of a concerted, systematic effort on the part of Hutton managers to obtain interest-free funds on an essentially permanent basis. It was this conclusion that resulted in the fraud charges being filed against Hutton. In fact, when the Hutton scheme was exposed, many of its banks immediately demanded restitution.[1]

Even though the overdrafts at the branch level were typically quite modest, when accumulated for all of Hutton's branches, the total was a staggering One-half billion dollars by the end of 1983. The collective impact of Hutton's cash management practices on its income statement was also dramatic. In 1981, interest profits accounted for almost three-fourths of the net income of the firm's retail brokerage division, an abnormally high percentage for the brokerage industry.

ARTHUR ANDERSEN'S INVOLVEMENT IN HUTTON'S CASH MANAGEMENT PRACTICES

Arthur Andersen was criticized for its role in the Hutton scandal by the business press and by several parties that testified before the congressional subcommittee investigating that scandal. Representative William Hughes, in remarks directed to Arthur Andersen officials appearing before the subcommittee, pointed out that the top executives of Hutton believed that Arthur Andersen had a responsibility to apprise them personally of the cash overdrafts: "Management at E. F. Hutton suggest that you were the culprits . . . that these practices weren't

---

1. The Justice Department also discovered that Hutton engaged in practices known as "chaining" and "crisscrossing" to create bank float. These methods, like the drawdown system, were used to manufacture large, short-term, interest-free loans for the brokerage firm. For a discussion of these methods, see B. Donnelly, "Cash Management: Where Do You Draw the Line?" *Institutional Investor*, September 1985, 69–79.

brought to their attention."[2] In fact, Arthur Andersen auditors did discover the overdrafts and questioned Hutton officials regarding their legality.

Exhibit 1 contains a memo included in Arthur Andersen's 1979 audit workpapers that describes a meeting between Arthur Andersen personnel and Hutton officials in which the brokerage firm's cash management practices were discussed. During that meeting, Joel Miller, the engagement audit partner, requested that Tom Rae, a Hutton executive vice-president responsible for legal affairs, provide Arthur Andersen with a written opinion affirming that Hutton's drawdown system was legal. Rae refused to provide such an opinion, maintaining that the system was obviously legal. Rae contended that Hutton's banks were fully aware of the drawdown system (a contention that proved to be untrue) and that Hutton's ability to pay any overdrafts precluded them from being illegal. This ability to pay, or "means," argument was used repeatedly by Hutton officials, particularly Rae, in responding to questions posed by Arthur Andersen auditors regarding the legality of the drawdown system.

The party testifying before the congressional subcommittee who was most critical of Arthur Andersen was Abraham Briloff, an accounting professor at Baruch College, City University of New York. Briloff castigated Arthur Andersen for failing to pursue the overdrafting problem once it was uncovered.

> Where has Arthur Andersen failed? . . . At the outset and most importantly, they failed to follow through on what they absolutely saw and understood, as early as 1980, as to what was going on. They questioned counsel, and counsel said, "Go away, we're too busy to respond." It is my view that had AA *really* fulfilled its responsibilities under the circumstances, the money-management excesses would have been stopped dead no later than 1980 or 1981.

Briloff was particularly alarmed that Arthur Andersen personnel assigned to the Hutton audit apparently failed to discuss the legality of the cash management practices with other parties following the meeting described in the workpaper memo reproduced in Exhibit 1.

> Note the concluding paragraphs of AA's March 7, 1980, memorandum in which the firm agreed to undertake some "homework." Note that it was going to inquire of its banking partners regarding prevailing practice. Did AA fulfill that assignment? If so, what contemporaneous documents are in its files describing its pursuits, and the results therefrom? If it was to turn out that AA did nothing to verify the glib responses from the Hutton people, then I maintain that the firm has failed to follow through in a most material respect . . . [Arthur Andersen was] extremely naive if they accepted as the last word the word of house counsel who was there to protect his own neck, his own turf.

Briloff maintained that Arthur Andersen, at the very least, had a responsibility to obtain an independent legal opinion regarding the legality of Hutton's cash management practices. Representatives of Arthur Andersen subsequently disputed Briloff's contention before the congressional subcommittee.

In fact, Arthur Andersen did not complete the follow-up procedures discussed in the 1980 memo. To explain why these procedures were not completed, Joel

---

2. This and all subsequent quotations were taken from U.S. Congress, House, Committee on the Judiciary, *E. F. Hutton Mail and Wire Fraud Case, Part 2* (Washington, D.C.: U.S. Government Printing Office, 1986).

EXHIBIT 1
Arthur Andersen
Workpaper Memo
Regarding E. F. Hutton's
Cash Management
Practices—1979 Audit

NEW YORK OFFICE
MARCH 7, 1980

MEMORANDUM FOR THE FILES

RE: E.F. HUTTON MONEY MANAGEMENT PROCEDURES

On March 5, 1980, representatives of AA & Co. and E. F. Hutton met to discuss the client's procedures in the area of "money management." Present in attendance were Joel Miller, Louis Lynn, Pat Gallagher, John Tesoro and Ted Chambers of AA & Co. and Thomas Rae, Michael Casteliano and Larry Volpe of E. F. Hutton. The purpose of the meeting was to obtain a greater understanding of the client's cash management procedures, whereby efforts are made by the firm to pay down bank loans and, thus, reduce interest expense. In addition, the meeting was also intended to discuss the company procedure of writing checks even though the balance per books is zero or negative. This is particularly relevant in light of the recent TI Industries lawsuit where the firm was found criminally at fault for writing checks in excess of book and bank balances.

Bill Sullivan explained Hutton's procedure with eleven different banks (client is presently exploring the possibility of using five more banks) where checks are drawn on these banks even though the balance per book would not cover the amount of the checks. Mr. Sullivan pointed out that in each of these banks Hutton has deposited funds which, even though they are legally segregated and cannot be used by the bank to cover shortages in Hutton's general account, are treated as "offsets" by the banks under a "global approach" which allows Hutton to overdraw its balances. In addition, Hutton has put up as collateral available customer securities to "cover" the various banks' uncollected funds. These funds result in deposits made by Hutton via check which have not cleared (normal clearing period is one day).

Similarly, the company also has a "check payable" or "zero balance" checking agreement with the Bank of America for payment to vendors and for issuing dividend payments to customers. Under this agreement, the Company writes checks overdrawing book balances, but maintains a zero or small deposit balance with the bank. This procedure is possible, according to William Sullivan, because the bank, each business day at 1 P.M., notifies the Company as to the required federal funds deposit to cover checks clearing the bank that day. The bank does not require any collateral for this particular arrangement.

The client maintains that the key to engaging in such transactions is that Hutton has the "means" to make ultimate payment. In other words, in the normal course of business the settlement of transactions will result in actual cash balances being deposited in the banks and, as a result, the balances per bank are rarely, if ever, overdrawn. Mr. Rae stated that the fact Hutton has the "means" to pay, precludes any possible illegalities in processing these transactions. Mr. Sullivan further pointed out that Hutton has always been "above board" in its dealings with the banks and that the banks are fully aware of the nature of these transactions (i.e., drawing checks on the account even though Hutton's records do not reflect a book cash balance large enough to cover the check at the time it is drawn). He also stated that several banks (Chase Manhattan, for example) have requested Hutton actually increase the scope of these activities.

After the discussion of the procedures employed and their legality, Joel Miller, AA & Co. engagement partner, requested that Tom Rae render a written legal opinion stating that Hutton's activities in this area don't present any potential legal problems. Mr. Rae declined to render such an opinion, stating that the banks are fully cognizant of Hutton's procedures, that this is an accepted banking practice and that there is no question as to the propriety of such transactions, again making reference to the "means of payment" principle. After Tom Rae declined to issue an opinion on this matter, Bill Sullivan offered to call one of the banks Hutton uses, Morgan Guaranty, and ask them what the banks would do if a company were to issue checks with no book balances. Joel Miller then stated that he would discuss the matter with other partners at AA & Co. whose clients include major money center banks to ascertain what the banks' point of view is regarding these transactions.

Louis T. Lynn

John Tesoro

Miller, the Hutton engagement audit partner, was called to testify before the subcommittee.

CONGRESSMAN HUGHES: Mr. Miller, what did you do after the meeting that took place on March 7, to check the accuracy of what was related to you?

MR. MILLER: Well, after the meeting, sir, I reflected on the entire meeting; the fact that I had a hundred bank confirmations with no exceptions noted . . . the fact that I found no evidence of checks bouncing, I found no unusual fees being charged by the banks to Hutton . . .

CONGRESSMAN HUGHES: That's not my question. My question is: what did you do after the meeting? Because, frankly, to your credit, you did see that there were some problems . . . Did you ever get to the banks' point of view on the system?

MR. MILLER: No, sir.

CONGRESSMAN HUGHES: Well, here's what you say, "Joel Miller then stated that he would discuss the matter with other partners of AA & Co. whose clients include major money-center banks, to ascertain what the banks' point of view is regarding these transactions."

MR. MILLER: Sir, I had a hundred confirmations from the banks. When I got back to my office and reflected on the entire meeting, I concluded that none of the banks had notified me of any problems—

CONGRESSMAN HUGHES: So you didn't follow through.

MR. MILLER: Well, I followed through in that I reflected on the entire problem and I concluded I would stick by the opinion that I believe Mr. Rae gave me.

The congressional testimony also indicates that Arthur Andersen raised the overdrafting issue with Hutton's audit committee. However, Briloff pointed out that the three-member Hutton audit committee was ineffectual. The audit committee was made up of three individuals, one of whom was actress Dina Merrill, granddaughter of Edward F. Hutton, who had little understanding or appreciation of complex accounting or auditing issues. Two business journalists who wrote a definitive history of the downfall of E. F. Hutton noted that top management recognized that "the audit committee was something of a joke"[3] and that it met at most only once or twice per year.

The lack of a strong audit committee was simply further evidence of what Representative Romano Mazzoli described as an environment of "plausible deniability" that Hutton's top management had created to insulate themselves from charges that they were responsible for the malfeasance of subordinates.

> We have fixed our posteriors to these chairs, now, for weeks in a row, and the only thing we're getting out of witnesses is "Well, don't look at me, look at the other guy. You know, I didn't know, I didn't ask a question, I didn't hear it, I wasn't there when it happened." Everything is built on plausible deniability—construct the situation, the scenario, so everybody can deny they were a part of it, and yet the thing goes on merrily down the road. And nobody but nobody is ever involved.

Briloff argued that this laxity in the control environment at Hutton made it incumbent on Arthur Andersen auditors to take their concerns regarding the

3. D. S. Carpenter and J. Feloni, *The Fall of the House of Hutton* (New York: Harper & Row, 1989), 117.

aggressive cash management practices of Hutton to the top level of the corporate hierarchy. By doing so, Arthur Andersen would have forced Hutton's top management to either eliminate the fraudulent practices or go on record in defense of them.

A final issue that Arthur Andersen representatives were questioned about involved the disclosure of the cash overdrafts in Hutton's financial statements. Briloff and Representative Hughes, the chairman of the congressional sub-committee, maintained that Hutton's financial statement disclosure of the over-drafts was inadequate. Exhibit 2 contains a memo included in Arthur Andersen's 1981 workpapers that addresses Hutton's cash management system. That memo discusses the fact that Hutton's cash management practices had been questioned by regulatory authorities. The last paragraph of the memo also discusses Arthur Andersen's rationale for the disclosure options selected for the cash overdrafts. Arthur Andersen agreed with Hutton management that "Drafts & Checks Payable" was a sufficiently descriptive caption for the overdrafts on Hutton's balance sheet and that no contingent liability disclosures for the overdrafts were necessary under *FASB Statement No. 5*, "Accounting for Contingencies."

Contrary to Arthur Andersen's position, Briloff maintained that the overdrafts should have been listed explicitly as "Cash Overdrafts" in the balance sheet and that Hutton's footnotes should have disclosed that these overdrafts were a source of interest-free loans for Hutton. In addition, Briloff contended that Hutton's footnotes should have disclosed the critical fact that customers' securities were being used as collateral for the overdrafts.[4] Representative Hughes was also concerned that third parties reading Hutton's financial statements were misled regarding the overdrafts.

> I'm not sure that I would be put on notice as to what was taking place by reading "drafts and checks payable." If you [addressing Arthur Andersen personnel] had described it as "overdrafts" I would know. The average person knows what an overdraft is. I don't think that you have fairly and honestly provided the information that would be needed for somebody reading that to understand what was going on.

Representative Hughes was also dismayed by the failure of Hutton's financial statements to disclose the ongoing Justice Department investigation from 1982 through 1984. Exhibit 3 contains the contingent liabilities footnote included in Hutton's 1984 financial statements. These financial statements were released approximately one month prior to the date Hutton pleaded guilty to the 2,000 counts of mail and wire fraud. The plea bargain agreement obligated the brokerage firm to pay millions of dollars in fines and restitution to the victimized banks. Hughes questioned Briloff regarding the adequacy of the footnote disclosure shown in Exhibit 3.

CONGRESSMAN HUGHES: In your opinion, was this disclosure adequate, given that it was a little more than a month before Hutton pleaded guilty to 2,000 counts of mail and wire fraud, that obviously, at this time, Andersen was on notice of the ongoing grand jury investigation, and, in fact, had been subpoenaed?

---

4. This was an important element of disclosure, since it would have alerted Hutton's customers that their investments were at risk if the brokerage firm became insolvent.

NEW YORK OFFICE
FEBRUARY 25, 1982

MEMORANDUM FOR THE FILES

RE: TRANSFERS OF FUNDS

  On February 25, 1982, Joel Miller and John Tesoro met with Tom Lynch (Executive V.P.), Tom Rae (Executive V.P., Legal), and Loren Schechter (Senior V.P., Legal) as well as Irwin Schneiderman of Cahill, Gordon & Reindel [the latter firm was Hutton's outside legal counsel] to discuss a situation concerning Hutton's policy of transferring cash balances between banks as well as "drawing down" cash from Hutton's branches to regional headquarters and finally to New York. It was brought to the attention of Hutton management that checks drawn on a bank in up-state New York had "bounced" as a result of "drawing down" balances for which subsequent deposits had not been made by the time such checks cleared. In addition, it was also brought to Hutton's attention by the New York State Banking Regulators that a significant amount of transfers took place between Manufacturers Hanover Trust and Chemical Bank in late December and January.

Concerning the first issue, Tom Rae stated that overdraft situations at the local bank should never have occurred and that the personnel responsible have been notified as to Company policy concerning drawdown procedures at the local bank level. Mr. Rae stated that the bank involved desires to continue doing business with EFH and did not seek to charge Hutton interest on the overdrawn balances (in answer to Joel Miller's question).

As far as the second issue is concerned, the Banking Regulators and the Federal Reserve Board expressed concern over the controls of Manufacturers Hanover concerning transferring of large balances when, in fact, there may not be sufficient funds to cover these transfers (i.e., from a credit risk point of view). Additionally, the Fed also apparently expressed concern over "creating float" as opposed to taking advantage of the float inherent in the banking system. We were assured of the fact that no action has been brought against Hutton nor unasserted claims, and in fact, the banks have not "lost" in the sense that EFH leaves money on deposit in the normal course of business (albeit *not* formal compensating balance arrangements).

Messrs. Schneiderman and Rae went on to state that Hutton is not regulated by the Fed or the New York State Banking Regulators and that this was more of a banking issue. They stated, however, that it was possible the SEC could have been notified of such occurrences. The major concern of management was potential negative publicity if the media were informed.

Concerning the financial statements, based upon our discussion, we concluded that no disclosure was warranted as promulgated by FASB Statement No. 5 and that the financial statements have a liability caption entitled "Drafts & Checks Payable," which is far in excess of "Cash." This clearly illustrates the fact that checks have been written for amounts in excess of bank balances. This very topic was addressed in our 1979 examination where we concluded, after conferring with Tom Rae, that an entity does not have a legal problem with such a "drawdown" or transfer procedure as long as it has the *intention* and means to make payment as EFH has done in the past. Additionally, Tom Rae stated that as a result of the aforementioned transaction, no customer of Hutton was disadvantaged. Messrs. Lynch, Rae, Schechter, and Schneiderman were of the opinion that there were no claims asserted or unasserted, that EFH would suffer no financial loss, and that the only exposure might be unfavorable publicity.

John Tesoro

Joel Miller

EXHIBIT 2
Arthur Andersen
Workpaper Memo
Regarding E.F. Hutton's
Cash Management
Practices—1981 Audit

EXHIBIT 3
E. F. Hutton's 1984
Contingent Liabilities
Footnote in Form 10–K

> The company and its subsidiaries are defendants in legal actions relating to its securities, commodities, investment banking, insurance and leasing businesses. Certainly these actions purport to be brought on behalf of various classes of claimants and seeks damages of material [*sic*] for indeterminant amounts. In the opinion of management, these actions will not result in any material, adverse effect on the consolidated financial position of the company.

PROFESSOR BRILOFF: This disclosure was very much like a bikini bathing suit, what it revealed was interesting, what it concealed was vital.

AUDITORS AND THE PUBLIC INTEREST

The congressional investigation of the E. F. Hutton scandal was another install-ment in a series of public relations disasters for the public accounting profession. The *Wall Street Journal* and other national newspapers reported blow by blow the daily verbal attacks of the congressional subcommittee on Arthur Andersen for its role in the debacle and the related criticism of the independent audit function as a whole. Representative Mazzoli leveled some of the most serious charges against the profession.

> Maybe some of the newer practitioners of accountancy have lost sight of the traditions and the lofty history of the profession because they walk into firms now that are groveling for money just like the most mercantile of companies. Maybe they are incapable of having this high fiduciary standard that we, at least in my generation, grew up with in law, and accountancy, and medicine.

Representative Hughes was also a vocal critic of the public accounting profession throughout the Hutton hearings. He admonished the profession to recognize the need for auditors to return to serving the public interest rather than focusing on serving the interests of their clients.

> As the U.S. Supreme Court recently noted, by certifying the public reports that collectively depict a corporation's financial statements, the independent auditor assumes a public responsibility transcending any employment relationship with the client. The public watchdog function demands that the accountant maintain total independence from the client at all times and requires complete fidelity to the public trust.

QUESTIONS

1. *Statement on Auditing Standards No. 47,*"Audit Risk and Materiality in Con-ducting an Audit," discusses the key components of audit risk that an auditor faces on any given engagement. Which components of audit risk were affected by the incentive compensation scheme that Hutton had established for its branch managers? Which audit risk elements did the "plausible deniability" nature of Hutton's corporate culture affect? How should each of these factors have influenced Arthur Andersen's audits of E. F. Hutton?

2. In your opinion, did Arthur Andersen have a responsibility to obtain an independent legal opinion regarding the legality of Hutton's cash management practices as suggested by Professor Briloff?

3. *Statement on Auditing Standards No. 31*, "Evidential Matter," identifies five key management assertions that underlie a set of financial statements. In the Hutton case, which of these assertions was most subject to question? Explain.

4. Representative Hughes maintained that "the average person" may have been misled by Hutton's financial statement disclosures regarding the massive over-drafts. Is it necessary for financial statements to be understood by nonexperts, or are accountants and auditors only responsible for ensuring that financial statements be comprehensible by individuals with some knowledge of accounting and financial reporting issues?

5. Hutton's 1984 financial statements did not disclose the plea bargain agreement with the Justice Department that was announced shortly after the release of those statements. Does *FASB Statement No. 5*, "Accounting for Contingencies," mandate disclosure of the terms of such an agreement and the expected financial statement impact?

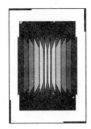

CASE 2.9

J. B. LIPPINCOTT COMPANY

In early 1978, Harper & Row, a large publishing company, was involved in merger negotiations with a smaller competitor, J. B. Lippincott Company. Founded in 1792 in Philadelphia, Lippincott specialized in publishing books and other materials for educational fields and the medical professions. In March 1978, the two companies announced the terms of a tentative merger agreement that called for Lippincott stockholders to receive one share of Harper & Row stock for each share of Lippincott stock they owned. In connection with this agreement, Harper & Row retained its independent auditors to perform a preacquisition review of Lippincott's 1977 financial statements, on which the audit firm of Lester Witte & Company had issued an unqualified audit opinion. Following the completion of their review, the Harper & Row auditors alleged that Lippincott's financial statements materially misrepresented the financial condition of the company. The most significant errors discovered were in Lippincott's various receivables accounts. As a result of the allegations by Harper & Row's auditors, the merger talks between the two companies were placed on hold.

Following the disclosure of the alleged errors in Lippincott's 1977 financial statements, the Securities and Exchange Commission (SEC) initiated an investigation of Lester Witte's 1977 audit of Lippincott—an investigation that focused on the audit of the company's receivables. The key audit procedure employed by Lester Witte on Lippincott's receivables was the mailing of positive confirmations to several hundred of the company's customers. Exhibit 1 summarizes the results of Lester Witte's confirmation procedures.

As Exhibit 1 indicates, Lippincott officials asked their Lester Witte auditors not to send confirmations to forty-eight of the accounts selected for that purpose. These forty-eight accounts were among Lippincott's approximately 14,000 "P", or problem, accounts—accounts for which the amount actually owed to Lippincott was in dispute. Many of these disputes were the result of errors made by Lippincott in the processing of cash payments by these customers. According to the SEC, customers' payments were sometimes applied to the wrong accounts, and cash discounts were often improperly recorded. Regarding the 119 accounts for which a discrepancy was reported on a returned confirmation, the SEC found

EXHIBIT 1
**Summary of the Results
of Lester Witte's
Receivables
Confirmation
Procedures**

Number of accounts selected for confirmation by Lester Witte	599
Customers who indicated that the account balance was correct	41
Customers who indicated that the account balance was incorrect	119
Customers who failed to return a confirmation	391
Customers who were not mailed a confirmation at the request of Lippincott management	48

that Lester Witte's workpapers did not disclose whether those receivables were subjected to follow-up audit procedures to determine if the recorded amount was in error. Nor did the workpapers indicate the procedures that were used to corroborate the balances of the large number of accounts for which no reply was received from the customer. The SEC alleged that if the confirmation procedures had been applied more appropriately, Lester Witte's auditors would likely have discovered significant errors that existed in Lippincott's receivables.

In addition to the P accounts, Lippincott also had apparent control deficiencies in accounting for consignment receivables and receivables from its "XX–YY" customers. The SEC found that the balances of the large consignment accounts were replete with errors caused by such simple mistakes as duplicate recording of sales invoices and failure to record credit memos. Lippincott's XX–YY receivables were from retail customers who purchased books via mail order. The balances of these accounts were generally quite small individually; however, their aggregate total was clearly material to Lippincott's financial statements. The SEC charged that the Lester Witte audit team was aware that the accounting procedures for the XX-YY accounts were extremely inadequate and that the result of these lax procedures was extensive errors in the balances of these accounts.

During the course of the year-end tests of Lippincott's receivables, the Lester Witte audit team requested a client-prepared reconciliation between the general ledger accounts receivable balance and the total of the accounts receivable subsidiary ledger. The reconciliation submitted to the auditors by Lippincott indicated a $79,713 unlocated difference between the two accounting records with the general ledger balance being the larger total. Despite this difference, Lester Witte, after applying nominal tests to the reconciliation, accepted the general ledger balance and allowed Lippincott to report that figure on its 1977 balance sheet. In fact, there were much larger errors in the subsidiary ledger than suggested by the unlocated difference of $79,713.

A final criticism of Lester Witte's year-end substantive tests of Lippincott's receivables involved a large amount owed to the company by Boston Educational Research (BER). In 1971, Lippincott had signed a contract to supply BER with a series of educational books for small children. From 1971 through the end of 1977, a receivable from BER had accumulated on Lippincott's books that represented, among other items, excess manufacturing costs incurred by Lippincott on BER's behalf. A new contract signed by the parties on December 22, 1977, reduced this receivable by nearly $400,000; however, Lippincott failed to record this reduction in its accounting records. Although Lester Witte was aware of the new contract, none of the auditors assigned to the Lippincott engagement actually read its stipulations. Instead, the auditors relied on the contention of

Lippincott's treasurer that the contract would not affect the company's operations until 1978.

Apparently, one of the causes of the substandard audit procedures performed by Lester Witte on the 1977 Lippincott engagement was the time pressure under which the individuals assigned to that audit were working. The SEC's investigation disclosed that officials of both Lippincott and Harper & Row were pressuring Lester Witte to complete the 1977 audit so that the merger between the two companies could be consummated. The SEC charged that because of this pressure, the Lester Witte auditors failed to adequately test Lippincott's internal controls for processing accounts receivable. If these controls had been properly tested, Lester Witte might have discovered the pervasive problems in the design and operating effectiveness of Lippincott's internal control structure.[1] In addition, the SEC's investigation demonstrated that the Lippincott audit team had not been properly supervised by the audit engagement partner. According to the SEC enforcement release that focused on this case, the audit partner did not become directly involved in the audit until it was nearly completed.[2] This lack of supervision and the lack of time to properly review the work of the subordinates assigned to the engagement resulted in audit procedures that were allegedly inadequate under the circumstances.

Epilogue

On August 4, 1978, Lippincott issued revised financial statements for 1977 that reported a net loss of $1,876,000. The original financial statements for 1977 issued by the company in April 1978 had reported a profit of $32,277. The following adjustments to Lippincott's receivables accounted for the majority of the change in the company's reported operating results: a $109,000 adjustment due to errors discovered in the accounts receivable subsidiary ledger, a write-down of $183,000 for the XX–YY accounts, an increase in the allowance for bad debts of $100,000 for the P accounts, a write-down of consignment receivables of $674,000, and a write-down of $387,000 of the amount due Lippincott by BER. Following the release of the corrected financial statements, Lippincott and Harper & Row agreed to new merger terms under which Lippincott's stockholders received a fractional share of Harper & Row stock for each share of Lippincott stock they owned. Within a year of the merger of the two companies, however, Harper & Row executives were being criticized for paying too much for Lippincott. In fact, Harper & Row was forced to write down the assets acquired in the Lippincott merger by an additional $14 million in 1979.[3]

1. In fact, the SEC found that during 1977, Lester Witte had performed a consulting engagement for Lippincott that included a review of certain segments of the company's internal control structure. Lester Witte's report to Lippincott management regarding the results of that review commented on "significant" problems that existed in the company's organizational structure, EDP accounting applications, and various internal controls. Given these findings, the SEC alleged that Lester Witte should have been aware of the possibility that Lippincott's controls were not effective.

2. See Securities and Exchange Commission, *Accounting Series Release No. 285,* 7 January 1981.

3. N. R. Kleinfeld, "Harper's Headache with Lippincott," *New York Times,* 9 August 1979, D1, D2.

QUESTIONS

1. Describe how an auditor's objectives would differ on a preacquisition review compared with a standard audit. In a preacquisition review, would an auditor be required to be independent of his or her client? Explain.

2. Professional standards require auditors to perform confirmation procedures on their clients' receivables in most audit engagements. Identify the circumstances under which auditors would not be required to use confirmation procedures on a client's receivables.

3. Given the circumstances, do you believe that Lester Witte should have used positive or negative confirmations, or a combination of both, during the 1977 Lippincott audit? Explain. If an auditor does not receive a reply from a positive confirmation request, what audit procedures should be performed at that point?

4. Was the request by Lippincott officials not to send confirmations to certain accounts a limitation on the scope of Lester Witte's audit? Under what conditions can an auditor permit a client to influence audit decisions?

5. What are the key objectives of audit workpapers? Did the Lester Witte auditors fail to comply with professional standards by not thoroughly documenting the nature and results of the follow-up tests used in conjunction with their receivables confirmation procedures? If so, what standards were violated in this regard?

6. Was it appropriate for the Lester Witte auditors to rely on the Lippincott treasurer's assertion that the new BER contract would not affect the company until the following year? How does an auditor identify major contractual agreements that a client has entered into during the period under audit? What are the key management assertions that an auditor should corroborate for such contracts, and what type of audit procedures should be used for that purpose?

Case 2.10

Porta-John Corporation

For many years, Earl Braxton worked as a tax accountant in the Detroit area. Eventually, Braxton decided that he wanted to be his own boss and sought out a company to acquire. In 1970, Braxton invested his money and dreams in a tiny company, Porta-John, which rented portable toilets, principally to construction companies. In a little more than a decade, Braxton built Porta-John into the largest company in the portable toilet industry.

Braxton continually searched for new opportunities to expand his business operations. Some of Braxton's ideas worked, some did not. In 1976, Braxton found himself involved in a lawsuit with the king of late-night television when he introduced a line of low-priced portable toilets marketed under the name-"Here's Johnny." When Johnny Carson sued Braxton for more than one million dollars for infringing on the trademark opening line of *The Tonight Show*, Braxton was forced to change the name of his new product. One of Braxton's more successful ideas was to begin franchising the rights to service portable toilets owned by his company. Franchisees paid Porta-John approximately one-third of their estimated first-year revenues. Ten percent of this franchise fee was paid in cash when the franchise agreement was signed. The balance of the fee was placed on a promissory note and paid over the ten-year term of the agreement.

Braxton's growing business empire consisted of Porta-John and several other small companies in the early 1980s when he decided to take on his most ambitious venture. This venture involved selling nearly four million dollars of stock to form a public company whose principal line of business was the production of human proteins that had several medicinal uses. About the same time, Braxton retained the Big Eight accounting firm of Deloitte Haskins & Sells, now Deloitte & Touche, because he wanted a prominent auditor to increase the credibility of his companies' financial statements.

According to Braxton, Deloitte convinced him to change the method of accounting for Porta-John's franchise revenues. Instead of the cash basis of accounting the company had been using for these revenues, Deloitte reportedly believed that the accrual basis of accounting would be more appropriate. This change in accounting method had a material impact on Porta-John's financial statements. When Porta-John adopted the accrual basis of accounting for franchise revenues, the company began recognizing the entire revenue on its ten-year franchise agreements in the initial year of those agreements. Again, Braxton insisted that this change in accounting method was Deloitte's idea. "I was just pumping toilets. We left the books to Deloitte, and they sold us on a method of accounting."[1]

In 1985, a new audit partner was assigned by Deloitte to supervise the Porta-John engagement. This individual disagreed with the decision to use the accrual basis of accounting for Porta-John's franchise revenues, since those revenues were subject to a high degree of collection risk. Apparently, Porta-John did not thoroughly check the credit status of new franchisees. As a result, many of the franchisees proved to be financially unstable and went out of business before paying a substantial portion of the franchise fee owed to Porta-John.

Porta-John switched back to the cash basis of accounting for its franchise revenues in 1985 and reissued its 1984 financial statements.[2] Porta-John's revised 1984 income statement reported a huge loss. Another large loss in 1985 eliminated its remaining stockholders' equity and caused Deloitte to question in its 1985 audit report whether the firm was a going concern. Porta-John's poor operating results in 1984 and 1985 were not due strictly to the change in accounting method. Braxton had become preoccupied with the new protein-production venture in the early 1980s and, as a result, paid little attention to Porta-John, his flagship operation. Much of the cash flow generated by Porta-John as well as a large portion of the company's assets were allegedly diverted to that new venture and other businesses owned by Braxton.

In 1990, Porta-John filed for bankruptcy. The company's bankruptcy petition reported that it had less than $60,000 in assets and over $4 million in liabilities. Two years earlier, Braxton had sued Deloitte & Touche, seeking damages of approximately $15 million. Braxton charged that the firm's "flip-flop" on accounting methods for the franchise revenues had contributed significantly to Porta-John's financial problems. Deloitte countersued Porta-John for unpaid professional fees of $157,000.

In a move that caught the accounting profession by surprise, Deloitte submitted the high bid for Porta-John's assets in May 1991 to the bankruptcy judge responsible for liquidating those assets. Deloitte acquired the legal title to the Porta-John name and trademark, the company's receivables, and its portable toilets.[3] More important, by effectively purchasing Porta-John, Deloitte voided the lawsuit filed against it by Braxton on behalf of the company. A large accounting firm reportedly incurs costs of at least $500,000 in defending itself against a professional malpractice lawsuit, such as the one filed against Deloitte by Porta-John.[4] Since Deloitte paid only $70,000 to "buy out" this lawsuit, the

---

1. K. Weisman and R. Khalaf,"Number Pumpers," *Forbes*, 11 November 1991, 110–11.

2. At this point, Porta-John was actually a subsidiary of another Braxton-owned firm. However, practically all of the consolidated revenues of the parent company resulted from Porta-John's operations.

3. B. Wernle,"Deloitte Buys Assets of Firm Once Suing It," *Crain's Detroit Business*, 10 June 1991, 3.

4. "Deloitte & Touche Buys the Bankrupt Plaintiff," *Public Accounting Report*, 15 November 1991, 3.

firm realized a significant saving as a result of its unique defense strategy. An attorney that has successfully sued several accounting firms suggested that the purchase of Porta-John's assets was unprofessional, since Deloitte's sole purpose was to eliminate the lawsuit pending against it.[5] Another prominent attorney had a different view.

> I certainly don't think it's unprofessional. If it works, it's going to be very creative. If it doesn't, it will end up in litigation anyway.[6]

Unfortunately for Deloitte & Touche, Earl Braxton eventually filed another lawsuit against the firm on his own behalf. At last report, there were numerous lawsuits stemming from the financial problems of Porta-John that were pending in various courts. Meanwhile, Deloitte & Touche has apparently discontinued its portable toilet line of business.

QUESTIONS

1. If an audit firm disagrees with an accounting method used by a client, how should this disagreement be resolved? What are the key factors that should be considered when resolving such a disagreement?

2. When a new audit partner is assigned to supervise an audit engagement, he or she is often more critical of a client's accounting practices than the prior audit partner. Explain why this is true. What steps should accounting firms take to ensure a smooth transition when there is a change in audit partners assigned to a client?

3. Large accounting firms have suffered huge financial losses in recent years because of lawsuits filed against them by clients and other parties. As a result, these firms have been forced to be innovative in defending themselves against lawsuits. Do you believe the defense strategy used by Deloitte in this case was unprofessional? Why or why not? When it comes to litigation, should accounting firms use an "anything goes" attitude to defend themselves? Explain.

---

5. Ibid.

6. Ibid.

CASE 2.11
FOUR SEASONS NURSING CENTERS OF AMERICA, INC.

On February 7, 1974, Kenneth Wahrman, an audit partner with Arthur Andersen, was sitting in an Oklahoma City federal courthouse. After a ten-week trial, he was awaiting a jury's verdict—a verdict that could mean spending the next five years of his life in a federal prison. Wahrman and two other Arthur Andersen employees had been indicted on criminal fraud and conspiracy charges in connection with the bankruptcy of an Arthur Andersen audit client, Four Seasons Nursing Centers of America, Inc., which cost investors and creditors an estimated $200 million. U.S. attorney Gary Naftalis, the federal prosecutor in the Wahrman trial, charged that Wahrman and his two subordinates conspired with executives of Four Seasons to conceal material misrepresentations in the company's audited financial statements. Prior to the Wahrman trial, Naftalis had obtained guilty pleas on similar charges from four other defendants in the Four Seasons case, two officers of Four Seasons and two individuals who served as the company's investment bankers.

THE SHORT AND TROUBLED HISTORY OF FOUR SEASONS

Four Seasons Nursing Centers of America was incorporated in 1967. The two principal founders of the firm, Jack Clark and his half-brother, Tom Gray, perceived a tremendous need for high-quality extended care for the elderly in the United States. At that time, the nursing home industry was a disorganized amalgamation of mom-and-pop operations. The typical nursing home of the mid–1960s was a converted motel or bowling alley and run by individuals with little or no medical training. Clark and Gray developed a prototype nursing home design with a physical layout in the shape of the letter X that allowed nursing personnel located in a central station to monitor all four corridors of the nursing home simultaneously. Clark and Gray's prototype design, which included a number of other innovative features, was quickly recognized within the

179

medical profession as a significant step forward in providing humane and cost-efficient extended care for the nation's elderly.

Four Seasons built and operated a number of nursing homes, but its officers were most interested in building the homes and then selling them to investors. Initially, physicians were the prime group toward which Four Seasons' executives directed their marketing efforts. Clark traveled from city to city in the Southwest making his sales pitch to small groups of doctors. Although this approach was successful, it did not allow Four Seasons to expand as rapidly as its officers wanted. In 1968, the company's executives and investment bankers devised a strategy to expand Four Seasons' operations by establishing an independent company that would buy the nursing homes from Four Seasons and then either operate them or sell them to other parties. This private company, Four Seasons Equity, was organized in November 1968 and capitalized with $20 million invested principally by insurance companies.[1]

The first public offering of Four Seasons Nursing Centers stock was at approximately $10 per share in May 1968. By the fall of 1969, the stock, which traded on the American Stock Exchange, had rocketed to $100 per share on the strength of the company's robust financial performance reported in its audited financial statements filed with the Securities and Exchange Commission (SEC). Also contributing to the surge in the market price of Four Seasons stock were the glowing profit and growth projections that Clark made for the company in speeches and news releases. In 1969, Clark reported that Four Seasons were well on its way to becoming the largest corporation in the world, a prediction that seemed reasonable, given the meteoric growth rates of the company's assets and revenues.

Unfortunately for investors in Four Seasons, Clark's glowing projections were unfounded. In fact, the company's impressive financial reports were largely a product of creative accounting gimmicks. One of the principal means Four Seasons' management used to inflate their company's net income was to misapply the percentage-of-completion method in accounting for the costs incurred and revenues recognized on nursing homes under construction. Initially, Four Seasons used the physical percentage-of-completion method to determine the amount of profit recognizable on the nursing homes it had under construction at the end of a fiscal year. For instance, Four Seasons would be entitled to record 20 percent of the profit on a project that was 20 percent complete at the end of a given year (assuming the project was also begun in that year). In 1969, the company switched to the cost-to-cost percentage-of-completion method, under which the percentage of profit recognizable on a long-term construction contract is a function of the proportion of the total projected costs for the project incurred to date. For example, if 80 percent of the total projected costs are incurred in a given year on a project, then a comparable portion of the total projected profit can be recognized that year.

---

1. Bill P. Jennings was one of several Oklahoma City bankers who channeled funds into Four Seasons. Although never formally charged, he was named in the federal indictment in the Four Seasons case as a co-conspirator. Years later, a small Oklahoma City bank Jennings owned, Penn Square Bank, would trigger a national banking crisis and become the focus of intensive congressional and regulatory scrutiny for its funding of speculative oil and gas ventures and its shoddy accounting practices.

U.S. attorney Naftalis alleged during the trial of Wahrman and his subordinates that the switch in accounting methods was spurred by the recognition of
Four Seasons' management that the company's 1969 profit would be less than
expected.[2] By switching to the cost-to-cost percentage-of-completion accounting
method, management could manipulate the amount of profit recognized in a
given year by distorting the expenditures incurred on construction projects in
process. Naftalis and his prosecution team charged that Four Seasons included
huge amounts of fictitious construction expenditures in its cost reports for 1969,
which resulted in illicit profits being reported in that year. Naftalis maintained
that Arthur Andersen auditors were aware that these costs were false, and that
the auditors thus were a party to the conspiracy to defraud individuals relying
on the Four Seasons financial statements. Attorneys for the Arthur Andersen
defendants disputed this contention by presenting copies of audit workpapers
for the Four Seasons engagement that demonstrated that the auditors challenged
fictitious costs they discovered during the audit and persuaded the client to
make the proper financial statement adjustments.

Four Seasons also misrepresented its financial results by including de facto
intercompany sales transactions in its income statement. Naftalis asserted that
from 1968 to 1970, Four Seasons Nursing Centers had considerable influence
over the operations of its principal customer, Four Seasons Equity. In Jack Clark's
guilty plea to the charge that he conspired to violate federal securities laws, he
admitted that major decisions made by the management team of Four Seasons
Equity were dictated by key executives of Four Seasons Nursing Centers.
Because Four Seasons Equity was essentially under the control of Four Seasons
Nursing Centers, the latter was, in reality, selling nursing homes to itself,
meaning that the gains on these transactions were nonreportable intercompany
profits. During the Wahrman trial, Naftalis attempted to establish that the Arthur
Andersen auditors were aware of the bogus nature of these sales transactions.

The Four Seasons scam came to an abrupt end in 1970. Industry insiders had
alleged repeatedly that Clark's profit projections for his ventures were grossly
overstated, allegations substantiated in early 1970 by security analysts who
obtained reliable cost and revenue data for several of Four Seasons' nursing
homes. The public disclosure that nursing homes, even the modern, cost-efficient
ones built by Four Seasons, were low-profit-margin operations quickly stemmed
the public's and bankers' enthusiasm for Four Seasons and left the company
without a source of new investment capital. Consequently, in 1970, when the $20
million in investment capital of Four Seasons Equity was depleted, there was
almost no market for the inventory of Four Seasons nursing homes under
construction.

The collapse of Four Seasons in June 1970 caused an abrupt change in the
public's perception of Jack Clark and Tom Gray. Once hailed as successful and
forward-looking entrepreneurs, they were castigated by the press as unscrupulous opportunists. Investigations of their backgrounds disclosed that neither had

---

2. Ironically, the SEC was at least partially responsible for Four Seasons' switch to the
cost-to-cost version of the percentage-of-completion method. Prior to the switch, the SEC had
complained to company officials that they were overestimating the physical state of completion of construction projects in process and, as a result, recognizing excessive amounts of profit
during the early years of those projects.

the requisite training or skills to oversee a multimillion-dollar operation. In fact, it was discovered that only a few years before founding Four Seasons, Clark had worked as a milkman in Oklahoma City, and Gray had operated a small motel in Henrietta, Texas.

Judge Luther Bohanon, the federal magistrate who presided over the trial of Wahrman and his associates, concluded that Four Seasons was simply an elaborate stock manipulation scheme designed to enrich Four Seasons' officers. Clark alone reportedly earned more than $10 million in capital gains on the sale of Four Seasons stock during the short time it was publicly traded. The evidence that most clearly supported Judge Bohanon's conclusion was an intercompany memo found in records subpoenaed by the court, a memo which was written by a Four Seasons executive: "Let's get Walston's [one of Four Seasons' investment bankers] opinion as to when we could sell a sizable portion of our stock, while the stock is at a good price, to guard against having to sell after the public realizes that nursing homes will not meet profit expectations."[3] After reading this memo, Judge Bohanon remarked that the Four Seasons debacle, which at that time was one of the largest securities frauds in history, would damage the investing public's confidence in the credibility of the securities markets for many years to come.

THE COSTS OF THE FOUR SEASONS SCANDAL TO ARTHUR ANDERSEN

On February 7, 1974, Kenneth Wahrman's two subordinates were found innocent of fraud and conspiracy charges; however, a hung jury caused the judge to declare a mistrial on the charges against Wahrman. Nine months later, Judge Bohanon dismissed the charges against Wahrman on the advice of a federal prosecutor. Although no Arthur Andersen employees or partners were convicted in the Four Seasons case, the lengthy scandal exacted a heavy price on the prominent CPA firm. Public records disclosed that the federal government spent more than $1 million unsuccessfully prosecuting the three Arthur Andersen auditors; however, Arthur Andersen reportedly spent several times that amount defending Wahrman and his two subordinates.[4]

The heaviest cost imposed on Arthur Andersen by the Four Seasons scandal was the damage inflicted on the CPA firm's reputation. Arthur Andersen officials were particularly disturbed by their firm being named as a co-conspirator in the Four Seasons federal indictment, although no charges were ever brought specifically against the firm. The managing partner of the Oklahoma City office of Arthur Andersen at the time was also named as a co-conspirator although he was not involved in the Four Seasons audit. This individual was named as a co-conspirator on the grounds that he was responsible for the supervision and ultimately the professional conduct of his subordinates. The national managing

---

3. R. Tempest, "Giant Fraud Probe Set," *Oklahoma Journal*, 29 February 1972, 66.

4. Arthur Andersen was also a defendant in a large civil suit filed by Four Seasons stockholders. The defendants in that case collectively agreed to pay $10.6 million to the plaintiffs, although the portion of the settlement paid by each defendant was not publicly disclosed.

partner of Arthur Andersen charged that the Justice Department had deliberately chosen, to the detriment of his firm, to use the Four Seasons case to send a warning signal to auditors nationwide that they could be held criminally liable when clients released materially misstated financial statements.

QUESTIONS

1. Arthur Andersen and certain of its personnel were defendants in both civil and criminal lawsuits for their involvement in the Four Seasons case. Compare and contrast the level of proof (certainty) that a plaintiff must establish in a civil suit versus a criminal suit.

2. Identify other litigation cases involving audit firms in which individual auditors faced criminal charges. What was the eventual outcome in each of those cases?

3. What responsibility does a managing partner of an office of a CPA firm have for the performance of subordinates? What responsibility does a senior auditor on an audit engagement have for the professional conduct of his or her subordinates?

4. *Statement on Auditing Standards No. 31,* "Evidential Matter," identifies five key management assertions that underlie a set of financial statements. Which of these assertions was violated in the Four Seasons case?

5. Four Seasons used both the physical and cost-to-cost variations of the percentage-of-completion method of accounting for costs and revenues on long-term construction contracts. Which, if either, of these two variations of the percentage-of-completion method is preferable? Why?

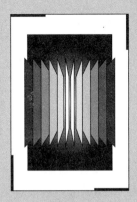

SECTION THREE
ETHICAL RESPONSIBILITIES OF AUDITORS AND ACCOUNTANTS

Case 3.1   Cardillo Travel Systems, Inc.

Case 3.2   Creve Couer Pizza, Inc.

Case 3.3   The PTL Club

Case 3.4   Leigh Ann Walker, Staff Accountant

Case 3.5   Phillips Petroleum Company

Case 3.6   Laurel Valley Estates

Case 3.7   Whittaker Corporation

Case 3.8   Suzette Washington, Accounting Major

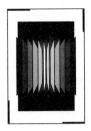

CASE 3.1

CARDILLO TRAVEL SYSTEMS, INC.

ACT 1

Russell Smith knew why he had been summoned to the office of A. Walter Rognlien, the seventy-four-year-old chairman of the board and chief executive officer of Smith's employer, Cardillo Travel Systems, Inc.[1] Just two days earlier, Cardillo's in-house attorney, Raymond Riley, had requested that Smith, the company's controller, sign an affidavit regarding the nature of a transaction Rognlien had negotiated with United Airlines. The affidavit stated that the transaction involved a $203,000 payment by United Airlines to Cardillo but did not disclose why the payment was being made or for what specific purpose the funds would be used. Also included in the affidavit was a statement that the net stockholders' equity of Cardillo was in excess of $3 million, a statement that Smith knew to be incorrect. Smith was aware that his company was involved in a lawsuit and that a court injunction issued in the case required Cardillo to maintain stockholders' equity of at least $3 million. Because of the blatant misrepresentation in the affidavit regarding the magnitude of Cardillo's stockholders' equity and a sense of uneasiness regarding the payment to Cardillo by United Airlines, Smith had informed Riley that he could not sign the affidavit.

When Smith stepped into Rognlien's office on that day in May 1985, he found not only Rognlien but also Riley and two other Cardillo executives. One of the other executives was Esther Lawrence, the firm's energetic forty-four-year-old president and chief operating officer and Rognlien's wife and confidante. Lawrence, a longtime employee of Cardillo, had assumed control of Cardillo's operations in 1984 after two of Rognlien's sons by a former marriage were forced out of the company in a power struggle.

As Smith sat waiting for the meeting to begin, his apprehension mounted. Although Cardillo had a long and proud history, in recent years the company had begun experiencing serious financial difficulties. Founded in 1935 and

---

1. The events discussed in this case were reconstructed from information included in Securities and Exchange Commission, *Accounting and Auditing Enforcement Release No. 143*, 4 August 1987. All quotations appearing in this case were also taken from that document.

purchased in 1956 by Rognlien, Cardillo was the fourth largest travel agency in the nation and the first travel agency to be listed on the American Stock Exchange. Cardillo's revenues had steadily increased since Rognlien acquired the company, approaching $100 million by 1984. However, operating expenses were increasing more rapidly, and the company's bottom line was being adversely affected by Rognlien's aggressive franchising strategy, which in 1984 alone had more than doubled the number of travel agency franchises operated by Cardillo. The net effect of these trends was a collective loss of nearly $1.5 million between 1982 and 1984 for the company.

Shortly after the meeting began, the overbearing and volatile Rognlien demanded that Smith sign the affidavit. When Smith steadfastly refused, Rognlien showed him the first page of an unsigned lease agreement between United Airlines and Cardillo. Rognlien then explained that the $203,000 payment was intended to cover expenses incurred by Cardillo in changing from American Airlines' Saber computer reservation system to United Airlines' Apollo system. Even though the payment was intended to reimburse Cardillo for expenses it would incur in switching to the new reservation system and was refundable to United Airlines if not spent, Rognlien wanted Smith to record the payment immediately as revenue without recognizing any offsetting liability. Not surprisingly, Rognlien's suggested treatment of the United Airlines payment would have allowed Cardillo to meet the $3 million minimum stockholders' equity threshold established by the court order outstanding against the company. Without hesitation, Smith informed Rognlien that recognizing the United Airlines payment as revenue without any offset would be improper. At that point "Rognlien told Smith that he was incompetent and unprofessional because he refused to book the United payment as income. Rognlien further told Smith that Cardillo did not need a controller like Smith who would not do what was expected of him."

Act 2

In November 1985, Helen Shepherd, the Touche Ross audit partner in charge of the 1985 audit being performed for Cardillo by her firm, stumbled across information in the client's files regarding the lease agreement Rognlien had negotiated with United Airlines earlier that year. When she inquired of other members of the Touche Ross audit team regarding that agreement, she was told of a $203,000 accrual that had been recorded in late June in Cardillo's accounting records as an adjusting entry. This accrual was apparently linked to the United Airlines–Cardillo lease agreement. The entry, which was approved by Lawrence, follows:

Dr Receivables—United Airlines	$203,210	
Cr Travel Commissions and Fees		$203,210

Shepherd's subordinates had discovered the adjusting entry during their second-quarter review of Cardillo's 10–Q statement and asked client executives about its nature. Lawrence had told the auditors that the entry was for commissions earned by Cardillo from United Airlines during the second quarter. The auditors had accepted Lawrence's explanation without attempting to corroborate it with other audit evidence.

After discussing the adjusting entry with her subordinates, Shepherd questioned Lawrence regarding the entry. Lawrence insisted that the adjusting entry had been properly recorded, at which point Shepherd requested that United Airlines be asked to provide a confirmation to Touche Ross regarding the major contractual stipulations of the lease agreement. Shepherd was concerned because the information she had reviewed regarding the lease agreement suggested that payments made to Cardillo were refundable to United Airlines under certain conditions and thus not recognizable immediately as revenue.

Shortly after her meeting with Lawrence, Shepherd was contacted by Rognlien, who also maintained that the $203,000 amount had been properly recorded as commission income during the second quarter. Rognlien also informed Shepherd that the disputed amount, which was paid by United Airlines to Cardillo during the third quarter of 1985, was not refundable to United Airlines under any circumstances. After some prodding by Shepherd, Rognlien eventually agreed to allow her to request a confirmation from United Airlines concerning certain parameters of the lease agreement.

On December 17, 1985, Shepherd received the requested confirmation from United Airlines. The confirmation stated that the disputed amount was subject to being refunded to United Airlines through 1990 if certain stipulations of the contractual agreement between the two parties were not fulfilled.[2] After receiving the confirmation, Shepherd called Rognlien and asked him to explain the obvious difference of opinion between United Airlines and Cardillo regarding the terms of their agreement. Rognlien informed Shepherd that he had a secret arrangement with the chairman of the board of United Airlines regarding the lease agreement; "Rognlien claimed that pursuant to this confidential business arrangement, the $203,210 would never have to be paid back to United. Shepherd asked Rognlien for permission to contact United's chairman in order to confirm the confidential business arrangement. Rognlien refused. In fact, as Rognlien knew, no such agreement existed."

A few days following Shepherd's conversation with Rognlien, she informed William Kaye, Cardillo's vice-president of finance, that the $203,000 amount could not be recognized as revenue until the contractual agreement with United Airlines expired in 1990. Kaye refused to make the appropriate adjusting entry, explaining that Lawrence had insisted that the payment from United Airlines be recorded immediately as revenue. On December 30, 1985, Rognlien called Shepherd and informed her that he was terminating Cardillo's relationship with Touche Ross.

In early February 1986, Cardillo filed an 8–K statement with the Securities and Exchange Commission (SEC) to notify that agency of the company's change in auditors. SEC regulations required Cardillo to disclose in the 8–K statement whether its officers or employees had been involved in any disagreements over technical accounting, auditing, or financial reporting issues with its former

---

2. Shepherd apparently never learned that the $203,000 payment was intended simply to reimburse Cardillo for expenses it incurred in connection with switching to United Airlines' reservation system. As a result, she focused almost exclusively on the question of when it was appropriate for Cardillo to recognize the United Airlines payment as revenue. If she had been aware of the true nature of the payment, she almost certainly would have been even more adamant regarding the impropriety of the $203,000 adjusting entry.

auditor prior to the latter's dismissal. The 8–K, which was signed by Lawrence, indicated that no such disagreements had preceded Cardillo's decision to dismiss Touche Ross. SEC regulations also required that the former auditor draft a letter regarding the existence of any disagreements with the former client and that this letter be filed as an exhibit to the 8–K statement. In Touche Ross's exhibit letter, Shepherd discussed the dispute that had arisen regarding the United Airlines payment to Cardillo. Shepherd also disclosed that the improper accounting treatment given the item had resulted in misrepresented financial statements for Cardillo for the six months ended June 30, 1985, and the nine months ended September 30, 1985.

In late February 1986, Raymond Riley, Cardillo's legal counsel, wrote Shepherd and insisted that she had misrepresented the United Airlines–Cardillo transaction in the Touche Ross exhibit letter filed with the company's 8–K. Riley also informed Shepherd that Cardillo would not pay the $17,500 invoice that Touche Ross had submitted to his company for the professional services Touche Ross had rendered prior to being dismissed by Rognlien.

Act 3

On January 21, 1986, KMG Main Hurdman (KMG) was retained by Cardillo to replace Touche Ross as the company's independent audit firm. A key issue that KMG soon addressed was the proper accounting for the United Airlines payment to Cardillo. When KMG personnel discussed the payment with Rognlien, he informed them of the alleged secret agreement with United Airlines that superseded the written contractual agreement. According to Rognlien, the secret agreement precluded Cardillo from being forced to return the disputed $203,000 payment under any circumstances. KMG refused to accept this explanation and informed Rognlien that the payment would have to be recognized as revenue on a pro rata basis over the five-year period of the agreement with United Airlines.[3]

In early 1986, Cardillo began experiencing severe liquidity problems. These problems were accentuated a few months later when a $685,000 judgment was imposed on Cardillo in the resolution of a civil suit in which the company was a defendant. Following the judge's ruling in that case, Raymond Riley informed Rognlien and Lawrence that the adverse judgment qualifed as a "material event" and thus had to be reported to the SEC in a form 8–K filing. In the memorandum he sent to his superiors, Riley clearly discussed the serious implications of not disclosing the settlement to the SEC: "My primary concern by not releasing such report and information is that the officers and directors of Cardillo may be subject to violation of rule 10b–5 of the SEC rules by failing to disclose information that may be material to a potential investor."

Within ten days of receiving Riley's memorandum, Rognlien sold 100,000 shares of Cardillo stock in the open market. Approximately two weeks after Rognlien sold the large block of Cardillo stock, Lawrence issued a press release that publicly disclosed for the first time the adverse legal settlement. However,

---

3. As was the case with the Touche Ross audit team, Cardillo executives were apparently successful in concealing from the KMG auditors the fact that the United Airlines payment was simply an advance to cover installation expenses for the new reservation system.

Lawrence failed to disclose the amount of the settlement or the fact that Cardillo was viable only because Rognlien had invested in the company the proceeds from the sale of the 100,000 shares of stock. Additionally, Lawrence's press release underestimated the firm's expected loss for 1985 by approximately 300 percent.

Following Lawrence's press release, Roger Shlonsky, the KMG audit partner responsible for the Cardillo engagement, met with Rognlien and Lawrence and informed them that the estimated loss for fiscal 1985 disclosed in the press release was grossly understated. Shortly after that meeting, KMG resigned as Cardillo's independent audit firm.

Epilogue

In May 1987, Cardillo Travel Systems, Inc., was forced into involuntary bankruptcy proceedings by its major creditors. Later that same year, the SEC concluded a lengthy investigation of the firm. The SEC found that Rognlien, Lawrence, and Kaye had violated several provisions of the federal securities laws. Among these violations were the making of false representations to outside auditors, failing to maintain accurate financial records, and failing to file prompt financial reports with the SEC. In addition, Rognlien was charged with violating the insider trading provisions of the federal securities laws. As a result of the SEC's findings, the federal agency imposed a number of permanent injunctions on each of the three individuals. In addition, the SEC attempted to force Rognlien to forfeit the proceeds of the 100,000 shares of Cardillo stock that he sold in April 1986. In January 1989, this latter issue was finally settled when Rognlien agreed to pay the SEC $60,000 to settle the insider trading charge.

Questions

1. Identify the accountants in this case who faced ethical dilemmas. Also identify the parties who had a stake in, or would be affected by, the outcome of each of these ethical dilemmas. What responsibility did the accountant in each case owe to these parties? Did the accountants fulfill these responsibilities?

2. Describe the procedures that an auditor should perform during a review of a client's quarterly financial statements. In your opinion, did the Touche Ross auditors who discovered the $203,000 adjusting entry during their 1985 second-quarter review take all appropriate steps to corroborate that entry? Should the auditors have informed the audit partner, Helen Shepherd, of the entry?

3. In reviewing the United Airlines–Cardillo agreement, Shepherd collected both evidence that supported the $203,000 adjusting entry as booked and evidence that suggested that the entry was recorded improperly. Identify each of these items of evidence she collected. What characteristics of audit evidence do the profession's technical standards suggest that auditors should consider when evaluating such evidence? Analyze the audit evidence that Shepherd collected regarding the disputed entry in terms of these characteristics.

4. What are the principal objectives of the SEC's rules that require 8–K statements to be filed when public companies change auditors? Did Shepherd violate the client confidentiality rule when she discussed the United Airlines–Cardillo transaction in the exhibit letter she filed with Cardillo's 8–K auditor change statement? In your opinion, did Shepherd have a responsibility to disclose to Cardillo executives the information that she intended to include in the exhibit letter to be filed with Cardillo's 8–K?

5. Do the profession's technical standards explicitly require auditors to evaluate the integrity of the key executives of prospective clients? Identify the specific measures that auditors can use to assess the integrity of a prospective client's executives.

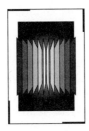

CASE 3.2
CREVE COUER PIZZA, INC.

Imagine this scenario. A few years after graduating from Rutgers, Arizona State, or the University of Idaho with an accounting degree, you find yourself working as an audit senior with a Big Six accounting firm. Your best friend, Rick, whom you have known since kindergarten, is a special agent with the Internal Revenue Service (IRS). Over lunch one day, Rick mentions the IRS's informant program.

"You know, Jess, you could pick up a few hundred dollars here and there working as a controlled informant for us. In fact, if you would feed us information regarding a few of those large corporate clients of yours, you could make a bundle."

"That's funny, Rick. Real hilarious. Me, a double agent, spying on my clients for the IRS? Have you ever heard of the confidentiality rule?"

Sound farfetched? Not really. Since 1939, the IRS has operated an informant program. Most individuals who participate in this program provide information on a one-time basis; however, the IRS also retains hundreds of "controlled informants" who work in tandem with one or more IRS special agents on a continuing basis. Controlled informants provide the IRS with incriminating evidence regarding individuals and businesses suspected of cheating on their taxes. In the early 1990s, the IRS revealed that more than forty of their controlled informants were CPAs.

Now consider this scenario. You, the audit senior, are again having lunch with your friend Rick, the IRS special agent. Rick is aware that you are under investigation by the IRS for large deductions you have taken in recent years on your federal income tax returns for a questionable tax shelter scheme. The additional tax assessments and fines you are facing significantly exceed your net worth. Your legal costs alone will be several thousand dollars. To date, you have been successful in concealing the IRS investigation from your spouse, other family members, and your employer, but that will not be possible much longer.

"Jess, I know this investigation is really worrying you. But I can get you out of this whole mess. I talked to my supervisor. She and three other agents are working on a case involving one of your audit clients. I can't tell you which one right now. If you agree to work with them as a controlled informant and provide them with information that you can easily get your hands on, they will close the case on you. You will be off the hook. No questions. No fines or additional taxes. Case closed . . . permanently."

"Rick, come on, I can't do that. What if my firm finds out? I'd lose my job. I would probably lose my certificate."

"Yeah, but face these facts. If the IRS proves its case against you, you are going to lose your job and your certificate . . . and probably a whole lot more. Maybe even your marriage. Think about it, Jess. Realistically, the agency is looking at a maximum recovery of $50,000 or so from you. But if you cooperate with my supervisor, she can probably squeeze twenty or thirty million out of your client."

"You're sure they would let me off . . . free and clear?"

"Yes. Free and clear. Come on, Jess, we need you. More important, you need us. Plus, think of it this way. You made one mistake by becoming involved in that phony tax shelter scam. But your client has been ripping off the government, big time, for years. You would be doing a public service by turning in these crooks."

Returning to reality, consider the case of James Checksfield. In 1981, Checksfield, a Missouri CPA, became a controlled informant for the IRS. The IRS special agent who recruited Checksfield had been his close friend for several years and was aware that Checksfield was under investigation by the IRS. Reportedly, Checksfield owed back taxes of nearly $30,000 because of his failure to file federal income tax returns from 1974 through 1977. At the same time the IRS was recruiting Checksfield, the federal agency was also investigating a Missouri-based company, Creve Couer Pizza, Inc. The IRS believed that the owner of this chain of pizza restaurants was "skimming receipts" from his business—that is, failing to report on his federal income tax returns the total sales revenue of his eight restaurants. Checksfield had been the accountant for Creve Couer Pizza for several years, although both the IRS and Checksfield denied that he was recruited specifically to provide information regarding that company.

From 1982 through 1985, Checksfield funneled information to the IRS regarding Creve Couer Pizza. Based upon this information, federal prosecutors filed a six-count indictment against the owner of that business in 1989. The owner was charged with underreporting his taxable income by several hundred thousand dollars and faced fines of nearly $1 million and a prison term of up to twenty-four years if convicted of the charges. Meanwhile, the IRS dropped its case against Checksfield. Both the IRS and Checksfield maintained that there was no connection between the decision to drop the case against him and his decision to provide the IRS with information regarding Creve Couer Pizza.

Following the indictment filed against the owner of Creve Couer Pizza, the owner's attorneys subpoenaed the information that the IRS had used to build its case against him. As a result, the owner discovered the role played by his longtime friend and accountant in the IRS investigation. Naturally, the owner was very upset. "What my accountant did to me was very mean and devious. He sat here in my home with me and my family. He was like a member of the family. On the other hand, he was working against me."[1] In another interview, the owner commented, "A client has the right to feel he's getting undivided loyalty from his accountant."[2] Contributing to the owner's anger was the fact that he

---

1. "Accountant Spies on Client for IRS," *Kansas City Star*, 18 March 1990, 2.

2. "The Case of the Singing CPA," *Newsweek*, 17 July 1989, 41.

had paid Checksfield more than $50,000 in fees for accounting and taxation services during the time that Checksfield had been working undercover for the IRS.

The case of the "singing CPA" was reported nationwide by the print and electronic media and resulted in widespread criticism of the IRS. The case also raised concerns by the public regarding the extent to which clients could trust their accountants to protect the confidentiality of sensitive financial information. When questioned regarding the matter, the IRS expressed no remorse for using Checksfield to gather incriminating evidence regarding the owner of Creve Couer Pizza. In particular, an IRS representative rejected the contention that communications between accountants and their clients should be "privileged" under federal law similar to the communications between attorneys and their clients.

> The IRS says the claim of a privileged [accountant-client] relationship is nonsense. "To the contrary," says Edward Federico of the IRS's criminal-investigation division in St. Louis, "the accountant has a moral and legal obligation to turn over information."[3]

The accounting profession was appalled by the Checksfield case and tried to minimize the damage it had done to the public's trust in CPAs. In particular, the actions of the IRS were condemned.

> Rarely has there been such a case of prosecutorial zeal that violated rudimentary standards of decency . . . turning the client-accountant relationship into a secret tool for government agents is an abominable practice. It demeans the service. It erodes trust in the accounting profession.[4]

EPILOGUE

In August 1990, the Missouri State Board of Accountancy revoked James Checksfield's CPA license for violating a state law that prohibits CPAs from disclosing confidential client information without the client's permission. In November 1991, the U.S. Justice Department suddenly announced that it was dropping all of the tax evasion charges against the owner of Creve Couer Pizza, Inc., although pretrial arguments had already been presented for the case. The Justice Department had little to say regarding its decision. However, legal experts speculated that the charges were dropped because the Justice Department believed the federal judge hearing the case would disallow the evidence collected by the IRS with the assistance of Checksfield.

QUESTIONS

1. Do CPAs who provide accounting, taxation, and related services to small businesses have a professional responsibility to serve as the "moral conscience" of those entities? Explain.

2. In a 1984 opinion handed down by the U.S. Supreme Court, Chief Justice Warren Burger noted that the "the independent auditor assumes a public

---

3. Ibid.

4. "IRS Oversteps with CPA Stoolies," *Accounting Today*, 6 January 1992, 22.

responsibility transcending any employment relationship with the client." If this is true, do auditors have a moral or professional responsibility to turn in clients that are cheating on their taxes or violating other laws?

3. Assume that you are Jess in the second hypothetical scenario presented in this case. How would you respond to your friend's suggestion that you become a controlled informant for the IRS? Identify the parties that would be affected by your decision and the obligations you would have to each.

4. In your opinion, should communications between accountants and their clients be "privileged"? Defend your answer.

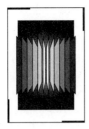

Case 3.3
The PTL Club

Jim and Tammy Bakker founded the PTL (Praise the Lord) Club, a religious broadcasting network, in 1974. A little more than one decade later, the PTL Club had more than 500,000 members and annual revenues of almost $130 million. Bakker and his close associates came under intense scrutiny in 1987 when it was disclosed that PTL funds had been used to pay a former church secretary to remain silent concerning a brief liaison involving herself and Bakker. That disclosure resulted in a series of investigations of PTL's finances by the Internal Revenue Service, the Federal Bureau of Investigation, the U.S. Postal Service, and numerous other federal and state agencies. In March 1987, Bakker was forced to resign as PTL's chairman. Two years later, he was convicted of fraud and conspiracy charges, fined $500,000, and sentenced to forty-five years in federal prison.[1]

The Bakker scandal spurred a nationwide debate concerning the lack of regulatory oversight of the financial affairs and fund-raising activities of religious broadcasting companies. Public documents disclosed that Bakker and his associates were being paid huge salaries and bonuses from the funds PTL raised through the use of televised appeals. In 1986, the Bakkers received almost $2 million, and in the first three months of 1987, when PTL was experiencing severe cash flow problems, the couple was paid $640,000. The organization was also criticized for the flamboyant life-styles of its officers. The executive suites at PTL's Fort Mill, South Carolina, headquarters were decorated in opulent style, including gold-plated bathroom fixtures and extravagant chandeliers. Bakker

---

1. In early 1991, a federal appeals court upheld Bakker's conviction on the fraud and conspiracy charges but voided Bakker's forty-five-year sentence, as well as the $500,000 fine, and ordered that a new sentencing hearing be held. According to the appeals court, the trial judge who imposed the lengthy sentence on Bakker may have allowed his personal religious predispositions to influence his sentencing decision. Following the re-sentencing hearing in August 1991, Bakker's sentence was set at eighteen years. In 1994, Bakker was transferred to a halfway house to serve the remaining few months of his sentence, which had been significantly reduced for good behavior. After being released from the halfway house, Bakker reported that he planned to return to the ministry.

and his wife enjoyed a rambling Palm Springs ranch house on their many trips to the West Coast, a $600,000 condominium in Highland Beach, Florida, and the use of a fleet of luxury automobiles, including Rolls-Royces.

Prior to 1987, Bakker's critics had persistently called for greater disclosure of PTL's financial affairs. Bakker resisted such demands, repeatedly asserting that such disclosure was not appropriate or necessary, since PTL had strong financial controls. In addition, Bakker often reminded his critics that PTL "had excellent accountants and that it had external audits by reputable [CPA] firms."[2] The results of the numerous investigations of PTL in 1987 and 1988, however, suggest that the organization's internal controls were extremely weak, and nonexistent in many cases. Investigators revealed that paychecks were being written to individuals who could not be identified, that large sums were being paid to consultants who admitted to not having provided any services to PTL, and that supporting documentation for millions of dollars of construction costs recorded in PTL's accounting records could not be found.

The most troubling weakness that investigators uncovered in PTL's accounting system was the existence of a secret executive payroll account that was used to disburse funds to Bakker and his closest aides. This account was so secretive that the organization's chief financial officer was not informed of the nature of the expenses being paid through it, and members of PTL's board of directors were totally unaware of its existence. Surprisingly, the check register for the account was maintained by a partner of Laventhol & Horwath, PTL's independent audit firm. In fact, that individual was the audit partner responsible for supervising the PTL audit engagement. Bakker or one of his aides would telephone the Laventhol partner when a check was written on the account. The partner would also be called periodically to determine whether PTL needed to deposit additional funds into the account.

Laventhol was widely criticized for its role in the PTL scandal and eventually named as a co-defendant in a $757 million class action lawsuit filed by former PTL contributors. The suit alleged that Laventhol assisted Bakker in misrepresenting the financial condition of PTL and was instrumental in facilitating Bakker's efforts to embezzle millions of dollars from PTL through the secret payroll account. Another co-defendant in the lawsuit was Deloitte, Haskins & Sells, PTL's audit firm up to 1984, which faced allegations similar to those leveled against Laventhol, even though Deloitte personnel did not maintain the check register for the secret payroll account.

PTL dismissed Deloitte as its audit firm in 1984 for undisclosed reasons and retained Laventhol shortly thereafter. Laventhol's decision to accept PTL as a client was apparently related to the CPA firm's aggressive marketing strategy it adopted in the 1970s. From 1980 to 1986 alone, the firm's revenues increased approximately 300 percent, growth that was largely a consequence of Laventhol's acceptance of high-risk audit clients, such as PTL, that other audit firms were reluctant to consider as clients. A former employee of Laventhol suggested that the firm "took too many risky clients like PTL—a strategy that, ironically, accountants often advise their clients to avoid."[3] In the civil lawsuit that named

2. L. Berton, "Laventhol & Horwath Beset by Litigation, Runs into Hard Times," *Wall Street Journal*, 17 May 1990, A1, A10.

3. Ibid., A1.

Laventhol as a co-defendant, the plaintiffs maintained that the CPA firm permitted the allegedly illegal payments from the secret payroll account "because PTL was the largest client for its [Laventhol's] Charlotte office."[4]

In the fall of 1990, Laventhol, the seventh-largest CPA firm in the United States at the time, filed for bankruptcy and was subsequently dropped as a defendant in the class action lawsuit initiated by former PTL members.[5] Two months later, the jury hearing that case rendered a $130 million judgment against Jim Bakker to be paid to the former members and contributors of PTL. However, the jury found that Deloitte & Touche, the successor firm of Deloitte, Haskins & Sells, was not guilty of any malfeasance in the case. In commenting on the jury's verdict, a Deloitte official noted that the suit was "a well-financed and well-executed attempt to recover enormous damages from an innocent accounting firm for the alleged wrongdoing of others."[6,7]

QUESTIONS

1. What ethical questions were raised by the maintenance of the secret payroll account for PTL by the Laventhol partner? Does the fact that PTL was a private organization not registered with the Securities and Exchange Commission affect the propriety of the partner's actions? Explain.

2. What procedures should an audit firm perform prior to accepting an audit client, particularly an allegedly high-risk client such as PTL?

3. Briefly define the so-called deep pockets theory as it relates to the litigation problems of large public accounting firms in recent years. What measures can these firms take to protect themselves from large class action lawsuits predicated upon allegations that are largely or totally unfounded?

4. M. Isikoff and A. Harris, "PTL Contributors Sue Ministry's Accounting Firms," *Washington Post*, 19 November 1987, C10, C16.

5. Although Laventhol was dropped as a defendant in this case, its partners and former partners did not escape financial responsibility for the firm's role in the PTL scandal. In a subsequent bankruptcy plan approved in 1992 by the U.S. Bankruptcy Court of New York, Laventhol's partners and former partners were required to contribute approximately $47 million to a settlement pool to liquidate outstanding claims against Laventhol. This pool was to be divided among the creditors of the firm and several parties that had sued the firm including PTL's former members. The individual contributions made by Laventhol partners to this settlement pool were reportedly as large as $700,000.

6. "Deloitte Victorious in PTL Case," *Public Accounting Report*, 31 January 1991, 5.

7. An excellent and comprehensive summary of the accounting and auditing issues involved in the PTL scandal can be found in *Anatomy of A Fraud* (New York: Wiley, 1993), by Professor Gary Tidwell of the College of Charleston.

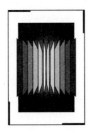

CASE 3.4

LEIGH ANN WALKER, STAFF ACCOUNTANT

Leigh Ann Walker graduated from a major state university in the spring of 1989 with a bachelor's degree in accounting.[1] During her college career, Walker earned a 3.9 grade point average and was involved in extracurricular activities, including a number of student business organizations. Her closest friends often teased her about the busy schedule she maintained and the fact that she was, at times, a little too "intense." During the fall of 1988, Walker interviewed with several public accounting firms as well as a number of large corporations, and she received six job offers. After considering all of her offers at length, she accepted an entry-level position on the auditing staff of one of the "Big Six" accounting firms. Walker was not sure whether she wanted to pursue a partnership position with her new employer, but she believed that the training programs the firm provided and the breadth of experience she would receive as a result of her varied client assignments would get her career off to a good start.

Walker spent the first two weeks on her new job at her firm's regional audit staff training school. On returning to her local office in early June 1989, she was assigned to work on the audit of Saint Andrew's Hospital, a large sectarian hospital that had a June 30 fiscal year-end. Walker's immediate supervisor on the Saint Andrew's engagement was Jackie Vaughn, a third-year senior. On Walker's first day on the Saint Andrew's audit, Vaughn informed her that her assignment included responsibility for auditing the cash accounts of the hospital, as well as assistance with the audit of accounts receivable. Walker was excited about her first client assignment and was particularly pleased that she would be working for Vaughn. Vaughn had a reputation in the local office as being a demanding

---

1. This case is based upon a true set of facts; however, the names of the parties involved have been changed. Much of the information incorporated in this case was provided by an employee of a job placement firm. The services of this individual's firm had been retained by the student identified in this case as Leigh Ann Walker.

senior who typically brought her engagements in under budget, but also as being a senior who was fair and knowledgeable and had an excellent rapport with clients.

Like many newly hired staff auditors, Walker was apprehensive about her new job. Although she believed that she understood the purpose of independent audits and had a general understanding of the nature of the work performed by auditors, she was not sure that her two-week staff-training seminar or her one college course in auditing had adequately prepared her for her new work role. After being assigned to work under Vaughn's supervision, Walker was some-what relieved. She perceived Vaughn as the type of individual who, although demanding, would be patient and understanding with a new staff auditor and as someone from whom she could learn a great deal. Walker resolved that she would work hard to impress Vaughn and had hopes that Vaughn would choose to be her mentor through the first few years of her career.

Early in Walker's second week on the Saint Andrew's engagement, Vaughn asked her during lunch whether she had taken the CPA examination in May. After a brief pause, Walker replied that she had not but was planning to do some intensive studying over the following five months and then take the exam in November. Vaughn indicated that was a good strategy and offered to lend Walker a set of CPA review manuals—an offer that she declined. In fact, Walker had returned to her home state during the first week of May and sat for the CPA exam. Because she was concerned that she had not done particularly well, she had decided not to tell her co-workers that she had taken the exam. Even though she realized that most of her peers would not pass all sections of the exam on their first attempt, she wanted to avoid the embarrassment of admitting through-out the remainder of her career that she had not been a "first timer."

Walker continued to work on the Saint Andrew's engagement throughout the summer. She completed the cash audit within budget and thoroughly docu-mented her work. Vaughn was pleased with Walker's work and was quick to compliment and encourage her. As the engagement was winding down in early August, Walker received her grades on the CPA exam in the mail one Friday evening. To her surprise, she had passed all four parts of the exam. She immediately called Vaughn to tell her the good news and was disappointed when her superior's response was much less than enthusiastic. At that point, Walker recalled having earlier told Vaughn that she had not taken the exam in May. She immediately apologized and explained why she had chosen not to disclose that she had taken the exam. Still, Vaughn seemed somewhat perturbed, and Walker decided that it was best to drop the subject and pursue it later in person with Vaughn.

The following week, Vaughn spent Monday through Wednesday with another client, while Walker and the other staff assigned to the Saint Andrew's engage-ment continued to wrap up the hospital audit. On Wednesday morning, Walker received a call from Don Roberts, the office managing partner, who was also the engagement audit partner for Saint Andrew's. Roberts asked Walker to meet with him late that afternoon in his office. She assumed that Roberts simply wanted to congratulate her for passing the CPA exam.

The usually upbeat Roberts was quite somber when Walker stepped into his office that afternoon. After she was seated, Roberts informed her that he had spoken with Vaughn several times during the past few days and that he had consulted with the three other audit partners in the office regarding a situation involving Walker. Roberts then explained that Vaughn was very concerned about Walker's having lied to her regarding the CPA exam. Vaughn had told Roberts that she did not want Walker assigned to any future engagements of hers, since she could not trust Walker to be truthful. Vaughn had also suggested that Walker be dismissed from the firm because of the lack of integrity that she had demonstrated. Roberts then told Walker that he and the other audit partners agreed with Vaughn. He informed Walker that she would be given sixty days to find another job and that he or the other partners in the local office would not disclose that she had been "counseled out" of the firm if they were contacted by employers interested in hiring her.

QUESTIONS

1. In your opinion, did Vaughn overreact to Walker's admission that she had been untruthful regarding the CPA exam? If so, how would you have dealt with the situation if you had been in Vaughn's position? How would you have dealt with the situation if you had been in Roberts's position?

2. Vaughn obviously questioned Walker's personal integrity. Is it possible that one can fulfill the responsibilities of a professional role while lacking personal integrity? Why or why not?

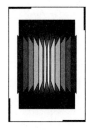

CASE 3.5

PHILLIPS PETROLEUM COMPANY

Bill Grant sat in the middle of a large jail cell with twelve other inmates as the long October night dragged on.[1] To pass the time, Grant and several other inmates played cards and talked about their hopes of soon being reunited with their families. The accommodations of the Tulsa County Jail were not unlike those of most jails: dirty, no lid on the toilet, and twelve beds for thirteen inmates. What made this scene unusual, however, was not the less-than-glamorous, overcrowded condition of the jail cell, but rather the presence of Grant, an audit partner with the international accounting firm of Arthur Young & Company.

On October 6, 1975, Bill Grant, at the time the managing partner of Arthur Young's Tulsa office, appeared at a hearing in a Tulsa federal courthouse. The presiding judge at the hearing was Judge Allen Barrow. Judge Barrow ordered Grant to produce certain audit workpapers that had been subpoenaed by a federal grand jury. These workpapers pertained to Phillips Petroleum Company, an audit client of Arthur Young's Tulsa office. When Grant respectfully denied the judge's request, he was cited for civil contempt, handcuffed, and led away to jail. Apparently, the judge hoped that an overnight stay in a crowded jail cell would convince Grant to change his mind.

The federal grand jury's interest in the Arthur Young workpapers stemmed from an ongoing investigation of Phillips. The focus of this investigation was possible tax fraud related to a secret, multimillion-dollar fund that Phillips' executives had allegedly established to make political contributions. One contribution made from the secret fund, which was maintained in a Swiss bank account, was an illegal donation of $100,000 to what became known during the Watergate era as CREEP—the Committee to Reelect the President (Richard Nixon). Under the terms of an earlier plea bargain agreement with Watergate

---

1. The facts of this case were drawn principally from the following articles: "Arthur Young Aide Cited for Contempt and Jailed in Tulsa," *Wall Street Journal*, 8 October 1975, 10; F. Andrews, "Arthur Young Faces Test on Protecting Client Audit Secrets," *Wall Street Journal*, 14 October 1975, 23; "Arthur Young & Co. Gives Grand Jury Data on Phillips Petroleum," *Wall Street Journal*, 15 October 1975, 28; "Pleas by Phillips Petroleum Filed on U.S. Charges," *Wall Street Journal*, 23 November 1977, 2.

205

special prosecutor Archibald Cox, Phillips' chairman of the board had admitted to the $100,000 contribution to Nixon's 1972 reelection campaign and pleaded guilty to one misdemeanor.[2] However, following that plea bargain agreement, a seven-count indictment was filed against Phillips. The key charge in this indictment was that Phillips had filed false federal tax returns by failing to report interest revenue earned on the secret Swiss bank account.

Prior to Bill Grant's appearance before Judge Barrow on October 6, 1975, Arthur Young had turned over to the federal grand jury approximately 12,000 pages of workpapers prepared during earlier audits of Phillips. However, Arthur Young had refused to submit to the grand jury several workpapers relating to two key issues: (1) certain tax accruals made by Phillips, and (2) attorneys' letters that Arthur Young had obtained from Phillips' law firms. Among other topics, these attorneys' letters were known to include discussions of "unasserted claims" of which Phillips' attorneys were aware. Apparently, the federal grand jury believed that both sets of workpapers would provide important insight on the allegations involving Phillips.

Arthur Young had refused to provide the contested workpapers to the grand jury on the grounds that they contained confidential information that, if disclosed, would be potentially damaging to Phillips. Tax accrual audit workpapers, for example, typically contain an audit firm's critical analysis of tax-related decisions made by their clients. Gaining access to an audit firm's tax accrual workpapers for a particular company makes it much easier for the Internal Revenue Service to build a case against that company.

Bill Grant was released from the Tulsa County Jail on October 7, 1975, but was ordered to make an appearance the following week before Judge Barrow. If Grant again refused to produce the workpapers requested by the grand jury, he faced the possibility of being cited for criminal contempt and a seventeen-month jail term. During the week between Grant's two court appearances, Arthur Young's attorneys worked out a compromise with Judge Barrow. Under the terms of this agreement, Arthur Young would turn over copies of the requested tax accrual workpapers to Judge Barrow. However, all matters other than those specifically identified by the grand jury subpoena would be masked in the copies of those workpapers given to the grand jury. Judge Barrow also granted Arthur Young the right to contest any subsequent court order to provide the original "unmasked" tax accrual workpapers to the grand jury.

Judge Barrow did not relent with respect to the contested attorneys' letters. Arthur Young was ordered to provide copies of those letters to Judge Barrow without any restrictions on their subsequent use. Phillips filed a motion to appeal this order, but that appeal was denied.

EPILOGUE

The Watergate-related problems of Phillips Petroleum continued to plague the company for two years following the resolution of the dispute concerning the

---

2. Phillips' chairman also revealed that he had personally delivered $50,000 to Mr. Nixon in a New York City apartment during the 1968 presidential campaign in which Mr. Nixon eventually defeated Senator Hubert Humphrey.

Arthur Young workpapers. In early 1976, Phillips' executives agreed to tempo-rarily turn over control of the company to its outside directors after the filing of a large class action lawsuit against the firm stemming from the charges of illegal campaign contributions. The following year, in November 1977, the case against Phillips was closed permanently when the company pleaded guilty to one felony charge of conspiracy to make illegal campaign contributions, pleaded no contest to four related tax evasion charges, and paid a fine of $30,000.

Ironically, Arthur Young's tax accrual workpapers for another audit client, the large oil company Amerada Hess, became the focal point of another major litigation case. The issue in this case was whether the IRS had the right to review copies of auditors' tax accrual workpapers. In 1984, the Supreme Court decided the case by unanimously ruling that the IRS has the right to review tax accrual workpapers prepared during an independent audit.

QUESTIONS

1. Do you believe that Bill Grant was justified in refusing to provide the requested workpapers to the grand jury? Explain.

2. What responsibility, if any, does a public accounting firm have to its partners and employees when they are subpoenaed to testify regarding a client?

3. What is the purpose of "attorneys' letters" obtained during the course of an audit? If attorneys are aware that these letters can be routinely subpoenaed from auditors, how will this fact affect the quality of the audit evidence provided by these letters?

4. How, if at all, are the documentation and other evidence included in tax accrual audit workpapers affected by auditors' knowledge that those workpapers can be obtained by the IRS?

5. Assume that Arthur Young had discovered during its 1973 audit of Phillips the illegal campaign contribution made to President Nixon's 1972 reelection campaign. How should this discovery have affected the remainder of the audit?

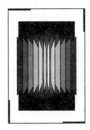

CASE 3.6
LAUREL VALLEY ESTATES

In 1978, two California businessmen, Claude Trout and Harry Moore, formed a real estate development company, which they named Laurel Valley Estates.[1] The partnership agreement signed by Trout and Moore stated that the two partners would make equal capital contributions to the new firm and would share equally in its profits. Trout's initial capital contribution to the partnership was a 400–acre parcel of undivided land that was appraised at $640,000, whereas Moore contributed an equal amount of cash. From 1978 through the end of 1981, Trout supervised the subdivision of the 400–acre property into residential lots, as well as the addition of improvements to the property. During that same period, Moore spent a considerable amount of time negotiating with several construction companies to build expensive tract homes on the partnership's land.

Near the end of 1981, Moore became restless with the slow progress that was being made in developing the Laurel Valley property. He was also concerned that Trout was not properly managing the partnership's dwindling cash funds and that, as a consequence, those funds might be depleted before the development project was finished. To allay his concern regarding the financial status of Laurel Valley Estates, Moore retained Newby & Company, an accounting firm that he had employed in connection with prior business ventures, to review the books of the partnership. When Moore informed Trout of his intentions, Trout indicated that he had no objection to Newby & Company's reviewing the partnership's accounting records. In fact, Trout told Moore that if he preferred, Newby & Company could be retained as the partnership's permanent accounting firm. Moore accepted Trout's offer, and a few days later Trout informed Douglas & Michaels, the partnership's accounting firm since its inception in 1978, of the decision to switch to Newby & Company.

---

1. The background information for this case was drawn from a legal opinion rendered in the 1980s. To protect the anonymity of the parties involved, their names were changed. In addition, certain of the factual circumstances reported in this case are fictionalized accounts of the actual facts disclosed in the legal opinion.

In early December 1981, Jay Kent Newby, a staff accountant with Newby & Company and the son of the firm's founder, arrived at the offices of Laurel Valley Estates to review the partnership's books. Newby requested Trout to provide a listing of all tangible assets held in the name of the partnership, as well as the partnership's general ledger, cash receipts and cash disbursements journals, and check register.

Late in the afternoon of his second day on the Laurel Valley engagement, a visibly upset Newby stormed into Trout's office and interrupted a conversation Trout was having with his secretary. Newby reported to Trout that he had uncovered major problems in the partnership's financial records. The property that Trout had contributed to the partnership was listed as an asset on the firm's general ledger; however, the legal title to that property had never been transferred to Laurel Valley Estates and instead was still in Trout's name. Then, Newby charged that over the past three years, Trout had "squandered" most of the cash invested in the partnership by Moore. According to Newby, Trout had paid exorbitant amounts to contractors he had retained to develop the Laurel Valley property. Newby also implied that many of the contractors were likely close friends or even relatives of Trout. Newby concluded his tirade by informing Trout, in the presence of Trout's secretary, that the partnership's records were fraudulent, that Trout owed hundreds of thousands of dollars to the partnership, and that Trout "could be looking at jail."

Trout was shocked and stunned by Newby's allegations. After regaining his composure, Trout immediately offered to deed the Laurel Valley property to the partnership. However, Newby informed Trout that "it was too late" to do that. Within minutes, Newby had packed his briefcase and was on his way out the door of the partnership's office. Trout stopped him. "What can I do to clear this up?" Trout asked. After a brief pause, Newby replied sarcastically, "Pray." Early the next morning, Harry Moore telephoned Trout and asked that he drive to Sacramento that day and meet with him, Jay Kent Newby, and Newby's father in the accounting firm's office. Trout immediately agreed to make the short drive to Sacramento.

Jay Kent Newby presided over the meeting that afternoon among the four men in the Newby & Company office. After presenting a brief summary of the problem he had uncovered the prior day, Newby reported that he had devised a way to resolve the situation without any legal action being taken against Trout. Because Trout was obviously "crooked and dishonest," Newby stated that Moore should be allowed to withdraw immediately from the partnership. Newby's plan called for Trout to return Moore's initial cash investment in the partnership and to pay Moore interest on his investment for the prior three years at a 12 percent annually compounded rate. When Trout asked Moore if that was what he wanted to do, Moore, who had yet to speak during the meeting, nodded affirmatively. Trout then agreed to the settlement and apologized for the mistake he had made, insisting that he had not been aware of the need for him to transfer the title of the 400–acre property to the partnership. Additionally, Trout insisted that he had made every effort to conserve the funds committed to the partnership by Moore. Within two weeks, Trout had arranged to borrow approximately $900,000, the amount that was required to liquidate Moore's interest in Laurel Valley Estates. One week later, Trout mailed a check for that amount to Moore.

Following the dissolution of the partnership, Trout lost interest in completing the development of the Laurel Valley property and eventually sold it at a significant loss to another party. Over the following months, Trout's health began to deteriorate, and he was eventually forced to seek psychiatric help. Trout attributed his physical and mental deterioration to the dissolution of his partnership with Moore and to the allegation of Jay Kent Newby that he was "crooked and dishonest." In late 1982, Trout told Jim Hardy, a partner of Laurel Valley Estates' original accounting firm, of the problem that had led to the breakup of his partnership with Moore. Hardy immediately informed Trout that state law did not require him to deed the Laurel Valley property to the partnership. According to Hardy, the stated intentions of partners is the controlling factor in determining whether personal assets of individual partners have been contributed to the partnership. Because the Trout and Moore partnership agreement clearly specified that Trout's initial capital contribution would be the 400–acre property, that property was legally an asset of the partnership even though the title was still in Trout's name. In fact, Hardy had researched that specific question when he set up the books for Laurel Valley Estates shortly after the partnership was formed in 1978.

Trout was livid after hearing Hardy explain that he had not been required to transfer the title of the 400–acre property to Laurel Valley Estates, as Jay Kent Newby had insisted. Trout immediately retained an attorney and filed a large civil suit against Newby & Company, charging the accounting firm with professional malpractice, fraud, and the intentional infliction of emotional distress. The judge who presided over the initial hearing of the case concluded that there was no basis for any of the three charges and dismissed Trout's suit. A few days following the dismissal of the suit, Trout died of a heart attack.

Several months following Trout's death, the executor of his estate appealed the dismissal of the lawsuit against Newby & Company to the state appeals court. The appellate court ruled that there was considerable evidence supporting Trout's allegation of professional malpractice by Newby & Company but agreed with the lower court's decision regarding the charges of fraud and infliction of emotional distress. The appellate judge who wrote the legal opinion in the case noted that Jay Kent Newby should have researched more thoroughly the legal question regarding Trout's initial capital contribution to the partnership before rendering any professional advice to Trout. Even though the appellate judge strongly suggested that Newby & Company was guilty of professional malpractice, he left the question of whether the firm's actions were the proximate cause of Trout's damages to be decided by a jury trial. The judge also noted that although Trout could not sue Newby & Company for the intentional infliction of emotional distress because of legal technicalities, plaintiff counsel might be able to prove that Jay Kent Newby had slandered Trout.

Shortly before the trial was to begin in the civil lawsuit filed against Newby & Company by Trout's executor, the accounting firm offered to make a sizable payment to Trout's estate to settle the case out of court. Trout's executor accepted the offer only after Newby & Company's partners extended a personal apology to members of the Trout family for the unfortunate incident involving Jay Kent Newby and Claude Trout.

QUESTIONS

1. What professional responsibilities did Jay Kent Newby fail to fulfill in his interaction with Claude Trout? Identify specific ethical rules and other professional standards that he violated. Would your answer be affected by the fact that Newby was not a CPA at the time? Given this additional fact, what other parties, if any, violated one or more of the public accounting profession's ethical rules or standards?

2. The controversy in this case focused on the legal question regarding whether or not Trout was required to deed the 400–acre property to the partnership. Are auditors required to be competent in such legal matters? If you had been in Jay Kent Newby's position, what would you have done when you discovered that the property in question had not been deeded to the partnership?

3. Trout was technically a client of Newby & Company when that firm reviewed the partnership's accounting records in late 1981. When Trout sued Newby & Company for professional malpractice, he filed a tort action against the accounting firm. Identify the general elements of proof that a client must establish when suing an accounting firm for professional malpractice. What other type of lawsuit could Trout have filed against Newby & Company, given that he was in privity with the accounting firm?

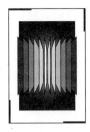

CASE 3.7

WHITTAKER CORPORATION

In the fall of 1971, Whittaker Corporation, a large, diversified manufacturing concern involved in the chemicals, metals, and housing industries, entered into negotiations to sell one of its major subsidiaries, Crown Aluminum Corporation. A tentative contract to sell the Crown subsidiary to Chamberlain Manufacturing Corporation was drawn up in late 1971. The sale was contingent on the outcome of a complete physical inventory of Crown's stocks of raw materials, work-in-process, and finished goods. To the alarm of Whittaker's executives, the physical inventory disclosed that Crown's general ledger inventory balance was over-stated by $6.3 million, or approximately 50 percent. When the shortage was discovered, Chamberlain immediately withdrew its offer to acquire Crown.

The majority of the inventory shortage was at one of Crown's production plants. Ironically, just a few weeks earlier, Whittaker's audit firm, Arthur Andersen & Company, had observed the taking of the physical inventory at that production plant in connection with its annual audit of Whittaker for the fiscal year ending October 31, 1971. An investigation by the Securities and Exchange Commission (SEC) in 1973 identified a number of alleged deficiencies in the audit procedures employed by the Arthur Andersen audit team at that inventory site. These alleged deficiencies apparently prevented Arthur Andersen from discovering a massive inventory fraud that Crown employees had perpetrated on Whittaker for several years.

The SEC investigation disclosed that during their observation of Crown's 1971 physical inventory, the Arthur Andersen auditors had failed to control the tags used by the Crown employees to record their inventory counts. In addition, the auditors had neglected to adequately investigate certain items that accounted for a large proportion of the dollar value of the production plant's inventory. For example, in one case, Crown personnel had listed the unit of measure of an inventory item, a large aluminum coil, as being 50,000 pounds, when the actual unit of measure was 5,000 pounds. As later pointed out, the Crown production facility was not physically large enough to accommodate an aluminum coil weighing 50,000 pounds. These oversights were particularly disturbing to the SEC because Arthur Andersen had a history of problems with Crown's annual physical inventories. For example, in both 1969 and 1970, Arthur Andersen discovered that Crown had recorded inventory quantities in its computerized inventory ledger from count tags that had not been used during the physical inventory. Because of such problems in the past with Crown, the SEC maintained that Arthur Andersen should have taken special precautions in auditing that subsidiary's inventory during the 1971 Whittaker engagement.

In 1972, following the discovery of the inventory shortage at Crown Aluminium, Whittaker and Arthur Andersen personnel jointly agreed that an extensive study of Whittaker's inventory controls and accounting system was necessary. Arthur Andersen offered to perform this study and to bill Whittaker for the work at approximately one-half of the audit firm's normal billing rates. Whittaker insisted, however, that Arthur Andersen perform the review free of charge, given the circumstances. Arthur Andersen eventually agreed to this arrangement under the condition that any subsequent "systems work" that was recommended as a result of the review would be billed to Whittaker at a 50 percent reduced rate.

During the course of the negotiations with Arthur Andersen, Whittaker retained outside legal counsel to determine whether it had a basis for filing a civil suit against the audit firm. Whittaker chose not to disclose to Arthur Andersen that it was pursuing its legal options, since the audit firm was in the process of completing its examination of Whittaker's fiscal 1972 financial statements. On December 28, 1972, Whittaker's board of directors decided to file a civil suit against Arthur Andersen predicated on the alleged deficiencies in the firm's 1971 audit of the Crown inventory site. When Arthur Andersen asked to review minutes of the board of directors meetings held in December 1972, a standard year-end audit procedure, Whittaker management reported that those minutes had not been prepared and instead submitted a condensed summary of the board meetings to Arthur Andersen. This summary failed to mention the legal action that Whittaker planned to take against Arthur Andersen.

On January 4, 1973, Arthur Andersen issued its audit report on Whittaker's fiscal 1972 financial statements. Two days later, Whittaker executives notified Arthur Andersen of their intention to file a suit asking for $3 million in damages as partial compensation for the inventory shortage that Arthur Andersen auditors had failed to discover in 1971. Over the next few weeks, officials of Arthur Andersen and Whittaker met several times to discuss the proposed lawsuit. During one of these meetings, Arthur Andersen representatives informed Whittaker management that they would not be able to sign off on amendments to Whittaker's 1972 financial statements because the proposed litigation threatened their firm's independence. This presented a major problem to Whittaker, since the company could not file its annual registration statement with the SEC until the amendments were approved by Arthur Andersen. Whittaker executives warned Arthur Andersen that if the amendments were not signed, they would recommend at the upcoming stockholders meeting that another audit firm be retained by the company.

Finally, on January 30, 1973, representatives of Arthur Andersen and Whittaker met and agreed to a compromise to settle their differences. The terms of this agreement included an $875,000 cash payment by Arthur Andersen to Whittaker and the provision of an additional $375,000 of professional accounting services to Whittaker at no cost. Prior to finalizing the agreement, an Arthur Andersen representative inquired whether Whittaker management would recommend at the stockholders meeting that Arthur Andersen be retained as the company's auditor. Whittaker officials responded affirmatively to that inquiry. Arthur Andersen also allegedly suggested that only the $875,000 payment be disclosed when the terms of the agreement between the two parties were released to the public, a suggestion apparently agreed to by Whittaker management.[1]

After the agreement between the two parties was reached, Whittaker requested that a meeting be arranged with the SEC to determine whether the federal agency would approve the agreement. Whittaker management was apparently concerned that the SEC might contend that the agreement adversely affected Arthur Andersen's independence and thus disqualified the firm from serving as Whittaker's independent auditor. During the meeting with SEC officials, which took place in early February 1973, neither Whittaker nor Arthur Andersen disclosed the services that Arthur Andersen had provided or intended to provide to Whittaker free of charge, the total value of which significantly exceeded $1 million. Nor did either party disclose the alleged flaws in Arthur Andersen's audit of the Crown inventory site. Instead, the two parties simply disclosed the cash payment of $875,000 by Arthur Andersen to Whittaker.

> No mention was made of the deficiencies in the Crown audit even though the Commission staff, concerned because of the apparent size of the settlement, asked Arthur Andersen representatives whether there were significant audit deficiencies. Arthur Andersen personnel at the meeting stated that they stood by the quality of their audit and were making a settlement solely to avoid protracted litigation.[2]

Apparently, if the SEC had known about the extent of the alleged deficiencies in Arthur Andersen's 1971 audit of the Crown inventory site, the agency would definitely have questioned Arthur Andersen's independence with respect to Whittaker. Theoretically, at least, the flawed Crown inventory audit might have placed Arthur Andersen in an intolerable position during the 1972 Whittaker audit. Whittaker management could potentially have used the existence of the deficiencies in the 1971 Crown inventory audit as leverage to extract concessions from Arthur Andersen auditors during the course of the 1972 audit engagement.

At the annual stockholders meeting in March 1973, Whittaker management recommended, and the stockholders approved, Arthur Andersen as the company's audit firm for the following fiscal year. However, shortly after the stockholders meeting, the SEC learned of the previously undisclosed aspects of the agreement between the two parties and immediately ordered a formal investigation. Following that investigation, the SEC ordered Whittaker to disclose to its stockholders the full details of the January 1973 agreement with Arthur Andersen, which the company did in a proxy statement released in March 1974. In late 1973, because of the controversy surrounding the undisclosed details of the

---

1. Following the release of the results of the SEC's investigation, Arthur Andersen officials reported that they never objected to disclosing all aspects of their negotiations with Whittaker. Arthur Andersen also disputed that its audit of the Crown production plant's inventory was deficient even though the SEC publicly reported that the audit firm had failed to comply with generally accepted auditing standards while auditing that inventory site.

2. This and all subsequent quotations were taken from Securities and Exchange Commission, *Accounting Series Release No. 157*, 8 July 1974.

agreement with Arthur Andersen, Whittaker management decided to dismiss Arthur Andersen and retain Coopers & Lybrand to serve as the company's audit firm.[3]

In July 1974, the SEC censured Arthur Andersen for its failure to disclose all aspects of the agreement it reached with Whittaker in January 1973. The SEC criticized Arthur Andersen most harshly for its lack of candor in the meeting arranged with SEC representatives in early February 1973: "Both Whittaker and Arthur Andersen, in seeking the advice of the Commission's staff in the manner in which they did, not only frustrated the purposes of the [federal securities] statutes but imposed upon the Commission and its staff by seeking advice without providing the staff with all of the material facts." In the enforcement release reprimanding Arthur Andersen, the SEC went on to stress that the credibility of the nation's financial reporting system ultimately depends on the integrity of the professionals who are the key participants in that system:

> The objectives of the securities laws can only be achieved when those professionals who practice before the Commission, both lawyers and accountants, act in a manner consistent with their responsibilities. . . . too much importance is attached to the word of the professional, to permit his or her word to become the subject of question. A professional's word is often the functional equivalent of his or her reputation.

QUESTIONS

1. Given the circumstances, do you believe that Arthur Andersen acted properly when it offered to perform a review of Whittaker's inventory system at reduced rates and then eventually agreed to perform that review at no cost? If not, what should Arthur Andersen have done at that point in time?

2. After learning of Whittaker management's proposed lawsuit, do you believe that Arthur Andersen should have resigned as the company's audit firm? Why or why not?

3. Did Whittaker management behave ethically when it deliberately concealed from the Arthur Andersen auditors the lawsuit that it was considering filing against the audit firm? Explain.

4. What parties were potentially most affected by the dispute between Arthur Andersen and Whittaker (other than the Arthur Andersen auditors and Whittaker management)? How were these parties affected by the dispute, and who violated or potentially violated their interests during the course of that dispute?

---

3. In September 1976, the directors and officers of Whittaker Corporation were named as co-defendants, along with Arthur Andersen, in a $50 million class action lawsuit filed on behalf of Whittaker's stockholders. The suit alleged that the defendants were responsible for issuing financial statements that materially misrepresented the financial condition of Whittaker, resulting in substantial losses for Whittaker's stockholders. No public record or comment on the resolution of this lawsuit was found, which suggests that the suit was unsuccessful or was settled for a nominal amount.

Case 3.8

Suzette Washington, Accounting Major

Suzette Washington financed her college education by working as an inventory clerk for Bertolini's, a clothing store chain located in the southeastern United States.[1] Bertolini's caters primarily to fashion-conscious young men and women. The company's stores carry a wide range of clothing including casual wear, business suits, and accessories. The Bertolini's store for which Suzette worked is located a few blocks from the campus of the large state university that she attended. Except for management personnel, most of Bertolini's employees are college students. Suzette's best friend and roommate, Paula Kaye, worked for Bertolini's as a salesclerk. Paula majored in marketing, while Suzette was an accounting major.

During Suzette's senior year in college, Bertolini's began experiencing abnormally high inventory shrinkage in the store's three departments that stocked men's apparel. Suzette's supervisor, an assistant store manager, once confided in her that he believed one or more of the salesclerks might be stealing merchandise. Over lunch one day in the student union, Suzette casually mentioned the inventory problem to Paula. Paula quickly changed the subject by asking Suzette about her plans for the weekend.

"Paula, rewind for just a second. Do you know something that I don't?"

"Huh? What do you mean?"

"Missing inventory . . . shrinkage . . . theft?"

After a few awkward moments, Paula put down her grilled chicken sandwich and looked her friend in the eye. "Suzette, I don't know if it's true, but I've heard a rumor that Alex and Matt are stealing a few things each week. Polo shirts, silk ties, jeans. Every so often they take something expensive, like a hand-knit sweater or sports jacket."

1. This case was developed from information provided by a former college student who is now a CPA employed with an accounting firm. The names, location, and certain other background facts have been changed.

"How are they doing it?"

"I've heard—and don't repeat any of this—I've heard that a couple of times per week, Alex stashes one or two items at the bottom of the trash container beneath the number two cash register. Then Matt you know he empties the trash every night in the dumpster out in the alley, takes the items out, and puts them in his car."

"Paula, we can't let them get away with this. We have to tell someone."

"No 'we' aren't. Remember, this is just a rumor. I don't know that it's true. If you tell a manager, there will be questions and more questions. Maybe the police will be brought in. You know that eventually someone is going to find out who told. And then . . . slashed tires . . . phone calls in the middle of the night."

"So, don't get involved? Just let those guys keep stealing?"

"Suze, you work in inventory. You know the markup they put on those clothes. They expect to lose a few things here and there to employees."

"Maybe the markup wouldn't be so high if theft wasn't a problem."

Now there was no doubt in Paula's mind that Suzette was going to inform management of the matter. "Two months, Suze. Two months till we graduate. Can you wait till then to spill the beans? Then we can move out-of-state before our cars are spray-painted."

One week following Suzette and Paula's conversation, a Bertolini's store manager received an anonymous typed message informing her of the two-person theft ring allegedly operating within the store. Bertolini's immediately retained the services of a private detective. Over a four-week period, the detective documented the theft by Alex and Matt of merchandise with a retail value of approximately $500. After the police were notified, criminal charges were filed against the two young men.

QUESTIONS

1. What would you do if you found yourself in Suzette's position?

2. Would it be unethical for Suzette to report to a store manager what she has been told, considering that it is only a rumor? Would it be unethical for Suzette not to report what she has heard to a store manager?

3. Accounting majors are preparing to enter a profession recognized as having one of the strongest and most rigorously enforced ethical codes. Given this fact, do you believe that accounting majors have a greater responsibility than other business majors to behave ethically?

4. Briefly discuss internal control procedures that might have prevented the theft losses suffered by Bertolini's.

SECTION FOUR
PROFESSIONAL ISSUES

Case 4.1 Hopkins v. Price Waterhouse

Case 4.2 When Auditors Become Lobbyists

Case 4.3 Tommy O'Connell, Audit Senior

Case 4.4 Sarah Russell, Staff Accountant

Case 4.5 When Auditors Change Sides

Case 4.6 Bill DeBurger, In-Charge Accountant

Case 4.7 First Blood Associates

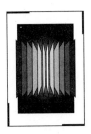

CASE 4.1
HOPKINS V. PRICE WATERHOUSE

In 1978, at the age of thirty-four, Ann Hopkins faced a dilemma that an increasing number of professional women are being forced to resolve. Hopkins was faced with making a choice between her family and her career. Although comfortable with her position at Touche Ross & Company, for whom she had worked several years, Hopkins realized that either she or her husband, also a Touche Ross employee, had to leave the firm because of its nepotism rules if either was to have an opportunity to be promoted to partner. Hopkins decided that she would make the sacrifice. She resigned from Touche Ross and immediately accepted a position in the consulting division of Price Waterhouse.

Four years later, Hopkins was nominated for promotion to partner with Price Waterhouse, the oldest and, arguably, most prestigious of the Big Eight public accounting firms. Of the eighty-eight individuals nominated for promotion to partner with Price Waterhouse that year, the other eighty-seven of whom were men, Hopkins had generated the most business for the firm, bringing in approximately $40 million in client revenues to the Washington, D.C., office for which she worked. Because client development skills are typically considered the most important criterion in partnership promotion decisions, Hopkins appeared to be a shoo-in for promotion.

Strengthening her case even more was the unanimous and strong support that she received from the seven partners in her local office, a factor also strongly considered by Price Waterhouse in evaluating candidates for promotion to partner. Much to her surprise, Hopkins was not awarded a partnership position. Instead, she was told that she would be considered for partnership the following year. Just a few months later, however, Hopkins was informed that she was no longer under consideration for promotion to partner, although the firm's top executives invited her to remain with Price Waterhouse in a nonpartner capacity.

Disenchanted and somewhat bitter, Hopkins voluntarily resigned from Price Waterhouse in January 1984 and accepted a position with the World Bank in Washington, D.C. Eventually, nagging uncertainty regarding why she was rejected for partnership caused Hopkins to file a civil action against Price Waterhouse.

Prior Criticism of Personnel Practices of Big Eight Firms

The lawsuit that Ann Hopkins filed against Price Waterhouse drew attention to an issue that had been simmering within the public accounting profession for many years. During a 1976 investigation of the accounting profession by the U.S. Senate, several parties had suggested that Big Eight firms' personnel practices discriminated against not only females but minority males as well.[1] At one point during these hearings, the Senate subcommittee sponsoring the investigation requested each of the Big Eight firms to disclose the average compensation of their partners and the number of females and nonwhite males in their partner ranks. The request for this information evoked uncooperative responses from several of the Big Eight firms. Two of these responses are shown in Exhibit 1. (Exhibit 2 presents a letter that Senator Lee Metcalf, chairman of the investigative subcommittee, wrote in response to a letter from Ernst & Ernst questioning the authority of the Senate to investigate the personnel practices of private partnerships.) Eventually, six of the Big Eight firms provided the requested information regarding the number of females and minority males among their partners. Collectively, these firms had only four partners who were black males and only seven female partners out of a total of more than 3,500 partners.

The criticism leveled at the personnel practices of Big Eight firms by the 1976 Senate investigation spurred academic researchers and investigative reporters to begin monitoring the progress of women and minorities within Big Eight firms.[2] Most studies following the Senate investigation suggested that women and minorities were making progress in obtaining entry-level positions with Big Eight firms. However, by the late 1980s when the Hopkins suit against Price Waterhouse was working its way through the courts, neither group had made significant inroads into the top hierarchy of these firms. For instance, in 1988 women held approximately 3.5 percent of the partnership positions with Big Eight firms, even though these firms had been hiring women in considerable numbers since the mid–1970s.[3]

Continued concern regarding the progress of women and minorities within Big Eight firms caused an inordinate amount of attention to be focused on Ann Hopkins's civil suit against Price Waterhouse. Although the Hopkins case provides only anecdotal evidence regarding the personnel practices of Big Eight (now Big Six) firms, it is noteworthy for a number of reasons. First, this case provided, for the first time, extensive insight into the partnership selection process employed by large accounting firms. Second, the case focused attention

---

1. U.S. Congress, Senate Subcommittee on Reports, Accounting and Management of the Committee on Government Operations, *The Accounting Establishment* (Washington, D.C.: U.S. Government Printing Office, 1977).

2. See the following sources: D. Rankin, "More Women Moving into Public Accounting, but Few to the Top," *New York Times*, 17 December 1977, 18; E. Berg, "The Big Eight: Still a Male Bastion," *New York Times*, 12 July 1988, D1; K. Rankin, "Minorities Seek Truce with Big 8," *Accounting Today*, 11 September 1989, 6.

3. Berg, "Big Eight," D1; "Women Comprise Half of 1986–87 Graduates," *Public Accounting Report*, 1 February 1988, 7.

EXHIBIT 1
Selected Responses to
U.S. Senate Request for
Information Regarding
Big Eight Firms'
Personnel Practices

June 11, 1976

The Honorable Lee Metcalf, Chairman
Subcommittee on Reports, Accounting,
    and Management
Committee on Government Operations
United States Senate
Washington, D.C. 20510

Dear Senator Metcalf:

I acknowledge receipt of your letter of June 7, 1976. As you know, this firm has responded and in considerable detail to the Committee's earlier requests. However, we consider the information sought in this letter to exceed the scope of the Committee's investigative authority. Moreover, the information sought includes data proprietary to this firm and its individual members. As a result, we respectfully decline to provide the requested data.

Very truly yours,

Russell E. Palmer
Managing Partner and
Chief Executive Officer
Touche Ross & Company

June 30, 1976

The Honorable Lee Metcalf, Chairman
Subcommittee on Reports, Accounting,
    and Management
United States Senate
Washington, D.C. 20510

Dear Senator Metcalf:

This will acknowledge your letter of June 7 which was received during the period I was away from my office.

We find it difficult to understand why the compensation of our partners is a matter of valid interest to a subcommittee of the Committee on Government Operations. We are even more perplexed with the suggestion that this could be a matter of importance in an assessment of our professional performance.

Along with these reservations we also confess to a deep-rooted belief that members of a private partnership have a right to maintain privacy over such matters if they wish to do so. Therefore, absent an understanding of its justification, we respectfully decline to furnish the compensation information you have requested.

Two partners (.5% of the total number of our partners) are female. None of our partners are blacks.

Yours very truly,

William S. Kanaga
Arthur Young & Company

on the need to rid performance appraisal methods of gender-based criteria in all disciplines, but particularly in professional fields. Finally, *Hopkins v. Price Waterhouse* is important because it stimulated discussion of measures that professional firms could take to facilitate the career success of their female employees.

EXHIBIT 2
U.S. Senate Response to Ernst & Ernst's Reluctance to Provide Requested Personnel Information

June 28, 1976

Mr. R. T. Baker
Managing Partner
Ernst & Ernst
Union Commerce Building
Cleveland, Ohio 64115

Dear Mr. Baker:

In your letter of June 24, you question the authority of this subcommittee to request information from your firm on various subjects. You note that our authority is primarily directed to the accounting practices of Federal departments and agencies.

Our requests for information from your firm are based on the unusual and substantial relationship which has developed between certain Federal agencies and influential segments of the accounting profession. This relationship has led to official recognition by Federal agencies of judgments on binding standards which have been made entirely within the private sector. The Securities and Exchange Commission has even formalized its acceptance of private decision-making through Accounting Series Release 150. The Moss amendment to the Energy Policy and Conservation Act also contemplates Federal recognition of private decisions on the manner of uniform accounting to be developed for the oil and gas industry.

The substantial reliance by Federal agencies upon decisions made in the private sector represents a significant delegation of the statutory authority vested in those agencies. This arrangement involves important decisions affecting the policies of the Federal government and other segments of our society.

Decisions made by Federal agencies are subject to review by Congress and the public. Much progress has been made both in Congress and the Federal government in opening the processes of decision-making to public scrutiny. The public has a right to know the identity and interests of those who act under the public's authority to determine the directions which this nation shall take.

When public decision-making authority is delegated to the private sector, the public has an even greater interest in knowing who is directing important national policies. As you are well aware, little information is available to Congress or the public concerning the activities of accounting firms. That is why it is necessary for this subcommittee to request information on various activities of accounting firms.

Your firm is substantially involved in the private decision-making process which develops accounting standards that are recognized by Federal agencies. The information which has so far been requested by this subcommittee is only a small fraction of the information that is publicly available regarding the identity and interests of Federal officials, or even major corporate officials. Yet, the decision-making area in which your firm is involved influences public policy as much or more than do many companies for which the requested information is publicly available.

This subcommittee has a responsibility to ensure that Federal accounting practices are responsive to the public interest. We must be informed on matters which are relevant to Federal accounting practices. That is why your firm has been requested to provide information to this subcommittee.

Very truly yours,

Lee Metcalf, Chairman
Subcommittee on Reports,
  Accounting, and Management

PRICE WATERHOUSE'S CONSIDERATION
OF ANN HOPKINS FOR PROMOTION TO PARTNER

Each year, the partners of Price Waterhouse are asked to nominate senior managers in their offices whom they consider to be viable partner candidates. Price Waterhouse's admissions committee collects these nominations and then provides a list of the nominees to each partner in the firm. Partners are then invited to provide either a "long form" or "short form" evaluation of the individual candidates. Typically, a partner who is well acquainted with a nominee provides a long form evaluation, whereas a partner who has had little or no contact with a given nominee submits a short form evaluation or no evaluation at all. Both forms require the partners to assess the partnership potential of the nominees on a number of scaled dimensions, including client development abilities, interpersonal skills, and technical expertise. After responding to the scaled items, the partners are asked to indicate whether the given individual should be admitted to partnership in the firm, whether he or she should be denied partnership, or whether the partnership decision should be deferred for one or more years. The partners are also asked to write a brief explanation of the key reasons for their overall recommendation for each candidate.

After studying and summarizing the evaluations, the admissions committee prepares a list of the candidates it recommends for admission to partnership, a list of candidates not recommended for promotion, and a final list of candidates for whom a "hold" recommendation is being made. These latter candidates are typically individuals who appear to have potential for partnership but have some weakness in their background that should be remedied before the individual is considered again for promotion. The recommendations of the admissions committee are then submitted to the firm's policy board, which reviews them and selects the final slate of candidates to be voted on by the entire partnership.[4]

In Ann Hopkins's case, the admissions committee received thirty-two evaluation forms commenting on her nomination for partner. Of this total, thirteen were positive recommendations, eight recommended denial of partnership, three suggested that she be held over for consideration the following year, and eight indicated insufficient information to make a firm recommendation. The most common criticism of Hopkins by the partners who recommended denial of partnership was that she had poor interpersonal skills and an abrasive personality. Specific comments in this respect suggested that she was too demanding of her subordinates, used profanity at times, and was generally harsh and overly aggressive. Likewise, one partner noted that she was "macho," while another observed that "she may have overcompensated for being a woman."[5]

After reviewing Hopkins's evaluations, the admissions committee recommended that she be held over for consideration, a recommendation accepted by the policy board. The admissions committee apparently decided that her inter-

4. This description of Price Waterhouse's partnership selection process was summarized from information presented in the 1985 court opinion issued in Hopkins v. Price Waterhouse, 618 F. Supp. 1109 (D.C.D.C. 1985).

5. This and all subsequent quotations were taken from Hopkins v. Price Waterhouse.

personal skills were too weak to allow her to function effectively as a partner. To increase her chances of being promoted to partner the following year, she was advised to undergo a "Quality Control Review" that would identify specific aspects of her job-related skills that needed improvement. Several partners also indicated that they would give her opportunities to demonstrate that she was remedying the deficiencies in her interpersonal skills. However, these partners never followed through on their commitments. Four months following the completion of the Quality Control Review, the managing partner of Hopkins's office informed her that she would not be renominated for partner and that it was unlikely she would be reconsidered for promotion to partner in the future.[6]

ANN HOPKINS'S CIVIL SUIT AGAINST PRICE WATERHOUSE

Ann Hopkins was informed by her office managing partner in mid-1983 of the "hold" recommendation that had been given to her nomination for partner by the admissions committee. At that time, the office managing partner discussed with her some of the reservations that were expressed regarding her nomination. In particular, he related that several partners believed that her appearance and interpersonal manner were overtly masculine and that these traits caused her to be less appealing as a partner candidate. The office managing partner, who still strongly supported Hopkins for promotion to partner, then suggested that she could improve her chances for promotion if she would "walk more femininely, wear make-up, have her hair styled, and wear jewelry." Following her resignation from Price Waterhouse, Hopkins recalled these suggestions and began to speculate that she was denied partnership not because she was unqualified to be a partner with the firm but, rather, because she was perceived as being unqualified to be a female partner. Eventually, she concluded that Price Waterhouse had established different standards for promoting females and males to partnership positions. In fact, this issue became the focal point of her civil suit against her former employer. The specific allegations that she brought against Price Waterhouse follow:

1. The criticisms of her interpersonal skills were fabricated by the Price Waterhouse partners.
2. Even if the criticisms of her interpersonal skills were valid, Price Waterhouse had promoted male candidates to partner who had similar deficiencies in interpersonal skills.
3. The criticisms of her interpersonal skills were a direct result of sexual stereotyping by Price Waterhouse partners.
4. The partnership selection process employed by Price Waterhouse did not discount the sexually discriminatory comments made regarding her candidacy.

---

6. Apparently, two of the partners in Hopkins's local office informed the office managing partner that they would not support her nomination for partner the following year. Without strong supportive nominations from the partners in the local office, it was a foregone conclusion that Hopkins would not be promoted. Although it is somewhat unclear why these individuals changed their minds regarding the partnership potential of Hopkins, they apparently decided that the concerns regarding her interpersonal skills were valid.

The judge in the *Hopkins v. Price Waterhouse* case ruled that Hopkins's first allegation was not supported by the evidence presented during the trial. According to the judge, the defense counsel clearly proved that Hopkins, in fact, did have poor interpersonal skills, particularly when dealing with subordinates. The judge also ruled that Price Waterhouse was well within its rights to deny an individual a partnership position who did not possess adequate interpersonal skills. However, the judge also pointed out that court testimony demonstrated that male candidates for partner who had been described as being "crude, abrasive, and overbearing" had been promoted to partnership positions with Price Waterhouse in prior years. A review of past promotion decisions made by the firm also disclosed that at least two earlier female partner candidates had apparently been disqualified from consideration for promotion by Price Waterhouse because they acted like "Ma Barker" or tried to be "one of the boys."

The judge in the Hopkins case observed that an earlier legal case had established the precedent that an employer who evaluates a woman with an aggressive or abrasive personality differently than a man with similar personality traits is guilty of sex discrimination. After reviewing all of the evidence presented during the trial, the judge concluded that Price Waterhouse, in fact, had evaluated Hopkins as a candidate for becoming a female partner rather than simply a partner with the firm.

> [Female] candidates were viewed favorably if partners believed they maintained their femininity while becoming effective professional managers. To be identified as a "women's liber" was regarded as a negative comment. Nothing was done to discourage sexually biased evaluations. One partner repeatedly commented that he could not consider any woman seriously as a partnership candidate and believed that women were not capable of functioning as senior managers—yet the firm took no action to discourage his comments and recorded his vote in the overall summary of the evaluations.

Although Hopkins was found to have been the victim of sex discrimination, the judge in the case concluded that the discrimination was not overt or intentional. In fact, Hopkins freely admitted during the trial that she had never perceived that she was being discriminated against because of her gender while she was employed with Price Waterhouse. Instead of overt discrimination, the judge ruled that Hopkins had been a victim of sexual discrimination that was latent within the culture of Price Waterhouse. That is, the partners who made the sexually biased remarks regarding Hopkins were not aware that they were evaluating her unfairly relative to male candidates for partner. Despite this lack of awareness on the part of individual partners, the judge ruled that Price Waterhouse was at fault for perpetuating an evaluation system that allowed sexual stereotypes to adversely affect the promotion opportunities of female employees.

> There is no direct evidence of any determined purpose to maliciously discriminate against women but plaintiff appears to have been a victim of "omissive and subtle" discriminations created by a system that made evaluations based on "outmoded" attitudes." . . . Price Waterhouse should have been aware that women being evaluated by male partners might well be victims of discriminatory stereotypes. Yet the firm made no efforts . . . to discourage comments tainted by sexism or to determine whether they were influenced by stereotypes.

EPILOGUE

In May 1990, six years after Ann Hopkins filed suit against Price Waterhouse, a federal judge ruled that Hopkins was entitled to approximately $400,000 in compensatory damages from Price Waterhouse as a result of having been victimized by sex discrimination. More important, the judge also ruled that the CPA firm had to offer Hopkins a partnership position. During a party to celebrate the court decision, Hopkins maintained that she would have no reservations joining a firm that had unfairly rejected her for partnership seven years earlier. She also joked with her male co-workers at the World Bank regarding several less-than-complimentary remarks made regarding her during the trial. In particular, she questioned the assertion of one Price Waterhouse partner that she needed to enroll in a charm school. Moments later, Hopkins took a long and noisy slug of champagne—straight from the bottle.

In late 1993, the AICPA reported that approximately 4.9 percent of the partnership positions with the sixteen largest accounting firms were held by women.[7] However, women account for a much larger percentage of the individuals most recently promoted to partnership positions with large accounting firms. For example, in 1993, 18 percent of Deloitte & Touche's new partners were women, compared with only 13 percent in 1992. Comparable figures for KPMG Peat Marwick for 1993 and 1992 were 16 percent and 10 percent, respectively.[8] Several of the Big Six firms have also adopted policies designed specifically to retain women employees. Both Deloitte & Touche and KPMG Peat Marwick have created career planning and mentoring programs for women. Likewise, KPMG Peat Marwick and Price Waterhouse have recently established gender-issue workshops for their employees and partners to attend.

QUESTIONS

1. Do you believe that public accounting firms have a responsibility to make a special effort to facilitate the career success of female employees? Why or why not? What specific measures could public accounting firms take in this regard, in addition to those mentioned in the case?

2. In business circles one will frequently hear references to the "old boy" network. Many women in professional firms have complained that their gender automatically precludes them from becoming a member of the old boy network within their firm. Define, in your own terms, what you believe is meant by the phrase *old boy network*. Should professional firms attempt to break down these networks?

3. The nepotism rules that have been adopted by many professional firms pose a major inconvenience for married couples who work for, or would like to work for, these firms. Discuss the costs and benefits of these rules in a public accounting setting. In practice, do you believe these rules are equally fair (or unfair) to both sexes?

---

7. "Footnotes," *Accounting Today*, 18 October 1993, 3.

8. "More Women Become Partners in Accounting," *Wall Street Journal*, 10 August 1993, B1.

4. In commenting on the career opportunities of women and minorities in public accounting firms, an executive partner of a national accounting firm noted that "client acceptance" was an important issue. That is, he believed that the reluctance of certain clients to accept female and minority auditors was a factor contributing to the lack of progress of these groups in public accounting. Assume an audit client objects to a given auditor because of the auditor's sex or race. What courses of action should the CPA firm consider taking in such a case?

5. Several of the large public accounting firms that were asked to provide information to the U.S. Senate during the 1976 investigation of the accounting profession claimed that disclosing such information would constitute an invasion of their privacy. Do you agree or disagree with these firms' view? Why? Even if such disclosures are considered an invasion of privacy, are they justified from a public interest perspective?

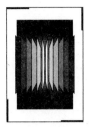

CASE 4.2

WHEN AUDITORS BECOME LOBBYISTS

In the early 1990s, the Financial Accounting Standards Board (FASB) was blindsided by an avalanche of controversy stemming from an accounting rule that it had proposed. This proposed rule, which was included in the FASB exposure draft "Accounting for Stock-Based Compensation," called for corporations to recognize compensation expense for certain stock options when they were granted to executives and employees. Shortly after the stock option exposure draft was circulated, the FASB was flooded with hundreds of letters, most of them extremely critical of the proposed change in accounting for stock options.

Even Congress and the President of the United States voiced opinions on the proposed stock option accounting rule. In early 1994, the Senate passed a resolution by a vote of 88-9 urging the FASB to drop the proposed standard. The debate in the Senate was led by two individuals who seldom agree on important policy matters but shared a similar opinion of the FASB's stock option proposal. Senator Barbara Boxer, a liberal Democrat from California, criticized the FASB for "pursuing an abstract theory" that will "damage the growth potential of many companies."[1] On the other side of the aisle, Senator Phil Gramm, a staunch Republican from Texas, observed in his typically blunt manner, "The bottom line here is that this is a stupid proposal."[2] About the same time, President Clinton expressed his concern that the stock option accounting standard might "undermine the competitiveness" of many of the nation's most important industries.[3]

By far, the most vocal critics of the FASB's stock option proposal were business executives of large public companies—the individuals who stood to lose the

---

1. K. Rankin, "Congress Rips FASB on Stock Options," *Accounting Today*, 1 November 1993, 1, 33.

2. Ibid.

3. C. Harlan, "Accounting Proposal Stirs Unusual Uproar in Executive Suites," *Wall Street Journal*, 7 March 1994, A1, A8.

most if the standard was adopted. The two-hundred-member Business Round-table, composed of chief executive officers of large public companies, waged a public relations war against the FASB's efforts to overhaul accounting for stock options. These individuals realized that the new standard would likely cause many companies to stop issuing stock options, which for many years had been a lucrative source of income for corporate executives. The president of one computer firm was so incensed by the FASB's efforts that he suggested disbanding the rule-making body.

> The arrogant, out-of-touch FASB bureaucracy should simply close its doors and stop damaging corporate America for the sake of accounting principles.[4]

Numerous editorials regarding the proposed stock option rule appeared in the business press, most of which were critical of the proposal. For example, an editorial in *Forbes* referred to the stock option proposal as "FASB's Folly."[5] This editorial noted that the proposed accounting rule was one of the FASB's "most asinine, destructive proposals ever" and then added that "the idea is utterly illogical."[6]

Many prominent members of the accounting profession became involved in the controversy surrounding the proposed stock option rule. Eventually, the debate within the profession took on a nasty tone. Charges that certain accounting firms were lobbying against the proposal to appease their large audit clients were met with angry rebuttals. Nevertheless, these charges raised anew important issues that have faced the accounting profession over the past two decades. Among these issues is whether the integrity and credibility of the independent audit function are undermined when accounting firms lobby on behalf of controversial positions supported by their audit clients. A related question is whether the authority for issuing accounting rules should remain in the private sector or be assumed by a governmental agency.

Stock Options As Compensation Expense

Companies often include stock options as a component of their compensation scheme for key executives and employees. A company that popularized this method of compensation was Chrysler Corporation. In 1978, the financially troubled automobile manufacturer wanted to hire Lee Iacocca as its chief executive, an individual who had enjoyed a long and successful career as a top executive of Ford Motor Company. Chrysler offered Iacocca a $1 annual salary and 400,000 stock options. The stock options gave Iacocca the right to purchase 400,000 shares of Chrysler common stock at a predetermined cost per share or "exercise price" at any time over a several-year period. If Iacocca succeeded in turning around Chrysler, the company's stock price would likely rise well above the exercise price of his stock options. He could then cash in those options by purchasing Chrysler's common stock at the exercise price and reselling it at the

---

4. T. J. Rodgers, "New FASB Rule Is Ill-conceived," *Business Credit*, June 1994, 20–21.

5. "FASB's Folly," *Forbes*, 31 January 1994, 26.

6. Ibid.

higher market price. In fact, Iacocca masterminded one of the most celebrated corporate turnarounds in U.S. history and realized a reported profit exceeding $40 million by exercising his stock options.

In recent years, the use of stock options as a component of executives' compensation has become an important corporate strategy for newly formed companies. Compensatory stock option plans are particularly prevalent among emerging companies in high-technology industries including the computer industry and the biotechnology industry. Newly formed companies in these industries typically cannot afford to pay the large salaries commanded by the executives they want to hire. As a result, these companies often use the "Chrysler" strategy to attract these individuals.

In 1972, the Accounting Principles Board, the FASB's predecessor, issued *APB Opinion No. 25*, "Accounting for Stock Issued to Employees." *APB No. 25* allows companies to ignore stock options issued to executives and employees if those options have an exercise price equal to or higher than the current market price of the company's common stock. That is, no compensation expense is recorded for such stock options. The FASB decided that this "nonaccounting" approach for out-of-the-money stock options was unreasonable and decided to change it. The FASB's position was simple. Although stock options may have an exercise price equal to or above the current market price of a company's stock on the date they are granted, they still have an economic value on that date. This economic value stems from the opportunity the holders of the options may have to purchase the company's common stock at less than market value at some point over the term of the options. This economic value, according to the FASB, is a component of an entity's compensation expense and should be recognized as such in its accounting records.

One of the more difficult issues addressed by the FASB's stock option proposal was the question of how companies should go about determining the economic or fair value of out-of-the-money stock options when they are granted. The FASB suggested that option-pricing models be used for this purpose. Such models have been used for years by sophisticated investors to determine the economic value of stock options that are publicly traded. However, to determine the economic value of a stock option using an option-pricing model, several assumptions must be made. For example, the future volatility of the underlying common stock must be estimated. Small changes in these assumptions can result in wide fluctuations in the estimated value of a stock option.

CRITICISM OF FASB's PROPOSED STOCK OPTION RULE

Opponents of the FASB's proposed change in the method of accounting for stock options presented two principal reasons why the proposal should not be adopted. The difficulty of establishing a reasonable estimate of stock options' economic value was one of these reasons. However, the primary argument against the FASB's proposal was that it would create financial problems for thousands of companies, particularly "start-up" companies.

Critics of the FASB's proposal maintained that because most new companies initially have minimal earnings, they could not afford to offer stock options to executives they wanted to hire if the value of these options had to be expensed immediately. As a result, these companies would have difficulty attracting highly qualified personnel for their key management positions. Carrying this argument to its logical conclusion, fewer new companies would be formed if the FASB's proposal was adopted. The resulting implications for the national economy, according to an editorial in *Forbes*, would be dire. *Forbes* pointed out that in the mid-1980s, fourteen million of the nearly nineteen million new jobs created nationwide were linked to new companies.[7] A federal official denounced the FASB for stubbornly refusing to take these alleged pervasive and negative economic consequences into account when considering the proposed stock option standard.

> Faced with these arguments, the FASB's rebuttal is simple: When it comes to accounting principles, economic consequences be damned; the truth will set investors free.[8]

Among the parties expressing strong disagreement with the stock option proposal were the Big Six accounting firms. In commenting on the proposal, a partner with Ernst & Young noted, "Why introduce an extremely subjective measure into financial statements?"[9] In an eleven-page analysis of the proposed rule, Arthur Andersen & Co. concluded:

> We believe it is in the best interests of the public, the financial community, and the FASB itself for the Board to address those issues that have a significant impact on improving the relevance and usefulness of financial reporting. In our view, employers' accounting for stock options and other stock compensation does not meet that test.[10]

Coopers & Lybrand, another Big Six firm, studied the potential impact of the proposal on the earnings of companies that issue stock options as a form of compensation.[11] This study, which considered seven hundred individual stock option grants, demonstrated that the proposed accounting rule would have a large negative impact on corporate earnings, particularly the earnings of new companies. Finally, the Big Six firms banded together and sent a joint letter to the FASB in July 1994. In that letter, these firms strongly encouraged the FASB to drop the stock option proposal from its agenda.[12]

SUPPORT FOR FASB'S STOCK OPTION PROPOSAL

Supporters of the new accounting standard for stock options maintained that it was needed to recognize a very material expense of corporations that was going unrecorded. These same parties also maintained that the arguments used by

---

7. Ibid.

8. J. C. Beese, "A Rule That Stunts Growth," *Wall Street Journal*, 8 February 1994, A18.

9. R. Khalaf, "If It Ain't Broke . . .," *Forbes*, 12 April 1993, 100.

10. Arthur Andersen & Co., *Arthur Andersen Accounting News Briefs*, "FASB Exposure Draft 'Accounting for Stock-based Compensation,'" August 1993, 8.

11. M. S. Akresh and J. Fuersich, "Stock Options: Accounting, Valuation, and Management Issues," *Management Accounting*, March 1994, 51–53.

12. P.B.W. Miller, "Ethics and Stock Options—An Update," *In The Public Interest*, Newsletter of The Public Interest Section of the American Accounting Association, October 1994, 3.

opponents of the proposed standard were flimsy, at best. For example, defenders of the proposal refused to accept the contention that the compensation expense associated with newly issued stock options should not be booked simply because this expense is difficult to estimate precisely. Warren Buffett, a billionaire investor and frequent critic of the FASB, noted that "It is both silly and cynical to say that an important item of cost should not be recognized simply because it can't be quantified with pinpoint accuracy."[13]

Supporters of the FASB's stock option proposal also rejected the economic consequences argument used by opponents of the proposal. The vice-chairman of the FASB, James Leisenring, insisted that it was not the FASB's responsibility to consider the economic consequences of new accounting standards such as their impact on job creation in the economy.[14] Likewise, Professor Paul Pacter of the University of Connecticut argued that the FASB must maintain a neutral attitude with respect to the economic impact of new accounting standards.

> Accounting standards seek to measure and report faithfully the economic events and transactions that have taken place. This objective applies equally to events and transactions that are favorable to the business and those that are unfavorable. Accounting standards are not and should not be designed to obscure or distort reality. If the reality is that stock options have value and are intended to motivate employees and to compensate them for their services, accounting should reflect that reality.[15]

Several supporters of the FASB's stock option proposal pointed to the fiasco in the savings and loan industry during the 1980s to support their contention that allowing economic considerations to dictate the choice of accounting methods can have disastrous results. In the 1980s, the accounting profession was forced to accept creative accounting methods for thousands of savings and loans. Regulatory authorities, including Congress, perceived that the financial problems being experienced at the time by the savings and loan industry would be short-lived. So, the argument went, the hundreds of savings and loans that were technically insolvent should be allowed to continue operating. Consequently, these institutions were allowed to use accounting methods that overstated their assets to make them appear solvent. Again, the eventual result of this policy decision was disastrous. The executives of many of these insolvent savings and loans made increasingly speculative investments, hoping to return them to a profitable condition. As a result, the losses of these savings and loans began piling up at an ever-increasing rate. Finally, in the late 1980s, the federal government was forced to step in and spend several hundred billion dollars bailing out the savings and loan industry.

Dennis Beresford, the chairman of the FASB and target of much of the criticism directed toward the stock option proposal, was particularly concerned by the suggestion that his organization consider the economic consequences of new accounting rules. Beresford noted that business entities in the past had often argued against new accounting standards because of their supposed negative economic consequences. In many of these cases, Beresford maintained, business

---

13. Harlan, "Accounting Proposal Stirs Unusual Uproar," A8.

14. Rankin, "Congress Rips FASB," 33.

15. P. Pacter, "FASB's Stock Option Proposal: Correcting a Serious Flaw," *CPA Journal*, March 1994, 60–61.

executives were simply attempting to avoid economic reality by not accounting for certain expenses. This latter point was well made by the *New York Times*, which strongly supported the stock option proposal in a series of articles.

> For both pensions and post-retirement health benefits, companies resisted accounting reforms. . . . But when corporate boards were finally forced to look at reasonable estimates of the costs, companies began to control these costs.[16]

Finally, several parties contended that the economic consequences argument used by business executives to campaign against the FASB's stock option proposal was a smoke screen used to conceal these executives' true motive in criticizing the proposal. These parties maintained that business executives' campaign against the proposed stock option accounting rule was simply an exercise in economic self-interest. For many years, corporate executives had been reaping windfall profits from the exercise of stock options, a job "perk" they did not want to see fall by the wayside because of the proposed new accounting rule. Consider just two examples of enormous profits realized by corporate executives as a result of stock option grants. In 1992, two top executives of U.S. Surgical Corporation realized more than $80 million by cashing in stock options granted to them in prior years.[17] Topping that figure was a nearly $200 million stock option profit realized by two Walt Disney Company executives in 1992.[18]

Of the hundreds of letters received by the FASB regarding the stock option proposal, one was a tongue-in-cheek correspondence from Mr. Beauregard T. Greede, the chairman of Sillicorp, Inc. Mr. Greede was quite upset with the FASB's suggestion that his firm record the expense associated with the stock options he had been granted.

> Do you think my handpicked board of directors would have awarded me options on a gazillion shares of Sillicorp stock if they'd had to tell the stockholders what the options were worth? And expense 'em![19]

A more direct point of view on this matter was provided by a financial analyst who supported the FASB's stock option proposal.

> To me, it doesn't make sense that you can give stock options to executives and not call it compensation. If it's compensation, it has to be accounted for. Right now, the companies have a free ride and they don't want to give it up. And that's what the uproar is about.[20]

THE DEBATE OVER STOCK OPTIONS TURNS NASTY

As the controversy over the stock option proposal escalated, the debate within the accounting profession became sidetracked. Instead of focusing on the

---

16. F. Norris, "In Accounting, Truth Can Be Very Scary," *New York Times*, 11 April 1993, sec. 3, 1.

17. L. Berton and J. S. Lublin, "Executives Say Accounting Idea Is Poorly Timed," *Wall Street Journal*, 4 December 1992, B1, B12.

18. Ibid.

19. G. M. Kang, "Hands Off My Stock Pile," *Business Week*, 12 April 1993, 28–30.

20. G. A. Cheney, "Stock Option Quest Sparks Questions about FASB's Future," *Accounting Today*, 10 October 1994, 10, 12.

soundness of the FASB's stock option proposal, accountants began debating whether it was proper for accounting firms to lobby the FASB on proposed new standards. Much of this debate centered on the Big Six accounting firms. Recall that in July 1994, the Big Six firms asked the FASB in a joint letter to drop the stock option proposal. An accounting professor questioned the motives of the Big Six firms in submitting this letter to the FASB.

> This letter is dreadful in several respects. Its arguments are strictly political and advance the interests of corporate management . . . . When I weigh this letter on the ethics scales, I find it wanting. The economic world is waiting for and needs responsible behavior and more complete financial statements, but these people advocate the opposite.[21]

The Chief Accountant of the Securities and Exchange Commission (SEC), Walter Schuetze, was probably the most prominent member of the profession to criticize the Big Six accounting firms' lobbying efforts against the stock option proposal. Schuetze pointed out that representatives of these firms had initially supported the proposal when it was placed on the FASB's agenda in 1984. Schuetze suggested that the switch in the position of these firms "was in response to fear of losing clients or other forms of retaliation."[22] A former Big Six partner and former member of the FASB, Schuetze went on to suggest that the Big Six's lobbying efforts against the stock option proposal called into question the independence of these firms.

> If public companies are pressuring their outside auditors . . . to take particular positions on financial accounting and reporting issues and outside auditors are subordinating their views to those of their clients, can the outside auditor community continue to claim to be independent?[23]

Schuetze's criticism of Big Six accounting firms did not go unanswered. An editorial in the bimonthly publication *Accounting Today* chastised Schuetze for his criticism of the Big Six firms. The editorial noted that Schuetze was "unnecessarily shrill" in his criticism and suggested that he did the profession "a disservice by his intemperate remarks."[24] Philip Chenok, president of the American Institute of Certified Public Accountants, also berated Schuetze for his criticism of the dominant firms in the accounting profession. Chenok said he found it "offensive and inappropriate for the Chief Accountant of the SEC to suggest a loss of independence [by the major accounting firms] over the stock option matter."[25]

INVITING GOVERNMENT INTERVENTION?

In criticizing Big Six firms for becoming "cheerleaders"[26] for their audit clients in the campaign against the stock option proposal, Walter Schuetze warned that

---

21. Miller, "Ethics and Stock Options," 3.

22. "Schuetze Wary over CPA Independence on Stock Option Proposal," *Journal of Accountancy*, March 1994, 9–10.

23. Ibid.

24. "No Option Left," *Accounting Today*, 7 February 1994, 3.

25. "Accountants Are Chided over Stock-Option Stance," *Wall Street Journal*, 12 January 1994, A5.

26. Ibid.

these firms might be damaging their own interests. Schuetze noted that such lobbying efforts could serve as an invitation for regulatory authorities "to regulate more heavily, and more directly, the auditing profession in particular and financial accounting and reporting in general."[27]

Schuetze's warning was not unfounded. During the 1970s, a U.S. Senate investigation of the accounting profession resulted in severe criticism of the large accounting firms that dominate the profession.[28] Among the specific charges leveled at these firms was that they lobbied rule-making bodies within the profession to adopt proposed accounting rules that would benefit the economic interests of their largest audit clients. Like Schuetze, the Senate suggested that such lobbying efforts were an indication that these firms' independence had been compromised. Although never seriously considered, one recommendation that resulted from the Senate's investigation was the creation of a federal agency to assume responsibility for the independent audit function.

A more credible recommendation that stemmed from the Senate's investigation of the accounting profession during the 1970s was the creation of a federal agency to establish accounting standards. The heated controversy over the FASB's stock option proposal raised again the possibility of intervention in the profession's rule-making processes by the federal government. A former Chief Accountant of the SEC, John Burton, recently questioned whether the FASB could survive much longer given the continuing pressure exerted on it by the business community.[29] In recent years, two members of the FASB, both former partners of Big Six accounting firms, have resigned. In each case, these individuals cited as reasons for their resignation the pressure exerted on them by corporate interests opposed to one or more of the FASB's proposals.

The Big Six accounting firms are strongly opposed to the federal government assuming a direct role in the establishment of accounting standards. However, when these firms criticize a proposed standard, they take the risk of further undercutting the FASB's authority and hastening its demise. As the controversy over the stock option proposal became very heated, the large accounting firms were careful to focus their criticism specifically on that proposal. While they were criticizing the stock option proposal, these firms expressed support for retaining the FASB as the principal rule-making authority for the accounting profession.

> We believe that setting financial accounting standards should remain in the private sector. We oppose direct involvement by Congress in establishing financial accounting standards. The current arrangements under which the FASB establishes financial accounting standards subject to oversight by the SEC generally work well.[30]

27. "Schuetze Wary over CPA Independence," 10.

28. U.S. Congress, Senate Subcommittee on Reports, Accounting and Management of the Committee on Government Operations, *The Accounting Establishment* (Washington, D.C.: U.S. Government Printing Office, 1977).

29. L. Berton, "FASB Finds That Criticism Increases Difficulty of Finding New Member," *Wall Street Journal*, 18 January 1991, B3.

30. Arthur Andersen & Co., "FASB Exposure Draft," 8.

EPILOGUE

In late 1994, the FASB rescinded its controversial stock option proposal. Under a new proposed accounting standard, companies would be allowed to expense out-of-the-money stock options when issued *or* to simply disclose the income statement effect of expensing such stock options in their financial statement footnotes. If this proposal is adopted, clearly most companies will choose the second alternative. Dennis Beresford, FASB chairman, commented on the FASB's decision to retract the original stock option proposal.

> No matter how hard we tried to convince people of the correctness of our stand, there simply was not enough support for the notion of requiring expense recognition.[31]

QUESTIONS

1. What are the principal advantages and disadvantages of having the rule-making bodies in the accounting profession controlled by the private sector rather than by the federal government?

2. Large accounting firms are among the parties most knowledgeable of accounting theory and the pragmatic or everyday problems of applying accounting standards. As such, these firms are well positioned to evaluate the soundness of proposed accounting rules. Should rule-making bodies make use of the expertise and insight of these firms when considering proposed accounting standards? Why or why not? If so, explain how this could be done while minimizing the risk that these firms would antagonize their clients or, conversely, be seen as catering to the economic interests of their clients.

3. Assume that you are the managing partner of an office of a large accounting firm. The chief executive officer of your office's largest client has contacted you and asked that you write a letter to the FASB, on behalf of your firm, which is critical of a new accounting rule being considered by the FASB. What should you do at this point? What factors should be considered in responding to the client executive's request?

4. Should the FASB consider the economic consequences of proposed standards when deciding whether to adopt these standards? Explain. Identify the key issues or factors the FASB should consider when deliberating on proposed accounting rules.

---

31. "FASB Revises Position on Stock Options," *Journal of Accountancy, February 1995, 18–19.*

CASE 4.3
TOMMY O'CONNELL, AUDIT SENIOR

Tommy O'Connell had been a senior with a Big Six accounting firm for less than one month when he was assigned to the audit engagement for the Altamesa Manufacturing Company.[1] Tommy realized that being assigned to the tough Altamesa job was a clear indication that Jack Morrison, the office managing partner, regarded his work highly. The assignment would allow Tommy to become better acquainted with Morrison, who served as the audit partner for the Altamesa engagement. Despite the challenge and opportunity posed by the Altamesa engagement, Tommy did not look forward to spending three months in Amarillo, Texas, which was a five-hour drive from his home in Fort Worth. This would be his first audit engagement outside Fort Worth since his marriage six months earlier, and he dreaded breaking the news to his wife, Suzie, who often complained about the long hours his job required.

Altamesa manufactured steel girders used in the construction and renovation of bridges in West Texas, New Mexico, Colorado, and Oklahoma. The company's business was cyclical and linked closely to the funding available to municipalities in Altamesa's four-state market area. To learn more about the company and its personnel, Tommy arranged to have lunch with Shay Jennings, the audit senior on the Altamesa job the two previous years. According to Shay, Altamesa's management took aggressive positions regarding year-end expense accruals and revenue recognition. The company's revenues were recorded under the percentage-of-completion method, since its sales contracts extended over two to five years. Shay recounted several disputes with the company's chief accountant regarding the estimated stage of completion of jobs in progress. In an effort to front-load as much of the profit on the jobs as possible, the chief accountant always insisted that the jobs were further along than they actually were.

---

1. The facts of this case were reconstructed from an actual series of events. Names and certain background information have been changed to conceal the identities of the individuals involved in the case.

After speaking with Shay, Tommy was apprehensive about tackling the difficult Altamesa engagement. But he realized that the job gave him an excellent chance to maintain and strengthen his fast-track image within his office. If he was to reach his goal of being promoted to manager by his fifth year with the firm, he would need to prove himself on tough assignments such as the Altamesa engagement.

It was late May, just two weeks before Tommy would be leaving for Amarillo to begin the Altamesa audit—the company had a June 30 fiscal year-end. Tommy, Jack Morrison, and an audit manager were having lunch at the Cattleman's Restaurant in the "Cowtown" district of north Fort Worth.

"Tommy, I've decided to send Carl with you out to Amarillo. Is that okay?" asked Jack Morrison.

"Ah . . . sure, Jack. Yeah, that'll be fine," Tommy replied.

"Of all people," Tommy thought to himself, "he would send Carl Wilmeth to Amarillo with me." Carl was a staff accountant with only a few months' experience, having been hired in the middle of the just-completed busy season. Other than being auditors and approximately the same age, the two young men had little in common. Tommy was from rural West Texas, while Carl was from the exclusive Highland Park community of north central Dallas. Texas Tech, a large state-supported university, was Tommy's alma mater, while Carl was a graduate of a small private college in the East.

Tommy did not appreciate Carl's cocky attitude, and his lack of experience made him a questionable choice for the Altamesa engagement, at least in Tommy's mind. As he tried to choke down the rest of his prime rib, Tommy recalled the complaints he had heard about Carl's job performance. Over the past three months, Carl had worked on two audits. In both cases, he had performed admirably—too admirably, in fact, coming in well under budget on the audit tasks that he had been assigned. On one engagement, Carl had completed an assignment in less than 60 hours when the budget was 100 hours; the previous year, 110 hours had been required to complete that same task. Both seniors who had supervised Carl suspected that he had not completed all of his assigned audit procedures, although he had signed off on those procedures on the audit program. The tasks assigned to Carl had been large-scale tests of transactions that involved checking invoices, receiving reports, purchase orders, and other documents for various attributes. Given the nature of the tests, confirming their suspicions would have been difficult for the seniors.

Six weeks later, in early July, the Altamesa audit was in full swing. Carl had just finished his third assigned task on the job, in record time, of course. "Boss, here's that disbursements file. Anything else you want me to do this afternoon? Since I'm way ahead of schedule, maybe I should take off and work on my tan out on the golf course."

"No, Carl. I think we have plenty to keep you busy right here." Tommy was agitated but he tried not to let it show. "Why don't you pull out the contracts file and then talk to Ellen in the sales office. Make copies of any new contracts or proposals over the past year and put them in the contracts file."

At this point, Tommy simply did not have time to review Carl's cash disbursements workpapers. He was too busy trying to figure out Altamesa's complex method of allocating overhead costs to contracts-in-progress. Later that afternoon, he had an appointment to meet with the chief accountant and a production superintendent to discuss the status of a large job. Tommy and the chief accountant had already argued on two occasions regarding a job's stage of completion. Shay had been right: the chief accountant's intention was to recognize profit on the in-progress jobs as quickly as possible. With four decades of experience, Scrooge—a nickname Shay had pinned on the chief accountant—obviously considered the young auditors a nuisance and did not appreciate their probing questions. Each time Tommy asked him a question regarding an important issue, the chief accountant responded with a rambling, convoluted answer that was intended to confuse rather than inform.

To make sense of Altamesa's complicated accounting decisions for its long-term contracts, Tommy spent several hours of nonchargeable time each night in his motel room flipping through copies of job order worksheets and contracts. Occasionally, he would refer to prior year workpapers, his firm's policy and procedures manual, or even his tattered cost accounting textbook from his college days. Carl spent most of his evenings in the motel's club being taught the Texas Two-Step and Cotton-eyed Joe by several new friends he had acquired.

During July and August, Tommy and Carl worked fifty to sixty hours per week on the Altamesa engagement. Several times Tommy wondered to himself whether it was worthwhile to work so hard to earn recognition as a "superstar" senior. He was also increasingly concerned about the impact of his fast-track strategy on his marriage. When he tried to explain to Suzie that the long hours and travel would pay off when he eventually made partner, she was unimpressed. "Who cares if you make partner? I just want to spend more time with my husband," was her stock reply.

Finally, late August rolled around and the Altamesa job was almost done. Jack Morrison had been in Amarillo for the past three days going over the Altamesa workpapers with a fine-tooth comb. Nothing seemed to escape Morrison's eagle eye. Tommy had spent twelve hours per day since Morrison had arrived, tracking down missing invoices, checking on late confirmations, and tying up dozens of other loose ends. Carl was already back in Fort Worth. Morrison had allowed him to leave two days earlier after clearing his review comments.

"Tommy, I have to admit that I was a little concerned about sending a light senior out to run this audit. But, by golly, you have done a good job." Morrison did not look up as he continued to sign off on the workpapers spread before him on Altamesa's conference table. "You know, this kid Carl does super work. I've never seen cleaner, more organized workpapers from a staff accountant."

Tommy grimaced as he sat next to Morrison at the conference table. "Yeah, right. They should look clean, since he didn't do half of what he signed off on," Tommy thought to himself. Here was his opportunity. For the past several weeks, Tommy had planned to sit down with Morrison and talk to him regarding Carl's job performance. But now he was reluctant to do so. How do you tell a partner you suspect that much of the work he is reviewing may not have been done? Besides, Tommy realized that as Carl's immediate supervisor, he was responsible for that work. Tommy knew that he was facing a no-win situation. He leaned back in his chair and remained silent, hoping that Morrison would hurry through the last few workpaper files so they could make it back to Fort Worth by midnight.

Epilogue

Tommy never informed Jack Morrison of his suspicions regarding Carl's work. Thankfully, no problems—of a legal nature—ever arose on the jobs to which Carl had been assigned. After passing the CPA exam in his first attempt, Carl resigned from the accounting firm and enrolled in a prestigious MBA program. At last report, Carl was a junior executive with a large investment banking firm. Tommy reached his goal of being promoted to manager within five years. However, a year later he decided that he was not cut out to be a partner and resigned from the firm to accept a position in private industry.

QUESTIONS

1. Compare and contrast the professional roles of a senior auditor and a staff accountant. In your analysis, consider the different responsibilities assigned to each role, the job-related stresses that individuals in the two roles face, and how each role contributes to the successful completion of an audit engagement. Which of these two roles is (a) more important and (b) more stressful? Defend your choices.

2. Assume that you are Tommy O'Connell and have just been informed that Carl Wilmeth has been assigned to work with you on the Altamesa audit engagement. Would you handle this situation any differently than Tommy did? Explain.

3. Again, assume that you are Tommy. Carl is badgering you for something to do midway through the Altamesa job. You suspect that he is not completing all of his assigned procedures, but at the time you are wrestling with a contentious issue in the contracts-in-progress file. What would you do at this point? What could you do to confirm your suspicions that Carl is not completing his assignments?

4. Now assume that Jack Morrison is reviewing the Altamesa workpapers. To date, you (Tommy) have said nothing to Morrison about your suspicions regarding Carl. Do you have a professional responsibility to raise this matter now with Morrison? Explain.

5. Assume that at some point Tommy did discuss Carl's questionable work performance with Morrison. Tommy did not have any tangible proof that Carl was failing to complete his assigned tasks. The only evidence Tommy had in this respect was that Carl had come in significantly under budget on every major task assigned to him over a period of several months. If you were Jack Morrison, how would you handle this matter?

CASE 4.4
SARAH RUSSELL, STAFF ACCOUNTANT

Sarah Russell grew up in a small town in the flatlands of western Kansas where she was born.[1] In high school, she was homecoming queen, valedictorian of her graduating class, starting guard on her basketball team for two years, and a candy striper at the local hospital. Since her parents had attended the University of Kansas, Sarah was off to Lawrence at age eighteen. After spending her freshman year posting straight A's in thirty hours of college courses, Sarah settled on accounting as her major after seriously considering journalism, pre-law, and finance. Although Sarah had yet to take any courses in accounting and had not been exposed to the subject in high school, she had been impressed by a presentation that a female partner of a large accounting firm had made at a career fair. Sarah was excited by the challenges and opportunities presented by public accounting, as described by the partner. Here was a field in which she could learn a great deal in a short period and advance rapidly to a position where she had important responsibilities. Plus, public accounting provided a wide range of career paths. If she really enjoyed public accounting, she could pursue a partnership position with a large accounting firm. Then again, she might "hang out her shingle" in her hometown, see the world on the internal audit staff of a large corporation, or return to college after a couple of years of real-world experience to earn an MBA.

Sarah completed the tough accounting courses at the University of Kansas with only two small blemishes on her transcript—B's in individual and corporate taxation. During the fall semester of her senior year, Sarah accepted a position as a staff accountant with a Big Six accounting firm. Although she considered staying in her home state, Sarah decided to request an assignment in her new

---

1. Carol Knapp wrote this case while an assistant professor at the University of Nevada Las Vegas. This case is based upon experiences related by a young woman who was employed by a large accounting firm. The names of the individuals involved in this case and other background facts, such as locations, have been changed.

employer's Chicago office. Sarah believed that exposure to big-city life would allow her to reach a more informed decision when it was time to make a long-term commitment to a career path and a life-style.

During her first year on the job, Sarah was assigned to six audit engagements with clients that included a pipeline company, a religious foundation, and a professional sports team. She worked hard on each engagement and earned impressive performance appraisals from each of her immediate supervisors. Somehow Sarah also squeezed a CPA review course into her hectic schedule that first year. And she was glad she did. She was among the few rookies in her large office to pass the CPA exam in one attempt. With that barrier out of the way, Sarah focused her energy on being promoted to audit senior as quickly as possible.

Several individuals were particularly supportive of Sarah during her first year, including R. J. Bell, an audit partner. Bell was forty years old and had been a partner for eight years. The rumor was that he was in line to become the new office managing partner within the next year or so. Bell tried to get to know the new staff accountants assigned to the audit staff and to help them adjust to their jobs in any way he could. Several times during the year, Bell invited small groups of staff accountants to his home to have dinner with him and his family. Recognizing that Sarah was new to Chicago, he made a special effort to insure that she was included in office social events and that she received complimentary tickets to cultural and sporting events that were often made available to the office. When Sarah's old car from college died, Bell helped her obtain a loan from a local bank. Sarah appreciated Bell's guidance and advice. She considered the firm to be very lucky to have an audit partner who took time from a busy schedule to be so helpful to staff accountants.

Shortly after her first anniversary with the firm, Sarah received a telephone call from Bell at home one Saturday afternoon. At first, Sarah thought there must be a client emergency that required her assistance, but Bell did not bring up any client business during the conversation. Instead, he told Sarah that he had just called to chat. Sarah felt mildly uncomfortable with the situation, but spoke with Bell for a few minutes before making up an excuse to get off the phone.

The following day, Sarah, who was an avid jogger, had just completed a four-mile run on her regular jogging trail in a city park when Bell pulled up as she walked toward her car. "Hi, Sarah. How was your run?" Bell asked nonchalantly. "I was just driving by and thought you might like to get a Coke after your workout."

As Sarah approached Bell's car she felt awkward but tried to act natural, as if his unexpected appearance was only a coincidence. "Thanks, R. J. But I really need to get back to my apartment. I've got several errands to run and phone calls to make."

"You sure? I'm buying."

"Yeah, I'd better get home."

"Well, okay."

Over the next several weeks, Bell made a concerted effort to develop a personal relationship with Sarah. Eventually, Bell, who was known for working long hours, was calling her nearly every evening from his office just "to chat." Once or twice per week, he would invite her to get a drink with him after work. On a couple of occasions, she accepted, hoping that by doing so he would stop asking her. No such luck. Finally, she began avoiding him in the office and stopped answering her home phone when she thought it was him calling. Twice, Bell dropped by her apartment in the evenings. Panic-stricken both times, Sarah refused to answer the door, hoping he would quickly decide that she was not home.

As Bell became more insistent on seeing and speaking with Sarah, she felt increasing levels of stress and powerlessness. She did not know what to do or to whom she could turn. She was reluctant to discuss the matter with her friends in the office, since she did not want a rumor mill to get started. Embarrassment prevented her from discussing the matter with her parents or other family members. Worst of all, Sarah began wondering whether she had somehow encouraged Bell's behavior. She racked her brain to recall each time that she had spoken or met with him during her first year on the job. She could not remember saying anything that could have been misconstrued by him. But maybe she had inadvertently said something that had given him the wrong impression. Maybe he had mistaken the sense of respect and admiration she had for him as affection. Maybe she had asked him an inappropriate question. Maybe . . .

EPILOGUE

After more than six weeks of enduring Bell's advances, Sarah mustered the courage to make an appointment with him during office hours one Friday afternoon. When Sarah informed Bell that she wanted to keep their relationship on a strictly professional level, he failed to respond for several awkward moments. Finally, he remarked that Sarah must have misinterpreted his actions in recent weeks. He was simply trying to make her feel more comfortable with her job. "I go out of my way to be as friendly and sociable with as many members of the audit staff as I can." Bell then informed Sarah that, given the situation, he would see to it that she was not assigned to any of his engagements in the future. After a few moments of silence, he tersely asked, "Is there anything else I can do for you, Miss Russell?" Sarah shook her head softly and then got up and left his office.

Sarah had no further contact or conversations with Bell following that Friday afternoon meeting in his office. A few months later, she decided to return to Kansas to be closer to her family. Sarah is now an assistant controller with a manufacturing company headquartered in her home state.

QUESTIONS

1. In your opinion, how should Sarah have handled this matter? Identify the factors that Sarah should have considered in dealing with the situation. Also, identify the professional and personal responsibilities of Sarah, R. J. Bell, and other relevant individuals in this matter.

2. What were the costs and potential costs to Sarah's employer in this case? How should accounting firms attempt to prevent these types of situations from occurring? Assume that rather than speaking to Bell, Sarah had informed the office managing partner of the problem she was facing. How should the office managing partner have responded to the situation?

3. This case occurred in the early 1980s. Do you think this type of situation could occur now? Explain.

CASE 4.5

WHEN AUDITORS CHANGE SIDES

A controversial issue that has faced public accounting firms in recent years is the hiring by audit clients of individuals who previously served as their independent auditors.[1] When a client hires a former auditor, particularly its former audit engagement partner, there is some risk that the integrity and independence of the client's subsequent audits will be questioned. In the following New York Times *article ("When Auditors Change Sides," 11 October 1992, sec. F, 15), Allison Leigh Cowan discusses this phenomenon.*

To some people, William J. Sanders's resume is a mere footnote in an otherwise sorry chapter of business history. To others, it holds a clue about what can go wrong when the relationship between companies and their accountants becomes too cozy.

As the partner at Deloitte & Touche who headed the audit of First Executive Corporation for many years, Mr. Sanders had much responsibility for the reassuring opinions that Deloitte issued each year about the insurance company's financial health.

Then, in May 1990, he became First Executive's chief financial officer. Court documents show that his pay package included a $300,000-a-year base salary, a guaranteed bonus of $100,000 the first year and $200,000 the next, a company car and 181,818 bargain-priced stock options. The deal was sweet enough that Mr. Sanders quickly added seven more Deloitte employees to First Executive's payroll, including three who had worked on the audit.

The good times did not last, and much of the group, including Mr. Sanders, had to get out their resumes again within a year. By then, the company's severe financial problems had become so unmistakable that regulators in California and New York seized its two insurance subsidiaries, forcing the parent company to file for bankruptcy.

EXHIBIT 1
Companies With Senior Executives Who Once Worked for Their Auditors, and Where Questionable Accounting Contributed to Millions of Dollars in Investor Losses

---

American Continental Corporation (parent of failed Lincoln S&L)
Jack Atchison
Came from: Arthur Young
Became: Vice-president at salary of $930,000 a year

Cannon Group
Barry J. Lublin
Came from: Mann, Judd, Landau
Became: Chief financial officer

Chambers Development
Richard A. Knight
Came from: Grant Thornton
Became: Chief financial officer

Dairy World Genetics Partnerships
John J. O'Shaughnessy
Came from: Laventhol & Horwath
Became: Held various financial and accounting jobs

First Executive Corporation (parent of failed Executive Life)
William J. Sanders
Came from: Deloitte & Touche
Became: Chief financial officer with cash pay of over $500,000 plus stock options

Phar-Mor Inc.
Jeffrey Walley and Stanley Cherelstein
Came from: Coopers & Lybrand
Became: Senior executives

Source: A. L. Cowan, "When Auditors Change Sides," *New York Times*, 11 October 1992, sec. F, 15.

Now some regulators and others are wondering whether the troubles at First Executive and other companies hold a lesson about the problems that can arise when the door leading from public accounting to the private sector swings too freely. In California, the State Board of Accountancy has been tracking six cases including First Executive in which auditors failed to spot questionable accounting that ultimately contributed to huge investor losses. [*See Exhibit 1.*] The common thread: Each had lured people who had been working for its auditors into its executive suite at a time when the company's financial condition was becoming too precarious and the auditor's annual opinion could decide the company's fate.

"One of the questions we are looking at is, 'Is there total independence when that opinion is rendered, or is it somehow affected by the enticement to switch over to the other side?'" said Gregory P. Newington, the board's enforcement chief.

On October 22, its administrative committee is scheduled to consider legislation it has drafted that would require auditors to notify employers when they receive job offers from clients. "Something needs to be done," said Ira M. Landis the board's president.

In government, hopping directly from an influential job to, say, a high-paid lobbyist's position is often taboo, and many federal agencies forbid former officials from cashing in on their contacts for a time.

But in accounting, such career moves rarely raise an eyebrow. Indeed, Mr. Sanders and others who have found themselves in his position insist that their judgment as auditors was never impaired by job offers from their clients. And experts say there simply is no rule that expressly prohibits someone from acting one day as a company's auditor and the next day as the auditor's client.

In fact, it happens all the time. The vast majority of people hired by accounting firms at the entry level never make partner. Instead, many go to work for clients.

"By hiring your chief financial officer from your independent auditor, you're hiring somebody who knows the capability and the shortcomings of the independent auditor and can take advantage of that knowledge," said Loren Kellogg, publisher of Financial Statement Alert, a Los Angeles–based research service that scrutinizes the accounting practices of public companies.

"This has been the situation in enough accounting and auditing disasters that it should be strictly prohibited," he continued. Short of that, however, he favors requiring companies to disclose when they have hired someone from their auditing firm, so that investors have the benefit of that red flag.

Of course, many companies and their accountants believe matters would be best left in their own hands. "As long as the firm is advised of the situation, it probably can make sure there was no loss of objectivity," said John A. Heyman, a partner with BDO Seidman, who heads all of that firm's audits of public companies. He notes that many firms routinely reassign employees who have received job offers or double-check their work.

Perhaps, but such an approach leaves a lot to judgment, and even companies that have experienced problems do not always hesitate about returning to the auditing well.

Cannon Group Inc., a Los Angeles–based film company, hired Barry J. Lublin to be its chief financial officer in the summer of 1985. He had been a top partner on Cannon's audit in the Los Angeles office of Mann, Judd, Landau since 1979. By late 1986, the company disclosed that its accounting was the subject of an SEC investigation, which it later settled, and it reassigned Mr. Lublin to another job. Subsequently, he agreed to have his accounting license suspended for one year.

So whom did the company hire to take his place? Susan Beazley, a partner at Arthur Young, Cannon's new accounting firm.

QUESTIONS

1. Identify legitimate reasons that a company may have for wanting to hire members of its audit engagement team.

2. Assume that you were a member of the audit engagement team of Vermeil, Inc., during the two previous years. Last year, you were the audit senior who supervised the fieldwork, the same role you will assume on the next audit of Vermeil that will begin shortly. The audit engagement partner for the Vermeil audit the previous five years, Richard McGee, was hired six months ago as Vermeil's controller. You are well acquainted with McGee, since you were assigned to several audits on which he was the engagement partner. McGee will be the primary client contact person during this year's audit. Briefly discuss the problems this situation may pose for you. Does this situation have the potential to affect your independence or appearance of independence? Explain.

3. What measures, if any, has the profession taken in recent years to minimize the problems associated with auditors "changing sides"? In your opinion, what additional measures, if any, are necessary in this regard?

CASE 4.6

BILL DeBURGER, IN-CHARGE ACCOUNTANT

"Bill, will you have that inventory memo done by this afternoon?"

"Yeah, Sam, it's coming along. I should have it done by five or so."

"Make it three . . . or so. Okay, Bub?"

Bill responded with a smile and a nod. He had a good relationship with Sam Hakes, the partner supervising the audit of Marcelle Stores.[1]

Bill DeBurger was an in-charge accountant with one and one-half years of experience with his employer, a large national accounting firm. The title "in-charge" was used by Bill's firm for the employment position between staff accountant and audit senior. Advanced staff and semisenior are titles used by some accounting firms for this position. Typically, individuals were promoted to in-charge after one year with Bill's firm. An additional one to two years and successful completion of the CPA exam was usually required before promotion to audit senior. The title "in-charge" was a misnomer, at least in Bill's mind. None of the in-charges he knew had ever been placed in charge of even a small audit. Based upon Bill's experience, an in-charge was someone a senior or manager expected to work with little or no supervision. "Here's the audit program for payables. Go spend the next five weeks completing the twelve program steps . . . and don't bother me," was the prevailing attitude in making work assignments to in-charges.

As he turned back to the legal pad in front of him, Bill forced himself to think of Marcelle Stores' inventory—all $50 million of it. Bill's task was to summarize in a two-page memo nine hundred hours of work that he, two staff accountants, and five internal auditors had done over the past two months. Not included in the nine hundred hours were eight inventory observations that had been sub-ordered out to other offices of Bill's firm. Marcelle Stores was a regional

---

1. The information for this case was provided by a former public accountant who is now a college instructor. The names, location, and certain other background facts have been changed.

chain of 112 specialty stores that featured a broad range of products for do-it-yourself interior decorators. The company's most recent fiscal year had been a difficult one. A poor economy, increasing competition, and higher supplier prices had slashed Marcelle's profit to the bone over the past twelve months. The previous year, the company had posted a profit of slightly less than $8 million; for the year just completed, the company's preaudit net income was hovering at an anemic $500,000.

Inventory was clearly the most important audit area on the Marcelle engagement each year. This year, inventory was doubly important. Any material overstatement discovered in the inventory account would convert a poor year profit-wise for Marcelle into a disastrous year in which it posted its first-ever loss.

Facing Bill on the small table that served as his makeshift desk were two stacks of workpapers, each two feet tall. Summarized in those workpapers were the results of extensive price tests, inventory observation procedures, year-end cutoff tests, an analysis of the reserve for inventory obsolescence, and various other audit procedures. Bill's task was to assimilate all of this audit evidence into a conclusion regarding Marcelle's inventory. Bill realized that Sam Hakes expected that conclusion to include the key catch phrase "presented fairly, in all material respects, in conformity with generally accepted accounting principles."

As Bill attempted to outline the inventory memo, he gradually admitted to himself that he had no idea whether Marcelle's inventory was materially accurate. The workpaper summarizing the individual errors discovered in the inventory account reflected a net overstatement of only $72,000. That amount was not material even in reference to Marcelle's unusually small net income. However, Bill realized that the $72,000 figure was little better than a guess. Especially troubling to Bill was the client's allowance for inventory obsolescence. Bill had heard rumors that Marcelle intended to discontinue two of the fourteen sales departments in its stores. If that were true, the inventory in those departments would have to be sold at deep discounts. The collective dollar value of those two departments' inventory was $6 million, while the client's allowance for inventory obsolescence had a year-end balance of only $225,000. When Bill had asked Sam about the rumor, the typically easy going partner had replied with a terse "Don't worry about it."

Bill always took his work assignments seriously and wanted to do a professional job in completing them. He believed that independent audits served an extremely important role in a free market economy. Bill was often troubled by the fact that certain of his colleagues did not share his view. Some of his co-workers seemed to have an attitude of "Just get the work done." These individuals stressed form over substance: "Tic and tie, make the workpapers look good, and don't be too concerned with the results. A clean opinion is going to be issued no matter what you find."

Finally, Bill made a decision. He was not going to sign off on the inventory account regardless of the consequences. He did not know whether the inventory account balance was materially accurate, and he was not going to write a memo indicating otherwise. Moments later, Bill walked into the client office being used by Sam Hakes and closed the door behind him.

"What's up?" Sam asked as he flipped through a workpaper file.

"Sam, I've decided that I can't sign off on the inventory account," Bill blurted out.

"What?" was Sam's stunned, one-word reply.

Bill stalled for a few moments to bolster his courage as he fidgeted with his tie. "Well . . . like I said, I'm not signing off on the inventory account."

"Why?" By this point, a disturbing crimson shade had already engulfed Sam's ears and was creeping slowly across his face.

"Sam . . . I just don't think I can sign off. I mean, I'm just not sure whether the inventory number is right."

"You're not sure." After a brief pause, Sam continued, this time pronouncing each of his words with a deliberate and sarcastic tone. "You mean to tell me that you spent almost one thousand hours on that account, and you're not sure whether the general ledger number is right?"

"Well . . . yeah. You know, it's just tough to . . . to reach a conclusion, you know, on an account that large."

Sam leaned back in his chair and cleared his throat before speaking. "Mr. DeBurger, I want you to go back into that room of yours and close the door. Then you sit down at that table and write a nice, neat, very precise, and to-the-point inventory memo. And hear this: I'm not telling you what to include in that memo. But you're going to write that memo and you're going to have it on my desk in two hours. Understood?" Sam's face was almost entirely crimson as he completed his short speech.

"Uh, okay," Bill replied.

Bill returned to the small conference room that had served as his work area for the past two months. He sat in his chair and stared at the pictures of his two-year-old twins, Lesley and Kelly, which he had taped to the wall above the phone. After a few minutes, he picked up his pencil, leaned forward, and began outlining the inventory memo.

QUESTIONS

1. What conclusion do you believe Bill DeBurger reached in his inventory memo? Put yourself in his position. What conclusion would you have expressed in the inventory memo? Why?

2. Would you have dealt with your uncertainty regarding the inventory account differently than Bill did? For example, would you have used a different approach to raise the subject with Sam Hakes?

3. Evaluate Sam Hakes's response to Bill's statement that he was unable to sign off on the inventory account. In your view, did Sam deal with the situation appropriately? Was Sam's approach "professional"? Explain.

4. Is it appropriate for relatively inexperienced auditors to be assigned the primary responsibility for such critical accounts as Marcelle Stores' inventory? Explain.

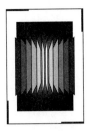

CASE 4.7
FIRST BLOOD ASSOCIATES

In late 1982, the movie *First Blood* was released to theaters across the nation and immediately became a box office success.[1] Starring Sylvester Stallone as the Vietnam veteran "Rambo," the movie's gross ticket sales approached $200 million and spurred its producers to develop two equally successful sequels.

In July 1981, a partnership entitled First Blood Associates was formed to acquire the rights to the film, which was in an early stage of production at that time. This partnership purchased *First Blood* the following year from the production company that developed and filmed the movie. In the fall of 1982, for the purpose of recruiting limited partner investors in the film venture, the general partners of First Blood Associates prepared a private placement offering memorandum that was registered with the Securities and Exchange Commission. Eventually, more than two dozen individuals invested approximately $250,000 each to become limited partners in the joint venture. According to the private placement memorandum, the limited partners of First Blood Associates were to share 98 percent of the net profits and cash flows generated by the movie.

Included in the private placement memorandum was a lengthy financial forecast that was entitled "Report on Projected Statements of Tax Basis Operations, Cash Flow and After Tax Results for an Investor in the 50% Tax Bracket for Eleven Years Ending December 31, 1992." The bulk of the forecast consisted of charts summarizing financial projections for the film, discussion of the key assumptions underlying the financial projections, and a three-page "Accountants' Report" prepared by the public accounting firm of Touche Ross. Exhibit 1 contains excerpts from the Touche Ross report.

Unfortunately for the limited partners of First Blood Associates, the private placement memorandum failed to fully secure their ownership interests in the movie. The wording of the private placement memorandum precluded the limited partners from sharing in profits resulting from the sale of key distribution rights to the film. As a result, even though the movie was a huge financial

---

1. The facts of this case were drawn principally from the following legal opinion: Block v. First Blood Associates, 743 F.Supp. 194 (S.D.N.Y. 1990).

EXHIBIT 1

**Excerpts from the
Touche Ross Report
Included in the Private
Placement Memorandum
Prepared by the General
Partners of First Blood
Associates**

> We have analyzed the accompanying financial projections referred to above, such analysis being comprised of reading the Confidential Private Placement Memorandum and statement of projection notes, hypotheses and assumptions, checking the compilation of the projections from stated hypotheses and assumptions, challenging the internal consistency of the projections, and inquiring about factors that may influence the financial results. Based on our analysis, we believe the projections have been properly compiled on the stated bases and the bases for the projections are adequately described.
>
> ... some of the assumptions inevitably will not materialize and unanticipated events and circumstances may occur . . . . Actual financial results achieved by the proposed partnership and the actual cash distributed and taxable income or loss and other tax results allocated to individual limited partners may vary from the projections, and the variations may be material.
>
> ... because relevant information which may be significant may not have been considered in developing the projections and [because] our analytical procedures were limited, we are unable to and do not express a conclusion on the completeness and reasonableness of the assumptions as a basis for predicting the financial results of the partnership and the availability and timing of income tax results to individual limited partners during the projection period.
>
> Because of the complexity of the federal and state laws which may be applicable for an individual partner, and of other legal and economic matters involved, each prospective limited partner should consult with his or her personal tax and investment advisors.

success, the limited partners received cash distributions of only $11,000 on their original $250,000 investments. To add insult to injury, in 1987 the Internal Revenue Service (IRS) ruled that the limited partners of First Blood Associates could not claim any deductions on their federal tax returns for the losses they had incurred. According to the IRS, since the contractual agreement signed by the limited partners precluded them from realizing any profit on their investments, the venture had to be treated as "tax-motivated," meaning that all losses incurred by the limited partners were disallowed for federal tax purposes.

The limited partners eventually filed suit against a number of parties to recover their losses. One of the parties named in that suit was Touche Ross. The limited partners of First Blood Associates alleged that the Touche Ross report on the financial projections contained in the private placement memorandum was misleading in several respects. The primary allegation against Touche Ross was that its report failed to disclose that it was impossible for the limited partners to realize a profit on their investments in the First Blood venture, regardless of how successful the film might prove to be. This problem was a consequence of the failure of the private placement memorandum to secure the limited partners' ownership interests in the film. The limited partners maintained that given this flaw in the memorandum, which was read and reviewed by the members of the Touche Ross engagement team, the accounting firm should have known that the financial projections prepared by the general partners were blatantly misleading. The suit filed in 1989 against Touche Ross charged the accounting firm with common law fraud and deceit, negligence and malpractice, and violating Rule 10b–5 of the Securities Exchange Act of 1934.

In an opinion handed down in 1990 by a U.S. district court, the civil claims filed against Touche Ross by the limited partners of First Blood Associates were all denied. The judge hearing the case disallowed the claims because the statute of limitations had expired prior to the time that the plaintiffs had filed suit against Touche Ross. The statutory provisions in such cases require plaintiffs to file their claims within two years of discovering the fraud or within six years of the fraud itself. The judge ruled that since the fraud had been perpetrated in the fall of 1982, when the private placement memorandum was prepared, the limited partners had, at most, until the fall of 1988 to file a claim against Touche Ross. Because the lawsuit was not filed until July 1989, the statute of limitations had obviously expired. As a result of the judge's ruling on the statute of limitations issue, the question of whether Touche Ross had been guilty of professional malfeasance in reporting on the financial projections included in the private placement memorandum became a moot issue.

Epilogue

A recent legal opinion suggests that an accounting firm can minimize its potential legal liability when it is associated with a financial forecast if the uncertainties related to that forecast are specifically and clearly identified. None of the parties to this litigation case—Donald J. Trump Casino Securities–Litigation Taj Mahal Litigation, no. 92-5350, 3rd Cir., Oct. 14, 1993—were accountants. Nevertheless, the ruling establishes a legal precedent for similar litigation cases in the future that do involve accountants. This case was highlighted in a recent article in the *Journal of Accountancy*.[2]

In the Trump case, thousands of investors purchased high-yield "junk" bonds that financed the construction of the Taj Mahal casino in Atlantic City. The prospectus used to market these bonds expressly and repeatedly documented the high risk associated with the casino venture. In the first few years of its operation, the new casino experienced disappointing financial results. In anticipation of a bankruptcy filing, the bondholders filed suit against the parties responsible for the financial forecast included in the prospectus. However, the plaintiffs' claims were quickly dismissed. The judge hearing the case ruled that the bond prospectus had clearly documented the uncertainties related to the financial forecast. As a result, there was no basis for the plaintiffs' allegation that the forecast was misleading.

> The basic point, as stated in this decision, is that forward-looking statements about anticipated financial performance may not constitute the basis for a securities fraud claim if the risks are described plainly and honestly.[3]

Questions

1. At present, what technical standard or standards define a CPA's responsibility when reporting on financial projections such as those included in the private placement memorandum discussed in this case? Was this standard or standards in effect when Touche Ross issued its report on the financial forecast prepared by the general partners of First Blood Associates?

2. Identify the three basic types of services that an audit firm may provide to a client that prepares and distributes financial forecasts or other financial projections. In this case, which type of service did Touche Ross apparently provide?

---

2. M. R. Young, "When Investors Rely on Financial Projections: Ruling Gives New Protection from Lawsuits," *Journal of Accountancy*, February 1994, 26–27.

3. Ibid., 26.

3. Draft a suitable opinion, given current technical standards, summarizing the results of the Touche Ross engagement performed for the general partners of First Blood Associates.

4. Assuming that the statute of limitations had not expired in this case, discuss the theories under which the limited partners of First Blood Associates could have attempted to recover their losses from Touche Ross. Limit your answers to charges of negligence under the common law against the audit firm and to the alleged violation of Rule 10b–5 under the Securities Exchange Act of 1934.

Section Five
Classic Litigation Cases

Case 5.1 Fred Stern & Company, Inc. (*Ultramares Corporation v. Touche et al.*)

Case 5.2 BarChris Construction Corporation

Case 5.3 1136 Tenants Corporation

Case 5.4 Yale Express System, Inc.

Case 5.5 First Securities Company of Chicago (*Ernst & Ernst v. Hochfelder et al.*)

Case 5.6 Equity Funding Corporation of America

CASE 5.1

FRED STERN & COMPANY, INC.
(*ULTRAMARES CORPORATION V. TOUCHE ET AL.*)

The decade of the 1920s in the United States was characterized by a number of excesses. In the business world of the Roaring Twenties, the scams and schemes of flimflam artists and confidence men were legendary. The absence of a strong regulatory system at the federal level to police the securities markets—the Securities and Exchange Commission was not established until 1934—aided, if not encouraged, financial frauds of all types. In all likelihood, the majority of individuals involved in business during the 1920s were scrupulously honest. Nevertheless, the culture of that decade did breed a disproportionate number of opportunists who adopted an "anything goes" approach to transacting business with others. An example of a company in which this self-serving attitude apparently prevailed was Fred Stern & Company, Inc., which duped three of its creditors out of several hundred thousand dollars in the mid–1920s.

Based in New York City, Fred Stern & Company was engaged in the importation and selling of rubber, a raw material demanded in huge quantities by a number of industries during the 1920s. The demand for rubber for industrial use in the United States more than tripled in the 1920s compared with the preceding decade. The nature of the rubber importation trade required large amounts of working capital. Unfortunately, Fred Stern & Company was chronically short of working capital and had to rely extensively on banks and other financial institutions to finance its day-to-day operations.

In March 1924, Stern requested a $100,000 loan from Ultramares Corporation, a finance company whose primary line of business was the factoring of receivables. Ultramares was familiar with Stern & Company and had engaged in a few small transactions with the company in the past. Given the size of the loan requested, however, Ultramares asked Stern's management to provide an audited balance sheet before deciding whether to grant the loan. Stern had been audited a few months earlier by Touche, Niven & Company, a prominent accounting firm based in London and New York City. The unqualified audit opinion issued by Touche on Stern's December 31, 1923, balance sheet is shown in Exhibit 1. After Touche completed the Stern audit, client officers had requested the accounting firm to provide them with thirty-two serially numbered copies of the audit report. Touche, Stern's auditor since 1920, was well aware that the audit reports were to be used by Stern's management to obtain external debt financing but did not know or ask which specific banks or finance companies would be given the audit reports.

After reviewing the audited balance sheet of Stern—which reported assets of more than $2.5 million and a net worth of approximately $1 million—and the accompanying audit report, Ultramares supplied the $100,000 loan requested by the company. Shortly thereafter, Ultramares extended two additional loans to Stern totaling $65,000. During the same time frame, Stern also obtained more than $300,000 in loans from two local banks after providing them with copies of the December 31, 1923, balance sheet audited by Touche.

Unfortunately for Ultramares and the two banks that granted loans to Stern, the company was declared bankrupt in January 1925. Subsequent courtroom testimony would prove that the company had been hopelessly insolvent at the end of 1923 when its audited balance sheet had reported a net worth of $1 million. An accountant with Stern, identified only as Romberg in court records, concealed the bankrupt status of Stern from the Touche auditors by making a number of false entries in the company's accounting records, the largest one being a debit of more than $700,000 to accounts receivable.

Following the bankruptcy of Stern, Ultramares sought to recover the funds it had loaned to the company by suing Touche. Ultramares alleged that the audit firm had been both fraudulent and negligent in auditing Stern's financial records. The *New York Times* reported that the negligence claim in the Ultramares suit was "novel" and would likely serve as a major "test case" for third parties hoping to recover losses from audit firms.[1] The novel aspect of the negligence claim was the fact that Touche did not have a contractual relationship with Ultramares. The only contract Touche had established was with the officers of Stern, the contract being to audit the December 31, 1923, balance sheet of that company. At the time, a well-entrenched legal doctrine was that only a party in privity with another— that is, having an explicit contractual agreement with another—could recover damages stemming from the second party's negligent conduct.

Another interesting facet of the Ultramares suit was that the founder of the accounting firm, Sir George Alexander Touche, was named personally as a defendant. Touche, who served for two years as the sheriff of London during World War I, agreed to merge his accounting practice in the early 1900s with that of a young Scottish accountant, John B. Niven, who had immigrated to New York City. The new firm prospered, and Touche, who was knighted in 1917 by King George V, eventually became one of the most respected leaders of the emerging public accounting profession. John Niven also became prominent within the profession and, ironically, was serving as the president of the American Institute of Accountants, the predecessor of the AICPA, when Fred Stern & Company was declared insolvent. One of the issues raised in the Ultramares suit was whether

---

1. "Damages Refused for Error in Audit," *New York Times*, 27 June 1929, 50.

February 26, 1924

Touche, Niven & Co.
Public Accountants
Eighty Maiden Lane,
New York

Certificate of Auditors

We have examined the accounts of Fred Stern & Co., Inc., for the year ended December 31, 1923, and hereby certify that the annexed balance sheet is in accordance therewith and with the information and explanations given us. We further certify that, subject to provision for federal taxes on income, the said statement in our opinion, presents a true and correct view of the financial condition of Fred Stern & Co., Inc., as at December 31, 1923.

EXHIBIT 1
Touche, Niven & Company's Audit Opinion on Stern's December 31, 1923, Balance Sheet

Sir George Touche and the other partners of his firm who were not directly involved in the Stern audit could be held personally liable for the malfeasance or alleged malfeasance of their subordinates.

ULTRAMARES CORPORATION V. TOUCHE ET AL.: A PROTRACTED LEGAL BATTLE

The Ultramares lawsuit against Touche was tried before a jury in a New York trial court. The principal allegation made by Ultramares's attorneys was that the Touche auditors should have easily discovered that Stern's December 31, 1923, balance sheet overstated the company's receivables by more than $700,000. That error, if corrected, would have decreased the reported net worth of Stern by nearly 70 percent and greatly reduced the likelihood that Ultramares would have extended the company a sizable loan.

Court testimony disclosed that most of the audit work on the Stern engagement was performed by a young man by the name of Siess. In early February 1924, when Siess arrived at Stern's office to begin the audit, he discovered that the company's general ledger had not been posted since the prior April. Consequently, he and his assistants spent the first few days on the engagement posting entries from the client's journals to its general ledger. When this work was completed, the balance of Stern's accounts receivable totaled approximately $644,000. Stern's accountant, Romberg, obtained the general ledger from Siess the day before the auditor was to prepare a trial balance of the company's accounts. After reviewing the ledger, Romberg recorded an entry crediting sales and debiting receivables for approximately $706,000. Beside the entry in the receivables account he entered a number cross-referencing the recorded amount to the company's sales journal. The following day, Romberg informed Siess of the entry he had recorded in the general ledger. Romberg told Siess that the entry represented the December sales of Stern that had been inadvertently omitted from the company's accounting records. Without questioning Romberg's explanation for the large entry, Siess included it in the receivables balance. In fact, the entry was totally fictitious. Romberg or one of his subordinates prepared seventeen sales invoices to support the entry, but the sales transactions reflected on the invoices had never occurred.

In subsequent testimony, Siess initially reported that he could not recall if he had reviewed any of the seventeen invoices allegedly representing the December sales of Stern. Later, however, he admitted that he had not examined any of those invoices, when plaintiff counsel demonstrated that "a mere glance" at the documents would have proved that they were bogus.[2] The invoices in question had been hastily prepared and lacked shipping numbers, customer order numbers, and other pertinent information. After admitting that none of the seventeen bogus invoices had been examined, Touche's attorneys attempted to justify this oversight by pointing out that audits involve "testing and sampling" rather than an examination of entire accounting populations.[3] Consequently, it was not surprising or unusual, they argued, that none of the fictitious December sales invoices were among the more than two hundred invoices examined during the Stern audit. The court ruled that auditing on a sample basis was appropriate in most cases but that Touche, nevertheless, had a responsibility to review the December sales invoices specifically, given the suspicious nature of the large December sales entry recorded by Romberg: "Verification by test and sample was very likely a sufficient audit as to accounts regularly entered upon the books in the usual course of business. . . . [However], the defendants were put on their guard by the circumstances touching the December accounts receivable to scrutinize with special care."[4]

Ultramares's attorneys were quick to point out during the trial that Touche had even more reason than just the suspicious nature of Romberg's December sales entry to question the integrity of the $700,000 year-end increase in receivables. In auditing the company's inventory account, the Touche auditors had discovered more than $300,000 in errors—errors that caused the preaudit inventory balance to be overstated by 90 percent. The auditors had also encountered problems while examining Stern's accounts payable and discovered that the company had improperly pledged the same assets as collateral for several different bank loans. Given the extent and nature of the problems discovered by the Touche auditors during the Stern engagement, the court ruled that the accounting firm should have been particularly skeptical of the accuracy of the company's accounting records. This should have been the case, the court observed, even though the Touche auditors had a good rapport with Stern's officers and apparently had not encountered any reason in prior audits of the company to question the integrity of those individuals. In commenting on this point, the court noted: "No doubt the extent to which inquiry must be pressed beyond appearances is a question of judgment, as to which opinions will often differ. No doubt the wisdom that is born after the event will engender suspicion and distrust when old acquaintance and good repute may have silenced doubt at the beginning."[5]

The jury in the Ultramares case dismissed the fraud charge against Touche, since the company's attorneys failed to establish that the audit firm had intentionally deceived Ultramares (intentional deceit being a necessary condition for fraud). Regarding the negligence charge, the jury ruled in favor of Ultramares and awarded the company damages from Touche of more than $186,000.

---

2. Ultramares Corporation v. Touche et al., 255 N.Y. 170, 174 N.E. 441 (1930), 449.

3. Ibid., 449.

4. Ibid.

5. Ibid., 444.

However, the judge who presided over the case subsequently overturned the jury's ruling, alleging that it was in error. In explaining his decision, the judge did not contest the fact that Ultramares's attorneys had clearly established that Touche had been negligent during its 1923 audit of Stern. Instead, the issue raised by the judge was the long-standing doctrine that only a party in privity could sue and recover damages resulting from a defendant's negligence: "Negligence is not actionable unless there is a breach of duty owing by defendants to the plaintiff. To hold that the defendants' duty extended to not only Stern but to all persons to whom Stern might exhibit the balance sheet, and who would act in reliance thereon, would compel the defendants to assume a potential liability to practically the entire world."[6]

The trial judge's decision to overturn the jury's verdict was quickly appealed by Ultramares's attorneys. The appellate division of the New York Supreme Court reviewed the case and, in a vote of 3 to 2, decided that the trial judge had inappropriately reversed the jury's decision on the negligence charge. As appellate justice McAvoy noted, the key issue in the case was whether Touche had a duty to Ultramares "in the absence of a direct contractual relation."[7] Justice McAvoy concluded that Touche did have an obligation to Ultramares, and to other parties relying on the Stern financial statements, even though the accounting firm's contract was expressly and exclusively with Stern.

> One cannot issue an unqualified statement [audit opinion] . . . and then disclaim responsibility for his work. Banks and merchants, to the knowledge of these defendants, require certified balance sheets from independent accountants, and upon these audits they make their loans. Thus, the duty arises to these banks and merchants of an exercise of reasonable care in the making and uttering of certified balance sheets.[8]

Although Justice McAvoy and two of his colleagues were unwavering in their opinion that Touche had a legal obligation to Ultramares, the remaining two judges on the appellate panel were just as strongly persuaded that no such obligation existed. In the dissenting opinion, Justice Finch maintained that holding Touche responsible to any party that might subsequently rely upon the Stern financial statements was patently unfair to the accounting firm: "If the plaintiff [Ultramares] had inquired of the accountants whether they might rely upon the certificate in making a loan, then the accountants would have had the opportunity to gauge their responsibility and risk, and determine with knowledge how thorough their verification of the account should be before assuming the responsibility of making the certificate run to the plaintiff."[9]

Following the appellate division's ruling in the Ultramares case, Touche's attorneys appealed the decision to the next highest court in the New York state judicial system, the court of appeals, which ultimately handed down the final ruling in the lengthy judicial history of the case. The chief justice of that court, Benjamin Cardozo, was a nationally recognized legal scholar whose opinions were given great weight by other courts. Justice Cardozo and his six associate

---

6. "Damages Refused for Error in Audit," *New York Times*, 27 June 1929, 50.

7. Ultramares Corporation v. Touche et al., 229 App. Div. 581, 243 N.Y.S. 179 (1930), 181.

8. Ibid., 182.

9. Ibid., 186.

justices ruled unanimously that the judge who presided over the trial in the Ultramares case had properly reversed the jury's decision on the negligence claim. In essence, Justice Cardozo reiterated the arguments made by Justice Finch by maintaining that it would be unfair to hold Touche legally responsible to a third party, unknown to Touche when its audit was performed, that happened to obtain and rely upon Stern's audited balance sheet. However, Justice Cardozo suggested that had Ultramares been clearly designated as a beneficiary of the Stern–Touche contract, his ruling would have been different.

Unfortunately for Touche and other accounting firms, Justice Cardozo's opinion did not end with his commentary on the negligence question in the Ultramares suit. After resolving that issue, he severely criticized the conduct of the accounting firm during the 1923 audit of Stern and then implied that Ultramares might have been successful in suing Touche on the basis of gross negligence: "Negligence or blindness, even when not equivalent to fraud, is none the less evidence to sustain an inference of fraud. . . . At least this is so if the negligence is gross. . . . [in the Ultramares case] a jury might find that . . . [the Touche auditors] closed their eyes to the obvious, and blindly gave assent."[10]

THE ULTRAMARES DECISION:
IMPLICATIONS FOR THE PUBLIC ACCOUNTING PROFESSION

In retrospect, the Ultramares decision had two principal implications for the public accounting profession. First, it clearly established that certain direct beneficiaries of an audit, generally referred to as primary beneficiaries, were entitled to recover damages from a negligent auditor. However, subsequent to the Ultramares ruling, very few plaintiffs were successful in establishing themselves as primary beneficiaries of an audit.[11] Consequently, this "expansion" of the auditor's legal exposure proved to be fairly insignificant.

The second key implication of the Ultramares ruling for the public accounting profession was that it provided a new strategy for plaintiff counsel to use in bringing suits against auditors on behalf of nonprivity parties. Following the Ultramares ruling, attorneys representing such plaintiffs began suing auditors for gross negligence. Prior to that ruling, an allegation of fraud was the only feasible approach for nonprivity third parties to take when attempting to recover losses from auditors. Because establishing the existence of gross negligence is much easier than proving actual intent to defraud, auditors were suddenly faced with a much greater degree of legal exposure to third parties who relied upon audited financial statements.

A secondary issue addressed by Justice Cardozo in the Ultramares case was the question of whether Sir George Touche, as well as the other partners of his firm who had no direct connection with the Stern engagement, could be held

---

10. Ultramares Corporation v. Touche et al., 255 N.Y. 170, 174 N.E. 441 (1930), 449.

11. Decades later, the *Credit Alliance* case established the conditions that third parties must satisfy to qualify as primary beneficiaries in the jurisdiction in which the *Ultramares* case was tried. See: Credit Alliance Corporation v. Arthur Andersen & Company, 483 N.E. 2d 110 (N.Y. 1985).

personally liable for the conduct of their subordinates who were assigned to the Stern audit. Although this issue was a moot one with regard to the negligence allegation, it was still pertinent to the fraud charge since Justice Cardozo stated that the plaintiff was entitled to a re-trial regarding the question of whether Touche's negligence was severe enough to infer fraudulent conduct or gross negligence.[12] Justice Cardozo, in no uncertain terms, ruled that all of the partners of Touche were legally responsible for the actions of the firm's employees during the course of the Stern audit, since those employees were the agents of the partners.

EPILOGUE

In the years following Justice Cardozo's ruling in the Ultramares case, the legal exposure of public accountants to third-party financial statement users was gradually extended. The first extension actually came on the heels of the Ultramares case with the passage of the Securities Act of 1933. That federal statute imposed on auditors a very significant legal obligation to initial purchasers of new securities marketed on an interstate basis. Under the 1933 act, plaintiffs do not have to prove fraud, gross negligence, or even negligence on the part of auditors. Instead, if the plaintiffs can establish that the financial statements issued in conjunction with the sale of new securities contain material errors or omissions, then the defendant audit firm assumes the burden of proving that its employees were "duly diligent" in performing the audit.[13] To sustain a due diligence defense, an audit firm must show that following a "reasonable investigation," it had "reasonable ground to believe and did believe" that the audited financial statements included in the securities registration statement were materially accurate. Unfortunately, the courts have generally not been receptive to the due diligence defense if the plaintiffs have clearly established that the financial statements in question contain material errors.

Public accountants' legal exposure has also expanded under the common law over the past several decades. In 1965, the American Law Institute's *Restatement of Torts*, a legal compendium that is relied on heavily in many jurisdictions, suggested that "foreseen" beneficiaries, in addition to primary beneficiaries, should have a right to recover damages from negligent auditors.[14] Foreseen beneficiaries are members of a limited group or class of third-party financial statement users. The auditor is typically aware of this distinct group of potential financial statement users but is usually unaware of the specific individuals or

---

12. For whatever reason, Ultramares apparently chose not to file an amended lawsuit against Touche predicated upon an allegation of gross negligence.

13. Of course, audit firms have other defenses available to them as well when they have been sued by third parties under the Securities Act of 1933. These include, among others, expiration of the statute of limitations time period specified by that law, the fact that the plaintiff knew the financial statements were misleading when he or she purchased the securities, and the fact that the plaintiff's losses were not a result of the misleading financial statements but rather the result of some other cause.

14. American Law Institute, *Restatement of the Law, Second: Torts* (Philadelphia: American Law Institute, 1965).

entities who are members of that group. Finally, the Rosenblum ruling of 1983 went beyond the boundary previously established by the *Restatement of Torts* when it implied that even "reasonably foreseeable" or "ordinary" third-party financial statement users should have a right of recovery from negligent auditors.[15] Reasonably foreseeable third parties include a much larger population of potential financial statement users than the class of "foreseen" third parties. The most liberal interpretation of the definition of reasonably foreseeable third parties would include individual investors who happen to obtain a copy of audited financial statements and make a decision based upon them.

QUESTIONS

1. Observers of the accounting profession have suggested that the gradual extension of auditors' liability to third-party financial statement users is an effort by the courts to "socialize" investment losses. Assuming this theory is true, discuss its benefits and costs to audit firms, audit clients, and third-party financial statement users, such as investors and creditors. In your view, should the courts have the authority to socialize investment losses? If not, what party or parties should determine how investment losses are distributed in our society?

2. The auditor's legal responsibilities under the Securities Exchange Act of 1934 are quite different from those he or she assumes under the Securities Act of 1933. Briefly point out these differences and comment on why they exist. How does the auditor's legal exposure differ under the common law and the 1934 act?

3. The current standard audit report is quite different from the version issued during the 1920s. Identify the key differences in the two reports and discuss the forces that accounted for the evolution of the audit report into its present form.

4. Why was it common in the 1920s for companies to have only an audited balance sheet prepared for distribution to external third parties? Comment on the factors that resulted in the adoption, over a period of several decades, of the financial statement package that most companies presently provide to external third parties.

5. When assessing audit risk, should auditors consider the type and number of third parties that may ultimately rely on the financial statements of the client? Refer to *Statement on Auditing Standards No. 47*, "Materiality and Audit Risk in Conducting an Audit," before responding. Should auditors require that audit engagement letters identify the third parties to whom the client intends to distribute the audited financial statements? Would this practice eliminate auditors' legal liability to nonprivity parties who are not mentioned in engagement letters?

---

15. H. Rosenblum, Inc. v. Adler, 461 A. 2d 138 (N.J. 1983).

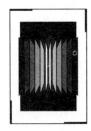

CASE 5.2

BarChris Construction Corporation

Christie Vitolo and Leborio Pugliese became business partners in 1946 when they pooled their resources to form a small construction company in New York City. Initially, Vitolo handled the financial affairs of the partnership, and Pugliese was responsible for supervising the construction projects undertaken by the company. As the company grew in size, Vitolo's limited understanding of financial management practices and accounting matters forced him to hire an accountant, Leonard Russo, who was given the title of executive vice-president. A few years later, Vitolo and Pugliese hired two accountants formerly employed by Peat, Marwick, Mitchell & Company, their audit firm, to serve as the controller and treasurer of the company. In 1955, Vitolo and Pugliese incorporated their business, forming what later became known as BarChris Construction Corporation, and then four years later took the company public by selling 560,000 shares of common stock at $3 per share. Shortly thereafter, the BarChris stock was listed on the American Stock Exchange.

The principal line of business of BarChris was the construction of bowling alleys. Bowling as a recreational sport received a tremendous boost in 1952 when automatic pin-setting machines were introduced in the United States. Over the following decade, the demand for bowling alleys grew at a phenomenal rate. Throughout that time, the construction of bowling alleys was dominated by two companies, AMF and Brunswick. BarChris, although much smaller than either of those companies, was by 1960 the third largest builder of bowling alleys in the United States. In 1956, BarChris reported total sales of $800,000; four years later, the company had total revenues exceeding $9 million and a net income of approximately $750,000. In a *Wall Street Journal* article in early 1961, Russo predicted that the company would achieve sales of $15 million that year and realize a profit of $1.2 million.

Most of the bowling alleys BarChris constructed were built for syndicates of small investors. On the date the construction contract was signed, the investment syndicate would advance a small down payment on the purchase price of the

271

bowling alley to BarChris. The investors would then give BarChris a note for the balance of the purchase price which was due in installments over a period of several years following the completion of the alley. In 1960, BarChris began engaging in sale and leaseback arrangements with finance companies. In such transactions, BarChris would construct an alley and sell it to a finance company, which would then lease the alley to a subsidiary of BarChris. This subsidiary would then operate the alley. Regardless of which of the two sales techniques was used, BarChris incurred large cash expenditures for construction costs prior to receiving any significant payments from the eventual purchaser of an alley. As a result, the company was constantly in search of external financing to bankroll its construction projects. In May 1961, to provide much-needed working capital, the company sold $1,740,000 of 5.5 percent, fifteen-year bonds to the general public under an S–1 registration statement filed with the Securities and Exchange Commission (SEC).[1]

Unfortunately for BarChris and its competitors, the construction market for bowling alleys collapsed in the early 1960s as the public's demand for new bowling alleys was finally satisfied. The sudden decline in new construction projects and the company's recurring need for additional working capital posed a severe financial crisis for BarChris in 1962. BarChris's liquidity problems were exacerbated by the fact that many of the investors who had contracted with the company for the construction of bowling alleys began to experience cash flow problems as their revenues failed to reach the levels they had expected. As a result, several of the investment syndicates defaulted on the notes due BarChris, forcing the company to assume the day-to-day operations of many of the bowling alleys it had constructed. Finally, in late 1962, after being unable to make the semiannual interest payments on its outstanding bonds, BarChris filed for protection under Chapter 11 of the federal bankruptcy code.

BONDHOLDERS SUE FOR RECOVERY OF THEIR INVESTMENTS

Following the bankruptcy filing by BarChris in late 1962, a class action lawsuit was initiated by individuals who had purchased bonds in the public offering made by the company in 1961. Named as defendants in this suit were the executive officers of BarChris, the company's investment broker, and its audit firm, Peat Marwick. The lawsuit was noteworthy for a number of reasons, the most important being that it was one of the first major cases brought under the Securities Act of 1933, which regulates the issuance of new securities.[2] For the public accounting profession, the BarChris case was important because it was one of the first lawsuits to address the extent and nature of auditors' legal

---

1. Companies are required to file an S–1 registration statement with the SEC when they offer new securities for sale to the general public.

2. From the date of the adoption of the Securities Act of 1933 through the mid–1960s, surprisingly few civil lawsuits were filed under that statute. One study found that fewer than two civil suits were filed annually under the Securities Act of 1933 during the first few decades it was in effect. During the 1960s and 1970s, the number of such lawsuits increased dramatically as plaintiff counsel recognized that huge judgments could potentially be obtained in class action suits filed against third parties, such as auditors and investment brokers, associated with S–1 registration statements.

liability under the Securities Act of 1933. In particular, the BarChris case provided important insights on the issues that federal courts would consider in determining whether financial errors proved to exist in S–1 registration statements were material and whether auditors had satisfied their due diligence responsibilities under the 1933 act.

The opinion handed down by the presiding judge in the BarChris class action suit focused on the following three issues:

1. Did the S–1 registration statement filed by BarChris in connection with the sale of the 5.5 percent, fifteen-year bonds contain false representations?
2. If the registration statement contained false representations, were they "material"?
3. Did the defendants satisfy their due diligence obligation to review the registration statement to determine whether it was free of material false representations?

Judge McLean, the federal judge who wrote the BarChris opinion, demonstrated a masterful understanding of the accounting and auditing issues implicit in each of these questions. As a result, many observers of the accounting profession predicted that the BarChris opinion would be relied upon heavily in future years by judges hearing cases involving independent auditors filed under the federal securities laws.

Issue 1: Were There False Representations in the BarChris S–1 Registration Statement?

The 1958 through 1960 annual financial statements of BarChris, all of which were audited by Peat Marwick, were included in the S–1 registration statement filed by the company with the SEC in the spring of 1961 in connection with its plans to sell the 5.5 percent, fifteen-year bonds. Also included in the registration statement were unaudited financial statements for the first quarter of 1961. For these latter statements, Peat Marwick performed what is commonly known as an S–1 review rather than a full-scope audit. In evaluating Peat Marwick's conduct in the BarChris case, Judge McLean focused principally on the firm's performance of the 1960 BarChris audit. Apparently, the judge concluded that prospective investors, in reviewing the S–1 statement, most likely concentrated on the audited 1960 financial statements rather than on the unaudited statements for the first quarter of 1961 or the audited statements for 1958 and 1959.

Shown in Exhibit 1 are the principal items that Judge McLean ruled were in error in the 1960 financial statements of BarChris.[3] The plaintiffs in the BarChris case alleged that the company had improperly applied the percentage-of-completion method in accounting for the profit recognized on the bowling alley construction projects. In fact, the plaintiffs implied that the completed contract method should have been used for the construction projects because of the uncertainty regarding the amount of profit that would ultimately be recognized on those projects. On this latter point, Judge McLean disagreed with the

---

3. Although not discussed in this case, similar errors were identified by Judge McLean in the unaudited financial statements of BarChris for the first quarter of 1961.

plaintiffs, ruling that the percentage-of-completion method was the proper accounting technique to use under the circumstances. However, he also concluded that the estimated stage of completion of two of the jobs in progress on December 31, 1960, had been overly optimistic, resulting in overstatements of revenue for the fiscal year ending on that date.

More than one-half of the alleged overstatement in sales shown in Exhibit 1 was the result of a sale and leaseback transaction involving the Heavenly Lanes construction project in East Haven, Connecticut. At the time, accounting standards allowed the total gain on sale and leaseback transactions to be included in the accounting period in which the transaction occurred.[4] However, Judge McLean ruled that allowing this treatment was improper even though it was permissible under generally accepted accounting principles. The judge defended his position by pointing out that the Heavenly Lanes transaction was, in reality, simply a "mechanism" used by BarChris to finance the completion of that project rather than being a true sale of the property.

The overstated revenues reported by BarChris in its 1960 income statement resulted, of course, in an overstatement in the company's net operating income and earnings per share figures for that year as well. Exhibit 1 documents the overstatements in those two items determined by Judge McLean as a result of his analysis of BarChris's operating results for 1960.

The liquidity problems BarChris had experienced throughout its existence focused considerable attention during the class action lawsuit on the effect of the alleged financial statement errors on the company's key liquidity ratios at the end of 1960. Of particular concern to Judge McLean in this regard was a transfer of approximately $145,000 to BarChris from one of its unconsolidated subsidiaries in late December 1960. What troubled Judge McLean was a stipulation of this transaction that required the cash to be returned to the BarChris subsidiary by January 16, 1961. In analyzing this transfer of funds, which was apparently arranged by Russo, Judge McLean made the following remarks:

> In any event, to treat it [the $145,000] as cash on hand without some explanation of the temporary character of the deposit was misleading. The incident is important for the light that it sheds upon BarChris's business practices. This has a bearing upon the credibility of some of BarChris's officers and the weight to be given to their testimony in other respects.[5]

In addition to ruling that the year-end cash balance was overstated, Judge McLean concluded that the December 31, 1960, accounts and notes receivable balances of BarChris were overstated. The judge ruled that a $50,000 reserve should have been established at the end of 1960 for a receivable that appeared unlikely to be collected, and that a receivable from a subsidiary should not have been included in the BarChris balance sheet, because it was an intercompany item. Regarding the company's notes receivable, BarChris often discounted with

---

4. In 1960, accounting standards only required that "the principal details of any important sale-and-leaseback transaction" be disclosed in the financial statements. For a discussion of this issue, see H. B. Reiling and R. A. Taussig, "Recent Liability Cases—Implications for Accountants," *Journal of Accountancy*, September 1970, 39–53.

5. This and all subsequent quotations were taken from the following legal opinion: Escott v. BarChris Construction Corporation, 283 F.Supp. 643 (1968).

EXHIBIT 1
Key Errors Noted in
1960 BarChris Financial
Statements by Judge
McLean

A. Sales	
As Per S–1 Statement	$ 9,165,320
Correct Figure	8,511,420
Overstatement	$ 653,900
% Overstatement	7.7%
B. Net Operating Income	
As Per S–1 Statement	$ 1,742,801
Correct Figure	1,496,196
Overstatement	$ 246,605
% Overstatement	16.5%
C. Earnings per Share	
As Per S–1 Statement	$ .75
Correct Figure	.65
Overstatement	$ .10
% Overstatement	15.3%
D. Current Assets	
As Per S–1 Statement	$ 4,524,021
Correct Figure	3,914,332
Overstatement	$ 609,689
% Overstatement	15.6%
E. Current Ratio	
As Per S–1 Statement	1.9
Correct Figure	1.6
% Overstatement	18.8%
F. Contingent Liabilities	
As Per S–1 Statement	$ 4,719,835
Correct Figure	5,095,630
Understatement	$ 375,795
% Understatement	7.4%

finance companies notes due from its customers.[6] A certain percentage of the face value of these notes was withheld by the finance companies as reserves for uncollectible amounts. When a note was paid in full, the reserve for that note was remitted to BarChris. For financial statement purposes, BarChris reported these reserves as current assets due from the finance companies. Judge McLean maintained that reporting the total amount of the reserves as a current asset was misleading, since (1) a certain percentage of the reserves was never remitted to BarChris because of defaults on some of the notes by customers, and (2) the remittances that were made often occurred several years after the notes were discounted.

The final substantive error that Judge McLean identified in the 1960 BarChris financial statements involved the company's contingent liabilities. The bulk of

---

6. Judge McLean implied, on occasion, that these notes were "factored," which was technically incorrect, since that term signifies that the notes were sold without recourse. The notes were actually assigned to, or discounted with, the finance companies, meaning that the latter could collect payments in default from BarChris.

these contingencies arose as a result of the notes receivable that BarChris discounted with finance companies. The judge ruled that the company had improperly estimated its contingent liabilities, resulting in them being understated in the 1960 financial statements by approximately $375,000, as shown in Exhibit 1.

ISSUE 2: WERE THE FALSE REPRESENTATIONS IN THE BARCHRIS S–1 REGISTRATION STATEMENT "MATERIAL"?

The second major issue addressed by Judge McLean in his review of the BarChris S–1 registration statement concerned whether the errors in the financial statements included in the S–1 were material. As he observed, a prerequisite for a defendant to be held civilly liable under the Securities Act of 1933 is that any false representations qualify as material errors. According to Judge McLean, the SEC's regulations define the concept of materiality in the following manner. "The term 'material', when used to qualify a requirement for the furnishing of information as to any subject, limits the information required to those matters as to which an average prudent investor ought reasonably to be informed before purchasing the security registered."

In analyzing the errors that affected the December 31, 1960, income statement of BarChris, Judge McLean posed the question of whether the overstatements of sales, net operating income, and earnings per share "would have deterred the average prudent investor from purchasing" the company's bonds that it offered for sale in the spring of 1961. Judge McLean ruled in each case that the errors were not large enough to have discouraged a prudent investor from purchasing the bonds. In explaining his decision, the judge commented on the fact that the bonds were considered a "speculative" security by the investment advisory services, and as a result, prospective investors were unlikely to have been deterred by what he characterized as "comparatively minor errors" in the reported sales and earnings figures for 1960.

The $375,000 understatement in the contingent liabilities of BarChris as of December 31, 1960, was also ruled to be an immaterial amount. Judge McLean noted that the total assets of BarChris as of that date were $6,101,085. In relation to that total, he observed that either the reported or actual contingent liabilities figure would have been considered a "huge amount" by prospective investors. According to Judge McLean, "If they [investors] were willing to buy the debentures in the face of this information, as they obviously were, I doubt that they would have been deterred if they had been told that the contingent liabilities were actually $375,000 higher."

Somewhat surprisingly, Judge McLean ruled that the overstatement of current assets and the consequent overstatement of BarChris's current ratio as of December 31, 1960, were material errors. As shown in Exhibit 1, in percentage terms, there was only a slight difference between the overstatement of the current ratio, which Judge McLean ruled to be a material error, and the overstatement of the company's earnings per share, which was ruled to be an immaterial amount by the judge. However, the judge apparently concluded that bondholders or prospective bondholders, as compared with equity investors, would be much more concerned by an overstatement of a company's liquidity position than by an overstatement of its earnings. This would be particularly true when the company in question had a history of liquidity problems and was facing significant working capital needs in the near future.

ISSUE 3: DID PEAT MARWICK SATISFY ITS DUE DILIGENCE OBLIGATION IN REVIEWING THE S–1 REGISTRATION STATEMENT?

The key defense that Peat Marwick pleaded in the BarChris civil suit was the so-called due diligence defense. The Securities Act of 1933 defines this defense in the following manner:

> After reasonable investigation [the defendant] had reasonable ground to believe and did believe, at the time such part of the registration statement became effective, that the statements therein were true and that there was no omission to state a material fact required to be stated therein or necessary to make the statements therein not misleading.

As suggested by this definition, to sustain the due diligence defense, Peat Marwick was required to establish that its auditors had performed a "reasonable investigation" of the S–1 statement and that the results of this investigation had caused the auditors to conclude that the financial data in the statement were materially accurate. In assessing Peat Marwick's due diligence defense, Judge McLean reviewed the procedures the firm's engagement team had completed during the 1960 audit and during the subsequent S–1 review performed during the spring of 1961.

The senior auditor assigned to the BarChris engagement in 1960 and 1961 was a young man named Berardi. Judge McLean suggested that the choice of Berardi to serve as the senior auditor on the relatively complex BarChris audit was a questionable decision, since he was not a CPA at the time, had no prior experience with the bowling industry, and had just recently been promoted to senior. Berardi's review of the sale and leaseback transaction involving the Heavenly Lanes construction project was of particular concern to Judge McLean. After scrutinizing the Peat Marwick workpapers, Judge McLean concluded that Berardi never realized that the Heavenly Lanes sale and leaseback was essentially an intercompany transaction. Interestingly, the audit manager assigned to the BarChris engagement apparently did discover this fact at one point during the audit. This individual made the following notation as a review comment on one of Berardi's workpapers: "When talking to Ted Kircher [the BarChris treasurer] in the latter part of '60 he indicated one subsidiary is leasing alley built by BarChris—the profit on this job should be eliminated as its ownership is within the affiliated group."[7] In response to the above review comment, Berardi added the following notation on a workpaper concerning the Heavenly Lanes

---

7. Technically, the Heavenly Lanes property was sold to a finance company and then leased by that company to a BarChris subsidiary. However, the terms of the lease were such that the judge ruled that BarChris remained the de facto owner of the property.

project: "Properties sold to others by affiliates." As Judge McLean observed, this note was somewhat vague, but it could be construed to suggest that Berardi believed the property had been sold to an external third party. If this were the case, Judge McLean argued, Berardi should have completed certain procedures to corroborate this sale—which he apparently did not.[8]

Judge McLean ruled that Berardi was not responsible for failing to discover that the year-end transfer of approximately $145,000 to BarChris by its unconsolidated subsidiary was required to be repaid shortly after the year-end. As noted by the judge, Russo did not inform Berardi or the other Peat Marwick auditors of this fact, and "it would not be reasonable to require Berardi to examine all of BarChris's correspondence when he had no reason to suspect any irregularity." Regarding the treatment of the reserves due from the finance companies, which were reported as current assets in the BarChris balance sheet, Judge McLean concluded that Berardi should have recognized that most of those reserves would not be released within one year and thus did not qualify as current assets.

Judge McLean's most severe criticism of Berardi was reserved for the senior's performance of the S–1 review during the spring of 1961. The legal opinion in the BarChris case provided the following definition of an S–1 review:

> The purpose of reviewing events subsequent to the date of a certified balance sheet (referred to as an S–1 review when made with reference to a registration statement) is to ascertain whether any material change has occurred in the company's financial position which should be disclosed in order to prevent the balance sheet figures from being misleading.

Shown in Exhibit 2 is a partial list of the audit procedures that Berardi was assigned to complete in connection with that review. Judge McLean specifically noted that the S–1 audit program provided to Berardi was in conformity with generally accepted auditing standards. However, the judge ruled that Berardi had failed to complete the audit procedures assigned to him in a satisfactory manner.[9]

> He devoted a little over two days to it [the S–1 review], a total of 20½ hours. He did not discover any of the errors or omissions pertaining to the state of affairs in 1961 which I have previously discussed at length, all of which were material. . . . he got answers [from management] which he considered satisfactory, and he did nothing to verify them. . . . as far as results were concerned, his S–1 review was useless.

As a result of his thorough study of the Peat Marwick audit workpapers, Judge McLean ruled that the audit firm had failed to establish its due diligence

---

8. Judge McLean noted in his opinion that he was not "satisfied" with Berardi's testimony regarding this transaction. At one point, Berardi testified that he believed the property in question was not a bowling alley under construction but rather a tract of vacant land. In Berardi's defense, BarChris had two names for the disputed property, Heavenly Lanes and Capitol Lanes, a fact that apparently confused not only Berardi but other members of the Peat Marwick engagement team as well.

9. Largely as a result of the BarChris case, the auditing profession adopted more definitive guidelines for auditors to follow when reviewing important events occurring subsequent to the client's balance sheet date.

1. Review minutes of stockholders, directors, and committee [meetings].
2. Review latest interim financial statements and compare with corresponding statements of preceding year. Inquire regarding significant variations and changes.
4. Review the more important financial records and inquire regarding material transactions not in the ordinary course of business and any other significant items.
6. Inquire as to changes in material contracts.
10. Inquire as to any significant bad debts or accounts in dispute for which provision has not been made.
14. Inquire as to newly discovered liabilities . . . direct or contingent.

EXHIBIT 2
Partial Audit Program
Used by Peat Marwick
during 1961 S–1 Review

defense.[10] Judge McLean reached a similar conclusion regarding the other key defendants in the case as well. Prior to a court-ordered judgment being rendered against the defendants, an out-of-court settlement was agreed to by all parties to the BarChris civil suit. Apparently, the terms of that settlement were never publicly disclosed.

QUESTIONS

1. Are the completed contract and percentage-of-completion methods mutually acceptable alternatives in accounting for long-term construction projects? If not, specify the conditions under which each method should be used.

2. *Statement on Auditing Standards No. 31*, "Evidential Matter," identifies five key management assertions that underlie a set of financial statements. Which of these assertions was violated by the year-end transfer of $145,000 to BarChris by its unconsolidated subsidiary? Would the preparation and auditing of a year-end bank transfer schedule by Peat Marwick have likely disclosed the violation of this assertion? Why or why not? What other audit procedures might have resulted in the discovery of this improper year-end bank transfer?

3. Judge McLean was forced to make a determination of whether the errors that existed in the 1960 financial statements of BarChris were material. Should the accounting profession adopt quantitative materiality guidelines for use by auditors and accountants? Discuss the advantages and disadvantages of such guidelines from the auditor's perspective.

4. Identify the key differences in the auditor's legal liability under the Securities Act of 1933, which served as the basis for the civil suit against Peat Marwick in the BarChris case, versus the auditor's legal liability under the Securities Exchange Act of 1934.

5. In 1961, accounting standards allowed companies to recognize immediately the total amount of gain on a sale and leaseback transaction. Shortly after the

---

10. As noted earlier, two of BarChris's financial executives were former Peat Marwick employees. Members of the Peat Marwick engagement team reportedly relied on these two individuals to inform them of any significant problems that BarChris was facing. Unfortunately, this reliance was not justified, since these two individuals apparently did not alert the Peat Marwick auditors to several important accounting and financial reporting issues confronting BarChris. For a discussion of this facet of the case, see W. A. Wallace, *Auditing* (New York: Macmillan, 1986), 641.

BarChris case was litigated, this accounting treatment was disallowed. Should auditors allow clients to use any method of accounting for a given transaction as long as the method chosen is not expressly prohibited by professional standards? Discuss the rationale for your answer.

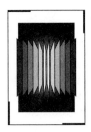

CASE 5.3

1136 TENANTS CORPORATION

For most of his life, New York City businessman I. Jerome Riker was a powerful man with an extensive network of influential friends and business associates. Possibly the most influential of his friends was Roy M. Cohn, the famed lawyer who served as the prosecuting attorney in the Julius and Ethel Rosenberg espionage trial following World War II and who later was the chief legal counsel of Senator Joseph McCarthy during the infamous McCarthy hearings held in the U.S. Senate during the mid–1950s. Cohn was known as one of the most important power brokers of his time, having close personal ties to numerous government officials, including J. Edgar Hoover and, years later, Ronald Reagan. Riker apparently benefited greatly from his friendship with Cohn, who was well known for the favors he did for close friends. Cohn steered business deals Riker's way and, for a time, was a co-owner with Riker of American Funding Corporation, a large finance company.

Riker's principal business interests were in the real estate industry. For four decades, he served as president of one of the largest real estate investment companies in New York City, overseeing Riker & Company from his stylish Madison Avenue office. From 1926 through 1965, Riker managed the most expensive and exclusive residential properties in the United States, the elegant cooperative apartment buildings that line Park Avenue and Fifth Avenue on the upper east side of Manhattan Island. In addition to being prominent within the inner circles of the Manhattan business and civic communities, Riker was also well known among the socialites who inhabited the posh "Hamptons" communities of Long Island. In fact, one of Riker's most prized real estate properties was the glitzy Bath and Tennis Club of Westhampton, Long Island, of which he was the principal stockholder.

During the early 1960s, Riker's infatuation with the Westhampton property apparently induced him to begin illegally diverting cash from the trust funds of several of the cooperatives he managed. Much of this cash was reportedly used to finance various capital improvement projects at the Long Island club. In March 1965, the New York State Supreme Court ordered Riker & Company to cease operations, charging that the firm had been engaging in "self-dealing" and the commingling of its funds with those of its clients. Three months later, Riker was indicted on thirteen counts of grand larceny in connection with his alleged theft of nearly $1 million from the trust funds of the cooperatives his firm had previously managed. In November 1965, after pleading guilty to the charges filed against him, Riker was given a suspended sentence and indefinite probation by Judge Gerald Culkin of the New York State Supreme Court. Judge Culkin defended the light sentence by explaining that Riker had paid back approximately $20,000 of the stolen funds and had intended to return the remainder but had been prevented from doing so by a series of poor investments.

One of the cooperatives from which Riker embezzled funds was the 1136 Tenants Corporation, located at 1136 Fifth Avenue on Manhattan. Riker admitted to stealing approximately $130,000 from the trust funds of that cooperative. Because they were unable to recover the stolen funds from Riker, the tenants of the Fifth Avenue cooperative filed a civil suit against the accounting firm Max Rothenberg & Company, which had prepared the annual financial statements and tax returns of the 1136 Tenants Corporation. The principal allegation leveled at the accounting firm was that it should have discovered, and reported to the tenants, the embezzlement of funds by Riker.

The central focus of the trial and subsequent appeals heard in the 1136 Tenants case was the contractual agreement between the tenants and Max Rothenberg & Company. This contract was never reduced to writing and instead was simply an oral agreement between a partner of the accounting firm and I. Jerome Riker. The plaintiffs alleged that the accounting firm had been retained by Riker, their agent, to provide an audit of the 1136 Tenants Corporation's trust funds in addition to preparing the entity's annual tax returns. The accounting firm disputed this contention, alleging instead that other than the preparation of the tax returns, the oral agreement with Riker was simply to perform so-called write-up, or bookkeeping, services for the cooperative. The courts found that the oral agreement between Riker and the Rothenberg firm, in fact, had been for the performance of write-up services rather than an audit.

> The affidavits and examination before trial ... show that the plaintiff orally employed defendant firm of accountants to "write up" its books from statements and facts submitted from time to time to the defendant by plaintiff's managing agent, Riker; and defendant made periodic reports thereof in regular accounting form to the plaintiff and its shareholders.[1]

Unfortunately for the cooperative tenants and the Rothenberg accounting firm, the information supplied by Riker to the firm was grossly in error. Of course, Riker submitted the false information to conceal his embezzlement from the tenants' trust funds. The accounting firm freely admitted that had an audit of the trust funds been performed, the irregularities perpetrated by Riker would almost certainly have been revealed. Even though Max Rothenberg & Company had agreed to provide only write-up services, the court ruled that the firm had a professional obligation to inform the tenants of certain "suspicious" matters coming to the firm's attention during the course of the engagement. The court was referring principally to a workpaper entitled "Missing Invoices" that an

---

1. This and all subsequent quotations were taken from the following legal opinion: 1136 Tenants Corporation v. Max Rothenberg & Company, 277 New York Supp., 2d 996 (1967), 998.

accountant with the Rothenberg firm had prepared during the 1136 Tenants engagement. This workpaper detailed more than $44,000 of expenses for which supporting documentation could not be located. As established by the plaintiffs, these expenses were fabricated by Riker to extract cash from the cooperative's trust funds.

Also damaging to the Rothenberg firm was an admission by one of its partners during the trial that the 1136 Tenants engagement had been somewhat more extensive than the provision of write-up services. The partner testified that his subordinates had reviewed bank statements and other documentary evidence during the engagement, ostensibly to corroborate the financial data included in the trust funds' accounting records. The plaintiffs' legal counsel then established that the tenants had some justification for believing that the Rothenberg firm was providing more than write-up services. For instance, the income statement compiled for the cooperative by Rothenberg personnel included an expense item labeled simply as "Audit." Even more important, the court ruled that the accounting firm had failed to issue a definitive disclaimer of opinion on the financial statements clearly documenting that the statements had not been subjected to a full-scope audit.

The original court that heard the 1136 Tenants case ruled in favor of the plaintiffs, awarding them a judgment exceeding $230,000. The size of the judgment was startling to the accounting profession, since the Rothenberg firm had been paid only $600 for the services it provided to the tenants. The judgment against the accounting firm was upheld by a New York appellate court by a narrow margin of 3 to 2. The two judges who voted to repeal the decision of the lower court argued forcefully that the Rothenberg firm had made a good faith effort to inform the tenants that "no independent verification" of the cooperative's compiled financial statements had been performed. Nevertheless, the three judges voting in favor of the original court's decision focused on the fact that the actions of the Rothenberg firm during the write-up engagement had introduced some degree of ambiguity regarding the nature of the services that the firm was providing to the 1136 Tenants Corporation. This ambiguity, when coupled with the fact that suspicious circumstances were uncovered by the accounting firm during the engagement and not disclosed to the tenants, was sufficient to convince the three judges that the lower court's decision should be upheld.

QUESTIONS

1. Implicit in the court decisions handed down in the 1136 Tenants case is the presumption that accountants have a responsibility to specify precisely to their clients the type of professional service that will be provided during the course of an engagement. Identify the current technical standards that focus on this issue. What are the principal requirements of these standards? Do the standards require that a written engagement letter be obtained by an accounting firm providing professional services to a client?

2. In recent years, the product line of services that accounting firms provide has expanded significantly. Identify the principal auditing and auditing-related services that accountants provide, and briefly compare and contrast these services.

3. Academic research suggests that the expanding product line of auditing and auditing-related services that accounting firms are offering to their clients may be confusing to the users of financial statements. (For instance, see C. M. Pillsbury, "Limited Assurance Engagements," *Auditing: A Journal of Practice & Theory*, Spring 1985, 63–79.) What measures could the profession adopt to eliminate or reduce this confusion? Would these measures, if in place at the time, have limited the legal exposure of Max Rothenberg & Company in the 1136 Tenants case?

4. What steps should CPAs take when they discover financial irregularities during the course of a compilation engagement? Are CPAs required to inform client management when irregularities are discovered during such an engagement? If so, briefly summarize the nature of the communications that the CPA should make to the client in this context.

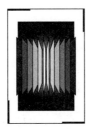

CASE 5.4
YALE EXPRESS SYSTEM, INC.

Irving Goldberg joined the accounting department of Republic Carloading & Distributing Company during World War II. Nearly two decades later, Goldberg's hard work and dedication to his employer were rewarded when he was promoted to treasurer of the company. Republic's principal line of business was freight forwarding, which involves consolidating partial railroad carloads of freight shipments into full carloads and then forwarding the individual items of freight to their ultimate destinations. In May 1963, Goldberg became an employee of Yale Express System, Inc., when that company acquired Republic. Yale Express, a publicly owned company, was much smaller than Republic and engaged principally in short-haul trucking at the time. Yale Express was founded in 1938 by Benjamin Eskow, and twenty-five years later the company was still effectively controlled by the Eskow family, which held 61 percent of its outstanding stock.

THE TRIALS AND TRIBULATIONS OF IRVING GOLDBERG

Following the takeover of Republic by Yale Express, Goldberg remained the treasurer of Republic, which was operated as a wholly owned subsidiary of its new parent company. Within a matter of months after the acquisition, executives of Yale Express began pressuring Goldberg to manipulate the reported operating results of Republic. Apparently, most of this pressure was applied by Fred Mackensen, the administrative vice-president of Yale Express and an individual who had been instrumental in arranging the takeover of Republic. In a subsequent trial, Goldberg testified that Yale Express's chief accounting officer informed him that Mackensen wanted to report a profit of $250,000 for Republic during September 1963 even though Goldberg's figures showed that the company had posted a small loss during that period. Three months later, Mackensen was upset by the $900,000 loss that Goldberg reported for Republic for the 1963 fiscal year. According to Goldberg, Mackensen would not accept Republic's operating results until the loss had been reduced to approximately $100,000.

Goldberg testified that he and Mackensen had serious disagreements over the accounting methods that Goldberg was employing for Republic. The most heated disagreement apparently concerned Goldberg's method of estimating Republic's unrecorded transportation expenses at the end of each fiscal year. Because the railroads and trucking companies that Republic dealt with were quite slow in submitting invoices for their services, Goldberg and his subordinates were forced to estimate the amount of such expenses that should be recorded as accrued liabilities at the end of each fiscal year. Historically, Republic had incurred approximately $.84 of transportation charges for each $1 of earned revenue. However, Mackensen decided that the accrual rate should be only $.78 per $1 of revenue for the fiscal year ending December 31, 1963. According to Goldberg's analysis, this change in the accrual percentage for transportation charges resulted in an overstatement of Republic's net income for 1963 of approximately $1 million after the posting of year-end audit adjustments. Even though Goldberg was aware of the errors in Republic's financial statements, he signed a report filed by the company with the Interstate Commerce Commission (ICC) that indicated that the statements were accurate. When asked to explain why he vouched for the accuracy of the erroneous financial statements, Goldberg replied that at the time he signed the ICC report, he was not "responsible mentally."[1]

In April 1964, Goldberg voluntarily took a leave of absence from Republic. Since January of that year, he had been under psychiatric care and had been taking sedatives to help him cope with the heavy stress being imposed on him by his superiors. When he returned to Republic in May 1964, Goldberg was informed that he had been demoted to a clerk's position, chief of disbursements. Shortly thereafter, he discovered that two large adjusting entries had been posted to Republic's accounting records during his absence. These entries, which had been initialed by Mackensen, reduced Republic's transportation expenses for the first quarter of 1964 by $600,000. At this point, Goldberg went to the board of directors of Yale Express and reported that Republic's operating results were being grossly misrepresented. As a result of Goldberg's allegation, Yale Express's audit firm, Peat Marwick, was retained by the company's board of directors to perform an independent analysis of Republic's transportation expenses. The results of the Peat Marwick study supported Goldberg's claim. Nevertheless, following the completion of that study, the president of the company asked Goldberg to resign. Goldberg refused, stating that his personal financial situation would not allow him to do so. A few months later, however, Goldberg was fired by Mackensen, who justified the dismissal by stating that Goldberg's position was no longer needed by the company.

GERALD ESKOW: AMBITION LEADS TO CONVICTION

The president and chief executive of Yale Express in 1963 was Gerald Eskow, who was known for his single-minded dedication to the company and his willingness to work extremely long hours. The ambitious, thirty-nine-year-old son of the

---

1. "Former Official of Unit of Yale Express Claims Mental Irresponsibility," *Wall Street Journal*, 14 October 1968, 8.

founder of Yale Express was extremely proud of his father and the fact that the senior Eskow, in just two decades, had transformed a small local trucking operation into a very profitable public company known for its excellent service to its customers. The success of his father motivated Eskow to add to the prestige of the family name and to the size of the family fortune. Reportedly, the younger Eskow's goal was to build Yale Express into one of the largest transportation companies in the nation, an ambition that apparently induced him to approve the acquisition of Republic Carloading & Distributing Company in the spring of 1963. In hindsight, the purchase of Republic, which was more than twice as large as Yale Express and in deteriorating financial condition at the time, proved to be a very poor decision for both Yale Express and Eskow.

Court testimony in the various lawsuits that were filed following the disclosure of Yale Express's financial problems suggested that Gerald Eskow was not aware, at least initially, of the misrepresented operating results of the Republic subsidiary. Court records document that Mackensen concealed the significant operating losses of Republic from Eskow by ordering various subordinates to falsify Republic's accounting records. In fact, Republic maintained a "black book" that documented the differences between the actual and publicly reported operating results.[2] The U.S. Attorney who prosecuted the top executives of Yale Express for criminal fraud alleged that by mid–1964, Eskow must have realized that Republic's operating results were being materially misrepresented and that the financial crisis facing that subsidiary was threatening the viability of Yale Express. Later that same year, Yale Express used financial statements drawn from its falsified accounting records to obtain a loan of several million dollars. It was the use of these bogus financial statements for this purpose that would eventually prove to be the downfall of both Mackensen and Eskow. The financial statements reported a profit of approximately $1.5 million for the first nine months of 1964 when the actual figure was a loss of nearly $2 million.

By March 1965, Yale Express could no longer conceal its severe financial problems. At that time, company executives revealed that Yale Express had lost approximately $3 million in 1964 in spite of the profitable figures, which the executives admitted were erroneous, that had been reported several months earlier for the first three quarters of that year. Company officials also disclosed that during 1963, rather than the profit of $1,140,000 that had been reported in Yale Express's audited financial statements, the company had actually realized a loss of more than $1.2 million. The disclosure of the misrepresented 1963 and 1964 financial statements spurred the stockholders of Yale Express to file a large class action lawsuit against the company's officers and its audit firm, Peat Marwick. It also resulted in a series of investigations of the company's financial affairs by the Securities and Exchange Commission (SEC), the ICC, and a federal grand jury. In May 1965, to stave off the company's creditors, Yale Express's board of directors filed for protection under Chapter 10 of the Federal Bankruptcy Act. Although the company had total assets of $47 million compared with total liabilities of $39 million at the time, a significant portion of the assets were intangible items such as goodwill. In fact, the company's 1964 audited financial statements disclosed that its liabilities exceeded its tangible assets by more than $4 million.

---

2. "Two Former Officials of Yale Express Plan to Appeal Convictions," *Wall Street Journal*, 7 November 1965, 28.

Following the company's filing for protection under the federal bankruptcy statute, Gerald Eskow called a news conference in which he criticized the directors of Yale Express for approving that action. Eskow argued that the bankruptcy filing had been too hasty and suggested that the reported losses of the company were overstated. Several months later, at a second news conference, Eskow announced that he and other members of his family had donated 800,000 shares of Yale Express stock, which represented nearly 75 percent of the family's holdings, to the employees of the company. Eskow hoped that the dramatic gesture would serve as an incentive for the employees to return the company to a profitable position: "If our good intentions of giving unsolicited gifts are not enough of an impetus to awaken those employees who have given less than their best, or who have stolen time, money or freight from this company, then our noble venture will have been wasted."[3]

In 1967, Gerald Eskow, Fred Mackensen, and the former chief accounting officer of Yale Express were indicted by a federal grand jury on various criminal fraud charges. The principal allegation against Eskow was that he knowingly used false financial statements to raise debt capital for Yale Express in late 1964. Mackensen and the former chief accounting officer of Yale Express were also charged with submitting false financial statements to the SEC. In August 1968, Eskow filed a $20 million civil lawsuit against Peat Marwick, alleging that the audit firm had fraudulently concealed the true financial condition of Yale Express from company executives.

> In Mr. Eskow's complaint is an allegation that a Peat Marwick staffer on or about August 21, 1964, prepared a "cash flow" workpaper that "advised and alerted" Peat Marwick and the other defendants that Yale Express's "alleged profit" of $717,000 in the first half of 1964 . . . "was false, misleading and fraudulent" and, instead, a loss of $1,615,000 had been sustained. But Peat Marwick "did nothing to correct these errors or to advise (Mr. Eskow) or third parties thereof."[4]

Peat Marwick officials responded to Eskow's allegation by charging that he was simply attempting to damage the credibility of the Peat Marwick auditors who were expected to testify against him and the other former Yale Express executives facing criminal indictments.[5]

Following a three-week trial, Eskow and Mackensen were convicted in November 1968 on thirty-two counts of using fraudulent financial statements to obtain loans for Yale Express. The following month, a federal judge fined Eskow $15,500 and gave him a one-year suspended sentence, and Mackensen was fined $4,650 and given a nine-month suspended sentence. Still professing his innocence, Eskow appealed the conviction. In June 1970, the U.S. Supreme Court rejected his appeal and ruled that the conviction would stand.

---

3. D. Dworsky, "Yale Truckers Get Pep Talk and Gift," *New York Times*, 24 December 1966, 25, 32.

4. "Yale Express System Former President Sues Auditor, Peat Marwick," *Wall Street Journal*, 23 August 1968, 4.

5. No public comment on the resolution of Eskow's civil suit against Peat Marwick could be found. Most likely, the suit was settled out of court for no damages or only nominal damages.

Peat Marwick: Auditor, Consultant . . . Defendant

Peat Marwick was retained by Yale Express in early 1964 to audit the company's 1963 financial statements. Irving Goldberg testified that the audit firm initially contested the adequacy of Yale Express's 1963 year-end accrual of transportation expenses. According to Goldberg, Peat Marwick believed that the Republic subsidiary had understated its accrued transportation charges by nearly $2 million. After an addition of $975,000, Goldberg reported, Peat Marwick accepted the adjusted balance of the accrued transportation expense account. Under cross-examination during one of the Yale Express lawsuits, Goldberg was asked if he informed Peat Marwick that the 1963 Yale Express financial statements about to be reported on by the audit firm were materially misstated, even after the posting of the large audit adjustment. Goldberg replied, "I did not. I couldn't have cared less."[6] Goldberg also admitted that he never brought to Peat Marwick's attention the adjusting entries approved by Mackensen in the spring of 1964 that materially reduced Republic's transportation expenses for the first quarter of that year.

Peat Marwick issued its audit opinion on the 1963 Yale Express financial statements on March 31, 1964. On April 9, 1964, Yale Express released its 1963 annual report to its stockholders and approximately two and one-half months later filed its annual 10–K statement with the SEC. Shortly after the completion of the 1963 audit, Peat Marwick was retained to perform what was referred to by Yale Express officers as the "special studies" consulting project. The purpose of this project was to investigate the allegation made by Goldberg to the Yale Express board that the company's financial records had been falsified. Reportedly, Peat Marwick assigned thirty-five auditors to pore over the transportation invoices received and/or paid by Yale Express during the first five months of 1964. As a result of this intensive study, Peat Marwick discovered that Yale Express, in fact, had materially understated its 1963 accrual for transportation expenses. Exactly when in 1964 Peat Marwick reached this conclusion was subject to dispute. Stockholders who filed suit against Peat Marwick alleged that the firm knew the accrual was understated prior to June 29, 1964, the date that Yale Express filed its 1963 10–K report with the SEC. Peat Marwick maintained, however, that its auditors did not discover that the accrual was materially understated until after the 10–K had been filed.

A severe liquidity crisis in late 1964 forced executives of Yale Express to seek immediate external financing. The executives approached eight insurance companies and asked them to extend Yale Express a multimillion-dollar loan. In connection with the proposed loan, the Yale Express officials agreed to supply the syndicate of insurance companies with unaudited financial statements for the first nine months of 1964. In early November of that year, Robert Conroy, the Peat Marwick partner who supervised the annual audit of Yale Express, met with Eskow and Mackensen in a Wall Street restaurant. According to sworn statements of Eskow and Mackensen, Conroy reportedly informed the two Yale Express

6. "Former Official of Unit of Yale Express Claims Mental Irresponsibility," *Wall Street Journal*, 14 October 1968, 8.

executives that the results of the Peat Marwick special studies consulting project should not be used in connection with the compilation of the financial statements requested by the eight insurance companies. Instead, Conroy allegedly recommended that those financial statements be compiled directly from the Yale Express accounting records—accounting records that had not been adjusted at that time for the significant understatement of transportation expenses discovered by Peat Marwick. Conroy allegedly informed Eskow and Mackensen that such statements would have the advantage of being consistent with the prior year's annual report and that any errors in the interim statements would be "picked up" by the year-end Peat Marwick audit.[7]

In an affidavit submitted by Conroy to the court hearing the class action lawsuit filed by the stockholders of Yale Express, Conroy disputed much of the prior testimony regarding his conversation with Eskow and Mackensen in early November 1964. Conroy testified that he had repeatedly warned the Yale Express executives that statements drawn from the company's unadjusted accounting records would be materially in error. He also testified that the decision to provide the insurance companies the erroneous financial statements for the first nine months of 1964 was made strictly by officials of Yale Express.

In a preliminary hearing in the Yale Express class action lawsuit, the presiding judge focused on three key issues regarding the conduct of the Peat Marwick auditors during that firm's tenure with Yale Express. The first of these issues was whether Peat Marwick, after completing the special studies project, had a responsibility to inform third parties that Yale Express had significantly understated its transportation expenses in its 1963 audited financial statements. In discussing this point, the judge made the following comments: "The elements of good faith and common honesty which govern the businessman presumably should also apply to the independent public accountant. . . . the common law has long required that a person who has made a representation must correct that representation if it becomes false and if he knows people are relying on it."[8]

The SEC, in a legal brief filed with the court hearing the Yale Express class action lawsuit, contended that if an audit firm discovers, after the fact, that an opinion it has issued on a client's financial statements is incorrect because of previously undetected errors, it has a responsibility to inform third parties of those errors. Apparently as a direct result of the SEC's stance on that issue, the AICPA in 1969 adopted *Statement on Auditing Procedures No. 41*, "Subsequent Discovery of Facts Existing at the Date of the Auditor's Report." This technical standard requires auditors to inform financial statement users of undisclosed material errors in financial statements that they have previously audited if client management refuses to do so.[9]

The second key issue concerning Peat Marwick in the Yale Express case was whether the audit firm had a responsibility to inform third parties relying on Yale Express's interim 1964 financial statements that those statements were

---

7. Fischer v. Kletz, 206 F. Supp. 180 (1967), 196.

8. Ibid., 186, 188.

9. This requirement is an exception to the ethical rule that prohibits auditors from disclosing confidential client information to third parties without first obtaining permission to do so from the client.

materially in error. On this point, the judge ruled that since Peat Marwick had not formally or informally contracted to audit the interim 1964 financial statements of Yale Express, the audit firm had no responsibility to inform interested third parties of the errors in those statements. That is, while performing the special studies project, during which the errors in the 1964 interim financial statements were discovered, Peat Marwick was acting strictly as a consultant to Yale Express, not as an independent auditor.

The final issue concerning Peat Marwick was whether the audit firm had aided and abetted the fraudulent actions of Yale Express by recommending that the 1964 interim financial statements be provided to external third parties. In the preliminary opinion handed down in the case, the presiding judge noted that the conflicting testimony on this issue would have to be resolved in court. However, since the case was eventually settled out of court, a final judgment on this point was never rendered.[10]

According to published reports, Peat Marwick contributed $650,000 to the settlement pool established by the defendants in the Yale Express class action lawsuit. Ironically, the reorganization plan subsequently approved by the bankruptcy judge for Yale Express resulted in Peat Marwick becoming the largest shareholder of the company. Professional fees owed to Peat Marwick by Yale Express, following the termination of their auditor-client relationship, caused the audit firm to be one of the largest unsecured general creditors in the bankruptcy hearing. Consequently, Peat Marwick was awarded approximately 12 percent of the new Yale Express common stock issued following the court-ordered reorganization of the company.

QUESTIONS

1. Identify the alternative courses of action that Goldberg had available to him in late 1963 when he was being pressured by Mackensen to manipulate Republic's reported operating results. Which of these alternatives would have been most appropriate for him to choose under the circumstances? Why? Assume Goldberg was a CPA. How would this additional fact affect your answer, if at all?

2. Do you believe that Goldberg had a responsibility to inform Peat Marwick of his concern that the 1963 and interim 1964 financial statements of Yale Express were materially misstated? Why or why not?

3. According to *Statement on Auditing Standards No. 55*, "Consideration of the Internal Control Structure in a Financial Statement Audit," which was issued several years subsequent to the Yale Express lawsuit, one of the fundamental elements of an internal control structure is the "control environment." Discuss the factors that affected the control environment at Yale Express. How should these factors have influenced the Peat Marwick audit of the company?

10. This was also true of the first issue concerning Peat Marwick that was addressed in the Yale Express case. That is, the judge never ruled specifically that Peat Marwick, following the completion of the special studies project, should have informed interested third parties that the 1963 financial statements of Yale Express contained material errors.

4. What audit risk factors arising subsequent to the acquisition of Republic by Yale Express should have been considered by Peat Marwick during its planning phase for the consolidated Yale Express audit?

5. Technically, Peat Marwick was serving as a consultant, not as an independent auditor, during the special studies project. Discuss the ethical questions that may arise when an audit firm provides both consulting and auditing services to a company, particularly questions stemming from the obligation of CPAs to protect the confidentiality of clients' financial records. Identify consulting services that audit firms are not allowed to provide to audit clients.

6. Identify the specific legal courses of action, under the common law and statutory law, that the Yale Express stockholders could have taken against Peat Marwick. In your discussion, identify the elements of proof that the stockholders would have been required to establish to prevail against Peat Marwick.

7. Why did the AICPA react so quickly and affirmatively to the position expressed by the SEC in the legal brief that agency filed in the Yale Express class action lawsuit? Does the SEC have direct or indirect influence on the standard-setting process in the auditing domain?

8. Is it appropriate for an auditor to inform a client not to be concerned with errors in interim financial statements, since such errors will likely be detected and corrected during the year-end audit? Support your answer.

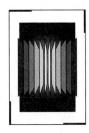

CASE 5.5

FIRST SECURITIES COMPANY OF CHICAGO (*ERNST & ERNST V. HOCHFELDER ET AL.*)

Ladislas Nay immigrated to the United States from Hungary in 1921 at the age of eighteen. The industrious young immigrant was excited about the opportunities that his new land offered him and promised himself that he would make the most of them. Shortly after his arrival in the United States, Nay made his way to Chicago, and almost immediately found employment in the booming securities industry with a small brokerage firm. For the next several years, Nay worked long and hard hours learning the brokerage business. Unfortunately for Nay, the Great Depression hit the securities industry particularly hard. Young stockbrokers like himself were nearly always the first to be released by their firms when personnel cuts were necessary. During the bleak 1930s, Nay, who by this time had Americanized his first name to Leston, endured a number of job changes and two failed marriages. Finally, in 1942, as World War II began to pull the United States out of the depression, Nay landed a permanent job with the brokerage firm of Ryan–Nichols & Company.

Within two years after joining Ryan–Nichols, Nay was promoted to president of the firm and eventually became its principal stockholder, accumulating more than 90 percent of the firm's outstanding common stock. In 1945, Nay's firm became a member of the Midwest Stock Exchange and shortly thereafter was renamed First Securities Company of Chicago. Over the next two decades, Nay's career and personal life flourished. His family, which included his wife and three children, eventually moved to the upper-class neighborhood of Hyde Park, near the University of Chicago. Nay and his wife, Elizabeth, became actively involved in community affairs, each holding appointments to prominent civic boards. Nay also made a number of close friends among the faculty and staff of the University of Chicago. In fact, many of his best customers were associated with the prestigious school.

Nay's personal attention to the financial needs of his customers earned him their respect and admiration. One of his customers described him as a kind and considerate man, much "like an old-fashioned English solicitor who took care of a family's affairs."[1] His conservative investment strategies were particularly appealing to his friends who taught at the University of Chicago, many of whom were nearing retirement when he became acquainted with them. Nay offered those customers with whom he developed a particularly close relationship an opportunity to invest in a lucrative fund that he personally managed, a fund that was not an asset of First Securities. Nay referred to this fund, of which no other First Securities personnel were aware, as simply the "escrow syndicate." The cash Nay collected for investment in the escrow syndicate was loaned to blue-chip companies that developed sudden and unexpected working capital shortages. These companies were willing to pay interest rates well above the prevailing market rates, because of the urgency of their working capital needs. As a result, Nay's customers who invested in the escrow syndicate earned rates of return ranging from 7 to 12 percent—returns that at the time were nearly double those paid by banks on savings accounts.

One of Nay's closest friends, Arnold Schueren, entrusted Nay with more than $400,000 over a period of nearly three decades and granted him a power of attorney to make all investment decisions regarding those funds. Another individual who relied heavily on Nay for investment advice was the widow of a close associate of the famed University of Chicago scientist Enrico Fermi. She subsequently testified that Nay had managed her family's investments for many years but did not offer her the opportunity to invest in the escrow syndicate until after her husband's death. According to her account, Nay reported that he offered this investment opportunity only to his "nearest and dearest friends."[2] Following the death of another of his customers, Norman Moyer, Nay convinced Moyer's widow to invest her husband's estate of $90,000 in the escrow syndicate. In total, seventeen of Nay's friends and/or their widows invested substantial sums in the escrow syndicate.

Dr. Jekyll and Mr. Hyde: A Tragic Ending

On the morning of June 4, 1968, Leston Nay drove to St. Luke's Hospital in Chicago to pick up his wife, who had fallen and broken her hip the prior week. Earlier that morning, Nay had called his firm and told his secretary that he would not be in the office that day because he had a stomach virus. Shortly before noon, as his wife, who was still on crutches, made her way to the kitchen of their apartment, Nay retrieved his 12–gauge shotgun and shot her in the upper back from close range. Nay then laid a suicide note on a dressing table in his bedroom, sat down on his bed, put the muzzle of the gun in his mouth, and pulled the trigger.

The Nays' friends and associates were shocked by the news of the murder-suicide. These same people were shocked again when the Chicago police

1. J. M. Johnston, "How Broker Worked $1 Million Swindle," *Chicago Daily News*, 13 December 1968, 42, 43.

2. Ibid.

released the contents of Nay's suicide note, which disclosed that the kindly stockbroker had led a Dr. Jekyll–Mr. Hyde existence for decades. In the note addressed "To whom it may concern," Nay admitted that he had been stealing from his customers for more than thirty years. The escrow syndicate in which his closest friends had invested did not exist. Instead, Nay had used the funds for his own purposes. Although the note did not disclose how the funds were spent, the police speculated that Nay had lost the money in the stock market. Nay was apparently successful in concealing the missing funds from the escrow investors for as long as he did because he periodically mailed them interest and dividend checks, payments that deterred the individuals from questioning the safety of their investments.

In the suicide note, Nay showed some remorse when he referred to the fact that the eighty-year-old Moyer was penniless as a result of his actions. He also explained why he had decided to take his life. After his friend Arnold Schueren died in 1967, the executor of Schueren's estate, a Montana bank, demanded a return of the funds Schueren had invested with Nay. Nay stated in the suicide note that he had "stalled" as long as he could but that the bank would not be put off any longer. So, he took his life. Most likely, Nay murdered his wife to "save" her from the shame she would feel when his fraudulent scheme, of which she was apparently unaware, was disclosed.

DEFRAUDED CUSTOMERS SUE TO RECOVER THEIR INVESTMENTS

The individuals who participated in Nay's escrow syndicate filed civil lawsuits against a number of parties in an effort to recover their investments, which collectively totaled more than $1 million. One of the early suits filed by these investors was against the Midwest Stock Exchange. In that suit, the investors alleged that the stock exchange had not properly investigated Nay's background before admitting him to membership. If a more thorough investigation had been performed, the stock exchange might have discovered that Nay, in fact, had a history, although well concealed, of unscrupulous business practices. The investors suggested that the discovery of Nay's unethical conduct in the past would have forced the exchange to deny his application for membership and thus likely prevented him from engaging in the escrow syndicate fraud. The court hearing the suit dismissed the investors' claims, concluding that the stock exchange had sufficiently investigated Nay's background before approving his membership application.

The seventeen escrow participants or their estates also sued First Securities Company of Chicago. However, since the brokerage firm was bankrupt, the escrow investors were thwarted again, even though the court ruled that the brokerage firm had clearly aided and abetted Nay's fraudulent activities. Finally, Nay's former customers filed suit against Ernst & Ernst, the public accounting firm that had audited First Securities Company for more than two decades. The principal allegation in the plaintiffs' suit was that Ernst & Ernst had also aided and abetted Nay's fraud by failing to detect and disclose what became known throughout the lengthy judicial history of the First Securities case as Nay's "mail rule." According to the plaintiffs' legal counsel: "Nay had forbidden anyone other than himself to open mail addressed to him, and in his absence all such

EXHIBIT 1
Rule 10b–5 of the
Securities Exchange Act
of 1934

Employment of manipulative and deceptive devices. It shall be unlawful for any person, directly or indirectly, by the use of any means or instrumentality of interstate commerce, or of the mails or of any facility of any national securities exchange,

    (a) To employ any device, scheme, or artifice to defraud,

    (b) To make any untrue statement of a material fact or to omit to state a material fact necessary in order to make the statements made, in the light of the circumstances under which they were made, not misleading, or

    (c) To engage in any act, practice, or course of business which operates or would operate as a fraud or deceit upon any person, in connection with the purchase or sale of any security.

mail was simply allowed to pile up on his desk, even if it was addressed to First Securities for his attention."[3]

Nay's mail rule allowed him to conceal the existence of the escrow syndicate scam from his subordinates at First Securities and from the brokerage's independent auditors. The escrow investors charged Ernst & Ernst with negligence in failing to discover the mail rule during its numerous audits of First Securities. Had Ernst & Ernst discovered the mail rule, the plaintiffs alleged, a subsequent investigation would have been warranted, and this investigation would have led to the discovery and eventual termination of Nay's escrow investment scam.

ERNST & ERNST V. HOCHFELDER ET AL.

The civil lawsuit filed against Ernst & Ernst by the defrauded investors was predicated on alleged violations of the Securities Exchange Act of 1934. That federal statute does not expressly provide stockholders of companies registered with the Securities and Exchange Commission (SEC) with civil remedies. However, since the adoption of the 1934 act, the federal courts have allowed stockholders to use the statute as a basis for civil suits against directors or officers, investment brokers, auditors, and other parties associated with a company that files materially misrepresented financial statements with the SEC. Most of these suits allege one or more violations of Rule 10b–5 of the 1934 act, which is shown in Exhibit 1.

In the First Securities case, the plaintiffs charged that Ernst & Ernst was negligent in failing to discover Nay's mail rule and that this negligence constituted a violation of Rule 10b–5.

> The premise [of the investors' suit] was that Ernst & Ernst had failed to utilize "appropriate auditing procedures" in its audits of First Securities. . . . Respondents [investors] contended that if Ernst & Ernst had conducted a proper audit, it would have discovered this "mail rule." The existence of the rule then would have been disclosed to the Exchange [Midwest Stock Exchange] and to the Commission [SEC] by Ernst & Ernst as an irregular procedure that prevented an effective audit.[4]

To support their claim that the mail rule was a critical internal control weakness that had important implications for the Ernst & Ernst audits of First

---

3. Securities and Exchange Commission v. First Securities Company of Chicago, 463 F.2d 981 (1972), 985.

4. Ernst & Ernst v. Hochfelder et al., 425 U.S. 185 (1976), 190.

EXHIBIT 2
Excerpt from Expert Witness Testimony Regarding Nay's Mail Rule

Expert Witness No. 3:

If I had discovered in making an audit of a security brokerage business that its president had established an office rule that mail addressed to him at the business address, or to the company for his attention should not be opened by anyone but him, even in his absence; and that whenever he was away from the office such mail would remain unopened and pile up on his desk I would have to raise the question whether such rule or practice could possibly have been instituted for the purpose of preventing discovery of irregularities of whatever nature; would, as a minimum, have to undertake additional audit procedures to independently establish a negative answer to the latter question; also failing such an answer either withdraw from the engagement or decline to express an opinion on the financial statements of the enterprise.

Securities, the escrow investors provided affidavits from three expert witnesses with impressive credentials in the accounting profession. Exhibit 2 lists a portion of one of these affidavits.

The federal district court that initially presided over the *Hochfelder et al. v. Ernst & Ernst* case quickly dismissed the lawsuit, contending that there was no substantive evidence in support of the allegation that Ernst & Ernst had been negligent in auditing First Securities.[5] When the investors appealed this decision, the U.S. court of appeals reversed the lower court decision and ordered that the case go to trial. In its decision, the appeals court stated that there was sufficient doubt regarding the negligence claim against Ernst & Ernst to have the case heard. The appeals court also suggested that if negligence on the part of Ernst & Ernst were established, the audit firm could be held civilly liable to the defrauded investors under Rule 10b–5 of the 1934 act.

Before the Hochfelder case went to trial in federal district court, Ernst & Ernst appealed the ruling of the U.S. court of appeals to the U.S. Supreme Court. Ernst & Ernst argued before the Supreme Court that the negligence allegation upon which the escrow investors' suit was based was not sufficient, even if proved, to constitute a violation of Rule 10b–5. In fact, the point raised by Ernst & Ernst had arisen in numerous prior civil cases filed under the Securities Exchange Act of 1934. In these earlier cases, the federal courts had generally ruled or suggested that negligent behavior did constitute a violation of Rule 10b–5. That is, fraudulent behavior or grossly negligent behavior, either of which is much more difficult for a plaintiff to prove than ordinary negligence, did not have to be established for a defendant to be held civilly liable to a plaintiff under Rule 10b–5. Ernst & Ernst contested these rulings by arguing that Rule 10b–5, as worded, could not be construed to encompass negligent behavior. Given the long-standing controversy surrounding this issue and the number of lower courts that had wrestled with the inherent ambiguity of Rule 10b–5, the Supreme Court decided to rule on the issue in the Hochfelder case and thus establish a precedent for all future lawsuits filed under Rule 10b–5.

Before Ernst & Ernst's appeal was heard by the Supreme Court, the SEC filed a legal brief with the Court supporting the defrauded investors' argument that Rule 10b–5 should be construed to encompass both fraudulent and negligent conduct. In this brief, the SEC pointed out that the end result of investors' acting

5. Hochfelder et al. v. Ernst & Ernst, 503 F.2d 1100 (1974). (One of the investors defrauded by Nay was Olga Hochfelder.)

on inaccurate financial statements is the same regardless of whether the errors in the statements are a result of fraud or negligence. Because a central purpose of the federal securities laws is to promote the credibility of financial reports and to ensure that investors receive reliable information upon which to base their investment decisions, the SEC argued, the ambiguity in Rule 10b–5 should be resolved in favor of investors.

Surprisingly, the bulk of the Supreme Court's opinion in the Hochfelder case was not in response to either the arguments of the defrauded investors or those of Ernst & Ernst but rather was a response to the SEC's legal brief. The Court rejected the largely philosophical argument of the SEC and instead focused on the more technical issue of whether the authors of Rule 10b–5 intended it to encompass both negligent and fraudulent behavior. In addressing this issue, the Court reviewed the legislative history of the 1934 act and did a painstaking analysis of the semantics of Rule 10b–5. Eventually, the Court concluded that the key signal to the underlying meaning of Rule 10b–5 was the term *manipulative*. As shown in Exhibit 1, the heading of the rule clearly indicates that it pertains to "manipulative and deceptive" devices. According to the Supreme Court, negligence on the part of independent auditors or other parties associated with erroneous financial statements could not be construed as being manipulative behavior. The Court suggested that in most cases, for behavior to qualify as manipulative, intent to deceive—the legal term being *scienter*—had to be present.[6] In commenting on this point, the Court noted that: "When a statute speaks so specifically in terms of manipulation and deception, and of implementing devices and contrivances—the commonly understood terminology of intentional wrongdoing—and when its history reflects no more expansive intent, we are quite unwilling to extend the scope of the statute to negligent conduct."[7]

Two of the nine Supreme Court justices dissented to the decision in the Hochfelder case, and one justice abstained. In disagreeing with the majority decision, Justice Harry Blackmun sided with the view expressed by the SEC. He noted that although the decision was probably technically consistent with the semantics of the Securities Exchange Act of 1934, it was not consistent philosophically with the underlying intent of that very important federal statute. He wrote, "It seems to me that an investor can be victimized just as much by negligent conduct as by positive deception, and that it is not logical to drive a wedge between the two, saying that Congress clearly intended the one but certainly not the other."[8] Justice Blackmun went on to comment on the "critical importance" of the independent auditor's role and the responsibility of the auditor to serve the "public interest."[9] Given this important responsibility,

---

6. A particularly troublesome issue for the Supreme Court to resolve was the underlying meaning of Subsection b of Rule 10b–5. Subsections a and c of that rule refer explicitly to fraud, thus implying that negligence is not a severe enough form of misconduct to constitute a violation of Rule 10b–5. However, Subsection b contains no explicit reference to fraudulent conduct. The SEC construed this omission to suggest that Subsection b covers both fraudulent and negligent misconduct. The Supreme Court rejected this argument, maintaining instead that the explicit references to fraud in Subsections a and c suggested that fraudulent conduct was the implied, although unstated, culpability standard in Subsection b as well.

7. Ernst & Ernst v. Hochfelder et al., 214.

8. Ernst & Ernst v. Hochfelder et al., 216.

9. Ernst & Ernst v. Hochfelder et al., 218.

Justice Blackmun argued, negligent auditors should be held accountable to investors who rely to their detriment on materially inaccurate financial statements.

AN UNRESOLVED ISSUE

At first reading, the Supreme Court's Hochfelder opinion appeared to decide, once and for all, the culpability standard that would be used in determining whether violations of Rule 10b–5 have occurred. Unfortunately, the opinion is not quite as precise or definitive as it first appeared. A footnote to the opinion suggests that in certain cases, scienter, or intent to deceive, may not be a necessary element of proof for a plaintiff to establish in a civil suit alleging a Rule 10b–5 violation. The Court noted that some jurisdictions equate scienter with willful or reckless disregard for the truth or, more simply, "recklessness."[10] When engaging in reckless behavior, a party does not actually possess conscious intent to deceive; that is, scienter is not present. For whatever reason, the Court specifically refused to rule on the question of whether reckless behavior would be considered equivalent to scienter and thus constitute a violation of Rule 10b–5. This omission has resulted in plaintiffs' predicating alleged Rule 10b–5 violations by independent auditors on reckless behavior, since that type of professional misconduct is much easier to prove than actual scienter.

EPILOGUE

Following the issuance of the Hochfelder opinion by the Supreme Court, congressional critics of the opinion argued that the alleged "flaw" in Rule 10b–5 should be corrected legislatively. A bill that would have held negligent auditors civilly liable to damaged investors who relied on materially inaccurate financial statements filed with the SEC was introduced in the U.S. House of Representatives in late 1978. Fortunately for independent auditors, that bill was rejected by Congress.

QUESTIONS

1. Under present technical standards, to whom, if anyone, would auditors be required to disclose a company policy similar to Nay's mail rule if it were discovered during the course of an audit? Would this disclosure, if required at the time Nay was engaging in his fraudulent scheme, have likely resulted in his discontinuing the mail rule?

2. During the litigation referred to in this case, Ernst & Ernst argued that the mail rule was not relevant to its audits of First Securities, since that rule only involved personal transactions of Nay and the escrow investors. Do you agree? Why or why not?

---

10. Ernst & Ernst v. Hochfelder et al., 194.

3. Define *negligence* as that term has been used in legal cases involving independent auditors. What is the key distinction between negligence and fraud? Between recklessness and fraud? For all three types of professional misconduct, provide an example of such behavior in an audit context.

4. Assume that the investors defrauded by Nay could have filed their suit against Ernst & Ernst under the Securities Act of 1933. How, if at all, do you believe the outcome of their suit would have been affected?

5. Assume that the jurisdiction in which the Hochfelder case was filed invoked the legal precedent inherent in the Rusch Factors case. Given this assumption, would the defrauded investors have been successful in pursuing a negligence claim against Ernst & Ernst under the common law? Why or why not?

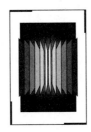

CASE 5.6

EQUITY FUNDING CORPORATION OF AMERICA

In 1960, Equity Funding Corporation of America was founded by four individuals who assumed equal partnership interests in the firm. Soon after its formation, two of the partners resigned, leaving the small company to Stanley Goldblum, who held the title of president, and Michael Riordan, who served as chairman of the board. The principal line of business of Equity Funding was the selling of life insurance policies and "funding programs" that merged life insurance and mutual funds into one financial package for investors. The development of creative financial investments was a trademark of Equity Funding in the early years of its existence. In fact, after going public in 1964, Equity Funding was soon recognized across the country as one of the most innovative companies in the ultraconservative life insurance industry.

TRAGEDY STRIKES EQUITY FUNDING

In January 1969, Michael Riordan was killed in a mudslide that destroyed his home in the exclusive Brentwood suburb of Los Angeles. Goldblum was immediately appointed chairman of the board and shortly thereafter retained Fred Levin, a company employee since 1967, to serve as the executive vice-president in charge of life insurance operations. Equity Funding's revenues and earnings increased dramatically under the aggressive, growth-oriented management policies of Goldblum and Levin. By 1972, Equity Funding was one of the ten largest life insurance companies in the United States and was the fastest-growing company in the industry. At the time, Equity Funding had total assets of approximately $500 million, compared with assets of only $9 million when the company went public eight years earlier. During that same period, the company's pretax earnings increased from $620,000 to $26 million. In late 1972, security analysts for the financial services and insurance industries chose Equity Funding's common stock, out of several hundred stocks in those industries, as their most popular investment recommendation.

The skyrocketing price of Equity Funding's common stock in the early 1970s made both Goldblum and Levin fabulously wealthy and allowed them to join the innermost circles of Los Angeles's celebrity social circuit. The fortune and notoriety achieved by these men was particularly impressive since both were from modest backgrounds. Levin earned a law degree from DePaul University in Chicago and then worked briefly for the Illinois regulatory agency responsible for overseeing that state's insurance industry. Levin's quick wit, his charming humor, and most important, his ruthless nature quickly endeared him to Goldblum after he joined Equity Funding in 1967. Levin reportedly had no qualms about humiliating employees publicly and kept a tight rein on the army of insurance sales personnel that he supervised.

As was the case with most of Goldblum's subordinates, Levin recognized the benefits of having a network of well-connected friends and business associates. At one point, when he encountered legal problems, he retained one such friend, Edmund Brown, an attorney and former governor of California, to represent him. Levin's wit made him much in demand as a speaker at meetings of insurance executives and financial analysts across the country. At one such meeting in January 1973, he summarized Equity Funding's management philosophy: "We're conservative in our financial management. . . . We are innovative in product development . . . and we are very traditional in our conviction that by serving the public's real needs, we will continue to grow in accordance to the objectives we set for ourselves."[1]

In many ways, Goldblum was a striking contrast to Levin. Goldblum was very much a loner who preferred to spend long hours working out with weights rather than wining and dining business associates. In the early 1970s, Goldblum's personal fortune was estimated at more than $30 million, an astonishing figure, given that a little more than a decade earlier he was a college dropout working in a meat-packing plant. In addition to attaining tremendous wealth, Goldblum was widely respected within his profession and held a number of important positions in professional and business organizations. One such position was chairman of the ethics committee of the Los Angeles branch of the National Association of Securities Dealers. Former associates recalled that Goldblum was a vigorous enforcer of that organization's code of ethics: "He was harsh on transgressors . . . [and gave] substantially stiffer penalties than had been anticipated."[2]

THE HOUSE OF CARDS COLLAPSES

In the spring of 1973, Equity Funding collapsed in a period of a few weeks when a disgruntled former employee disclosed the existence of a massive financial fraud within the company. The stories told by the former employee were so incredible that many parties associated with the company refused to believe the

1. L. J. Seidler, F. Andrews, and M. J. Epstein, *The Equity Funding Papers: The Anatomy of a Fraud* (New York: Wiley, 1977), 55.

2. R. L. Dirks and L. Gross, *The Great Wall Street Scandal* (New York: McGraw–Hill, 1974), 36.

revelations when they were first made public. The individual charged, and federal and state investigators later confirmed, that the majority of Equity Funding's life insurance policies were bogus. A lengthy audit by the accounting firm of Touche Ross, at the request of Equity Funding's court-appointed bankruptcy trustee, disclosed that the company had generated more than $2 billion of fictitious insurance policies. Most of these bogus policies had then been sold to reinsurance companies.[3] Goldblum and other company executives were forced to disguise the fictitious nature of these policies from insurance examiners and outside auditors by regularly holding midnight "file-stuffing" parties. The purpose of these parties was to generate supporting documentation for the thousands of nonexistent policyholders that had allegedly purchased life insurance from Equity Funding.

The Equity Funding fraud, like most financial frauds, had a modest beginning. Prior to taking their company public in 1964, Goldblum and Riordan were reportedly concerned that its earnings for that year were too low. To correct this "problem," Goldblum decided that Equity Funding was entitled to rebates or kickbacks from the brokers through whom the company's sales force purchased mutual fund shares. (These mutual fund shares were one component of the "funding programs" that Equity Funding sold to the general public.) Goldblum referred to these rebates, which were purely illusionary, as reciprocal income, or reciprocals. The reciprocal income was used by Goldblum to boost Equity Funding's 1964 net income to the level he thought the company should have reached during that fiscal year. According to one account of this scheme, "Goldblum supplied [a subordinate] with an inflated earnings per share figure—attributing the overstatement to 'reciprocals.' [The subordinate] was instructed to make whatever increases were necessary to support the inflated earnings per share figure."[4]

In subsequent years, the reciprocal income had to be supplemented with other fraudulent amounts to achieve Goldblum's predetermined earnings targets. In truth, Equity Funding was never profitable. Prior to collapsing in the spring of 1973, the company was technically insolvent even though Goldblum had just issued a press release reporting record earnings for 1972, up 17 percent over 1971. In that same press release, the brassy Goldblum reported that Equity Funding had increased the dollar value of the life insurance policies it had in force by nearly 50 percent over the previous twelve months.

One of the most alarming features of the huge Equity Funding fraud was the number of individuals who were aware of its existence. Dozens of individuals, both Equity Funding employees and external third parties, helped perpetuate and/or conceal the company's fraudulent schemes. Eventually, federal prosecutors would convict or obtain guilty pleas from twenty-two individuals associated with the company, including three of the company's independent auditors. As many as fifty additional Equity Funding employees, primarily clerical personnel, participated directly or indirectly in the fraud; however, prosecutors chose not to bring criminal charges against these individuals.

---

3. Life insurance companies often sell a portion of their outstanding policies to reinsurance companies. This practice effectively dilutes the business risk associated with selling life insurance.

4. A. I. Briloff, *More Debits Than Credits* (New York: Harper & Row, 1976), 323–324.

The extensive federal and state-level investigations of Equity Funding and the numerous books and articles that documented the life insurance industry's most infamous scandal suggest that Goldblum and Levin gradually and deliberately induced their co-conspirators to become involved in the fraud.[5] More often than not, these individuals were persuaded with significant monetary rewards in the form of stock rights, large salaries and bonuses, and exorbitant expense accounts.[6] Goldblum and other company executives who masterminded the fraud reaped their biggest financial benefits from the sale of Equity Funding stock. Goldblum alone reportedly earned more than $5 million from the sale of a fraction of his large holding of Equity Funding common stock. In fact, maintaining the company's stock price at a high level appeared to be the key motive underlying Goldblum's fraudulent activities. During 1972, several of the Equity Funding co-conspirators met with Goldblum and pleaded with him to report flat earnings for a period of years. They argued that by doing so, the company would have an opportunity to stop the fraudulent practices and become a totally legitimate operation. Goldblum refused to cooperate, pointing out that if reported earnings did not increase each year, the company's stock price would fall.

One of the seamiest anecdotes from the annals of Equity Funding, and one that graphically characterized the company's amoral culture, came to be known as the Cookie Jar Caper. Several lower-level Equity Funding employees devised a scheme to enrich themselves at the expense of several reinsurance companies. These individuals "killed off" a number of fictitious policyholders who had "purchased" Equity Funding life insurance policies—policies subsequently sold by Equity Funding to reinsurance companies. The employees then diverted to themselves the payments made by the reinsurance companies to the beneficiaries of the allegedly deceased policyholders. When Goldblum and Levin discovered this scheme, they ordered the individuals involved to continue it on a much larger scale but to channel the beneficiary payments by the reinsurance companies to Equity Funding's corporate bank accounts.

The numerous insurance examiners and independent auditors who reviewed and reported on Equity Funding's financial records over more than a decade were also victims of the criminal mischief of the company's executives. At one point, Levin ordered the Equity Funding offices being used by state insurance examiners to be bugged so that he would know the specific questions or issues they were addressing. Three independent auditors who were involved for several years in the annual audits of Equity Funding were eventually convicted of complicity in the fraudulent scheme. However, the large majority of Equity Funding's independent auditors were apparently never aware of the huge fraud. Equity Funding executives went to great lengths to conceal their fraudulent activities from these individuals. As an example, on the pretense of lunch at an

---

5. The Equity Funding Scandal is possibly the only financial fraud that has served as the basis for a movie, *The Day the Bubble Burst*, starring eventual Academy Award winner James Woods, Christopher Guest, and several other notable actors.

6. Many of these individuals expressed sincere remorse when they testified regarding their involvement in the massive fraud. For example, one reported, "I simply lacked the courage to do what was right." (H. Anderson, "12 More Ex–Equity Officials Get Jail, Fine or Probation," *Los Angeles Times*, 25 March 1975, section 3, pp. 9, 11.)

elegant and busy local restaurant, company officials rushed several auditors out of their office, hoping that they would leave their files unlocked. The auditors did just that, and other company employees spent the lunch hour copying the insurance policy numbers that had been randomly selected by the auditors for testing. Of course, with those numbers in hand, client executives were able to ensure that the selected files were totally "clean."[7]

THE AFTERMATH OF EQUITY FUNDING

The stockholders of Equity Funding and those of companies that Equity Funding had defrauded suffered losses of hundreds of millions of dollars. In fact, the disclosure of the Equity Funding scandal rocked all of Wall Street, dropping the collective market value of publicly owned stocks by more than $15 billion within one week. In comparison, Goldblum, Levin, and their co-conspirators paid a seemingly modest price for their transgressions. Goldblum would eventually serve four years in the Terminal Island federal prison in Long Beach, California, before being paroled, whereas Levin would serve only two and one-half years in the same facility.

At his sentencing hearing, a contrite Levin had pleaded for leniency: "Someday when this nightmare is over, I will conduct myself in a highly ethical manner, which hopefully will repay for some of the crimes and fraud I committed."[8] Within a few years after his release from prison, Levin was living in Beverly Hills and was president of a small plastics company. In 1984, he was indicted for embezzling $250,000 from the company's pension fund. Among the more than two dozen other fraud charges listed in the indictment against Levin were several that involved preparing forged invoices and other documents to support fictitious transactions allegedly engaged in by his company.

Goldblum also returned to the business world when he was released from federal prison. In 1984, he was elected president and chief executive officer of a company that operates a chain of medical care clinics. Goldblum remarked that he hoped to "put the company on a sound financial basis" and eventually "build it into a more substantive venture."[9] Ironically, Goldblum's new company was audited at the time by Seidman & Seidman, the accounting firm that had served as Equity Funding's independent auditor during its final year of existence. Shortly after Goldblum joined the company, Seidman & Seidman resigned as its audit firm, forfeiting a $40,000 annual audit fee in the process. Ostensibly, Seidman & Seidman resigned because it did not want to be associated with another company that had Goldblum as its chief executive.

---

7. The various public accounting firms that were unfortunate enough to have been associated with Equity Funding at some point in its existence collectively paid $44 million to settle the civil lawsuits filed against them following the collapse of the company.

8. H. Anderson, "Goldblum Gets 8–Year Term in Equity Scandal," *Los Angeles Times*, 18 March 1975, section 3, pp. 8, 9.

9. S. J. Sansweet, "Man Who Presided over Massive Fraud Picked to Head Firm," *Wall Street Journal*, 7 September 1984, 7.

QUESTIONS

1. Is it necessary or appropriate for independent auditors to trust the executives of a client? If so, to what extent should auditors trust client management? In your answer, consider integrating the concept of professional skepticism discussed in *Statement on Auditing Standards No. 53,* "The Auditor's Responsibility to Detect and Report Errors and Irregularities."

2. In evaluating the integrity of the executives of a prospective client, what types of information should auditors obtain, and from what sources would they generally collect this information?

3. In your view, was it appropriate for Seidman & Seidman to resign as the audit firm of Goldblum's new company after he was elected its president and chief executive officer? Under what conditions is it appropriate for a professional firm, such as a CPA firm, to choose not to provide professional services to a company or individual requesting such services?

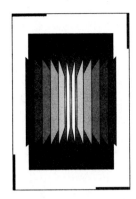

INDEX

Accountant(s). *See also* Accounting firms; Auditor(s)
changing sides by, 62–63, 118–19
ethical codes for, 217–18
exposure of, to third-party financial statement users, 263–70
importance of personal integrity in, 201–3
privileged communication with client, 195–96
professional responsibilities of staff, 241–44
recruitment of, as controlled informant, 193–97
responsibilities of, 156
   to specify type of professional services, 280–84
Accounting
accrual basis of, 175–76
cash basis of, 140, 175, 176
cost-to-cost percentage-of-completion method of, 180–81, 183
percentage-of-completion method of, 118, 120, 180, 183, 241, 273–74
problem of creative methods of, 56–59, 180, 235
Accounting and Auditing Enforcement Release No. 13, 137n
Accounting and Auditing Enforcement Release No. 30, 125n
Accounting and Auditing Enforcement Release No. 81, 129n
Accounting and Auditing Enforcement Release No. 109A, 30n
Accounting and Auditing Enforcement Release No. 143, 187n
Accounting and Auditing Enforcement Release No. 200, 92n
"Accounting-driven" deals, 65
Accounting firm(s). *See also*

Accountant(s); Auditor(s); *specific firms*
buy out of lawsuit by, 176–77
concerns over economic viability of, 113
and handling of technical disagreements in audits, 134
legal liabilities of, 257–60
liability of partners in, 28
lowballing by, 76, 78
partnership acquisition policies in, 221–29
pressures placed on partners in, 27
product line of services of, 280–84
Accounting Principles Board Opinion No. 25, 233
Accounting Series Release No. 153A, 150n
Accounting Series Release No. 157, 215n
Accounting Series Release No. 285, 173n
Accounting Series Release No. 292, 6n
Accounts payables
bogus debit memos for, 78
confirmation procedures for, 137, 147–51
   telephone, 149, 151, 153
   written, 147–48, 153
determining material accuracy of, 153
irregularities in, 147–51
management assertions for, 152
overstating, 75
search for unrecorded liabilities in, 152
Accounts receivables
allowance for uncollectible, 97
backlog of uncollectable, 95
confirmation procedures for, 8, 137, 171–72, 174
internal control structure for, 173
year-end tests of, 8, 172
Accounts receivable subsidiary ledger, transactions in, 7

Accrual basis of accounting, 175–76
Achison, Jack, 68
Acosta, Fernando, 56
Adjusting entries, 188–89, 191
   to tooling cost account, at Mattel, 9-10, 13
   treatment of, as prior period adjustments, 100
Administrative agreement, 81
Adverse judgment, qualification of, as material event, 190
Adverse publicity, 17
Affidavit, misrepresentations in, 187–92
Aggressive franchising strategy, 188
Aging summaries, misleading, 93–94
Aiding and abetting, 76–77
Akroyd, Dan, 71
Akst, Daniel, 42
Alexander Grant & Company, 15, 134. *See also* Grant Thornton
American Airlines, 188
American Continental Corporation (ACC), 55, 63
American Funding Corporation, 281
American Institute of Certified Public Accountants (AICPA) Code of Professional Conduct, 68, 114, 121
Anderson, Arthur, & Company
and audit of Four Seasons Nursing Centers of America, Inc., 179–83
and audit of Fund of Funds, 104–10
dual relationship with King Resources and, 103–4
legal action involving, 110–13
and audit of Lincoln Savings and Loan, 59–63
and audit of Mattel, Inc.
   alleged deficiencies in, 5–11
   deficient statements of, 12

involvement in cash management
    practices, 162–68
SEC criticism of, 11
and audit of Whittaker Corporation,
    213–16
costs of Four Seasons Nursing
    Centers of America, Inc. scandal
    to, 182–83
and proposed stock option rule
    change, 234
Annual percentage change in "same
    store" sales, 75
Antar, Eddie, 69–78
Antar, Sam E., 72, 78
Arizona, state privilege statutes and
    ethic rules in, 64
Arky, Steve, 17, 22, 26–27
Arm's length transactions
    in Funds of Funds, Ltd. case, 106, 107,
        109, 111, 114
    inventory shipments as, at U.S.
        Surgical Corp., 30, 34
Arnott, Gregory, 130, 132, 133–34
Assets
    disruption of, 55
    exchange of dissimilar, 63
    useful lives of, 39
Atchison, Jack, 60, 61–62
Attorneys' letters, purpose of, 207
Audit(s)
    comparison of review with, 53
    measures for strengthening
        procedures in, 12
    peer review of, 127
Audit clients, opinion shopping by, 89
Audit engagement team, responsibilities
    of, 13
Audit evidence
    acceptance of client representations
        as, 11, 100
    confirmation procedures in collecting,
        138–40
    evaluative criteria in assessing, 39
    in letter of representations, 114
    quickness in acceptance of, 64
    standards in evaluating, 191–92
Auditing the Allowance for Credit Losses of
    Banks, 89
Audit market, competitive nature of, 60
Audit objectives, and performance of
    year-end sales cutoff tests, 13
Audit opinions
    qualified, 108, 114
    unqualified, 15, 22, 61, 64–65, 79, 82,
        85, 87, 106, 121, 152
    withdrawal of, 28
Auditor(s). See also Accountant(s)
    changing sides by, 249–52
    imbalance of power in relationship
        with client, 35

liability of
    to bondholders, 271–80
    under Rule 10b-5, 293–300
    under Securities Act of 1933, 279
    under Securities and Exchange Act
        of 1934, 279
    to third-party financial statement
        users, 263–70, 285–92
as lobbyist, 231–39
objectives in observing inventory, 127
"placements" of, 76, 78
professional responsibilities of,
    241–44
and public interest, 168
public interest role of, 168
relationship with clients, 39
reliance of, on client management,
    301–6
responsibilities of, in reviewing tax
    returns, 27
and sexual harassment, 245–47
Audit plan, 95
    impact of client industry on, 78
    testing in, 95
Audit program for delinquent accounts,
    96
Audit reports, withdrawal of, 15–16
Audit review process, 24–25, 28
Audit risks, 89, 134
    assessment of, 127
    documenting, 130
    level of, 78
Audit scope, 25
    effect of time budget on, 100
Audit teams, communication between,
    40
Audit tests, 9–10
    confirmation procedures for
        receivables and payables, 137
Audit workpapers, 8
    citing of auditor for failing to produce
        in court, 205–7
    key objectives of, 174
Aune, Charles, 129

Bakker, Jim, 197–98
Bakker, Tammy, 197–98
Bank accounts, foreign, 77, 78
Bank float, chaining and crisscrossing in
    creating, 162n
Banking scandal
    Lincoln Savings and Loan Association
        as part of, 55–68
    and Penn Square Bank, 79–90
Bank of America, 161
Bankruptcy
    of Cardillo Travel Systems, Inc., 191
    Chapter 11, 77, 119–20
    of Fund of Funds, Ltd., 103

Barbie product line, 3
BarChris Construction Corporation,
    271–80
Barden Corporation, 34–35, 37
Barnard, Doug, 85
Barrow, Allen, 205, 206
BDO Seidman, 251
Beazley, Susan, 251
Beller, Eldon, 81
Beneficiaries, rights of primary, to
    recover damages, 268
Beresford, Dennis, 235–36, 239
Berkshire Hathaway, Inc., 143–45
Bill and hold sales, 6–8, 11, 12–13
Bills of lading, bogus, 6, 7, 8
Blackman, Alan, 29, 32
Blackmun, Harry, 298–99
Blanton, Jim, 83–84, 86–87
Block v. First Blood Associates, 257n
Bohanon, Luther, 182
Bondholders, liability of auditors to,
    271–80
Boston Educational Research (BER), 172
Boxer, Barbara, 231
Braxton, Earl, 175–77
Breeden, Richard, 61, 64
Briloff, Abraham, 163, 165–66, 168
Brown, Edmund, 302
Budget method of writing off
    uncollectible receivables, 99
Buffett, Warren, 144, 235
Burger, Warren, 195–96
Burke, William, 35
Burton, John, 238
Business interruption insurance claim, 13
    improper computation of, 10–11
Business risk, 89
Business Roundtable, opposition to
    stock option rule change, 232

California Society of Certified Public
    Accountants, 67
California State Board of Accountancy,
    67, 250–51
Campos, Edward, 135–36
Cannon Group Inc., 251
Capitalization, 17
    of legal expenses, 32
    of tooling costs, 35–38
Capital markets, 16
Cardillo Travel Systems, Inc., 187–92
Cardozo, Benjamin, 267–70
Carr, Phil, 106–8
Carson, Johnny, 175
Carter, Jimmy, 81
Cash basis of accounting, 140, 175, 176
Cash controls, 155–57
Cash drawdown system, abuses of,
    161–62, 163

Cash flow, 19
Cash management system, 160–68
Cash transactions, problem of large,
    140–41
Cassini, Oleg, 101
Cayman Islands subsidiaries, 132–33
Chaining, 162*n*
Chamberlain Manufacturing
    Corporation, 213
Chapter 11 bankruptcy, 77, 119–20
Chase Manhattan, 81
Checksfield, James, 194–95
Chenok, Philip, 237
Chrysler Corporation, and stock
    options, 232–33
Civil trial, level of proof in, 183
Clark, Jack, 179–82
Classic litigation cases
    BarChris Construction Corporation,
        271–80
    Equity Funding Corporation of
        America, 301–6
    First Securities Company of Chicago,
        293–300
    Fred Stern & Company, 263–70
    Tenants Corporation, 281–84
    Yale Express System, Inc., 285–92
Client acceptance, 229
Client confidentiality rule, 40, 105, 112
Client management, reliance of auditors
    on, 301–6
Client representations, acceptance of, as
    audit evidence, 11, 100
Cohen, David Jacob Levi, 77
Cohn, Roy M., 281
Collective losses, 16
Committee to Reelect the President
    (CREEP), 205
Common-sized financial statements, 39
Compensation, stock options as form of,
    232–33
Confidentiality agreements, 49, 54
Confirmation letter, 36
Confirmation procedures, 24, 28
    for accounts payable, 137, 147–51, 153
    for accounts receivable, 8, 137,
        171–72, 174
    in collecting audit evidence, 138–40
Consent decree, 58–59
Consigned merchandise, inclusion of, in
    year-end inventory, 75, 78
Continental Vending, 25
Control environment, 68
Cookie Jar Caper, 304
Coopers & Lybrand
    and audit of Whittaker Corporation, 216
    and proposed stock option rule
        change, 234
Cornfeld, Bernie, 101–2, 113
Cost amortization, 9

Cost-to-cost percentage-of-completion
    method of accounting, 180–81, 183
Cox, Archibald, 206
Cranston, Alan, 59
Crazy Eddie, Inc., 69–78
    charges of accounting irregularities, 75
    Peat Marwick audit of, 83–88
Creative accounting as problem, 56–59,
    180, 235
Credit memos, 8
    fictitious, 149–50
Creve Couer Pizza, Inc., 193–96
Criminal trial, level of proof in, 183
Crisscrossing, 162*n*
Crown Aluminum Corporation, 213
Culkin, Gerald, 282
Culpability standard, 299
Cumulative trading losses, 19
Currency and Foreign Transactions
    Reporting Act, 140, 141
Customer account confirmation
    procedures, 138–40
Customer account information, internal
    control policies regarding recording
    of, 140–41
Customer order forms, 6

Debit memos, preparation of bogus, 75
Deceive, intent to, 112, 299
Deep pockets theory, 199
Delinquent accounts, audit program for, 96
Deloitte Haskins & Sells. *See also*
        Deloitte & Touche
    and audit of Porta-John Corporation,
        175–77
    and PTL Club, 198, 199
Deloitte & Touche, 120. *See also* Deloitte
        Haskins & Sells
    and audit of First Executive
        Corporation, 249–50
    and audit of Lincoln Savings and
        Loan Association, 67
    and audit of PTL Club, 199
    promotion policies at, 221
Dingell, John D., 25, 42, 120
Direct investment rule, 59
Disagreement memorandum, 132
Disagreement procedure, 132
Diversification, 4, 102
Dixon, Bruce, 35–36, 36
Doughtie's Foods, Inc., 125–27
Drawdown system, 163
Drysdale Securities, 25
Due diligence defense, 277–79
Due diligence obligation, 44
Dumping of stock, 4

Earnings manipulation scheme, 5
Economic fallout, 16

Economic quantity model, 161
Economic valuation of stock options,
    231–39
8-K statements, filing of
    by Berkshire Hathaway, Inc., 144
    by Cardillo Travel Systems, Inc.,
        189–90, 191–92
    by ZZZ Best, Inc., 49–50
1136 Tenants Corporation, 281–84
Elliot, Anthony, 66
Embezzlement, 156
Engagement letter, 45
Equity, 18
Equity Funding Corporation of
    America, 25, 301–6
Ernst & Ernst v. *Hochfelder et al.,*
    293–300
Ernst & Whinney
    and audit of U.S. Surgical
        Corporation, 30, 33–38
    disagreement with USSC over
        capitalization of alleged tooling
        costs, 35
    retention and resignation of, at ZZZZ
        Best Company, 44–51
Ernst & Young, 89
    and proposed stock option rule
        change, 234
Escrow syndicate, 293–300
Eskow, Benjamin, 285
Eskow, Gerald, 286–88
ESM Government Securities, Inc., 15–28
    audit issues raised by debacle
        at, 22–27
    bookkeeping scam at, 19–22
    history of, 17–19
Ethics
    Cardillo Travel Systems, Inc., 187–92
    Creve Couer Pizza, Inc., 193–96
    Laurel Valley Estates, 209–12
    Leight Ann Walker, Staff Accountant,
        201–4
    Phillips Petroleum Company, 205–7
    The PTL Club, 197–99
    Suzette Washington, Accounting
        Major, 217–18
    Whittaker Corporation, 213–16
Ewton, Ronnie, 17, 18, 22, 25, 26, 27
"Excess inventory" item, 8–9
Expert witnesses, 23

Fair market value, establishing, 104, 108
Falwell, Jerry, 53
Federal Bureau of Investigation (FBI),
    investigation of
    Flight Transportation Corporation by,
        129
    Lincoln Savings and Loan Association
        by, 60

PTL Club by, 197
Federal Deposit Insurance Corporation (FDIC), 16, 79
Federal Home Loan Bank Board (FHLBB), 55
Federal Savings and Loan Insurance Corporation (FSLIC), 57
Federico, Edward, 195
Fermi, Enrico, 294
50 percent rule, 97
File-stuffing, 60
Financial Accounting Standards Board (FASB)
    FASB Statement No. 5, 166, 169
    and proposed rule change on stock options, 231–39
Financial Statement Alert, 251
Financial statements
    bogus, 129
    common-sized, 39
    ignoring fraudulent misrepresentations in, 16
    issuance of false and misleading, 5–6
    management assertions underlying, 53–54, 68
    red flags in, 78
First Blood Associates, 257–60
First Executive Corporation, Deloitte & Touche as audit firm for, 249–50
First Penn Corporation, 82
First Securities Company of Chicago, 293–300
Flight Transportation Corporation, 129–34
    Fox's audits of, 130–33
Florida Board of Accountancy, 27
Ford Motor Company, and stock options, 232–33
Foreign bank accounts, 77, 78
Four Seasons Equity, 180, 181
Four Seasons Nursing Centers of America, Inc., 179–83
    cost of scandal to Arthur Andersen, 182–83
    history of, 179–82
Fox & Company, audits of Flight Transportation Corporation by, 130–33
Fox-Raff brokerage firm, 106, 107
Fraud
    exposure of, at Wedtech, 116–17
    payroll, 135–36
    wire and mail, 160
Front-ending of lease income, 92n
Fund of Funds, Limited, 101–14
    allegations and court rulings, 110–13
    Arthur Andersen's audit of, 104–10
    Arthur Andersen's dual relationship with King Resources and, 103–4

Fund of Funds, Limited v. Arthur Andersen & Co., 110–13

Garcia, E. C., & Company, 56
Garcia, Ernie, 56, 67
Gardner, Leroy, 53
GEICO, 143–45
General Foods, 143–45
General ledger, transactions in, 7
Generally accepted accounting principles (GAAP), 33, 61, 66, 99, 274
Giant Stores Corporation, 147–53
    accounts payable irregularities, 147–51
    collapse of, 152
    SEC criticism of Touche Ross audit of, 151–52
Gladstone, William, 61, 62–63, 64
Glenn, John, 59
Goldberg, Irving, 285–86, 289
Goldberg, Stanley, 137–38, 141
Goldblum, Stanley, 301–5
Gomez, Jose, 15–28
Gonzalez, Henry, 56, 58, 62–63
Goodman & Company, audit of Doughtie's Foods, Inc. by, 126
Government securities markets, leverage available to investors in, 17
Gramm, Phil, 231
Grant, Alexander, 15–28
Grant, Alexander, & Company. See Grant Thornton
Grant, Bill, 205–6
Grant Thornton, 17, 27, 134. See also Grant, Alexander, & Company
Gray, Larry, 45, 47–48, 48, 51
Gray, Tom, 179–82
Greede, Beauregard T., 236
Greenspan, Alan, 59
Greenspan, George, 44, 45, 54
Guaraglia, Anthony, 118–19

Hanauer, J. B., & Co., 137–42
    assessment of internal controls, 137–38
    customer account confirmation procedures, 138–40
    judgment day for, 141
    money laundering allegations, 140–41
Handler, Elliot, 3–14
Handler, Ruth, 3–14
Harper & Row, 171
Harrington, John, 130, 132, 133–34
Hasbro, 11–12
Hess, Amerada, 207
Heyman, John A., 251

High-risk accounts and internal control issues
    Berkshire Hathaway, Inc., 143–45
    Doughtie's Food, Inc., 125–27
    E. F. Hutton & Company, Inc., 159–69
    Flight Transportation Corporation, 129–34
    Four Seasons Nursing Centers of America, Inc., 179–83
    Giant Stores Corporation, 147–53
    Howard Street Jewelers, Inc., 155–57
    J. B. Hanauer & Co., 137–42
    J. B. Lippincott Company, 171–74
    Porta-John Corporation, 175–77
    Trolley Dodgers, 135–36
Hirsch, Leon, 29, 38–39
Home State Savings, 16
Hoover, J. Edgar, 281
Hope, Michael, 35, 36, 37
Hopkins, Ann, 221–29
Hopkins v. Price Waterhouse, 221–29
Hot Wheels, 8–9, 10
Howard Street Jewelers, Inc., 155–57
Hubbard, Congressman, 61, 64
Hughes, William, 162, 165, 166, 168, 169
Hutton, E. F., & Company, Inc., cash management system at, 159–62
Hutton, Edward F., 159, 165

Iacocca, Lee, 232–33
IFG Leasing, 91–100
    accounting and control problems at, 92–94
    Touche Ross audit of, 94–99
In-depth review, 24
Industry knowledge, applications of, 11
Influence peddling at Lincoln Savings and Loan, 56–59
Inherent risk, level of, 12
Initial public stock offering, 71–72, 76
Insider trading, 191
Insolvency, 16
Intercompany transactions, 23, 25
    "mirror," 19
Internal controls
    assessment of, 137–38
    establishing, 155–57
    risks in, 141–42
    structure of, 93
    weaknesses in, 141
Internal Revenue Service (IRS)
    controlled informants of, 193–96
    investigation of
        into J. B. Hanauer & Co., 140–41
        into PTL Club, 197
    rights of, to tax accrual audit workpapers, 205–7
International Air System (IAS), 130

Interstate Appraisal Services and
     Assured Property Management, 44
Inventory
     auditor's objectives in observing, 127
     computer-based, 77
     inclusion of consigned merchandise
          in year-end, 78
     inflation of, 125, 126
     internal controls for, 126
     method used to misrepresent, 126
     obsolete, 38
     overstating, 69, 75
     shortage of, 74, 213–16
     test-counting, 127
     turnover of, 127
Inventory count sheets, falsification of, 78
Inventory memo, ethical issues in
     signing off on, 253–55
Inventory obsolescence reserve, 13
     intentional understatement of, 8–9
Inventory records, errors in, 6–7
Inventory shipments, as arm's length
     transactions, 30, 34
Inventory theft, ethical issues in
     reporting, 217–18
Investors Overseas Service (IOS), 101–2
Invoices, handling of forged, 118
Ito, Lance, 67

Jennings, B. P. "Beep," 79, 80–81, 180n
Joint and several liability, 28
Junk bonds, marketing of, 61, 66, 67
Justice, U.S. Department of
     filing of mail and wire fraud charges
          against E. F. Hutton & Company,
          Inc., 160
     investigation of
          into E. F. Hutton & Company, Inc.,
               161, 166
          into J. B. Hanauer & Co., 140–41
          into Lincoln Savings and Loan
               Association, 60
          into Penn Square, 89

Kaye, William, 189
Keating, Charles, III, 58, 67
Keating, Charles, Jr., 55, 56, 58–59, 67, 68
Keating Five, 59
Kellogg, Loren, 251
King, John McCandish, 102–3, 105, 106,
     107, 109–10, 112, 113
King Resources, 102–3
     Arthur Andersen's dual relationship
          with Fund of Funds and, 103–4
KMG Main Hurdman (KMG), 121. See
     also Main Hurdman
     and audit of Cardillo Travel Systems,
          Inc., 190–91

and audit of Wedtech, 117–20
KPMG Peat Marwick. See also Peat
     Marwick Mitchell & Company
     and audit of Wedtech, Inc., 119–20
     promotion policies at, 221

Lacey Manufacturing Company, 34, 36
Laissez-faire management style,
     159–60
Landis, Ira M., 251
Lasser, J. K., & Co., and audit of J. B.
     Hanauer & Co., 137
Laurel Valley Estates, 209–12
Laventhol & Horwath, and PTL Club,
     198–99
Lawrence, Esther, 187, 189–90, 191
Leach, Jim, 55, 65–66
Lease income, front-ending of, 92n
Lease receivables, 91, 92
     allowance for uncollectible, 93, 95–96,
          97, 98
     altering aging summaries of, 93–95
     budget method of writing off
          uncollectable, 99
Legal expenses, capitalization of, 32
Lehman, Congressman, 62–63
Leisenring, James, 235
Lent, Congressman, 44, 48
Letter of representations, audit evidence
     in, 114
Leventhal, Kenneth, & Company, 56
     investigation of, into Lincoln, 64–65
Levi, Alvin, 155
Levi, Julius, 155
Levi, Lore, 155
Levin, Fred, 301–5
Liabilities, unrecorded, 152
Lincoln Savings and Loan Association,
     55–68
     abuses at, 56–59
     audit history of, 59–63
     criticism of Arthur Young following
          collapse of, 63–66
Line of credit, 77, 92
Lippincott, J. B., Company, 171–74
Litton Industries, 4
Loan documentation problems, 85n
Lobbying, and influence peddling, 59
Lobbyist, auditor as, 231–39
Long-term asset account, charging of
     inventoriable production costs to,
     30, 34
Lowballing, 76, 78
Lublin, Barry J., 251

Mackensen, Fred, 285–86, 288
Mail fraud, 77
Mail rule, 295–99

Main Hurdman, 76. See also KMG Main
     Hurdman
     and audit of Crazy Eddie, Inc., 77
Malfeasance, 28
Management letter, 86
Mann, Judd, Landau, 251
Margin requirements, 17
Mariotta, John, 115, 116
Market manipulation, 101
Market value, 4, 41
Markup percentage, 102
Material errors, 15
Material event, qualification of adverse
     judgment as, 190
Materiality, concept of, 276
Material overstatements, 10
Material scope limitation, 142
Mattel, Inc., 3–14
     alleged deficiencies in Arthur
          Andersen's audits of, 5–11
     SEC criticism of Arthur Andersen's
          audits of, 11
Mazzoli, Romano, 165, 168
McCarthy, Joseph, 281
Mead, George, 17
Mecom, John, 107, 112, 114
Memorialization, use of, with loan files,
     61
Merrill, Dina, 165
Metcalf, Lee, 222
Millbrook Distributors, 149
Miller, Joel, 163, 165
Minkow, Barry, 41–54
Minority-owned businesses, 115
"Mirror" intercompany transaction, 19
Misrepresentation, 16
Missouri State Board of Accountancy,
     195
Mitchell & Company, and audit of Penn
     Square Bank, 79–90
Money laundering allegations, 140–41
More, Robert, 36, 37
Moyer, Norman, 294, 295

Naftalis, Gary, 179, 181
Nashwinter, William, 125–27
National Association of Securities
     Dealers, 25
Natural resources proprietary account
     (NRPA), 102, 103
Nay, Elizabeth, 293, 294
Nay, Ladislas (Leston), 293–96
Neary, Robert, 36
Negligence, 268–69
Nepotism, 221, 228
Net asset value as basis of distributing
     proceeds to shareholders, 104
Net income, overstatement of, 126
Net worth of Mattel, Inc., 3

Neuberger, Fred, 115, 116
Newington, Gregory P., 250
Niven, John, 264
Nonrecourse notes, 56, 68
Novick, Alan, 15, 17, 19–20, 22, 27

Obsolete inventory, 38
Office of the Comptroller of the
    Currency (OCC), 81
Oil and gas ventures, financing of, 81
Old Boy network, 228
O'Malley, Peter, 135–36
O'Malley, Walter, 135
100 percent participations, 81
Organization of Petroleum Exporting
    Countries (OPEC), 81
Orr, John, 103

Pacter, Paul, 235
Padgett, Tom, 43, 44
Partnership acquisition policies, 221–29
Partnership agreement, ethical issues in
    reviewing, 209–212
Patent expenses, amortization of, 32–33
Patterson, William, 80–81, 88
Payroll account, ethics in maintenance
    of secret, 198, 199
Payroll fraud, 135–36
Payroll transaction cycle, audit
    objectives of, 136
Peat, Marwick, Mitchell & Company. See
    also KPMG Peat Marwick
    and audit of Berkshire Hathaway,
        Inc., 143–45
    and audit of Crazy Eddie, Inc., 76, 77
    and audit of Penn Square Bank,
        79–90
    and audit of Yale Express System,
        Inc., 289–91
Peer review of audits, 127
Penn Square Bank, 79–90, 180n
    dismissal of Arthur Young by, 82–83
    history of, 80–82
Percentage-of-completion method of
    accounting, 118, 120, 180, 183, 241,
    273–74
Performance-based compensation
    schemes, 93
Performance reports, 125
Personal integrity, importance of, in
    accountant, 201–3
Phillips Petroleum Company, 205–7
Placements, 76, 78
Plea bargaining agreement
    in Lincoln Savings & Loan
        Association case, 67
    in Mattel, Inc. case, 5

in Penn Square Bank case, 88
in Phillips Petroleum Company case,
    205–6
Ponzi scheme, 41
Porta-John Corporation, 175–77
Postal Service, U.S., investigation of PTL
    Club by, 197
Preacquisition review, auditor's
    objectives on, 174
Premier growth companies, 4
Price-earnings ratio, 4
Price Waterhouse
    and audit of ZZZZ Best Company, 50
    and Doughtie's Foods, Inc., 125
    promotion policies at, 221–29
    review of Andersen's audit of Mattel,
        Inc., 5
Principal, Victoria, 101–2
Prior period adjustments, treatment of
    adjusting journal entries as, 100
Private placement offering
    memorandum, 257–60
Privileged communication, between
    accountant and client, 195–96
Production costs, description of, as
    capitalizable expenses on invoices,
    34–35
Professional issues
    change of sides by, 249–52
    DeBurger, Bill, 253–55
    First Blood Associates, 257–60
    Hopkins v. Price Waterhouse, 221–29
    O'Connell, Tommy, 241–44
    Russell, Sarah, 245–47
    when auditors are lobbyists, 231–39
Proportionate redemptions, 143, 145
PTL Club, 197–199
Public interest, and auditors, 168
Pugliese, Leborio, 271

Qualified audit opinion, 114
Quality control procedures, 28, 134
Quality control standards, compliance
    with, 127
Quick & Reilly, 137

Racketeering, 59, 77
Rae, Tom, 163
Reagan, Ronald, 116, 281
Recession, impact on sales, 4
Recourse notes, 68
Reevaluation transactions, 104, 107–8,
    112, 114
Registered broker-dealers, 138, 140
Registration statements, 45
    filing with Securities and Exchange
        Commission (SEC), 69

Regulatory oversight, 17
Related party transactions, 130, 134
Repo transactions, 18, 19, 22, 28
Republic Carloading & Distributing
    Company, 285
Repurchase agreements, 18
Reserve for obsolescence, 8–9
Resolution Trust Corporation, 59, 66
Retail sales, recording of transhipping
    transactions as, 75, 78
Revaluation transactions, validity of, 105–6
Reverse engineering, 29
Reverse repos, 18, 19, 28
Reversing entries, 7, 8
Review, comparison of, with audit, 53
Richard A. Eisner & Co., and audit of J.
    B. Hanauer & Co., 137
Riker, Jerome, 281
Riker & Company, 281–82
Riley, Raymond, 187, 190
Riordan, Michael, 301, 303
Risk assessment questionnaire in
    planning audit engagement, 130–31
Roberts, Don, 202–3
Robinson, John, 106
Rognlien, A. Walter, 187–92
Rosenberg, Ethel, 281
Rosenberg, Julius, 281
Rosenberg, Seymour, 4, 5
Rothenberg, Max, & Company, 282–83
Royalties, 13
    underpayment of, 10
Rozefsky, Inc., 149–50
Rubin, William, 130–31, 134
Russell, Harold, 82
Russo, Leonard, 271
Ruthton Corporation, 12
Ryan-Nichols & Company, 293

S-1 registration statement, 273–77
    due diligence obligation in reviewing,
        277–79
S-1 review, 273, 277–79
St. Germain, Fernand, 79
Sale and leaseback transaction, 274, 279–80
Sales
    annual percentage change in "same
        store," 75
    bill and hold, 6–8, 11, 12–13
    impact of recession on, 4
    recognizing revenue from, 12–13
Sales invoices, 6
Salvage values, 39
    establishing, for assets, 33
Sanders, William J., 249, 251
Schueren, Arnold, 294, 295
Schuetze, Walter, 237–38
Scienter, 112, 299

Seattle First National Bank, Continental Illinois, 81
Secondary dealers, 17
Second-party confirmations, 24
Securities Act (1933)
  due diligence defense under, 277–79
  legal responsibilities of auditor under, 263, 270
  liability of auditors to bondholders under, 271–80
Securities and Exchange Commission (SEC)
  and accounting problems at IFG Leasing, 92–94
  and Andersen audit of Mattel, 4, 7, 11, 12
  and audits of Doughtie's Foods, Inc., 126–27
  filing of 8-K statements with
    by Berkshire Hathaway, Inc., 144
    by Cardillo Travel Systems, Inc., 189–90, 191–92
    by ZZZ Best, Inc., 49–50
  filing of registration statements with, 69
  filing of S-1 registration statement with, 271–80
  filing of SEC Form S-1 with, 44
  filing of 10-K registration statements
    by Giant Stores, 152
    by IFG Leasing, 94–95, 100
    by Yale Express System, Inc., 289
  and internal control procedures at J. B. Hanauer & Co., 138
  investigation of
    "bill and hold" program, 6–8
    Investors Overseas Services, 101–2
    into J. B. Hanauer & Co., 140–41
    USSC's financial affairs, 30, 32
    Witte's audit of J. B. Lippincott Company, 171, 173
  responsibility for accounting method switch at Four Seasons Nursing Centers of America, Inc., 181*n*
  review of Andersen procedures at Crown Aluminum Corporation, 213–16
  shutdown of Flight Transportation Corporation by, 129
  signing of consent decree with Keating, 58
  and Touche Ross audit
    of Giant Stores Corporation, 151–52
    of IFG Leasing, 95–99
  and USSC, 38
  and ZZZZ Best Company scam, 42
Securities Exchange Act (1934), 112
  legal liability of auditor under, 270, 279

registered broker-dealers under, 138, 140
  Rule 10b-5 under, 258, 260, 296–99
Seidman & Seidman, 305, 306
Self-dealing, 281–84
Seneca, Bobby, 17, 27*n*
Set-aside program, 115–16
Sex discrimination, 221–229
Sexual harassment, 245–47
Shearson Lehman Brothers, purchase of E. F. Hutton & Company, Inc. by, 160
Shepherd, Helen, 188–92, 191
Shlonsky, Roger, 191
Side agreements, negotiation of, 104, 106, 107, 110, 112
Site visitations, bogus, 49
Slush fund, 118, 121
Small Business Administration (SBA)
  responsibility of auditors to report irregularities to, 118, 121
  responsibility of for set-aside program, 115–16
Smith, Russell, 187
Snyder, Tom, 53
Spear, Albert, 4
Statement on Auditing Procedures No. 41, 290
Statement on Auditing Standards No. 7, 54, 60, 83*n*
Statement on Auditing Standards No. 21, 13
Statement on Auditing Standards No. 31, 53–54, 68, 152, 169, 183, 279
Statement on Auditing Standards No. 47, 89, 168, 270
Statement on Auditing Standards No. 53, 114, 120, 306
Statement on Auditing Standards No. 55, 68, 291
Stern, Fred, & Company, Inc., 263–70
Stewart, Charles, 113
Stockholders' equity, 187
Stock options, proposed FASB rule change on, 231–39
Strauss, Norman, 35
Straw buyer, 57
Subsidiary fixed asset ledger, costs of assets in, 33
Substance-over-form rule, 65, 68, 144

Taj Mahal casino, financing of, 259
Technical review, 24
10-K registration statements, filing of, with SEC
  by Giant Stores, 152
  by IFG Leasing, 94–95, 100
  by Yale Express System, Inc., 289
10-Q statement, 188
Third-party financial statement users, liability of auditors to, 263–70, 285–92

Tooling costs
  capitalization of, 35–38
  overstatement of deferred, 9–10, 13
Touche, George Alexander, 264–65
Touche, Niven & Company, 263–70
Touche Ross & Company
  and audit of Berkshire Hathaway, Inc., 144
  and audit of Cardillo Travel Systems, Inc., 188–90
  and audit of Crazy Eddie, Inc., 76
  and audit of Equity Funding Corporation of America, 303
  and audit of Giant Stores Corporation, 147–53
  and audit of IFG Leasing, 94–99
  and audit of J. B. Hanauer & Co., 137
  and audit of Lincoln Savings and Loan Association, 63, 67
  and audit of Wedtech, Inc., 119–20
  and private placement offering memorandum, 257–60
Transhipping transactions, 71
  recording of, 75, 78
Trolley Dodgers, 135–36
Trump, Donald J., 259

Ultramares Corporation v. *Touche et al.*, 263–70
Underperforming companies, identifying and acquiring, 4
United Airlines, 187, 188, 189
U.S. government securities market, 17–19
U.S. Oil of Louisiana, 107
U.S. treasury bills, notes, and bonds, average daily dollar volume of, 17
United States Surgical Corporation, 29–40
  abusive accounting practices at, 30–33
  allegations of audit deficiencies, 33–35
  chronology of USSC–Ernst & Whinney disagreement regarding capitalization of alleged tooling costs, 35–38
Unqualified audit opinions, 15, 22, 61, 64–65, 79, 82, 85, 87, 106, 121, 152

Vesco, Robert, 113
Vincent, Janice, 63, 67
Vitolo, Christie, 271

Wahrman, Kenneth, 179, 181, 182
Ward, Lou, 157
Ward, Margie, 157

Weber, Congressman, 88
Wedtech Corporation, 115–21
    criticism of auditors, 117–20
    exposure of massive fraud at, 116–17
Welbilt Electronic Die Corporation, 115
Wescon, 56
Whittaker Corporation, 213–16
Wholly owned subsidiary, 91
Wilson, Thomas, 126–27
Wire and mail fraud, 160
Witte, Lester, & Company, and J. B.
    Lippincott Company, 171–74
Women
    sexual discrimination and promotion
        policies for, 221–29
    and sexual harassment, 245–47

Working capital, 92
Working papers, 5
Wortley, George, 86
Wyden, Congressman, 45, 50–51

Yale Express System, Inc., 285–92
Yamont, Paul, 35
Year-end account balance
    confirmation of, 133, 172
    procedures in handling, 139–40
Year-end sales cutoff tests, 8, 13
Year-end test, unrecorded liabilities as,
    152
York, Dean, 85

Young, Arthur, & Company, 60, 251
    and audit of Phillips Petroleum
        Company, 205–7
    criticism of, following Lincoln
        collapse, 63–66
    dismissal of, by Penn Square, 82–83

ZZZZ Best Company, Inc., 41–54
    collapse of, 51–52
    early history of, 42–43
    going public with, 43–44
    retention of Ernst & Whinney by,
        44–49